PeopleSmart

Developing Your Interpersonal Intelligence

People**Smart**

Developing Your Interpersonal Intelligence

Mel Silberman, Ph.D.

Author of the bestselling *Active Training*

with Freda Hansburg, Ph.D.

BK

BERRETT-KOEHLER PUBLISHERS, INC.
San Francisco

Berrett-Koehler Publishers, Inc.
450 Sansome Street, Suite 1200
San Francisco, CA 94111-3320
Tel: 415-288-0260   Fax: 415-362-2512
Website: www.bkpub.com

Ordering Information

Individual sales. Berrett-Koehler publications are available through most bookstores. They can also be ordered direct from Berrett-Koehler Publishers by calling, toll-free; 800-929-2929; fax 802-864-7626.

Quantity sales. Special discounts are available on quantity purchases by corporations, associations, and others. For details, contact the "Special Sales Department" at the Berrett-Koehler address above.

Orders for college textbook/course adoption use. Please contact Berrett-Koehler Publishers toll-free; 800-929-2929; fax 802-864-7626.

Orders by U.S. trade bookstores and wholesalers. Please contact Publishers Group West, 1700 Fourth Street, Berkeley, CA 94710; 510-528-1444; 1-800-788-3123; fax 510-528-9555.

Printed in the United States of America

 Printed on acid-free and recycled paper that is composed of 50 percent recycled waste, including 10 percent postconsumer waste.

Library of Congress Cataloging-in-Publication Data
Silberman, Melvin L.
    People smart : developing your interpersonal intelligence / by Mel Silberman ; with Freda Hansburg.—1st ed.
        p.   cm.
    Includes bibliographical references and index.
    ISBN 1-57675-091-4 (alk. paper)
    1. Emotional intelligence.   2. Interpersonal relations.   I. Hansburg,Freda, 1950–.   II. Title
    BF576 S57 2000
    158.2—dc21   99–042244

First Edition
05   04   03   02   01   00   10   9   8   7   6   5   4   3   2   1

Contents

Preface

vii

What Does It Mean To Be People Smart?

1

Becoming People Smart

8

How People Smart Are You?

12

People**Smart Skill 1**

Understanding People

19

People**Smart Skill 2**

Expressing Yourself Clearly

51

People**Smart Skill 3**

Asserting Your Needs

71

People**Smart Skill 4**

Exchanging Feedback

95

People**Smart Skill 5**

Influencing Others

119

People**Smart Skill 6**

Resolving Conflict

143

People**Smart Skill 7**

Being a Team Player

175

People**Smart Skill 8**

Shifting Gears

201

Putting It All Together

225

References

239

Index

241

About the Authors

251

*People**Smart** Seminars*

252

Preface

Are you less successful at times than you ought to be, given your intelligence and work ethic?

Do you reach out to others on the job or at home but your efforts are sometimes rejected?

Is your energy drained by conflicts with certain individuals?

Do you wish your relationships with people close to you were more harmonious and fulfilling?

People**Smart** is a book for those who ask themselves these questions, which means most of us at some time or other, with a supervisor, coworkers, teammates, clients, spouse, partner, children, relatives, or friends. The aim of People**Smart** is to give you a *one-stop*, all-in-one guide to healthier and more productive relationships. It saves you the time of reading a library full of self-help books on listening, communication, assertiveness, feedback, influence, conflict resolution, collaboration, and flexibility.

That's not to say that you should ignore the many wonderful books that exist on these subjects. (You will find just a brief sample in the *References*.) But, if you are short on time, you will find

People**Smart** to be a concise collection of the wisdom that I have culled from 40 years of reading and reflecting on my own life. (The first 18 years of my life I was too busy playing at life to get anything from reading and reflecting about it.)

People**Smart** was also written with the idea that there is more to developing your interpersonal effectiveness than just *reading* and *reflecting* about it. A Chinese philosopher, Lao Tzu (6th century BC), said: "If you tell me, I will listen. If you show me, I will see. If you let me experience, I will learn." People**Smart** is a book designed for *experiencing*. Becoming effective with people is a life-long challenge. Each decade presents unique opportunities to get good at it. But only if you do it!

Of course, none of us do anything unless we really want to. I hope that People**Smart** will inspire you to work at becoming interpersonally fit in the same way as you would work at becoming physically fit. And I want to be your personal trainer.

How did I get the nerve to apply for the job? Three big reasons come to mind.

1. I've been a psychologist for over 30 years. In the past 10 years, I have focused exclusively on developing practical ways to facilitate professional and personal development for adult learners. My guiding philosophy has been called active training.

   When training is active, you, not the trainer, do most of the work. You use your brain—studying ideas, solving problems, and applying what you learn. The adult trainer's job is to steer you in the right direction, give you enough basics to get you started, and gently push you to explore on your own. That's what I'm prepared to do.

   I've also found that people do not actively develop skills unless they are usable. I know how often I felt that the advice

I read in self-help books seemed impossible and inappropriate. I'm prepared to give you advice you can use immediately. I'll also help you fight the tendency to go right back to your accustomed, but perhaps unproductive, ways of handling people.

2. I am a survivor of lung cancer. During my two-year battle with this illness, I learned that you can't face cancer and fight it without the love, support, feedback, and prayers of others. Of course, the blessing of your family and closest friends is paramount. I am especially blessed with a loving wife of 36 years, Shoshana, who has been my steadfast life partner through times of joy and anguish. But, also knowing that everyone you knew who knew you had cancer was rooting for you was an additional gift you can never fully appreciate until it happens. Next to faith in God, I came to the conclusion that the best source to place your faith is in other people. That assumes, however, that you have invested enough in your relationships with people to reap the dividends. Luckily, I was taught to invest in people. Now, I want more than ever to teach that lesson to anyone who wants to profit from it.

3. I did not write People**Smart** alone. I am fortunate that Freda Hansburg agreed to assist me in the writing of this book. Freda is a superb psychologist, trainer, and writer. Her insights and common sense have shaped the advice contained in People**Smart** from beginning to end. You will enjoy your interpersonal workout a lot more because Freda had a major role in creating it.

Will you let me be your trainer?

Mel Silberman
Princeton, NJ
May 2000

What Does It Mean to Be People Smart?

Check off the "people" activities below that apply to you:

- ☐ supervising employees
- ☐ parenting children (and one's parents)
- ☐ working on a team
- ☐ being in a committed relationship
- ☐ dealing with your boss
- ☐ participating in religious or community groups
- ☐ helping others understand how to do something
- ☐ coping as a consumer
- ☐ obtaining business
- ☐ interviewing others or being interviewed
- ☐ relating to doctors, nurses, and mental health professionals
- ☐ selling to a customer
- ☐ attending a party
- ☐ networking
- ☐ interacting with coworkers or classmates
- ☐ chatting on the Internet

Chances are you checked several of these items. It used to be said that some of us were in the business of working with people and some of us were in the business of working with facts, figures, and machinery. This distinction was probably never accurate, but its inaccuracy is now beyond dispute: Good people skills are a must for any job, including technical ones. Our lives at home also demand superior people skills as we try to juggle new roles and new living conditions. The people business is no longer the domain of the few. It includes you and everyone you know.

The twenty-first century will feature a rapidly changing and highly interrelated world. You will probably accomplish very little on your own, but with other people you may be able to accomplish a lot. Increasingly, success will depend on being people smart.

Ask the person on the street what it means to be people smart, and you may get an answer such as, "Oh, that's a person who is really a smooth operator . . . a person who knows how to get others to join his side." A second person might answer, "someone who is personable, friendly, fun to be with." While few people would complain about having those two attributes, they represent a very limited view of what it means to be gifted with people. Being people smart is a multifaceted intelligence, not limited to your political skills or your social graces but including a wide range of interpersonal abilities. Being people smart means that you are good at eight skills:

People**Smart Skill 1**
Understanding People

How well you understand others has considerable impact on how successful you will be in every arena. People who understand others communicate more effectively, influence what others think and do, and resolve conflicts in a healthy manner. To discover what makes people tick, you must learn to listen actively, empathize, and acknowledge other viewpoints. You need to know how to ask questions that clarify what a person is trying to say. Understanding people means going beyond the words they speak and learning how to interpret the unspoken. You must also know how to read other people's styles and motives so that you can work with them effectively.

People**Smart Skill 2**
Expressing Yourself Clearly

Being people smart means knowing how to get your message across. Expressing yourself clearly is important to any relationship, personal or business. When you go on and on to make a point, you don't get the results you want. You must know how to get to the point when brevity is required, yet provide enough details so that you don't confuse people. And it's important to say things so that your words are memorable. You must also sense when the other person can help you be clearer by checking understanding of what you've said.

People**Smart Skill 3**
Asserting Your Needs

In order to be people smart, you've got to be your own person. You have to have limits and you have to establish those limits. If you try to be all things to all people, you'll wind up disappointing them. You also need to be straightforward with your wishes. Hinting at what you need from others only leads to disappointment and frustration. Once that happens, you often become angry at others and lose the calm and confidence you need to be at your best.

People**Smart Skill 4**
Exchanging Feedback

Being people smart means having the ability to give feedback easily and do it without giving offense. The feedback you provide must be descriptive, concrete, and intended to be helpful. It should also be well timed, nonblaming, and practical. It's also smart to get in the habit of asking for feedback as well as giving it. If feedback is withheld from you, it's as though you have blinders on. Without feedback, you're always left wondering what the other person is thinking about you. To encourage others to respond to your requests for feedback, you must give them time to organize and express their thoughts, and you must listen to what they're saying with an open mind.

People**Smart Skill 5**
Influencing Others

The people smart person is able to motivate others to action. To be in a more commanding position to influence others, you must become the kind of person who is able to connect with others, unearth their needs, and link them in an effective way to what you have to offer to them. You must also know how to reduce resistance to change and how to make persuasive appeals.

People**Smart Skill 6**
Resolving Conflict

The previous five skills become especially valuable when the situation is taking place in a tense arena. When emotions are running high, all the previous skills must come to the fore and some new skills come into play as well. Interpersonally brilliant people are exceptional conflict resolvers. The key to a person's ability to be a conflict resolver is to know how to get the subject right out on the surface. That's hard if you're scared or anxious. The other person may also be scared or anxious, and maybe even explosive. Besides getting the problem on the table, you must figure out what's bothering you and what's bothering the other person and be able to suggest creative solutions.

People**Smart Skill 7**
Being a Team Player

A person's ability to be interpersonally intelligent is really challenged when it comes to teamwork. All of us are involved in some kind of teamwork, whether at work, with another parent, in a neighborhood group, or in a service organization. Being a part of a team is challenging because you have less personal control over the outcome than you might have in a one-to-one relationship. It's often frustrating since you have fewer opportunities to get your point across and persuade others. Working in a team takes special skills, such as complementing the styles of the others, coordinating the efforts of team members without bossing them around, and building consensus.

People**Smart Skill 8**
Shifting Gears

Finally, people who are interpersonally adept are flexible and resilient; they understand that there are different strokes for different folks. One of the ways you can get a stuck relationship to change is to change the way you act in it. People who are successful in improving relationships are people who can get out of ruts and habits, even if they are helpful in some situations, and do things that are new and different. That's risky, so it's important to know how to avoid sticking your neck out too far.

These eight ways to be people smart give you the tools you'll need to establish and maintain strong relationships with everyone with whom you come into contact—from the perfect stranger to your most intimate partner. You will discover that these eight aspects of interpersonal intelligence fit together almost like a child's building blocks, each one offering a firm foundation for the next. Developing skill in one area also brings benefits in other areas. You'll come to think of these integrated abilities as keys for repairing and developing relationships that haven't always reached the levels you would like.

As you develop these skills, you will discover that many benefits follow:

When you understand someone else, you are appreciated. We like people who take time to understand what we think and feel. Being listened to and understood makes people feel more important and reassured.

When you explain yourself clearly, you are understood. If you can make your point clearly the first time, there may be less confusion to sort out later. This could help things go more smoothly at work, decrease misunderstandings at home, and save you time and energy.

When you assert yourself, you are respected. People respect individuals who are forthright. When you are straightforward, other people will admire your courage and personal strength. Your quiet firmness also goes a long way toward influencing others to honor your needs.

When you exchange feedback, you are enlightened. When you seek feedback, you discover the impact of your behavior on others. When you give feedback to others, you learn whether your views are on target. In the exchange, your relationships with others become fuller and more meaningful.

When you influence others positively, you are valued. Lots of people give advice, but people will welcome your advice only if you do it in a constructive manner. Your counsel will be sought because it is sincere, compelling, and helpful.

When you resolve conflict effectively, you are trusted. If you are soft on people and tough on issues, you don't bruise egos or make enemies. That inspires others to negotiate fairly.

When you collaborate with teammates, you are prized. People with good team skills are the employees most employers covet. You will be given more responsibility and greater rewards if you are a team player.

When you shift gears, your relationships are renewed. That's because a change in *your* behavior is often the catalyst for a change in the *other person's* behavior. You create the opportunity for problem relationships to be mended.

In short, you will find that it is *smart* to become people smart. What will it take to become more people smart? Let's find out. . . .

Becoming People Smart

While some kinds of abilities remain stable or even decline as you age, your ability to be people smart can grow continuously. That's the good news. The bad news is, it won't be easy. We adults are often not open to change. If you don't believe this, try this simple experiment:

> *Fold your arms without thinking. Now, fold them the opposite way so that you switch which arm is on top. Feel awkward? You bet. Well, stay that way for a minute. Now, cross your legs without thinking about it. Yep, the upper part of your body is still uncomfortable but your lower part is nice and comfortable. Now cross your legs the opposite way. Your whole body is now out of your comfort zone. Now go back to the way you normally fold your arms and cross your legs. Feel better? That's the real you. It's comfortable to do things in familiar ways.*

For better or worse, we have gotten used not only to folding our arms and crossing our legs in certain ways, but to relating to other people in certain ways. And it will be uncomfortable to change.

By the time we are grown up, we have tried many times to change some things in our lives and haven't succeeded. After all, look at how many times most of us have failed to lose weight, exercise regularly, spend more quality time with loved ones, donate blood, or do a host of other things we know are important. We undoubtedly have failed to keep New Year's resolutions so many times that we've lost count.

Perhaps our most stubborn source of resistance to change comes from the fact that, by now, we have a highly developed interpersonal style. The temperament with which we were born, the environments to which we've been exposed, and the relationships we have formed all contributed to the creation of a preferred way to relate to others. This style is so dominant that it will probably not change dramatically for the rest of our lives. Our social style develops around two core issues:

How we respond to others: When doing something with others, whether support, work, sex, or whatever, do we focus more on the activity itself or the person with whom we are doing the activity? Some of us are extroverted while others of us are more self-contained.

How we pursue our needs: Do we press our needs, (take initiative) or wait to consider the needs of others? Some of us are forceful while others are patient.

Where we fall with regard to these two core issues goes a long way in determining how we relate to others. Because our style is somewhat set, no one should expect or desire a radical change. But we can look ourselves in the mirror, take pride in our strengths and take stock of our weaknesses, and look for ways to work with and around them.

Think of getting interpersonally fit just as you would think of getting physically fit. While your body type, genetic makeup, and age limit the physical prowess you can achieve, you can still become much more physically fit than you presently are. The same thing is true of interpersonal fitness.

In People**Smart**, you will find a four-step process for boosting your interpersonal intelligence that is realistic and doable.

1. **You've got to WANT IT.** Since changing long-standing habits won't come easily, you have to pay special attention to motivation. You are more likely to be motivated if you are aware of when and where you need the skill the most. To help you make this connection, we will provide you with a list of situations where you might find the skill in question to be particularly relevant in your life at the moment. Choose a situation or two in which you want to excel and focus on them.

2. **You've got to LEARN IT.** Interpersonally intelligent people do certain things very well. Become familiar with the skills possessed by people who exemplify each of the eight People**Smart** skills. While you don't need a whole course in each area to make some changes, it is important to acquire a few basics. Even if you are familiar with this material, we urge you to review it.

3. **You've got to TRY IT.** Reading about what others do well will not suffice-you must do it yourself. With each aspect of interpersonal intelligence, we will encourage you to conduct an "experiment in change." These experiments will allow you to try on a small change in behavior for size. You will test your wings and may find the initial success necessary to sustain further practice

4. **You've got to LIVE IT.** One of the reasons that changes don't last is that after people get pumped up about doing something, they try to make it on sheer inspiration and willpower. They may make some headway but then quickly relapse. Real change comes only by overcoming obstacles that are in the

way in our daily life. We will help you to confront *your* difficulties with each People**Smart** skill. The skill may be difficult for you for reasons that are different than for someone else. If you face the reasons the skill is difficult for *you*, you will be more likely to incorporate the skill into your life.

If you think about it, these four steps apply to any area of self-improvement. For example, assume you are overweight. Even if you admit it to yourself, you really have to **want** to do something about it—especially if you love to eat. Therefore, it may prove necessary to increase your motivation by thinking about specific situations in which you want to enjoy the benefits of being lighter. Next, you might find it helpful to **learn** about the latest diets, ways to lose calories through exercise, and psychological tips to modify your eating behavior. When you decide to **try** something different, it will feel like an "experiment in change." If the experiment is successful, you may be able to build the approach you have been employing into your lifestyle. You will start to **live** it. Along the way, there will be plenty of obstacles to identify and find ways to overcome. If you do, the weight lost will stay off.

These four steps—*want it, learn it, try it*, and *live it*—are especially important when you are seeking changes in your interpersonal effectiveness. You cannot develop your people smarts merely by osmosis.

Before you begin the process of changing, it makes sense to take stock of your current effectiveness. How people smart are you?

How People Smart Are You?

Intelligence tests yield an intelligence quotient or IQ. You may have some idea of your IQ, but do you know your people smart quotient or PQ?

We have devised a rating scale called the *PeopleSmart Scale* to give you an estimate of your PQ. Just like an IQ scale, it is designed so that the average score is 100. Because it is a rating scale, however, your answers will be subjective. Therefore, the more honest you are when you rate yourself, the more accurate your PQ score will be. Also, your standard of comparison may be different from other readers; use people you know as your benchmark. Finally, you might find it difficult to make an overall judgment of yourself at all times and with all people. For example, your PQ at work may be higher than your PQ at home. As you take the test, consider choosing one or two of the following as your frame of reference:

- your partner
- your children
- your boss
- your assistants
- your friends
- your parents
- your colleagues
- your customers

You would then ask yourself how effective you are in your relationships with whomever you choose. Better yet, invite some of these people to give you their views about your People**Smart** skills. You can ask them to rate you on the *PeopleSmart Scale*. Or you can ask them to look over the content of each skill and discuss how they perceive your interpersonal effectiveness in each area. Whatever approach you use, you will find that focusing on a particular relationship is the best way to take stock of your People**Smart** skills. And now, for the rating scale!

The People**Smart Scale**

In the blank in front of each statement, write a number from 1 to 4 according to the following scale:

4 = excellent

3 = good

2 = fair

1 = poor

After you've attached a number to each statement, add the numbers and write the total in the box provided.

People**Smart Skill 1**

- How would you rate your ability to understand people?

_____ 1. I listen attentively to grasp what someone is thinking.

_____ 2. I take notice of other people's body language to understand them better.

_____ 3. To avoid misunderstanding, I ask questions that clarify what the speaker is saying.

_____ 4. I am able to sense what another person is feeling.

_____ 5. I can decipher the underlying reasons why people I know act the way they do.

Skill 1 score:

13

People**Smart Skill 2**

• How would you rate your ability to express your thoughts and feelings clearly?

____ 1. I give just enough detail so that I'm understood.

____ 2. People enjoy listening to me.

____ 3. I can take something complicated and explain it clearly.

____ 4. I say what I mean and what I feel.

____ 5. When I'm not clear, I let the other person ask questions rather then go on and on explaining myself.

Skill 2 score:

People**Smart Skill 3**

• How would you rate your ability to assert your needs?

____ 1. I am decisive about what I will do or not do for others.

____ 2. I speak up when my needs are not being met.

____ 3. I keep calm and remain confident when I get opposition.

____ 4. I stand my ground.

____ 5. I can say no with grace and tact.

Skill 3 score:

PeopleSmart Skill 4

• How would you rate your ability to exchange feedback?

_____ 1. I give appreciation and compliments freely.

_____ 2. When I criticize people, I offer suggestions for improvement.

_____ 3. To get different perspectives, I ask for feedback from a wide range of people.

_____ 4. I ask others for feedback to improve myself, not to fish for compliments.

_____ 5. I listen to feedback I receive from others.

Skill 4 score:

PeopleSmart Skill 5

• How would you rate your ability to influence how others think and act?

_____ 1. I establish rapport with people before trying to persuade them to do something.

_____ 2. I explore other people's viewpoints before trying to convince them of my own.

_____ 3. I give compelling reasons for adopting my viewpoint.

_____ 4. People are not defensive when I give advice.

_____ 5. I give people time to mull over what I've presented to them.

Skill 5 score:

People**Smart Skill 6**

- How would you rate your ability to get conflict resolved?

___ 1. I get the tensions between the other person and myself out on the table.

___ 2. Right from the start, I seek agreement over victory.

___ 3. I learn all I can about the other person's needs and interests when negotiating.

___ 4. I work to solve problems, not blame others, when we hit a stone wall.

___ 5. When I reach an agreement with someone, I make sure we both stick to it.

Skill 6 score:

People**Smart Skill 7**

- How would you rate your ability to collaborate with others?

___ 1. I request help from others and give them assistance in return.

___ 2. I pitch in when the group needs something done.

___ 3. I focus on other people's welfare as much as my own.

___ 4. I keep others informed about what I'm doing if it affects them.

___ 5. I help to facilitate and coordinate the efforts of others.

Skill 7 score:

PeopleSmart Skill 8

- How would you rate your ability to shift gears?

___ 1. When a relationship is not going well, I take the initiative to do something about it.

___ 2. I can see the patterns I fall into with other people.

___ 3. Even if I'm not at fault, I am open to making significant changes in my behavior when necessary.

___ 4. I am willing to take risks when they are called for.

___ 5. I am resilient. If things don't work out, I bounce back.

Skill 8 score:

Now add the numbers in the boxes and write the total here:

That is your PQ rating. If your score is over 150, you have superior People**Smart** intelligence. Keep it up! A score between 125 and 150 indicates that you have very good People**Smart** skills but you should keep working on them. If you scored between 100 and 125, your People**Smart** skills need some improvement. Remember, the scale is designed for 100 to be average or typical. A score under 100 suggests that you need considerable improvement.

You can also identify specific areas where you are especially weak by looking at the totals for each skill. Interpret a score of 10 or less on any one skill as an indication that you have a lot of work to do.

Consider starting a People**Smart** workout program by concentrating on your weakest areas. Or, if you wish, design your program so that you do a light to medium workout in each area. (This will be worthwhile even if you have a total PQ well over 100). You will find that the skills build in complexity if you do the workout in the order given. You can always decide later to go back to one or more of them for a heavier challenge. Regardless of your approach, keep in mind these cautions:

- Don't make your People**Smart** workout a burden! People don't persist with a physical fitness program if they don't enjoy it; the same is true with getting interpersonally fit. Have fun. Experiment. Explore.

- Don't try for a complete makeover! You may do yourself more harm than good. Even though we will give you a slew of advice, pick and choose what appeals to you. Trying to master it all will be counterproductive.

So, are you ready to start boosting your PQ? If so, let's begin by working on People**Smart** Skill 1: understanding what makes people tick.

People**Smart Skill 1**

Understanding People

You can see a lot, just by listening.

—YOGI BERRA

The existentialist philosopher, Jean Paul Sartre, observed that hell is other people! We agree in one sense. If understanding others were an easy proposition, people wouldn't have so many idiomatic expressions to express its difficulty:

"I just can't get inside his head."

"I don't get where she's coming from."

"I don't know what makes him tick."

"I just don't have her number."

"She's a tough nut to crack."

"I can't relate to him at all."

"She's a mystery to me."

Despite the challenge, trying to understand others is the cornerstone of interpersonal intelligence. When you don't understand other people, you can't influence, collaborate, or resolve conflicts with them. On the other hand, when you do understand how others think, feel, and perceive—when you can see through their eyes—all kinds of connection are possible:

Consider the case of a busy patent attorney we'll call Larry. He's not a bad guy, but sometimes he's a bad listener and doesn't tune in to others well. Larry puts in long hours and is usually drained when he finally gets home at the end of the day. A typical evening conversation between Larry and his wife, Laura, goes something like this:

> *Laura: Hi, dear. How was your day?*
> *Larry: Huh? Oh, okay. How are you?*
> *Laura: Well, all right. Actually, I'm really worried about the presentation I have to give tomorrow.*

Larry: *(Opening newspaper) So, what's for dinner?*

Laura: *(Sighs) There's some spaghetti I can zap . . . want some?*

Larry: *Sure. So, how are you?*

Laura: *(Sounding annoyed) I told you . . . I'm very anxious about my presentation. My client's new marketing director is coming to the meeting and I've heard he's been supercritical with the other account execs.*

Larry: *Oh, I wouldn't worry.*

Laura: *Well I am worried! I've changed the approach for the ad campaign three times already, and I . . .*

Larry: *(Interrupting) It'll be fine.*

Laura: *No, but . . .*

Larry: *You always do okay. Say, we got a favorable decision on the Vector opposition in Europe. So now the client wants to provoke an interference in the U.S. counterpart patent after all, because . . .*

Laura: *(Slamming down plate) Here's your pasta!*

Larry: *. . . we can move for invalidity on the prior art we discovered without a presumption of validity going for them. (Puts down paper) So, how was your day? Laura? (Notices she's left) I'll never understand that woman!*

Compare Larry to Pete. Pete is a doctor who conveys to his patients that they are the only important people in his life at the moment he is seeing them, even though he's got a packed waiting room. How does he do it? For starters, his staff is instructed not to interrupt patient visits except when there is an emergency. He listens to them as they tell their problems in detail and uses paraphrasing to show that he understands. Dr. Pete used to think that as soon as he heard enough to make a diagnosis it was expedient to interrupt the patient and make his recommendations. However, he has learned over the years that cutting people off too soon often leads to a misdiagnosis. He's also noticed that when patients feel listened to, they are more informative.

Dr. Pete has also learned that people may have their own reasons for not following through with his treatment recommendations. They may have fears or misinformation or cultural injunctions against following some of his instructions. So he tries to delve below the surface to understand their feelings and opinions. He also watches for important clues about people's concerns by paying attention to their body language. Knowing that each patient is unique, he evaluates his patients' needs, values, and personalities to better tailor their treatment to their temperaments. It may seem to take longer this way, but invariably he ends up saving time and achieving better outcomes in the long run.

In this chapter, we will show you how Dr. Pete and other people-gifted individuals are successful in understanding other people. Before we get to that, we would like you to think about your motivation to begin a workout program in this vital area of interpersonal intelligence.

"Want It"
Motivating Yourself to Be More Understanding of Others

One way to show yourself that you are serious about understanding people better is to choose a specific place to begin. Ask yourself *when* you want to understand someone better. Check the situations below that apply for you:

On the job:

- ☐ When you are interviewing a job applicant.
- ☐ When someone on your staff is less cooperative than usual.
- ☐ When your boss has expectations that don't make sense to you.
- ☐ When a client tells you he dislikes your proposal.
- ☐ When your secretary says she feels overwhelmed.
- ☐ When a colleague's suggestion doesn't make sense.
- ☐ When a coworker's ideas are confusing.
- ☐ When a customer has a complaint.

On the home front:

- ☐ When your partner seems on edge.
- ☐ When your child is irritable.
- ☐ When your child's teacher calls about your child's behavior in school.
- ☐ When your best friend is angry at you.
- ☐ When your partner seems despondent for no apparent reason.
- ☐ When your son complains that kids at school are picking on him.
- ☐ When your mother complains about something that seems very petty.
- ☐ When your teenage daughter stops talking to you.

When you want to make changes, set small, realistic goals. Don't attempt to understand effectively 100% of the time, everywhere, with everyone. Instead, think about the where, when, and who of your own life situations and pick a starting point. Don't begin with your most difficult scenario. You can work up to that. Look for people and circumstances you encounter regularly and where you have the motivation to handle those encounters differently.

Learn It
Three Ways to Understand People Better

Interpersonally intelligent people, those with high PQs, see understanding as an active process. They know that it takes deliberate effort and requires them to use their eyes, ears, voices, brains, and bodies. In a nutshell, here is how they do it: they **listen** and **observe** in order to take in words and body language; they **clarify the meaning** of what they hear by asking open-ended questions and responding to others' feelings and perceptions; and they **interpret behavior** in order to identify the motivation behind people's actions. Let's examine each of these skills in more detail.

1. Listening and Observing

It goes without saying that the most direct way to understand people is to really listen to their ideas and feelings and attend to their body language. When you are absorbed by an entertaining movie or suspenseful novel, attending is easy. However, if you have to sit through a long, boring speech, you know it can be a real chore.

Often, you will need to make a conscious decision and effort to listen and observe carefully, which is why we describe it as an active process. The key steps involved are to *put the speaker in the spotlight, show interest,* and *read body language.*

Put the Speaker in the Spotlight

The Greek philosopher Zeno stated: "We have been given two ears but a single mouth, in order that we may hear more and speak less." Decide that the other person is someone worth listening to and give him or her your full concentration.

Imagine a spotlight shining on the speaker. If you are doing something else that could distract you, stop. Instead of working at your desk, for example, consider getting up and moving to another location, in or outside your office, to help you focus on the speaker. If necessary, instruct others to not interrupt your time with this person.

Obviously, there are situations when you can't pay attention properly: When you are in the middle of something else, rushing out the door, in pain, in the shower, or otherwise engaged. To allow yourself to pay attention, choose a time and place when you are reasonably free of distraction. Sometimes you will be better off postponing an important conversation than dividing your concentration and risking misunderstanding. In this case, consider saying: "In order to give you my undivided attention, can we talk later?"

Paying attention also means refraining from interrupting. Let the speaker finish! Then pause to reflect. Interrupting or finishing the speaker's sentences will only cause frustration and distraction. Remind yourself that you will get your turn to talk. The other person is much more likely to listen to you if you've listened to him or her. When you feel the impulse to interrupt, just notice what you're feeling and file it in your mind for later. In short, paying attention means putting yourself in "receive" mode and keeping yourself there long enough to hear the other person out. If you do, even the most confusing people start to make sense.

Consider Tamara, who is discussing her problems with computer crashes with her colleague Kelly:

> *Tamara: My computer is really giving me grief. It keeps crashing on me.*
>
> *Kelly: Tell me what's happening.*
>
> *Tamara: It just crashes all the time. (Kelly remains attentive but silent.) I don't know what's going on. I think my computer and I weren't meant for each other! What should I do?*
>
> *Kelly: Tell me more about it first.*
>
> *Tamara: Well, it just freezes on me. Nothing moves. Maybe it's not a real crash, but I can't do any work on it right now. I've tried restarting the computer but I get the same result. I wonder if everything is connected right. (Tamara looks at her computer.) Oh my God, one of my connections is loose. I can't believe I didn't think about checking. (Tamara secures the connection.) I feel like an idiot, but thanks for listening. I probably would have gone through the whole day without discovering the problem.*

It's natural, of course, to find it hard to hang in there with people who are droners or ramblers. Unfortunately, some people "talk to think." They work out their thoughts by expressing everything that occurs to them. In such cases, don't get bogged down in the details. Focus on the broad picture of what they are saying but give them enough time to express themselves.

Finally, try to empty your mind as you listen attentively. Patricia Ann Ball, a former president of the National Speakers Association, tells the following story:

When my daughter was a little girl, she made a brilliant statement that has stuck with me ever since. "What did you say, Mom? I didn't hear you. I had my own answer running!" She said that because I was chastising her. Be very careful when you are listening to someone that you are not listening with your "answer running." (Straight Talk Is More Than Words, p. 35.)

Show Interest

By showing interest in what people have to say, you get more information. That's because other people are more likely to communicate openly when you actively tune into them. For example, can you recall having a conversation with a person who kept looking around the room, or drumming his chair with a pencil? Or with someone who fixed you with a blank, expressionless stare and kept her arms crossed while you talked? How did you respond? Most people tend to respond to this kind of behavior by backing off or clamming up.

Individuals who are skilled at reading people make a point of connecting with them. They make comfortable, flexible eye contact, neither avoiding the speaker's gaze nor staring excessively. They send encouraging signals by facing the speaker and leaning forward, nodding and mirroring with their facial expressions what they are hearing. (Smiling is good, but not if the speaker is describing his mother's funeral.) Your actions are the most basic element of your communication. If your nonverbal signals fail to match your speech, others will sense that something is off and feel mistrustful or guarded.

Of course, you also show interest through your words. At the simplest level, you can offer encouragement by interjecting expressions such as "ah-ha," "I see," "go on," or "no kidding."

You can also acknowledge the other person's point of view, even if you don't completely agree with it. Acknowledging means considering the circumstances and recognizing the kernel of truth or good in what the speaker is trying to communicate. Imagine, for example, a child who is berated by her mother for being argumentative. The child then counters: "But you argue with Daddy a lot." Should the mother interpret this as a mere diversion? Or say something more like: "You're right. I do. Both of us should argue less!"

You can also encourage the speaker by *not* responding in ways that negate or reject, even if we do this with good intentions. Here are some examples of "pseudo-accepting" responses that fail to demonstrate respect and acceptance:

Denying the validity of what the speaker feels or believes—"Oh, you shouldn't feel that way!" "That's silly." "How can you think like that?" It's not that you can't disagree. At an appropriate point in the conversation you can share your own perspective. But when your goal is to listen and understand, you will not succeed by negating the speaker's point of view.

Judging the speaker—"That's horrible!" "I can't believe you did that!" Avoid rushing to judgment. Hear the person out. If there really are grounds for arrest, you can call the police later.

Giving unsolicited advice—"If I were you . . . " "Honey, you should dump the creep!" "Look, I've been there, and, believe me, you don't want to . . . " We do owe constructive feedback to people who ask us for it, but volunteering advice when someone may just want us to listen leaves the speaker feeling discounted. He or she may just give up.

When you want to show interest as a listener, try to hear what it is that the speaker wants to have recognized or appreciated. Convey understanding of its importance to him or her. Acknowledgment is an important way to build trust and encourage others to be more open with you.

Read Body Language

Actions speak louder than words. It is estimated that only 7% of the impact we have on others comes from our word choices. The rest of the 93% is due to our body language and how we say what we say (tone of voice, speed of speech, volume). Also, our body language is mostly unconscious and possibly the most honest form of communication. Therefore, it's impossible to understand people without paying close attention to their body movements, facial expression, and vocal qualities.

There is a danger, however, in jumping to conclusions on the basis of a single behavior. When a person has folded arms, does it mean he or she feels threatened or merely skeptical? Does a person's silence mean anger? Or fear? Or a sense of awe? Does standing with hands in one's pockets mean a person is secretive or just critical? (Or has cold hands?)

Reading nonverbal signals correctly depends on noticing a cluster of behaviors. For example, when a person closes his eyes, folds his arms, and remains silent, chances are he is rejecting what you are saying! The following table provides a reasonable guide to reading a person's emotional state.

Anxiety — fidgeting, hand wringing, shifting from side to side, blinking, high pitched voice, throat clearing

Lack of interest — blank stare, doodling, looking around, monotone voice, tapping feet, drumming table

Involvement	leaning forward, open hands, moving to speaker's rhythm, direct eye contact, uncrossed legs, smile
Anger	redness of skin, loud voice, finger-pointing, steely eyes, legs/arms crossed, frown
Reflection	chin-stroking, nodding, index finger to lips, eyes glancing upward, glasses in mouth, ear turned toward speaker
Secretiveness	nose-touching, sideways glance, squint, covering mouth, smirk, low volume, mumbling
Disdain	hands on hip, hands behind neck, staccato voice, leg over chair, feet on desk, fingers hooked in belt

Variations from an individual's usual body language may be signals that something out of the ordinary is going on. Sudden changes in body language may indicate that an individual has been caught off guard—lying, for example. A vocal change, such as more rapid speech or a higher pitch, breaking eye contact, nervous gestures, or covering one's eyes or mouth can be telltale signs of dissembling. It is also important to notice when people rely on conversational ploys to control or direct interaction. When people avoid giving a reasonable response, answer curtly, change the subject, go off on tangents, or answer with a question, there's often something he or she is trying to conceal or evade.

Although it's important to avoid making pat judgments about people based on observations of their body language, persistent trends do reflect personality traits. Dramatic variations from the norm can alert you to stress or changes that may be affecting people. Your observations of others can contribute to your understanding of them.

2. Clarifying Meaning

The deeper level of understanding is recognizing the significance of what the other person tells us—the meaning behind the words. To understand others is to go beyond "just the facts, ma'am," asking yourself: "How must he feel?" "What does this mean to her?" When you want a deeper understanding of someone, use these three key techniques: *ask open-ended questions, paraphrase,* and *respond to feelings*.

Ask Open-ended Questions

It's fairly obvious that you can learn more about what someone means by asking questions. When you ask questions, you also succeed in showing your interest in what the other person is saying. There are different categories of questions: direct and open-ended questions can be useful tools for clarifying meaning, while leading questions can impede good communication.

Direct questions are those that require a simple factual response. "Did you like the movie?" "How late did you work last night?" "Is Lee okay?" "Would you rather have chicken or fish for dinner?" "Who do you think will get the promotion?" These are all examples of direct questions. They tend to be straightforward, and we can use them when you want specific information. Because their scope is precise, direct questions don't usually invite much elaboration from the speaker. Since they are usually "low demand," in this respect, direct questions are usually a nonthreatening way to request clarification, especially from someone who is shy or anxious. (An exception to this would be, "Do you care about me or not?")

Open-ended questions invite the speaker to expand or elaborate on her message. They offer more leeway to respond and share.

31

"What was the upsetting part for you about what he said?" "How do you foresee things getting better on the job?" "Why do you think Emilio was so quiet at dinner?" Use open-ended questions to encourage others to "open up" and share thoughts, feelings, and opinions. By doing so, you increase your chances of learning what's really important to them.

Leading questions, in contrast, are really statements masquerading as questions. "Don't you think he was tacky to say that?" "Are you really going to wear that dress?" "Why didn't you call first?" Like judging, denying, or giving unsolicited advice, asking leading questions puts others on the defensive. Rather than clarifying, they sidetrack communication. Many questions that start with a negative ("didn't he," "aren't you," "can't you") are leading questions.

Paraphrase

When you paraphrase, you reflect back to the speaker what you have heard. Do this by restating his or her message, accurately and succinctly, in your own words. Paraphrasing helps clarify meaning in two important ways. First, by offering the speaker your version of what you've heard, you test your understanding. If you've misconstrued, you give the speaker the opportunity to restate and correct the message. If you got it right, you'll get confirmation. Second, a paraphrase demonstrates your attention and interest, thus "rewarding" the speaker and encouraging further sharing, and at a deeper level. This maximizes your chances of learning what's really on his or her mind.

People sometimes reject the notion of paraphrasing, usually because they have had negative experiences with it. Paraphrasing is not effective if it turns into parroting:

Lou: *Man, she made me so mad!*

Sam: *So, like, she really made you mad.*

Duh! Instead, use your own words:

Lou: *Man, she made me so mad!*

Sam: *She really ticked you off.*

People also get turned off by overuse of trite formats for paraphrasing, such as "So, what I hear you saying is . . ." Avoid rote formulas. Just stating your own translation of the other person's message will be more immediate and genuine. The following exchange took place between Suzanne Gallo, a manager, and one of her employees, David Johnson, who was being "called on the carpet."

Gallo: *Come in, David. Have a seat. I suppose you're wondering why I want to talk to you.*

Johnson: *Yes, I guess I am.*

Gallo: *Well, David, recently something has come up that I want to know your feelings about. Remember the Adamson report?*

Johnson: *What about it?*

Gallo: *To be frank with you, there was a lot of disagreement on the figures that were used, and the boss wants the whole thing done over. It wasn't up to the level of the reports you've been turning out in the past. I have to admit that myself. But I want to hear your views about it.*

Johnson: *Well, there isn't much to say. I sort of figured it would get rejected anyway. I wasn't happy about the damn thing either. (Getting a little emotional.)*

Gallo: You weren't pleased with it either?

Johnson: No, I wasn't. Look, it takes about 25 to 30 hours, at least, for me to write up a report like that even when I've already worked up the figures! You know how long I spent on that report? About 5 hours! And I wasn't as sure on the figures as I should have been either.

Gallo: You didn't get to put in much time on the report, is that it?

Johnson: No, I didn't. In fact, I don't blame them for rejecting it at all. Like I said, it was a lousy job. But it won't be the last lousy job they get from me unless I get some help down here. There's no way I can run a research department and do the odds and ends that get sent in my direction. When we were a smaller outfit, it was possible, but not now.

Gallo: You're saying that you have too many assignments then?

Johnson: Yes, that's exactly what I'm saying! (Getting more upset.) I'm expected to do everybody's odds and ends. Production wants this, marketing wants that, cost accounting wants something else. Then along comes the Control Committee and their report. They give me a week's notice to get it out. I know I'm running a staff department, but there's no way one person can handle it all.

Paraphrasing may feel awkward at first and takes some practice to do smoothly and skillfully. When you succeed in concisely restating the core of the speaker's message, you'll probably know it. People usually respond to an effective paraphrase by saying "exactly!" or words to that effect, letting you know that you've grasped the meaning of what they've said.

Respond to Feeling

Feelings are a crucial aspect of meaning. Often the way someone feels about an event is far more important than the circumstances surrounding it. Yet many of us are hesitant to respond to others at a feeling level. We may see feelings as too personal to discuss. If you avoid acknowledging how others feel, you sacrifice a crucial aspect of understanding and connecting with them. In contrast, when you can translate your observations into an accurate reflection of someone's current feeling state, you are sharing a powerful acknowledgement of meaning.

Like paraphrasing, responding to feeling entails reflecting the speaker's message, essentially filling in the blank: "you feel _____." Feeling responses are particularly valuable to share when the speaker's tone and body language are conveying strong emotion (e.g., eyes tearing or teeth clenched), or when the words are laden with feeling ("it's just so *nerve*-wracking to go through this!"). In situations like these, the speaker's feelings may be the most salient part of the picture.

Two elements contribute to an effective feeling response: choosing the right feeling category and the right level of intensity. Examples of feeling categories include anger, sorrow, happiness, and fear (mad, sad, glad, and scared, in brief). All feelings can be experienced at low, medium, or high levels. A low level of anger, for instance, might be irritation; a medium level, resentment; a high level, rage. For sorrow, a low level could be disappointment; a medium level, sadness; a high level, despair. It's important to gauge the speaker's feeling intensity when making a response. To say to someone who is livid with rage "you seem a little annoyed" does not convey understanding. The more you expand your feeling vocabulary to encompass a range of feeling categories and intensity levels, the better your ability to deliver a response that is on target will be. You can expand your feeling word vocabulary by completing a "feeling matrix." See how many words you can add to each of the following feeling categories and intensity levels:

	Angry	Sad	Happy	Frightened
High	Enraged	Devastated	Overjoyed	Terrified
Medium	Resentful	Melancholic	Gratified	Startled
Low	Miffed	Discouraged	Pleased	Uneasy

When you are able to recognize not only *what* someone is feeling, but *why* he or she is feeling that way, you have come a long way toward understanding the meaning of his or her experience. If you can listen carefully to another person and accurately reflect: "you feel _____ because _____," you will truly be standing in his or her shoes. (If you are unsure of the reasons for a person's feelings, say something like: "I sense how disappointed you are but I don't know why. Help me understand.")

Sometimes speakers send mixed or confusing signals. When someone contradicts himself or displays body language that is not in sync with his words, it's hard to know what he really means. Skilled responding can be very helpful in situations like this. A tactful way to deal with a speaker's inconsistency is to say something like: "On the one hand, you're saying x, but on the other hand, you seem to be saying y. I'm confused." Then carefully listen and observe how the speaker responds. Paraphrase, or make a feeling response that reflects what you hear. The chances are good that the picture will become clearer.

Obviously, it takes conscious effort to use the skills involved in clarifying meaning. Initially, you may feel as if you are operating in slow motion when you practice these skills. If you stick with it, you'll begin to notice that you are starting to understand others at a deeper level, and that you are more often on the same wavelength with people.

3. Interpreting Behavior

Most of us agree with the maxim: "actions speak louder than words." However, understanding someone's actions is often difficult. You may understand why people who are similar to you behave the way they do. But when you need to deal with individuals whose needs, styles, and backgrounds are significantly different than yours, things can get confusing. Three essential skills that assist you in interpreting the behavior of others are to *evaluate their goals, assess their personal styles*, and *recognize their differences*.

Evaluate Goals

There are three basic goals we all pursue, in varying degrees, in order to feel safe and worthwhile: *control, connection, and competence*.

Being in *control* means having power over your life—sitting in the driver's, rather than the passenger's, seat. Individuals who grow up in environments with too much or too little control may develop deep concerns about control as adults. Children with an alcoholic parent, for example, often grow up in a chaotic family environment where behavior is erratic and unpredictable. As adults, they may be particularly concerned with maintaining orderly homes and regular routines. Often, people with excessive needs for control try to control others, instead of accepting that all any of us can do is control ourselves. Others leave people alone but overly control themselves. An extreme example is someone with an eating disorder.

In contrast, people who cope by abdicating control (say,

someone who learned early in life how to accommodate a strict or bullying parent) appear weak, indecisive, or deferential. They tend to let others control them. Instead of seeking control, they become dependent on others. A clinical example is someone who is agoraphobic.

Connection with others means inclusion, involvement, affiliation, support, love, affection, and membership. People with concerns about connection are fearful about being left out or ignored. Extreme concerns with connection can develop out of early experiences of being either abandoned or smothered. Individuals who are overly concerned with connection may come across as needy or intrusive. They may tend to live through others.

People who are uncomfortable with connection may be withdrawn or have a tendency to avoid others. Often people are ambivalent about connection: They may want it, but fear it or believe they don't deserve it. Instead of connection, they obtain distance. Such individuals may seek attention through rebellion or deviant behavior. The responses they get usually reinforce their ambivalence. These are the people who live according to the maxim: "negative strokes are better than no strokes."

When *competence* is the goal, people are concerned about being successful and demonstrating achievement and mastery to themselves and others. Too much or too little praise and recognition from authority figures early in life can shape an individual who is preoccupied with his or her competence. When people are overly concerned with their competence, they may be obsessed with accomplishment, often at the expense of relationships, or they may become perfectionists who hound themselves and others. Bragging, driven, or "Type A" individuals are usually worried about whether they're competent enough.

People who have simply given up any hope of proving their

competence come across as helpless and impotent. They may be chronic failures or individuals who aim too low and don't try to succeed for fear of failure.

When you are having difficulty understanding someone, think about these three Cs. If you can accurately "diagnose" the person's concerns, his or her behavior will start making more sense to you. It's also important to understand your own agenda, which can sometimes cause you to see others in distorted ways. For example, a supervisor who is trying to connect with subordinates may ask many questions or even hover over subordinates a bit. If one of her subordinates has a strong need for autonomy, he may misread her attention as controlling, micro-managing behavior. Let's look at a couple of further examples:

> *An elderly widower recently moved into an assisted living facility. Although he's of sound mind and not suffering from dementia or any other major psychiatric disorder, he has been refusing to change his clothes from one day to the next. His son and daughter-in-law become frustrated when he refuses to respond to their efforts to get him to change. They view him as someone who is trying to separate himself from the family. His behavior makes more sense if they recognize that he's been experiencing sudden and sweeping changes in his life, and not by any choice of his own. His wife is gone and he no longer has his familiar home. His "inexplicable" stance about not changing his clothes may be a way for him to feel some measure of control over his circumstances. Perhaps it will be more helpful to offer him some empathy for what he's been going through, as well as more choices in his day to day routine.*

Then there's the couple who recently broke up:

The young man bitterly tells his friend: "It drove me crazy how she kept asking me to do all these things for her! I mean, this girl can and did install an air conditioner in her bedroom. She changed the oil in her car, for crying out loud! And then she'd keep asking me to do stupid things for her, like changing the print cartridge in her fax machine, or checking her tire pressure. It was ridiculous!" Meanwhile, she tells her friend: "He never showed me any affection! Never put his arm around me or called me pet names. And then, when I'd ask him to do simple little things like, say, check my tire pressure, just to show he really cared about me, he wouldn't do them!" He's focused on her competence, while she's pursuing a goal of greater connection.

You can use the three *C*s as a checklist to help yourself think more objectively about what may be motivating someone whose behavior you find confusing. Just be careful not to read into a situation what's not there. And don't be afraid to ask: "I don't understand why you (supply puzzling behavior). Could you help me understand?"

Assess Personal Style

In addition to variations in goals, people have a range of personality styles. Although we each have our own preferences in other people, it's important to recognize that *different* doesn't necessarily mean *better* (or worse). Are right-handed people "better" than lefties?

One widely used tool for identifying different personality types is the *Myers–Briggs Type Indicator* or *MBTI* (Myers, 1993). Based on the work of Carl Jung, the *MBTI* defines eight personality preferences that people use in dealing with the world. These preferences are organized into four scales, each with two preferences:

- Where do you focus your attention?

  Extraversion **(E)**: you are energized by the outer world

  Introversion **(I)**: you are more tuned into your inner world

- How do you learn?

  Sensing **(S)**: by attending to facts, data, the "givens"

  Intuition **(N)**: by attending to possibilities, overall patterns, the "big picture"

- How do you decide?

  Thinking **(T)**: through logic, objective standards

  Feeling **(F)**: through values, inner harmony

- How do you orient to the outer world?

  Judging **(J)**: by being structured, organized, decisive

  Perceiving **(P)**: by being flexible, spontaneous, adaptive

Based on your preferences within each scale, the *MBTI* yields a four-letter code expressing your individual personality style. Someone with the code ENTP, for example, tends to be innovative, versatile, analytic, and attracted to entrepreneurial ideas, while the counterpart, ISFJ, tends to be sympathetic, loyal, kind, and concerned with helping those who need support. There is no one "right" code. Each has its unique strengths and developmental needs.

When you understand an individual's personal style and preferences, you will have a better idea of how to talk effectively with him or her. Some brief tips for the types described above are:

E: • let them think aloud

  • try to respond to them quickly

I: • give them time to think

• don't overwhelm them with too many questions

S: • show them evidence (details, examples)

• be practical, realistic, orderly

N: • give them the global concept first and let them ask for details

• tell them the challenges, changes, or benefits of an idea

T: • be calm, concise, logical

• list pros and cons of alternatives

F: • be friendly and get to know them before getting to business

• show them how an idea will affect and be of value to people

J: • set a timetable and stick to it

• give advance warning of changes

P: • be flexible, allowing for options and changes

• bring in new information and ideas

Many organizations use the *MBTI* to help people understand themselves and others, communicate better, and approach problem solving more creatively and constructively. (If you want to investigate *MBTI* further, go to www.mbti.com.)

Recognize Differences

The dimensions on which people differ are almost infinite, and each contributes something to our view of the world. Our size, shape, intelligence, ability, and birth order are just a few of the factors that make us each who we are. We won't try to offer an exhaustive checklist of the variables to keep in mind when you want to make sense of other people, but some demographic factors strongly impact the way people perceive, understand, and respond to the world, and it's helpful to keep them in mind:

Gender: Authors John Gray, Carol Gilligan, Deborah Tannen, and others have described the ways in which men and women think differently, talk differently, and often pursue very different agendas. Men may feel a more urgent need to fix things, for example, while women may be more concerned with empathy when something goes wrong. Differences in sexual orientation can also create barriers to understanding. Gay and lesbian individuals often feel discounted and disapproved of by the dominant culture and may perceive some events and circumstances accordingly.

Race: We are not yet a color-blind society. Racism and racial differences have a powerful impact on how we perceive relationships and interpersonal behavior. Whites are often quite unaware of privileges they enjoy that people of color may not. (For example: being able to rent an apartment or get a cab when and where you like, without hassles, or get a promotion without worrying whether others think it was due only to an affirmative action policy.) In some situations, racial minorities may perceive racism when none is intended. Whites, in turn, may fail to recognize the racist implications of their behavior. Few of us are comfortable confronting racial issues that impede our understanding of one another, but that doesn't mean they aren't there.

Culture and ethnicity: Our backgrounds and origins can create differences in how we look at time, individuality, family, nonverbal behavior, modes of address, authority, foods and beverages, illness and caretaking, etc. In the Middle East, for example, results-oriented Americans should avoid talking about business until they get to know their prospective clients. When visiting Germany, guests are expected to stand when a German host enters the room. People attempting to do business in Japan should be forewarned of the Japanese expectation for preparation for meetings.

Religion: Our faiths and beliefs can be a source of profound differences in how we see ourselves, our world, and other people, affecting our most basic values and assumptions. At a very simple level, we need to recognize that we don't all observe the same holidays and customs. We also differ in our views of sexuality, forgiveness, afterlife, and the nature of God.

Socioeconomic status: People live very different realities based on wealth and class. Attitudes and behavior are shaped not only by our current circumstances, but by those in which we were raised. Many people who achieve financial success after an impoverished childhood never feel they've "made it," while individuals who grow up in prosperous circumstances may have high expectations about their standard of living.

Age cohort: Older adults, who grew up during the Depression, may never feel truly secure financially. Baby boomers tend to define themselves as the dominant culture and grew up with an expectation that their standard of living would keep improving. Generation X learned to live with a constantly changing world of technological possibilities. No wonder we have generation gaps.

Our differences pose many challenges to understanding and appreciating one another. They are part of the fabric of our lives. When you can hear and see others in the full richness of their diversity, you gain in wisdom.

Try It
Exercises to Improve Understanding

Think of these activities as "experiments in change." They are opportunities to try out each of the skills of understanding others in preparation for implementing your own goals for personal change. Try one or more of these experiments and feel free to invent some of your own.

Listening and Observing

1. For a couple of days, keep a log of your conversations, either at home or at work, and record how often you interrupt others. You can do this informally by placing an object, like a coin or paperclip, in a particular pocket each time you catch yourself interrupting. Calculate the percentage of your conversations that included interruptions. How do you feel about your interruption rate? If you're unhappy with it, choose a specific person or situation and, for one full day, do not interrupt at all. Notice how this makes you feel and how others respond. See if you can identify what makes it hard for you to hear people out, then read the barriers and prescriptions we will discuss soon in order to select possible remedies.

2. Think of the person you consider the best listener you know, someone you invariably feel comfortable talking with. For a week, study his or her nonverbal behavior during conversations the person has with you or others. What does the person do that conveys interest and acceptance? Write down some of the behaviors you notice the person using. Next, notice whether any of these behaviors are part of your own present repertoire. If not, which of the behaviors would you be willing to try out? Choose one or two and practice them.

Clarifying Meaning

1. Ask someone you feel comfortable with to help you practice paraphrasing or responding to feelings. Ask the person to talk to you about some situation he or she feels strongly about. Listen and make a paraphrase or feeling response to every significant point the person shares with you. Tape the conversation, then review it with him or her. Ask the person to rate each of your responses as

"on" or "off." For at least one "off" response, see if you can come up with a response the other person thinks is more accurate. Practice paraphrases and feeling responses separately at first so you don't get confused.

2. Make a commitment to ask open-ended questions in conversations with others whom you want to understand better. See if you can avoid direct yes or no questions and use openers like "what . . ." "why . . ." "how . . ." If the other person seems defensive about your questions, add: " I want to be sure I understand what you're saying."

Interpreting Behavior

1. Think of someone you simply don't understand at all. Think about this person's behavior in a few key situations. What seems to be his or her primary goal: control, connection, or competence? Is this person's goal different from yours? When you recognize his or her usual goal, do you understand the person better? Would you change any of your own behavior in dealing with this person in the future?

2. Identify someone you know who's as different as possible from you. On a 1 to 10 scale, where 1 is the lowest and 10 the highest rating, rate how well you understand this person's values, behavior, and motivation. Now list some of the ways this person is different from you, including goals, personal style, and demographic factors. Which of these differences may be interfering with your ability to understand this person? Try to imagine yourself as this person, seeing the world through his or her eyes. How do you feel? How do things seem different to you? Now re-rate your understanding of the person. Is there a change?

Live It
Overcoming Your Own Barriers
to Lasting Change

There's a saying: "Everyone wants to grow and no one wants to change." Change is difficult, especially for adults. It's realistic to expect that you'll encounter barriers and setbacks, even when you truly want to become better at understanding. It helps to be aware of where your pitfalls are likely to be and to think ahead about how to navigate them.

There are many reasons why people have difficulty understanding others. See which of the following common barriers may apply to you and think about how our "prescriptions" could help you overcome them:

It's hard to pay attention because you're eager to talk yourself.

> Practice being fully present, having no other thoughts of your own. (Don't have your "answer running.") Listen to capture every word. Having the power to restrain yourself this way may give you more credibility with the speaker. Then, when you've listened and understood, state that you'd like to be heard without interruption.

You know exactly what the person is going to say. You could practically finish her sentences.

> And accomplish what? You knew what she'd say, she knew you'd interrupt. Try to break the habit of interrupting people, which only produces frustration. Go for the higher ground and hear the person out. There may even be the remote possibility that she'll surprise you this time and say something you didn't expect.

You have a short attention span.

Give yourself a little push by pretending you will have to take a test on what the other person is saying. Do lots of paraphrasing and summarizing to keep yourself focused. Imagine you are a journalist or interviewer who is taking careful notes.

You have a strong need to give advice.

Ask yourself how you feel when others give you unsolicited advice. Think of advice as a seasoning you want to use sparingly. Try to empathize and ask yourself how the person feels, instead.

The person goes on and on, or keeps repeating himself.

Listen for feelings, as well as content, which may be the real point of the speaker's message. Interject paraphrases and feeling responses to let the person know he's being heard. Ask questions to try to get to the heart of the issue (e.g., "so what's the most important part of that for you?").

You have a hard time understanding people who are very different from you.

First, remind yourself that different doesn't mean wrong or inferior. Instead of discounting or trying to change the person, make an extra effort to listen without judging. Acknowledge and show empathy. Ask yourself what the other person's goals and values are and recognize how your own assumptions may be getting in the way of hearing the person.

You totally disagree with what the person is saying and you're afraid that showing understanding will convey acceptance.

Let go of the notion that understanding equals agreement. They are separate activities. Tell yourself that listening simply means showing the other person that you understand where he is coming from, even if you yourself wouldn't be caught dead there. Feel free to disagree after you have fully grasped what the person has to say.

You get mad when the other person starts saying negative things about you.

Breathe. Listen and breathe. Losing your temper will only make things worse. Recognize that the person's negative words reflect his feelings, not your worth. Try to listen with an open mind and to understand his point of view. If you still conclude that his anger is without merit, simply say so.

The other person takes advantage of your interest by monopolizing the conversation.

Don't let it happen. After you've listened, you've earned the right to be the speaker. Change the subject.

The other person doesn't make sense.

Probe for understanding and use the skills of clarifying meaning. It may be that the person is confused or coming from a frame of reference very different from yours. Ask questions, paraphrase, and respond to feelings to get a better handle on the person's meaning. Think about what the person's goals may be.

When you feel upset or angry, the last thing you want to do is be understanding.

> Perhaps the most important time to do this is when you are in conflict with someone else. If you can channel your energy into trying to understand the other person, you will feel less defensive and may help defuse the situation. Understanding is not the same as giving in.

Give yourself plenty of praise for small successes with understanding others. Even though change can be difficult, it is certainly possible when you approach it in realistic, manageable steps and reward yourself for progress.

Understanding is the first and most fundamental of the abilities of interpersonally intelligent people. Improving your understanding skills will not only bring direct benefits, but will prepare you to perform other skills, such as expressing yourself clearly.

Expressing Yourself Clearly

Nothing is so simple that it cannot be misunderstood.

—Jr. Teague

The manager says to the assistant: "I'm looking at our unpaid bills. Would you check on the number for Acme?" The assistant replies, "We owe them $200." "No!" replied the manager. "What's their **phone** number?!"

Have you recently said something to another person that was absolutely clear to you, but a mystery to the listener? It happens to all of us. We sometimes assume people can read our minds. We simply don't appreciate that the approximately 800 words we use in daily conversation have, in total, about 14,000 meanings! Every time we use a word, we run the risk that the listener will misinterpret what we say.

Good communicators don't force others to be mind readers. They express themselves clearly and colorfully and make a point succinctly. People with poor communication skills are hard to listen to and understand:

A truly terrible communicator who stands out in memory (let's call her Marcia) infuriated the members of a work team over a period of months with her endless, meandering, circumstantial speech. Marcia never came to the point. People aged visibly waiting for Marcia to finish a sentence. By the time Marcia did finish a sentence, they had forgotten what her original point was. Marcia was self-absorbed, oblivious to the effect she had on other team members. On one occasion, after a lengthy monologue about how overworked she was, Marcia wondered aloud whether she ought to just take a sabbatical and go to an island for some rest. When team members expressed concern, Marcia went right on talking, explaining that she couldn't go now because she had library books due.

Compare Marcia to Sally. Sally is a car salesperson who connects with both female customers and male customers. Sally gets asked lots of questions, from the features of the cars she sells to the leasing options available to the customer. She has an uncanny ability to explain technical information in terms that any person, even automobile "dummies," can understand. One of her talents, for example, is to compare the features of a car to common household items. She also tells people no more than they want to know at the moment. When asked to make comparisons to a competitor's cars, she answers directly and honestly. She closes many sales in large part because she speaks enthusiastically about her own experience with the product she sells. Plus, she is such a friendly, warm person and engaging conversationalist, you just have to like her. If she can give you the deal you want, you want to buy from her.

What does Sally know that Marcia doesn't? In this chapter, we will help you sharpen your skills at clear self-expression by learning how excellent communicators do it. We'll also look realistically at what makes good communication hard for people and offer strategies and experiments to move you up the scale. Are you ready to get to work on being a better communicator?

Want It
Motivating Yourself to Become a Better Communicator

As we've said before, change doesn't come easily. All of us tend to be more or less set in our ways. This is not to say that you can't change but you've got to have reasons that motivate you to try. If you consider the situations in your day-to-day life in which better communication can help you, you may be able to identify specific rewards for brushing up your skills. The more personalized the benefit, the more powerfully it can motivate you to change.

In what situations do you most need to express yourself more clearly? If you think about the different arenas of your life, where could skillful communication most enhance your success and happiness? Do some of these situations suggest times when you have been less than satisfied with how you got your message across? Check them.

On the job:

☐ Giving a ten minute presentation to clients on a complicated project.

☐ Orienting a new employee to office procedures.

☐ Presenting your ideas for improving an unsuccessful product to skeptical team members.

☐ Giving detailed instructions to a temporary office worker.

☐ Conducting a performance review with a subordinate who doesn't recognize his work deficiencies.

☐ Updating your busy, impatient boss on the status of your projects.

☐ Conversing with important clients over a business lunch.

☐ Getting your point across to colleagues during meetings.

☐ Presenting your experience and qualifications during a job interview.

On the home front:

☐ Explaining the highlights of your day to a tired partner.

☐ Giving instructions to a new babysitter.

☐ Helping your kids with their homework.

☐ Talking with a new acquaintance at a party.

☐ Responding to your father-in-law's questions about your job.

☐ Telling someone how to get to your house by car.

☐ Talking to your teenager about the dangers of drugs.

☐ Describing your worrisome symptoms to a busy doctor.

☐ Coaching your child's soccer team.

☐ Expressing your tastes and preferences to a new friend.

We hope these examples prompt you to pinpoint circumstances of your own where better communication could pay off for you. Think about where, when, and with whom you need to sharpen your self-expression, and go for it!

Learn It
Three Ways to Become a Clear Communicator

High PQ people do three things very well: they **get their message across** by being concise, direct, and expressive; they **talk straight** by saying what they think and feel and don't beat around the bush; and they **include the listener** by allowing him or her to ask questions and clarify what they've said. Let's look more closely at each of these three ways to communicate effectively.

1. Getting Your Message Across

What does it take to get your point across? Good communicators do it by *thinking before they talk, orienting and summarizing*, and *painting with words*.

Think Before You Talk

Imagine you are selecting the camera focus for a photo. You can set the focus on "infinity" to capture a wide landscape, or you can zoom in for a portrait, but you can't do both simultaneously. Similarly, when you want to make your points effectively, you have to decide how much information to include. For example, the next time you describe to someone the week you've had, decide in advance whether you want to give the big picture or the juicy details. Meandering Marcia, whom we met earlier in this chapter, consistently packed too many irrelevant facts into her speech. On the other hand, if you've tried listening to someone who leaves out important pieces of information, or jumps from one topic to another with no connections in between, you know how confusing that can be.

Good communicators don't think out loud. They organize and prioritize the messages they want to convey, highlighting the essentials. They are easy to listen to because they think before they talk. You can be like them by preparing what you want to say rather than speaking impulsively. This is especially true if your message is complicated.

Imagine that you are giving a synopsis of a movie plot to a friend. How effectively would you convey the main points without bogging down in excessive detail? Or imagine that you had to give a detailed assignment to another person. By thinking before you talk, you will be more likely to be understood. When you think out loud, lots of extraneous information (what communication people call "noise") gets in the way.

Orient and Summarize

If you prepare the listener to receive new information and recap key points at the end, you are likely to be more effective at getting your point across. Orienting sets the stage by briefly introducing a topic or task so that the listener knows what you are going to talk about. Poor communicators plunge right in, giving the listener no opportunity to focus. We all use orienting, at least informally. "Are you sitting down?," for example, cues a listener to be ready for a shock. "I have good news and bad news" prepares him or her for a mixture of pleasure and disappointment. We do brief orientations frequently at work ("We need to talk about the sales figures for the last quarter") and at home ("Honey, about last night").

When you want someone's full attention and participation in a task, a more detailed orientation can be helpful. Suppose that, as a manager, you are about to conduct a performance review with Joe, a new employee. Joe is anxious about the review and doesn't really know what to expect. You could help Joe participate in the review process through a brief orientation like this:

Joe, we're going to spend the next hour or so discussing your work performance over the past year and completing this evaluation form together. (You show Joe the form.) I'd like us to do this collaboratively, so that we share our thinking about how you're doing. Let's start by talking about your strengths and accomplishments, then discuss areas for improvement, then goals for the next year. For each of those areas, I'd like you to share your thoughts first, then I'll add mine. If we have any disagreements, we'll discuss them in more detail. Does that make sense? Do you have any questions about the process?

Notice the elements of this detailed orientation. The upcoming task is described. A blank evaluation form provides a visual back-up. The benefits of the task and roles of participants are stated, the duration of the task estimated. Finally, there's a brief check to see if the listener understands or needs more information. All of this is done in less than a minute, but leaves Joe with a clear sense of what to expect, which in turn will help to enhance his participation in the review. Consider doing this kind of orientation when you need to give instructions or introduce new procedures or activities.

Whereas orienting is a way to introduce communication, summarizing is a way to close. By briefly restating key decisions or agreements and action items for the future we can promote clarity and understanding. Let's go back to Joe and his performance review:

> So, Joe, we agreed that you had a strong work perform-
> ance last year, that you're well organized and very effec-
> tive in face-to-face sales situations. Your sales figures for
> the last two quarters were in the top 5% of your division.
> We agreed that you need to work on improving the time-
> liness and quality of your written reports and that you'll
> attend the seminar Human Resources is offering next
> month on "Writing for Success." Also, you want me to
> give you immediate feedback on your future reports.
> Does that sound to you like the gist of our discussion?
> Anything you'd add or change?

This type of brief recap helps to underscore important points from the discussion, ensuring that everyone ends up on the same page.

Paint with Words

Finally, if you want to get your message across, you can't afford to be a lazy communicator. A child may answer the question, "How was your day?" with an "OK" and nothing more, but you must take the time and effort to be informative. It's better to say, "I don't think this proposal will work because . . ." rather than "This is no good," and it's better to reply to someone's idea with, "I don't agree with . . . because" rather than "What?!"

In addition, try to use fresh, vivid language that includes examples, metaphors, and analogies that help get your point across. For example, we recently asked an expert why women, on average, are more creative than men. He replied, "The corpus callosum that connects the left and right hemispheres of the male brain is like a dirt road. In the female brain, it is more like a super-highway." We got the point.

We can hear someone out there saying: "Yeah, fine, but I'm not a poet or an English major! We don't all have Pulitzer Prize vocabularies, you know." Point taken. But you *can* put some energy into expanding your vocabulary and using more of what you already know. Our teachers and parents weren't wrong when they told us to go look up the definitions of words we didn't know. And it helps to read books and newspapers so that you continue to learn. Many people also find that joining a group like Toastmasters gives them opportunities to practice speaking to others and get feedback. You can learn to have a way with words, if you want to.

At the very least, it's important to watch for unclear references. If you say, "Would you get the report for me?" be careful that the listener knows which report you mean. If you say, "Why are you still working on it?" does the listener know what *it* refers to? If you say, "You need to take your work to a different level," do you mean that a superior must approve your work or do you mean that the listener needs to do a better job?

Good communication takes thought and effort. When you take the time to get clear on what you want to say and find the right words to say it, you can go a long way toward getting your points across effectively.

2. Talking Straight

Good communicators are "straight shooters" who make their feelings and intentions clear. They don't confuse or mislead others by hinting, avoiding, or beating around the bush. But for many of us, talking straight can be difficult. We become shy or self-conscious at the prospect of being too direct with others, or worry that we'll come across as pushy or overbearing. The key elements of straight talk are to *stand behind what you say, make the listener comfortable*, and *be consistent*.

Stand Behind What You Say

Make "I" statements when you want to share your feelings or views. If what you mean is, "I don't think Joey is putting enough time and effort into his homework," then you should say *that* and not, "Don't you think Joey is spending a lot of time out with his friends?" If you are not sure you have been understood, don't say, "Do you understand?" Say instead, "Am I making sense?"

Everyone is entitled to a perspective. You don't have to air all of your views all of the time, but when you choose to share what's on your mind, accept the fact that it is *your* opinion, not the absolute truth. Say, "I think this plan is misguided," rather than, "This plan is misguided." Or, "It seems to me that you are trying to control my life," rather than "You're controlling my life."

At the same time, avoid qualifying what you think and feel by using phrases like *kind of, sort of, maybe, really, a little* as you make your point. Don't hedge so much. Be loud and clear: "I'm angry." "I disagree." "I don't believe you." "I admire you." "You're cool."

Make the Listener Comfortable

Talking straight doesn't mean you have to make others defensive. People get uptight when their control is removed or when their self-esteem is under attack. Avoid words like *always* and *never* even if you are complimenting someone. It's infuriating to be told, "You never apologize." And think about the impact of saying to someone, "You always look great!" You might be implying that the person better not have a "bad hair day."

Another tip is to describe someone's behavior without interpreting it. Better to say, "You are not letting me finish" than, "You don't care what I have to say, do you?!" In addition, don't control the solution by saying something such as, "We must stay within our budget," when you could share the problem by saying, "I'm worried that we are over budget. What can we do about it?"

Be Consistent

A straight talker is consistent over time. She doesn't say one day, "I don't care what we do this Saturday night," and the next day, "Why do we have to go to the movies again?" The other person really gets confused when we sometimes approve an action, and sometimes we don't.

In addition, if our lips say "No, no" but our eyes say "Yes, yes," people are going to be confused. Clear, sincere communication contains congruent verbal and nonverbal messages. Often, people are unaware of discrepancies between their words and their body language. They don't recognize, for example, that they are avoiding eye contact with the boss while assuring him the project will be completed on time, or assuring their spouse that they're listening, while glued to the TV.

If people frequently don't seem to buy what you're saying, try to notice your body language every so often. If someone yelled "freeze!" to us at random points during our conversations, many of us would be surprised at our own gestures, expressions, and positions. Watching yourself on videotape can be a useful way to increase your awareness of your body language.

3. Including the Listener

Good communicators talk *with* people, not at them. Have you ever been in a situation where you were walking along and talking with someone and suddenly realized they stopped a half block ago to look in a store window while you kept on talking? Communication doesn't happen if the other person doesn't stay with you. You can reduce the risk of leaving others behind if you try to *speak their language, let the other person speak*, and *confirm understanding* of what you've said.

Speak Their Language

Use what you know about the other person in order to speak from his or her frame of reference. If you have practiced the skills of effective listening in PeopleSmart Skill 1, you are able to pay attention to others and remember important material they have shared with you. By incorporating their own words and experiences, you can gain their attention and keep them at your side when you converse with them.

> *A couple of years ago, a colleague, who lives at the shore with her family, had described in vivid detail how an intense storm with high winds actually tore the roof off her home. Recently, a new administrator announced some rather sweeping and unpopular policy changes in the way our department would operate. The colleague, who had missed the meeting where these announcements were made, asked: "So, how did it go? Just how bad is it?" Our response: "Remember when the wind blew the roof off your house?" She got the message loud and clear.*

When talking with others, ask yourself: "What is the life experience of the listener?" Susan Boyd, a computer instructor we know, uses these points to help her students:

1. Computer hardware is like the pieces of a board game that you see and touch. Software is like the instructions for the game.

2. Your computer's hard disk is like a vast closet with a sophisticated closet organizer.

3. Passwords are like toothbrushes. Change them often and never share.

Your efforts to speak the other person's language will not only promote understanding, they will help you feel more connected to him or her.

Let the Other Person Speak

If you want to include the listener, *give up the microphone.* Sometimes providing the listener a chance to react or ask questions is enough to keep him with you. If there are a few seconds of silence, don't rush in to fill the void. Count to ten to give the other person the opportunity to say something.

Moreover, don't go on and on flooding people with information and expect them to remember what you said. A speaker talks on average at a rate of 150 words per minute. That's a lot to think about. What happens after a minute or more of non-stop talk? The listener has given up concentrating on what you're saying and is now hearing (but not truly listening) at the rate of 400–500 words per minute. No wonder people's minds wander in the face of an overly talkative person.

Confirm Understanding

It's not what you *tell* another person that counts. What counts is what that person *takes* away. Too often, people don't let the listener help them to be clearer. Everything we say to someone else is interpreted by that person in some fashion. If you said to someone something as simple as, "Fold a piece of 8½ x 11 inch paper in half," how do you know if the person will fold down the 8½ or 11 inch side? When you ask if you are clear, that leaves some space for the person to ask you, "Which way?" Let the listener help you get your message across.

Sometimes, you might be expressing complicated ideas and are not sure that you have been clear. Do you keep talking until you finally have gotten across what you wanted to say? It's often more productive to stop yourself early on and ask questions to check out the listener's understanding. Simply by asking, "Does that make sense?" or "So what do you think?," you can invite the listener in, give him a turn to talk and confirm whether your message was received. If the listener doesn't get what you're saying, you then have the opportunity to rephrase your message. Drew and Leslie were talking on the phone about their long-distance relationship.

> Drew: You should get into the habit of e-mailing me more
> often. Does that make sense?
> Leslie: Why are you saying that? (a little agitated)
> Drew: Oh, I thought you could cut down on your phone bill
> that way. You know what I mean?
> Leslie: Yeah, I thought you were implying that we'd have
> fewer arguments if I e-mailed you.
> Drew: No way! I'm glad we got that cleared up. Otherwise,
> we would really have had an argument.

Try It
Exercises for Improving Your Communication Skills

If you were setting out to do a five-mile run, you'd undoubtedly do some stretching first to loosen up. Consider these experiments in change as warm-up exercises to help you practice being a better communicator. Choose one or more to try out, or adapt them in ways that fit your own situation.

Getting Your Message Across

1. For one week, focus on choosing your words. Strive to select the best ways to convey your message in important conversations. To help you in this regard, try to build your vocabulary by obtaining a "word power" book, reading good literature, or looking up unfamiliar words. Listen to other people's use of language. When you think about using a word that's not specific enough (such as "nice," "bad," "okay," "cool,"), brainstorm other possibilities. Also, give examples that spell out what you mean.

2. Choose a specific assignment you want to give someone. Write, word for word, how you would explain the task to that person, incorporating the key elements of effective orientation:

   Name and brief description of the task:
   Example of the task:
   Benefit of doing the task:
   Expected duration of the task:

   Here is an example:

   I want you to conduct exit interviews with our students when they graduate from the program. For example, you might ask them for their reaction to the clinical practicum. We hope to obtain useful feedback about our program. My guess is that each interview will take 30 minutes. We have eight students graduating this semester. Now, let's go over the details.

   You may want to go ahead and try out your verbatim orientation on the person you chose, asking him or her how clear you were.

Talking Straight

1. Choose a specific context or situation in which to practice making "I" statements. (For example: a regular team meeting, social gathering, or when talking with a significant other.) For a week, keep track of how often you speak in your own voice. Are you doing it more or less often than you want to? What makes it difficult for you to make "I" statements?

2. Keep a record of situations in which you were not upfront with someone else—when you hinted and hedged but didn't say what was on your mind. Or you brought up a different subject than the one you really wanted to raise. Think about the reasons why you were evasive. Select one or two situations that might arise again and plan how you can be more straightforward.

Try out your plan and see how it goes.

Including the Listener

1. Select a topic—a work situation, a problem, an experience, an idea—that you might share with a family member, friend, or coworker. Choose three different individuals you could see yourself discussing this topic with. Jot down some notes about how you might present the information to each of them in a unique and personalized way. Would you use more or less technical language? Different examples? After you're satisfied with your notes, take the next step and actually share your individualized presentations with each person. How do they turn out?

2. Practice confirming understanding for a week. Whenever you've talked at length or introduced a complicated subject, make a point of checking out the listener's understanding by asking questions such as, "Was that clear?" or "So, what do you think?" Based on

people's responses, would you say you're usually coming across clearly? If not, what changes could you try?

Live It
Overcoming Your Own Barriers
to Clear Communication

Since the world is not teeming with great communicators, we can safely assume that many of us find it difficult to express ourselves openly and honestly. Let's look at some of the common problems people experience in communicating effectively, along with our suggested prescriptions for dealing with them.

You talk while you think.

> Many people, especially extroverts, are quite comfortable thinking out loud and it may work fine for them some of the time. But there are other times when talking while you think prevents you from choosing your words or focusing on your main point. Experiment. Try deliberately pausing to formulate what you want to say. See whether you end up expressing yourself differently. It's nice if you *can* talk while you think, but it's even better to have a choice.

You fail to explain your thoughts and feelings in enough detail.

> Have a talk with yourself about when and why it might be important to put in the extra effort. Choose one or two high priority scenarios to practice in and ask someone you trust to give you feedback. Getting this input may give you some additional incentive for change.

You've had a lifelong habit of speaking too quickly, or mumbling, or using filler words like "um," " okay," " er," and so forth.

Listen to yourself on tape. This may help you become more conscious of how you sound to others. Slow down and speak up in selected situations. Pretend you're onstage or on camera. You might want to make a "bad" tape that features your worst communication behaviors, then a "good" version without them. Compare them and decide whether it's worth trying to change.

You have difficulty finding the right words to express yourself.

Try to get a handle on why this is. Are you shy or afraid of misusing words? Or are there gaps in your vocabulary? Work on expanding your repertoire. Make sure you keep a dictionary and thesaurus accessible. When you find yourself stuck for words, make a point of sitting down later and noting alternative ways you could have expressed yourself. Look up unfamiliar words and make a point of using them. And give yourself permission to take some risks and speak up more often.

You tell yourself that others need all the details in order to understand the situation.

Remember that sometimes less is more. If you give too much background or hide your main point in trivia, you lose the listener. Try to convey the big picture and then ask the other person if she needs clarification.

Other people aren't paying attention to me when I speak to them.

When we ask "somebody" to make coffee, it's often "nobody" who gets it done. Broadcasting is seldom effective. When you talk to individuals, make eye contact. Use the person's name. Unless you're talking on a phone or intercom, don't talk from another room.

You try to express something very important or sensitive while you're too upset to say it carefully and end up attacking the person.

Often people feel pressured to react in the moment, when what they really need is some time to reflect and formulate a response. This is especially true for introverts. It's okay to slow things down. Tell the other person you need some time to think and get back to him. Wait until you're ready before you try to answer.

You're afraid of the anger you might incur by speaking honestly.

Ask yourself why your true thoughts and feelings should anger others. Have you held onto resentments so long that you're ready to erupt like a volcano? Or have you had bad experiences with someone who led you to believe your ideas and feelings were wrong or dangerous? People often over-generalize from these experiences and start to see the whole world as a critic. If this sounds like you, give yourself permission to start speaking up more. Make "I" statements. Be calm and specific. When the other person responds, listen and paraphrase. If it helps, you can preface your honest remarks by saying, "I'm a little uncomfortable sharing this, but____," or "This may be hard for you to listen to, but please hear me out."

You don't want to come on too strong.

Being direct is not the same as coming on too strong. If you're calm, clear, reasonable, and specific, you're not showing disrespect. Remember, you can always check out how others are receiving your messages by saying something like, "I hope I wasn't too blunt. Are you okay with what I just said?"

When you feel unsure of yourself, you tend to preface your communication with disclaimers.

> "This may sound silly, but____" "I haven't really thought this through, but____" "Unaccustomed as I am to public speaking____" If we lead off this way too often, we diminish the significance of what we want to say and signal our listeners to tune out. Try to become more conscious of doing this. You may want to ask someone you trust to help by flashing you a sign when you start disclaiming. At the signal, try taking a nice, deep breath, then say what you want to say.

If some of these barriers seemed to apply to you, rest assured you are not alone. All of us have difficulties being honest, clear, and direct, at least some of the time. Decide which of our prescriptions you're willing to try. They will prepare you well for the next People**Smart** skill: asserting your needs.

PeopleSmart Skill 3

Asserting Your Needs

Since people cannot read minds, you must tell them what you want.

—PATRICIA JAKUBOWSKI

You can't be all things to all people. If you try, you'll wind up disappointing them. That's because others will come to expect too much from you, and you're bound to fail from time to time.

We all have limits, even those among us who are "superhuman." And that is healthy. There are some things you shouldn't do for others, either because they need to do it for themselves or because it will rob you of your ability to care for yourself and for those who really need your help.

Besides having healthy limits, you also need to speak up so others know what they are. Holding back what you need from others only leads to frustration. Once that happens, you may become angry at others and lose the calm and confidence you need to be at your best:

Don is a people pleaser. He doesn't like disapproval and organizes his day around doing what will be popular with others. At work, Don lives by the motto, "You won't rock the boat if you follow the waves." He watches for clues and listens for statements about what others want and makes sure he's on the popular side. Being agreeable and willing to comply, he stays afloat but goes largely unnoticed when new opportunities arise. If you asked Don if his needs were being met, he would probably say they were. Resentment builds up slowly in him, but it begins to surface with sarcasm and erupts on occasion with uncontrollable anger.

Compare Don to Hank.

Hank is a devoted father and a supportive manager of people. Yet he knows that if he stretches himself too far, he'll lose his perspective and inner balance, so he lets people know when he has reached his limit of giving. You don't feel intimidated by Hank's assertiveness, but you do get the message that he's his own person—kind of like most cats we've had. Hank respects other people's

72

needs as he respects his own. When you want something from Hank, he's more than willing most of the time. He also anticipates what you may need from him and provides it even before you ask for it. But if he can't fulfill a request, or just doesn't want to, he says, "I'm sorry I can't right now," or "I have to decline." He adds just enough explanation so that you know why. Consequently, you admire his directness and still feel that he's a nice guy.

What sort of feedback have others given you about the way you assert yourself? Do your friends and coworkers know what you want from them and what you would be willing to do for them? Who are you more like: Don or Hank?

Want It
Motivating Yourself to Become More Assertive

Think about when being more assertive would get your needs met. With whom do you want to be assertive? When? Do any of these situations apply to you?

On the job:

- ☐ Getting too much work from your boss.

- ☐ Wishing for more praise or appreciation from others.

- ☐ Dealing with colleagues who want to schedule a meeting time that is inconvenient.

- ☐ Getting repeated tongue-lashings from a coworker.

- ☐ Being sexually harassed.

- ☐ Unwanted overtime and unwelcome business travel.

☐ Being pestered by sales calls.

☐ Being visited by a coworker too often.

☐ Wanting your budget increased.

☐ Someone talking about you behind your back.

☐ Turning down a subordinate's request for reassignment.

☐ Receiving slow service from a supplier.

On the home front:

☐ Not receiving enough help with chores.

☐ Restricting TV viewing or computer usage.

☐ Requesting quality time with your partner.

☐ Demanding privacy.

☐ Coping with interfering parents.

☐ Expecting communication from your teenager.

☐ Being treated with disrespect by teachers, doctors, and others.

☐ Saying no to a charitable contribution.

☐ Feeling harassed by family members who want you to visit them.

☐ Arguing about attending religious services.

☐ Refereeing sibling disputes.

We hope these examples prompt you to pinpoint circumstances of your own where assertive communication could pay off for you.

Learn It
Three Ways to Become More Assertive

High PQ people become assertive by **being decisive**, by **remaining calm and confident**, and by **being persistent**. They are clear to themselves and to others about where they stand. They stay relaxed and self-assured as they express their needs and wishes. And they obtain what they need by sticking to their guns. By looking at each of these skills in more detail, you will get a better idea of what they involve and how to use them as your building blocks.

1. Being Decisive

Non-assertive people are fuzzy about both what they will do *for* others and what they want *from* others. They often operate by the seat of their pants, rarely thinking about how they feel and what they need. If a situation arises that they've been in many times before, they face it with fresh apprehension rather than with the security of knowing how they want to react. It's far better to be in the driver's seat, anticipating problems and being prepared.

How clear are you about such matters as:

- rules about your children's bedtime?

- requests to stop what you're doing and assist others?

- keeping within a budget?

- employee tardiness?

- the use of your car?

- last minute assignments?

- seeking and receiving affection?

- the amount of time you require to do a job?

- compensation for your services?

- the whereabouts of your child?

- telemarketing calls?

- noise and other distractions?

- returning unsatisfactory work or service?

- off-color humor?

Needless to say, we could list hundreds of issues! Little wonder that one might become confused and uncertain with others, but indecisiveness can carry a high price:

> *Lisa complained that her twelve-year-old daughter Dawn was constantly on the phone. "It's really very stupid," Lisa told me. "She and her friends call each other as soon as they get home from school." When asked what she wanted of Dawn, Lisa retorted: "To stay off the phone!" Lisa was then asked to clarify her position: When could Dawn use the phone? How long per call? Under what conditions would Lisa allow a separate phone line? It took time for Lisa to decide how she wanted to answer these questions, but once she did, Lisa realized how unclear she had been and was eager to tell Dawn the new telephone rules.*

We are not suggesting that merely deciding what you want will automatically lead to *getting* what you want. Naturally, resistance can occur to even the most carefully thought-out requests. However, when you know what you want, you have taken a long stride toward obtaining it. As it is often said, "The more you know where you are going, the easier it is to get there."

There are three important steps in being decisive: *separate needs from wishes, take a stand,* and *communicate your position.*

Separate Needs from Wishes

Most of us wish for lots of things, but we don't need them all. Interpersonally intelligent people know the difference between needs and wishes. They ask themselves, "Is this something important? Do I really care about this matter?" Consequently, the weight of concerns they carry is light. By contrast, other people get bogged down with lower priorities. They give equal importance to everything that crosses their path. Their load is heavy.

Make a list of things other people do that get you upset. Think about your boss, your employees, your partner, your family, and even your neighbors.

Things People Do That Get Me Upset

I don't like it when: _____

_____

_____

_____

_____

_____

_____

_____

_____

Now, review each item and ask yourself, "Is this something I must deal with now, or can it wait?" For example, imagine someone listing, "I don't like it when my assistant sometimes treats people as if he's annoyed to answer their questions." The question this boss must ask is whether this is a problem that should be addressed now or not. There might be more pressing priorities. You will be more successful asserting your needs if you let go of low-priority items, and concentrate your energy on those that remain. This fact is especially true for people who get easily upset at others.

A good way to assess each "I don't like" statement is to ask the following question: *Do I really want to press this matter at this time?* When doing this exercise, Jesse wrote the following:

> *"I don't like it when I'm asked to start a project and just as I'm getting into it, I'm pulled off into another assignment."*

An interviewer then asked: *Do you really want to press this matter at this time?* Jesse responded:

> *"Yes, I really do. It's happened many times before and I have always let the matter drop and behaved like a dutiful employee. I **need** to say something the next time this happens."*

Take a Stand

Even if you separate needs from wishes, you can't spend every waking hour clarifying all the important interpersonal issues that occur in your life. With so much going on, you probably tend to put things on hold. The danger, of course, is that you may never get back to them. As a result, things pile up and you never decide where you stand.

Think of three piles. The pile on the left includes behaviors you find acceptable. The pile on the right contains actions you find unacceptable. The pile in the middle is where you place matters you are unsure about.

acceptable   **unsure**   **unacceptable**

For most people, the *unsure* pile is very high, so much so that many items are buried and forgotten. Individuals who are people smart frequently do a spring cleaning. They sort through the pile and place as many items as possible in the *acceptable* or *unacceptable* piles. The rest of us keep piling on more issues.

To assert your needs, it is imperative that you review where you stand on the most important matters you face. You can't use the excuse that you are too busy. Imagine if you got clear about one issue every week of the year; by the end of the year, you would have taken a stand on 52 issues!

Of course, lots of situations are difficult and you might waffle about what stand to take. Remember that your positions do not have to be permanent. When you are really unsure what stand to take, experiment for a week with a particular position and see how it feels. Don't get frozen by indecisiveness. When you straddle the fence, you'll never learn where you want to stand. Don't worry if you decide to change your mind. Others will see you as thoughtful rather than indecisive.

It is especially helpful to take a stand first on matters where people want something from you rather than the other way around. That's because you have far more power to say "No" to someone's request than to make a successful request of others. Write down a list of possible "no's" you would like to express:

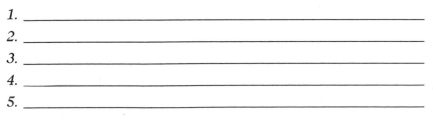

When I Need to Say No

I would like to say no when:

1. _____
2. _____
3. _____
4. _____
5. _____

6. _____

7. _____

8. _____

Review this list and select a few to act on immediately, then move on to situations where you want to say to others, "Do this." Spend some time clarifying what you want others to do by focusing on two key questions:

- What specifically do I want to see changed?

- Am I willing to accept a partial change, or do I want the entire situation improved?

Jesse was asked these questions about her objection to starting a project and then being pulled off it into another assignment:

> *Interviewer: What specifically do you want to see changed?*
> *Jesse: I would like a week's notice before being given a new assignment.*
> *Interviewer: Are you willing to accept a partial change or do you want the entire situation improved?*
> *Jesse: Well, I guess I'm not in a position to insist on this advance notice. I would settle for this gesture: When my boss decides he needs me on another assignment before I have finished a previous one, I want him to give me the opportunity to discuss the situation first with him and see if there are other solutions rather than simply being told to quit what I'm doing in favor of something else. If it can't be helped, then I'll live with it.*

Communicate Your Position

Having clarified what you want, you are now ready to express your need to the other person. Don't beat around the bush. That makes others suspicious and defensive. Go through the front door instead of the back! Use phrases such as:

- I would appreciate it if you____(call me first thing in the morning).

- I will not____(be able to come to the meeting).

- It would be great if you____(could give me a day's notice).

- I will have to____(turn down your request).

- Please____(tell me when you are taking the car).

- I would prefer that you____(get assistance from someone with more free time).

- It works best for me if____(you put it in writing).

- I've decided not to____(volunteer this time).

Avoid questions such as, "How about a thank you?" or, "Don't you think you could knock first?" Rhetorical appeals almost never get results. To help you avoid them, focus on what you want from the other person whenever he or she is doing something that interferes with your needs. Often, there is a tendency to comment on the person's behavior instead. A comment such as, "You're being a nag," for example, is far less direct than a statement such as, "I'd like you to tell me just once when you want me to do something for you." Commenting on other people's behavior often happens because we are uncomfortable about owning up to our feelings of anger. Instead of talking directly about our anger, we often cover it by accusing someone. For example:

Assume it's Sunday and a brother and sister, Joel and Debby, are playing so noisily that they wake their baby sister in the middle of her daily nap. They know how important it is to be quiet in the vicinity of the baby's room, but lately they have been quite forgetful about this. Their father, Marty, is livid and yells, "How many times do you need to be told to keep quiet during the baby's nap? You're both totally inconsiderate." Marty would have been better off saying more directly, "Now the baby is awake, my afternoon is loused up, and I really resent it."

In some cases, you may feel that it is important to convey some sensitivity to the other person while still standing up for your needs. You can accomplish this by adding some recognition of the other person's situation as in, "I realize you have been really busy, but I want you to make time for me." On the other hand, you may want to convey firmness if your prior assertive statements have been rejected. It may even include the mention of some type of consequence as in, "I am warning you that I will take this matter to Human Resources if we can't resolve it ourselves."

2. Remaining Calm and Confident

No matter how direct and straightforward you are about your needs and requests, there is no guarantee they will be honored. Communication is a two-way street. You will get a response, but it may be one you will not like. Being truly successful in meeting your needs is a result of how you react to unfavorable responses. You can undo all your hard work in expressing yourself directly at the beginning of the encounter if you become frustrated or angry in the middle of it. The key is to stay calm and confident in the face of resistance.

The problem is that few people can calm down just by being told to do so, or even by making their own personal resolution to relax. It takes a lot more. While there is no complete cure for over-reaction, there are three steps you can take to remain calm and confident under fire: *stay on track, give reasons nondefensively,* and *watch your body language.*

Stay on Track

As soon as you get any resistance to your request, the smart thing to do is to ask yourself: *What is my goal?* This action works like a circuit breaker so that you do not blow a fuse. It keeps you focused on what you want to accomplish rather than setting off your emotions:

> Sandy just finished giving a report to his team about how to improve the company's website. He worked long and hard on this report and was pleased with the quality of his recommendations. He was eager to find out how others felt. Rather than receiving kudos for his report, all he got was nitpicking. Showing his annoyance, he then said: "I would really appreciate it if you would discuss the value of my core recommendations and not get bogged down in little details." A teammate retorted: "Sandy, don't get so uptight. Aren't you open to feedback?" When he heard this remark, Sandy was about to lose control but he remembered to say to himself: "What's my goal?" Steadying himself, he calmly replied: "I do want your feedback, but it needs to focus on my core recommendations to be helpful to me and the team at this juncture."

Notice that Sandy essentially restated his needs rather than react to his teammate's remarks. People can get us off the topic by saying things to divert us or by sulking or acting miffed. One of the best ways to fend off the first maneuver is to calmly repeat what you want. Another strategy to add to your arsenal is a quick response to people's protests, such as "that may be," "that's not what we're talking about," or "Maybe, I am (stubborn, uptight, etc) but____." When resistance is silent, the best thing to do is ask a question, such as: "Tell me what you're thinking."

Finally, don't be afraid to say things such as, "Let me think about it for a few minutes," when you feel pressured to do something you would rather not do. Enjoy the pause that refreshes. People often have the notion that they have to respond instantly to other people's requests. Saying no gracefully and with tact comes easier if you take your time to clarify thoughts and decisions, especially when you're unsure where you stand or you've given a quick response under pressure and would like to rethink matters. If your eventual decision turns out to be unpopular with the other person, so be it.

Give Reasons Nondefensively

Often asserting your needs requires an explanation. The key is to explain yourself so that you are informative, without being defensive. Give a brief, respectful, honest explanation for your position as in, "I don't want to go out for dinner because I think we need to watch our spending right now." Too often, however, people go on and on as if their position were not justifiable until others agree with them (something they seldom do).

If you stop rather than go on and on, you give breathing room for the other person to reply and even to object. Don't be concerned about that. You can't filibuster forever. Giving room for a response shows your confidence that you can handle whatever happens. Notice in the following example how Ray holds the line with regard to his position about dinner and takes the knocks along the way:

Ray: I just think we can't handle that expense right now.

Chris: You always say that when it's something important to me, but if it's important to you, you somehow find the money!

Ray: That may be. I know I can be inconsistent, but right now, I don't think we can afford it.

Chris: Stop wiggling out of this one. You drive me crazy with your righteous attitude.

Ray: I'm sorry you feel that way, but I think we should not do this.

Chris: You can be so stubborn.

Ray: You're right about that.

It's also smart not to offer too many apologies. Being overly apologetic leaves the impression that you are guilt-ridden and uncertain. You might even say, "I wish we could see eye to eye, but unless we come up with a novel solution or great compromise, I am not prepared to change my stance." Sometimes a simple, "I'm sorry" without further defensive talk is the best course of action.

Watch Your Body Language

People pick up subtle cues in your body language that suggest that they can get the upper hand. Doreen goes to Jim's office and says to him:

"Jim, I've been meaning to talk to you about the off-color jokes you tell around the office. They make me uncomfortable." As she says this, her eyes look away nervously, her voice quivers, and her body is cringing. She realizes this, but hopes her fragility will bring a sympathetic response. However, Jim says: "Doreen, I didn't know you were so upset about the jokes. But why are you picking

*on me? All the men around here do it. No big deal."
Doreen feels defensive and she shows it by saying, in a
soft, halting tone, "I . . . I don't want you to be upset,
really I don't. OK? I'm talking to you because you tell
more off-color jokes than anyone else. At least, that's the
way it seems to me." Sensing that Doreen is serious but
still uncomfortable, Jim replies: "I didn't know you felt
that way. I'll try to knock it off." Doreen accepts Jim's
half-hearted commitment with a weak smile and leaves
his office.*

Tone of voice, gestures, and eye contact greatly affect the way
another person decides how insistent you are—no matter how
carefully you select your words. Work at improving your assertive
body language and voice tone by looking over the chart below and
selecting areas where you need improvement.

Vocal Nonverbal Behavior		
Nonassertive	*Assertive*	*Aggressive*
voice too soft	moderate loudness	voice louder than needed
frequent pauses	even, fluent speech	fast speech
questions	declarative sentences	exclamatory sentences
Facial Nonverbal Behavior		
Nonassertive	*Assertive*	*Aggressive*
little eye contact	open, direct contact	glaring, staring
tense facial muscles (fear)	relaxed, friendly	tense facial muscles (anger)
pleading, timid look	confident, engaged look	impassive, stony look
Postural Nonverbal Behavior		
Nonassertive	*Assertive*	*Aggressive*
fidgeting, wringing hands	open hands	clenched fists
hands behind back or in pockets	hands at side	finger pointing
nervous, shifting body	relaxed body position	rigid body position

3. Being Persistent

We all face situations in which problems persist even though we have been very clear and firm about our expectations. We thought that a matter was settled, only to find that the other person continues doing something we find unacceptable. Many people get discouraged when this happens and abandon their efforts to obtain a change in behavior, or they postpone them until another time. As a result, they let the person off the hook.

The key to getting a lasting solution is persistence. When you are persistent, you send the message that you are really serious. If the other person has never experienced your persistence before, he or she is apt to slack off.

Persistence does not mean nagging. Nagging is usually an expression of frustration rather than confidence. The person who persists is in control rather than out of control.

Three techniques are worth considering to be persistent in your efforts to inspire change: *reminding, requesting*, and *encouraging*.

Remind

Although you have asserted yourself until you're blue in the face, the other person may continue to behave as before. One option is to remind the person frequently what behavior is acceptable and what is not, until change occurs. Through repetition of your expectations, the other person learns that you will persist regardless of his or her forgetfulness or attempts to discourage you.

There are three key elements in using reminding as an option:

1. Select a specific behavior you'd like to change, such as keeping the family room tidy or getting to the meeting on time.

2. Communicate your expectation on a regular basis: Don't wait for infractions to occur.

3. Avoid other remarks and criticism. Give the plan a week. Express appreciation for any encouraging efforts during the week.

You can state your expectation verbally or in writing. If you verbalize your reminder, keep it simple and brief. For example, you might say: "Please remember to_____" or "I'm counting on you to_____" If you feel like a nag, try leaving written messages or creating a small sign. A short note that says, "REMINDER:_____" can be very effective.

Reminding is a slow but steady method. Its success depends on systematic, quiet repetition. Some people resist using this approach by claiming, "She should know what she's supposed to do." That may be true, but she may not know how serious you are about the matter. Repeated reminders, not done in the spirit of nagging, can convey your determination.

Request

It's amazing how often people assume that undesirable behaviors can be changed only if they tell the other person what has to happen. Requesting involves asking, not telling. Rather than setting down the law yourself, you can use the alternative of bringing your concerns to the other person and requesting him or her to work out a plan for altering the problem. You can demonstrate confidence when doing this procedure by approaching the other person with the attitude that you expect a serious consideration of your needs.

When you use this approach, take the following two steps:

1. State what the other person is doing that is unacceptable to you: "You still leave the kitchen a mess," or "You still give me last minute assignments."

2. Ask: "Are you willing to talk about changing this situation?" If the answer is yes, don't rush into giving advice. Instead ask, "What would you be willing to do about it?"

If the person makes an acceptable offer, respond with words like, "I appreciate your promise and I am counting on you to keep it." More than likely, you will get a vague promise to change. Accept it, but also press for a more specific commitment. If the person wants to strike a bargain with you, you have the option to accept or refuse. If the person dismisses your invitation with a shrug, try repeating yourself: "No, I really mean it. Are you willing to_____?" If you still get nowhere, then make a request to think over the conversation and return to the discussion at a time you think appropriate. Be persistent. Don't let one attempt at this strategy suffice.

Naturally, any commitment you obtain needs to be monitored. Be persistent about keeping the person to his or her promise.

Encourage

Encouraging is a plan to promote positive behaviors by complimenting any actions that are steps toward the desired results. Often, when a person is not behaving as we'd hoped, the usual response is to bear down on the failures. If you look hard enough, you can notice positive signs that, if nurtured, will bring about the overall result you are seeking.

The key to this approach is to eliminate any criticism for awhile. Persist with positive messages only. For example, you might note and reinforce the following:

- an occasional attempt to keep a room tidy

- a better than usual report from a member of your staff

- a willingness to assist you in a chore

- an attempt at friendliness

- taking initiative

- handling something instead of asking you to do it

Don't defeat your own purposes by giving exaggerated praise. People don't believe overly effusive compliments. They may also feel manipulated. Straightforward, no-fuss messages produce the best results: "That was better." "Nice going." "Thanks." Remember to keep a positive focus for at least a week to demonstrate your sincerity and persistence.

Try It
Exercises for Developing Your Assertiveness

Armed with some motivation and tips, it's time to try it out. Here are some experiments you can undertake right away to work on your goals and find out if you like the results:

Being Decisive

1. Make a list of requests people make of you that are a burden. Review the list and select one or two requests that you will refuse in the next week. Think about how you will politely, but firmly, inform someone of your need to say "no," then carry out your plan.

What happened? Did you feel less guilty than you thought you would?

2. Review the requests you want to make of others to help you meet your own needs. Select one or two. Get clear in your mind what you specifically want. Formulate each request so that it is as reasonable as possible for the person you will ask, then make your request(s).

Did you get a positive response? Are you happy with the support you obtained?

Remaining Calm and Confident

1. Work on staying calm and confident in situations that usually cause you stress. Plan in advance how you might handle these situations in order to feel more confident. When the situation occurs, take a deep breath, slow yourself down, and talk just enough to express your wishes. Don't get defensive or caught up in power struggles or blow your cool. If you lose control of your emotions, recognize when it is happening and gain a grip on yourself.

What were the results? Do you like how you handled yourself?

2. Take one of the following strategies and practice it for one week with a variety of people and in a variety of situations. Work on it until it becomes second-nature.

   • Repeat yourself rather than respond to someone's remarks.

   • Avoid arguments with others by using phrases such as, "That may be," "We see it differently," and "That's true, and_____"

   • Give brief, non-apologetic explanations for your position.

Being Persistent

1. Work on your persistence. Identify times when you give up too easily or flip-flop on an issue on a day to day basis. Make a small list of decisions you would like to stick to in the coming week. After the week is up, look over your list and give yourself a grade: A=stuck to my guns; B=persisted most of the time; C=persisted some of the time; D=gave up.

2. Select one of the three creative options for persisting (*reminding, requesting, encouraging*), and try it for one week with someone who might benefit from it.

Live It
Overcoming Your Own Barriers
to Lasting Change

As you attempt to develop your assertiveness, you should expect that the road ahead will be full of personal land mines. As you navigate this road, be aware of those factors that have prevented you in the past from acting assertively. Here are some obstacles most of us have to overcome to create lasting change; use our prescriptions to help yourself move forward:

I am afraid that I will offend someone or hurt his or her feelings.

> Think about whether you are taking on the responsibility for the other person's feelings. You have not signed a contract that says you must protect others from feeling upset. There is no way of handling all situations so that nobody feels badly. Ask yourself: "What will be the long-term effects on this relationship, on the other person, and on myself if I don't say what I want, feel, or believe? Will these long-term effects be worse than the short-term discomfort I or the other person may feel if I am assertive now?

I want to be accepted.

> When you appease someone, you don't win acceptance; you give that person encouragement to push you around again. Continual non-assertion erodes your sense of self-acceptance and in some cases leads to a general sense of worthlessness.

I can't help getting into power struggles and arguments with certain people.

> As you wait for these people to stop being argumentative, they are waiting for you to stop as well. Make the first move!

Even if you feel that the other person is extremely difficult, you can decide not to argue. Express your needs. Give brief, nondefensive reasons for them. End the conversation before it turns into a full-blown argument by saying, "Please think it over."

I am unsure if I have a right to say "no."

Sometimes, it's difficult to make this determination. But, if you continue to err on the side of caution, you will never find out if saying "no" is the best decision for you and possibly for the other person. The test question to apply is, "Will saying "no" help me to be more effective?"

I have a bad temper and lose hold of my emotions too quickly.

Slow down in the middle of a confrontation by taking a few breaths and doing a goal check (What is my goal right now?). You might want to say to the other person, "Can we start over again? I feel like things are getting out of control."

I am just not very decisive.

Making no decision is often worse than making the wrong decision. We learn something from trying out decisions—even poor ones. Remember that you do not have to make permanent commitments to a course of action. Try it for a week and see if you like the results. If not, reverse gears. Take prudent risks and evaluate the outcome.

I take a stand, get the result I want, but eventually the person goes right back to the same old behavior.

It is hard to be persistent. Review the three options, remind, request, and encourage on pages 89–91.

With some people, I don't know where to begin. They do so many things that drive me crazy.

> The key is to start somewhere specific. Give yourself a week to work on one matter at a time. Once you get compliance in one area, it becomes easier and faster to get other issues resolved to your satisfaction.

Don't give up on yourself. When you experience the occasional setback, remind yourself to take it a day at a time. It's the only way to go the distance! The confidence you gain by becoming more assertive will help you master the next skill, exchanging feedback.

Exchanging Feedback

Flatter me, and I may not believe you.
Criticize me and I may not like you.
Ignore me and I may not forgive you.
Encourage me and I will not forget you.

— WILLIAM ARTHUR WARD

Do you remember the fairy tale about the emperor's new clothes? Convinced by conniving tailors that he was clad in magnificent cloth of an extraordinarily light weave, the arrogant emperor unwittingly paraded naked through the streets of his kingdom. Daunted by his authority, none of his subjects dared speak up, until a small boy blurted out, "But he has no clothes on!"

Like the emperor, *all* of us can learn from the feedback of others. However, the prospect of hearing honest feedback from others can arouse powerful, sometimes conflicting feelings for many of us. We like to think we know ourselves, and most of us do in many important respects. We know our likes and dislikes, our feelings and beliefs, what makes us laugh and cry. But others have a vantage point we can never hold. They are our *mirrors*. If we hide from or deny their perspectives, we miss out on vital information.

Feedback is something we give as well as receive. Whether the gift is welcome or not depends on knowing when and how to share our reflections so that others accept, value, and seek out our point of view. When we exchange feedback in a caring and skillful way, we open a window on the world. But for most of us, this is not so easy:

Maya is the editor of a community newspaper. She's a hard worker, maybe a little driven, and often pretty hard on herself. She doesn't usually make a point of seeking feedback from the people around her—after all, who knows better than she when she messes up?

Besides, Maya gets very uncomfortable with negative feedback, as those of us who are hard on ourselves often do. When criticized, Maya gets defensive, gives excuses, or even bursts into tears. She tends to deny or minimize praise. Although she really is a kind person, Maya's perfectionism spills over into the feedback she gives others. She always finds the typos in subordinates' copy. Sometimes she just rewrites their work, rather than confronting them with negative reviews.

So, what's wrong? Maya gets the work done and tries to spare everybody pain. But by not being people smart about feedback, Maya misses the boat in some important ways. She doesn't learn that people appreciate her, even when she makes mistakes. She ends up doing more than her share of the workload. She misses the chance to grow and help others grow.

Kim, in contrast, is feedback savvy. The owner and manager of a beauty salon, Kim has a loyal clientele and seems to coax the best out of the young stylists she trains. She knows that information is power, and she cultivates a steady stream of input from customers and staff alike. When she does a client's hair, Kim will make a point of asking what the client really thinks. She doesn't just say, "Do you like it?," but asks "How is this for you?" She'll encourage the client to come back within the week if she's unhappy with anything, and, when she returns for the next appointment, Kim will ask whether the new style was difficult to manage. Not surprisingly, customers sometimes tell Kim they're dissatisfied, but Kim listens, and they always come back.

Kim is also comfortable and adept about giving her staff constructive feedback that helps them improve their skills. She's quick to point out their strengths and successes and, when she does critique, she's respectful, clear, and specific. Her employees routinely seek out her advice. When they move on to new opportunities, word of mouth helps Kim fill vacancies quickly.

<u>Want It</u>
Motivating Yourself to Develop
Your Feedback Skills

Only you can decide how important it is to improve your feedback skills. Think about the particular circumstances in which seeking and receiving feedback could improve your life. If some of the following situations are places where you are not satisfied with the feedback you are receiving or giving, check the boxes.

On the job:

- ☐ When one of your staff really goes the extra mile.
- ☐ When you want to know what your supervisor really thinks about your work.
- ☐ When you conduct a performance review.
- ☐ When you want to understand how your customers see your service or product.
- ☐ When you're displeased with a subordinate's work performance.
- ☐ When you want to know how your behavior helps and hinders your team.
- ☐ When your boss asks you how a project is going.
- ☐ When a coworker isn't carrying his or her weight.
- ☐ When someone does something you really admire or appreciate.
- ☐ When a colleague keeps intruding on your space, stealing credit for your work, or getting on your nerves.
- ☐ When someone asks you to write a letter of recommendation.

On the home front:

- ☐ When you want to know if your partner feels loved and appreciated by you.

☐ When you tell your kids how their behavior is perceived by others.

☐ When you explain to your partner how his or her nagging, yelling, spending, etc. affects you.

☐ When you tell contractors your opinion of the work they did.

☐ When you discuss your kid's report card.

☐ When you want to improve your sex life.

☐ When you deal with neighbors who borrow, and don't return, your things.

☐ When you coach sports teams.

☐ When you want to deepen your relationship with friends.

☐ When you express appreciation to others for helping you.

We hope these examples help you zero in on the situations where feedback skills can make a difference for you. Keep in mind the situations you checked as you read ahead.

Learn It
Three Ways to Be Effective at Exchanging Feedback

In the give-and-take of effective feedback, you need the skills to create a zone of safety in which honest and constructive information can be exchanged. High PQ people are adept at **inviting others** to give them constructive feedback. They are also talented at **getting invited** by others to give them feedback. Finally high PQ people give feedback that is **constructive** and **enlightening**. Let us explain how they use these three skills.

1. Inviting Others

By seeking feedback, we expand our horizons, intelligently using others as a source of information rather than just sticking to our own thoughts. But before we can help others feel comfortable sharing their views with us, we need to feel secure about accepting feedback and to believe that hearing it will be beneficial.

Many of us had have bad experiences with feedback. Perhaps we were on the receiving end of too much criticism from people in authority (parents, teachers, supervisors), or felt put down by peers when we were most vulnerable (would *anyone* want to be 13 again?). So it's understandable that some people would rather undergo root canal work than ask someone for personal feedback.

But we can exercise control of the process when we seek feedback. We can structure the experience in ways that create a sense of safety—not only for ourselves, but for others. The three important steps in doing this are to *convey receptiveness, make people comfortable*, and *broaden the circle* of our feedback sources.

Convey Receptiveness

People are more likely to share feedback if you convince them you are sincerely interested in hearing it. Many of the skills involved in effective listening and clear communication can be useful in conveying receptiveness to feedback. Let's look at a case study to see how a manager might improve the way he comes across to subordinates from whom he's seeking input.

> *Carlo is a unit director in an engineering firm. He supervises a small group of professional and technical staff. Carlo himself is a technician and not a particularly "touchy-feely" guy. His boss has instructed him to seek out more input from his staff about his own performance as a manager, as part of an overall quality improvement initiative in the organization. The idea makes sense to Carlo (he does care about what his employees think), but*

asking them for feedback in such a direct way is not something he routinely does or feels comfortable doing.

Carlo starts by meeting with Sarah, the clerical supervisor. He explains that he's been instructed to ask everyone to tell him how he's doing as a manager. He doesn't look Sarah in the eye when he asks her for feedback and he interrupts her to answer his phone twice during the meeting. Sarah does her best to be open with Carlo. She tells him that she appreciates the hard work and long hours he puts in and his obvious commitment to the company. Then she tries to offer him some constructive criticism:

Sarah: You know, as long as you're asking, it would really be a help if you could make a point of acknowledging the secretaries when they go the extra mile. Like when they stay late to meet a project deadline. They're always willing to pitch in, but it would mean a lot if you could say something to them.

Carlo: (Wincing) Aw, come on, Sarah! Everyone has to do her share. Besides, didn't I take them all out to lunch last month for Secretaries' Day?

Sarah: Yes, you did, but...

Carlo: All right, all right! I get the message. (Sighs)

Afterwards, Sarah felt worried. Had she gone too far? Hurt Carlo's feelings? Jeopardized her own position? She talked with one of the engineers, Michelle, and described the session to her. Although Michelle told Sarah not to worry, she made a mental note to watch her tongue when it was time for her own meeting with Carlo.

101

Obviously, Carlo gave out signals that he wasn't really open to negative feedback. His staff will respond accordingly. They'll go through the motions, trying to tell him what they think he wants to hear. Odds are, he won't get much useful information.

Let's try Take #2 and see how Carlo could have been more skillful at conveying receptiveness to his staff. He might have started his meeting with Sarah by providing a convincing and personal rationale for seeking her input:

> *Carlo:* *Sarah, the more I'm learning about quality improvement, the more I'm coming to understand that a manager's job is to make his people's jobs easier. I really want to make an effort to understand the impact my behavior has on people in our work group. I'd like you to help me with this by sharing your honest opinions with me. Would you be willing to do that?*

Carlo could also have used effective listening skills like paying attention and showing interest to eliminate distractions (like phone calls) and show Sarah that he values her input.

Because feedback makes him anxious, Carlo will have trouble conveying receptiveness unless he takes more control over the feedback process. He can structure the feedback Sarah will give him by telling her exactly what he's looking for:

> *Carlo:* *Sarah, you can help me today by answering two questions. What are some things I do that make it easier for you to do your job, and what's one thing I could do differently to make your job easier?*

By being specific, Carlo becomes more convincing to Sarah. By asking her to limit her negative feedback to just one item, he can keep his own anxiety under control. If Carlo felt he wasn't yet ready to hear any negative feedback, he could simply ask Sarah to answer only the first question in today's meeting. Perhaps after hearing enough positives from his staff, Carlo would feel more prepared to handle some of their negative impressions.

Using the effective listening skill of clarifying meaning would have also helped Carlo. By asking questions, paraphrasing, and summing up what he heard Sarah saying, Carlo would have ensured he understood her feedback and conveyed his sincere interest. Finally, Carlo needed to thank Sarah for sharing her views with him.

Conveying receptiveness is a way of giving others a green light when you want their feedback. You also need to make the feedback process as painless for them as possible.

Make Others Comfortable

People can be as intimidated by the prospect of giving feedback as they are at receiving it. There's usually some level of risk inherent in telling others what we think—especially what we think about *them*. If we want people to be frank with us, we need to help them feel that they can do so safely.

When seeking feedback, avoid putting others on the spot. By asking, "Are you willing to share some feedback with me?" you can give others a sense of control. Of course, if you have successfully conveyed your receptiveness to feedback, people are likely to feel more willing to give it. Defining a specific area in which you want feedback can also help put people at ease by making their task more manageable. Asking for positive feedback, at least initially, also helps to lower the level of risk.

Remember that not all feedback is related to self-appraisal. You may want other people's input on anything from room temperature to menu planning to office procedures. When you're trying to encourage more input, or input from new sources, it's a good idea to start by requesting impersonal feedback. Which question would you rather answer from your boss: "How do you think our staff meetings are going?" or, "How am I doing at chairing our meetings?" Similarly, would your comfort level be higher if your spouse asked, "What do you think of that suit in the window?," or, "How would I look in this suit?" It's not that there's anything wrong with seeking personal feedback. But if your goal is to create a comfort zone so feedback can begin to flow, starting with more neutral topics can help.

Here are some helpful expressions to use when requesting feedback:

- I'd like a suggestion about _____
- I'm not sure how I'm doing with _____
- I'm new around here and any suggestions you can give me will be appreciated.
- Could I have a regularly scheduled time with you to discuss _____
- I want to improve my _____

Think of feedback as an ongoing process, rather than a one-shot deal. As you help others grow more comfortable sharing with you, they will do so more spontaneously and frequently. And you will have more information available to you.

Broaden the Circle

How wide is your circle of feedback sources? As an experiment, look at the circle at the top of the next page. Let the space inside the circle represent one environment or arena of your life (your work group, your family, your social life, etc.) Pick one.

Now, list on the right side of the page the names of people in that environment with whom you have any relationship: Your boss, your coworkers, your parents, your children, your close friends. Go ahead.

Next, think about each person on the list and ask yourself, "Do I seek feedback from this person?" If you do, cross out the person's name on your list and write it *inside* the circle. If you rarely or never seek feedback from someone on the list, leave his or her name *outside* the circle. Continue doing this with each name on your list until you have placed everyone. What does the resulting diagram tell you about your circle of feedback? Are most people inside or outside of the circle?

Most of us do not routinely seek a 360 degree circle of feedback. More importantly, we're usually completely unconscious of this failing. As a result, we have blind spots like the ones drivers have in their rearview mirrors. There are people around us every day whose input we never receive. We just freeze their views out of our self-awareness and never realize what we're missing.

A 360 degree feedback circle on the job would include feedback from managers, subordinates, colleagues, customers, suppliers, competitors, and regulators. People with diverse feed-back sources receive input from both sexes, people of different ages and life positions, people of different cultures and ethnicity than their own. Stretch yourself in this way, so that you will feel enriched and find the world a more interesting and less predictable place.

2. Getting Invited

Just as it is valuable to receive feedback, it is also important to give it. But feedback is useful only if it's heard. And to hear feedback, people need to be receptive. Otherwise, they are likely to switch into 3-D mode and *deny, discount,* or *defend* themselves instead of listening. How do you get others to want your feedback? Getting invited entails four key behaviors: you need to *ask for permission, share rather than insist, time your input,* and *check others' perceptions*.

Ask for Permission

The ideal time to offer feedback is when the person wants to hear it. By asking permission to share feedback, you can set the stage for your input and assess the recipient's readiness to listen. Some ways to seek permission might be:

Is this a good time for you to hear some feedback about_____?

Would you be open to hearing some input about_____?

I have some thoughts on how you handled_____. Would you like to hear them?

May I share some reactions with you about_____?

Often people will respond affirmatively, but if it really is a bad time to offer feedback, it's better to know. Waiting until the person is more receptive will enhance the likelihood of your feedback being heard. Moreover, asking permission cues the other person and helps put him or her in the listening mode.

Share Rather Than Insist

Maybe your feedback will be right on target, and maybe not. Either way, it's best if you offer feedback in the form of a hypothesis rather than a proven fact:

> *Sean has accepted Terry's offer to share some feedback about a presentation Sean just gave to their clients. Sean wonders whether the clients were losing interest toward the end. Terry says: "I'm not sure, but perhaps a few concrete examples might have helped them get your point. What do you think?"*
>
> *Having noticed that Sean seemed to be trying to cram too much information into his talk, Terry asks: "I was wondering if you felt pressured to cover every aspect of the project today." When Sean agrees that this was the case, Terry asks, "Do you think it might have been better to just orient them today and save the details for another time?"*

By not insisting that you are right, you help your recipient trust you and feel safe. No one wants to believe his or her deficits are glaringly obvious. Speaking provisionally helps to equalize roles and promote collaboration in processing an experience.

Time Your Input

If you can recall a situation in which someone complained about what you did two months ago (or, worse, two years ago), you know how irrelevant and annoying feedback can be when it's poorly timed. It isn't helpful to be confronted with behavior that's ancient history. Feedback is most effective when it's immediate.

Whenever possible, go for an instant replay and time your feedback closely to the person's performance. The behavior in question is likely to be fresh in the other person's mind, making the feedback more relevant and meaningful. Details of the person's actions are easier to remember and describe. Often it can be helpful to "contract" with the person for ongoing instant feedback around a particular behavior. For example, you might agree that you will raise an eyebrow to cue the other person whenever he or she fidgets or uses filler words during a presentation.

Good timing also means being sensitive to the circumstances when others are receiving feedback. It may be kinder and easier all around to give a subordinate a negative review at the end of the work day, when he or she can go home and react to it privately, than first thing in the morning. Similarly, negative feedback is amplified tremendously when it's given in public. Some individuals are also sensitive about being complimented in front of others and will feel embarrassed, rather than pleased. By thinking through the impact that time and setting will have, you can reduce distractions and increase the usefulness of your input.

Check Perceptions

After offering feedback, seek a response from the recipient. How did he or she feel about what you said? Was there agreement or disagreement? Was your input helpful or confusing? Does the person need more information?

> *After their initial discussion, Terry asks Sean, "What do you think, Sean? Does this make sense?" Sean agrees that limiting the scope of the presentation would have*

been more effective, but admits he's not sure how he could have done that. After determining that Sean would like to hear some suggestions, Terry offers some concrete ideas, then asks, "Does that seem more manageable?"

It helps to use effective listening skills like paying attention to people's words and body language and clarifying the meaning of their reactions, after sharing feedback. If the other person felt hurt by your feedback, or misconstrued your meaning, it's important for you to know this. Often a clarification will help you salvage the situation and keep your invitation open in the future.

3. Being Informative

Feedback is most useful when it's constructive, concise, and specific. Most people are not looking for a complete makeover and won't be receptive to a sweeping critique. In addition, people are usually more receptive to feedback that accentuates the positive. If you can tell someone what he or she is doing right, the person will probably listen and will be more likely to repeat the behavior in the future. The three key elements of giving informative feedback are to *refer to concrete behaviors, limit the amount*, and *offer suggestions for improvement*.

Refer to Concrete Behaviors

Direct your feedback to specific actions and behaviors and avoid making global statements or judgments about the person. Consider the differences in the following examples:

Global: *"You really have an attitude problem."*

Specific: *"You sounded rather impatient on the phone just now with that customer."*

Feedback is most helpful when you can point out specific examples of the behavior in question. People understand better when given examples and it's harder to deny or discount feedback that's supported with specific instances. When you are the one giving the feedback, prepare yourself ahead of time with good examples to illustrate your points.

Personal: *"You're sloppy and disorganized."*

Behavioral: *"There seems to be a lot of clutter on your desk. How do you find things quickly when you need them?"*

Sometimes it may be difficult to avoid being personal in your feedback. When you find yourself labeling the individual, instead of describing behavior, ask yourself: "What does she *do* that makes me see her that way?" "Under what circumstances do I perceive her in this light?" Keep peeling the onion until you have identified behaviors contributing to your perceptions. Below are some examples of common personal labels and their underlying behaviors.

Label: *"Lazy"*
Specific behaviors: *Procrastinates, leaves tasks uncompleted, returns late from breaks.*

Label: *"Aggressive"*
Specific behaviors: *Interrupts others, speaks loudly, stands close to others.*

Label: *"Well organized"*
Specific behaviors: *Prioritizes assignments, sets deadlines, keeps materials in consistent places.*

Label: *"Confident"*
Specific behaviors: *Makes eye contact, accepts compliments graciously, expresses needs to others*

In each of these examples, the specific behaviors convey more information than the labels do. The behaviors are also less emotionally charged, so that people can hear them more easily. Whether your goal is to reinforce actions you want more of or redirect those you want to reduce, feedback that is behavioral and specific will be more effective.

Limit the Amount

The less feedback you give, the more effective you will be. Sounds crazy? It doesn't once you recognize that people are not able to hear and retain a lot of feedback at one time. If you keep the focus narrow, they will be all ears. So, don't include the kitchen sink when you offer feedback. Be selective! Here is a case in point:

Sam felt that a discussion with his college age son Darin was overdue. He had many things on his mind and felt that his son should hear them. Sam called Darin on the phone and, after some small talk, asked Darin if he had the time to listen to some concerns Sam wanted to express. Curious about what Sam had in mind, the son readily agreed:

Sam: I'm not sure that you are getting enough from the overall college experience. Would you like me to be more specific?

Darin: Sure. What do you mean?!

Sam: You go to classes and study several hours a day, but from what you've told me, you don't go to campus activities much or hang out with other students or take advantage of the cultural attractions in Boston. Do I have it right?

Darin: Well, I guess so. But, so what? I'm getting good grades.

At this point Sam was tempted to go into every area of activity he could think of that Darin was missing out on, but he stopped himself and narrowed his focus:

Sam: Yes, you are getting good grades, but let me limit this discussion to participating in campus activities. You haven't joined any clubs. I'm concerned about that. That was an important part of my college experience and I thought it would be for you also. What do you think?

Darin: Well, Dad, I guess I waited too long and the clubs have been going on for awhile and it would be difficult to fit in one right now.

Sam: Well, I am relieved that you think that being in a club is a good idea. Would you be willing to go over with me some possibilities and let's see if there is a way to comfortably join one of them this far into the school year?

Darin agreed to Sam's suggestion and they had a productive discussion. Darin decided to join the hiking club. With this activity as a start, he found a group of friends that he was comfortable with and enjoyed many other activities with them besides hiking. As a result, Darin enjoyed a more well-rounded college experience. Sam couldn't be happier that he held back during that phone call and narrowed the scope of his feedback.

Offer Suggestions for Improvement

Show your concern for other people's welfare and growth by suggesting ways they can build on their strengths and overcome deficits. When there's a problem, it helps to hear ideas about how to fix it. Suggestions are most helpful when they are:

Specific: Spell out exactly what the person can do differently.

Realistic: Make sure you're proposing something that's under the person's control. Don't suggest solving his financial problems by winning the lottery.

Positive: Instead of telling the person to stop doing something, suggest an alternative behavior (e.g., "How about taking a deep breath and hearing me out, rather than interrupting?").

Tactful: Avoid giving orders. Ask, "Would you be open to a suggestion?" Offer encouragement by saying, "I think you would be more effective if you_____"

Your informative feedback and constructive suggestions can help you become a resource to others, someone whose input is valued and sought.

Try It
Exercises for Developing Feedback Skills

If you're ready and willing to work on your feedback skills, choose one or two of these activities to flex your muscles:

Inviting Others

1. Make a list of people who don't give you feedback even though you would welcome it. Review your list and develop some hunches about why these people don't give you feedback, or as much feedback as you'd like. Then try this experiment to test out your hunches: Approach one or more of these people and say, "I don't want to put you on the spot, but I've never gotten your reactions to my (*select a quality, skill, or behavior*). Can you tell me why?" Give the person an opportunity to answer. If the answer is, "I thought

you knew how I felt," tell the person that you're not sure, and would he or she please tell you now. If the answer is, "You never asked me before," encourage the person to tell you now.

2. Identify someone from whom you'd like to get feedback. Approach the person and say, "I'd like to improve my (*select a quality, skill or behavior*). Could you tell me how well I'm doing right now, and also let me know in the future if there's any change for the better or worse? Could we set a time to do this?" Evaluate the results.

Getting Invited

1. Identify two people to whom you'd like to give feedback, even if you're not sure they want it. Select one of them to whom you have never given feedback, or haven't done so in a long time. Think carefully about what you will say to that person, then find an opportunity to do so. What were the results?

2. Think of someone you know who seems to have difficulty accepting feedback. Write down, word for word, three ways you might ask that person for permission to share some feedback with him or her. Then write down two positive things about the person that you share initially to improve your chances of being heard more easily in the future.

Being Informative

1. Think about the suggestions for improvement you have given people lately. Evaluate whether they have been *specific, realistic, positive,* and *tactful*. If you're not sure, keep these criteria in mind. During the next week, pay attention to yourself when you give suggestions.

2. Think of someone to whom you have recently given negative feedback. If you did not give the person suggestions for improvement,

write down two things the person could do to improve. When you next have an opportunity to speak with the person, tell him or her, "I've been thinking about the feedback I gave you the other day, and I'm not sure I was as helpful as I could have been. Could I take a moment to explain more clearly what I meant, and try to give you some concrete suggestions?" If the person agrees, give your improved feedback, then check out whether this was helpful to the person.

Live It
Overcoming Your Own Barriers to Lasting Change

In real life, change rarely takes a straight upward course. We all tend to backslide when we try to make new behaviors part of our daily routine. As we try to prepare for these inevitable relapses, it helps to anticipate where our personal stumbling blocks are likely to be. See whether some of these typical barriers to sharing feedback seem relevant to your own situation and consider using our prescriptions to cope with them.

I am reluctant to put others on the spot by asking them for feedback about me.

> Remember to ask others if they'd be willing to share feedback with you and to show receptiveness. Share a convincing and genuine reason why you're asking for the person's feedback. Structure the process to make the other person comfortable by asking for feedback that's specific to one or two behaviors, or for feedback that's positive. Remember to thank others for their feedback.

I honestly don't think the other person has feedback that will be useful to me.

> Ask yourself why you think that. Is it because the other person is outside your normal circle of feedback sources? Or because you find him or her difficult in some way? Is there a *remote* chance that this person has a viewpoint you don't usually hear? Might there be some advantage in at least listening to it? Try seeking the person's feedback, strictly as an experiment. Then assess how what you heard compared with what you expected.

I don't feel prepared for a lot of criticism.

> Of course not; who does? You needn't volunteer to be run over by a truck. Instead, focus the feedback process by asking for what you want. If you want someone to tell you what your strengths are, say so. If you think you could handle hearing about just one or two things you might do better, tell the person that. Don't fall into the trap of all or nothing thinking by telling yourself you have to avoid feedback altogether in order to protect yourself from a barrage of criticism.

The person I want to give feedback to is very touchy.

> Make sure you ask permission to give feedback. Accentuate the positive, making sure to be sincere. If you must give negative feedback, try for a ratio of two positives to each negative you share. Be certain to focus on behaviors, instead of labeling the person, and to offer constructive suggestions. Check to see how he or she is receiving what you say, and correct any misimpressions. Let the person know that you, in turn, will be happy to hear feedback from him or her.

I feel phony holding back my true feelings.

> Recognize that there's a difference between feedback and free fire. Focus on your goal: Is the important thing to unload or to get the other person to hear you? No one is asking you to lie, just to share the truth skillfully. If you make "I" statements, there's no reason you can't share your feelings. However, if you can slow down long enough to identify what you appreciate, in addition to what you resent about the person, you'll make your point more effectively.

The other person is strong-willed and closed to suggestions.

> But you're up to the challenge. First ask whether you may offer a suggestion. If he says yes, he's already put himself into a more receptive mode. If the person says no, accept it. You establish yourself as safe by giving him control. Next time, he may be willing to listen. Couch your suggestions in positive terms (e.g., "You do____well, and I think you could do it even better if____"). Be careful to be provisional in your feedback ("I could be wrong, but it seems to me____"). And, again, check out how the person perceives the feedback; ask if it made sense to him. Suggest he let you know whether your suggestion turns out to be helpful.

If you're like most people, you'll be pleasantly surprised at what you'll hear when you start asking others for their feedback. Don't be afraid to take the plunge. And we think you'll find that further rewards will come from improving the quality of your feedback to others. For instance, you will be more effective at influencing people.

Influencing Others

Power lasts ten years; influence not more than a hundred.

—Korean Proverb

Dale Carnegie captured the wishes of millions of people when he entitled his best-selling book, *How to Win Friends and Influence People*. We don't just want to have friends and loved ones; from time to time, we want to be an influence in their lives.

Influencing others has to do with getting them to be receptive to your views, advice and recommendations. It is not about getting them to admit you are right or forcing them to do as you wish. You can't *make* someone see the world as you see it, but you can sometimes open their minds to new attitudes and effective courses of action.

Unfortunately, many people are intent on making people over in their own image. Typically they get nowhere:

Maureen is one of the brightest people we've ever met. And one of the best read and best informed as well. She can be interesting to listen to—until the point when she wants you to agree with her. If you see things differently, she barrels ahead, stating with complete certainty how right she is. She does provide facts and figures to support what she's saying, but if you still have misgivings, her posture is that "you simply don't understand." Maureen also has little patience when others express views that she disagrees with. You seldom get the impression that she considers what you think or feel. The net result is that she rarely influences the views of others. She may be admired for her brilliance, but people keep her at arm's length. Sensing the rejection of others, Maureen retreats until the next time she is intent on changing people's minds. Her efforts are always short-lived and unsuccessful.

Compare Maureen to Andrea. Andrea is the training manager of a financial services company. She recently convinced her company to increase their commitment to training by $2 million dollars annually. This was accomplished by a painstaking personal campaign that lasted two years. When Andrea first suggested to senior management that a greater investment in training its work-force was essential, she was soundly rebuffed with the explanation, "In our experience, training is usually a waste of time and money. People will learn what they really need to on their own or by getting help from their coworkers and supervisors." Although disappointed by this response, Andrea was determined to do whatever it took to influence a change in thinking.

The first thing Andrea did was to talk with senior management about their personal experiences with training when they were first entering the company. She probed into many areas and listened with interest and understanding to the answers she obtained. It was not difficult for her to identify with the negative training experiences people had because she had had similar ones. She also asked senior management to share with her the business results they were seeking for the coming two years. Armed with this information, she put together a powerful presentation that featured newer, more effective training strategies. She also suggested how they could be utilized to impact the company's bottom line. Andrea was careful to benchmark the best training practices of other similar companies and establish their return on investment. This time, Andrea received a better response. Although no commitments were made, she did receive a promise to review her proposal after the next quarter's results.

To make a long story short, the proposal was kicked about for several months before given serious consideration. During that time, Andrea occupied herself with other projects, but also made a point of periodically checking in with her supervisor on the status of her proposal. After a year went by, senior management was becoming convinced of the merits of Andrea's views but still did not commit as much money as she had been seeking. Andrea graciously accepted the small budget, conducted some pilot programs that were well received, and provided data to support their value. Now, finally convinced of training's effectiveness, senior management gave Andrea the backing she had long been seeking.

Want It
Motivating Yourself to Develop
Your Influence Skills

It's people smart to develop your influence skills, but let's get more specific. With whom do you want to be influential? When? Where? Check the situations where you can picture yourself having more impact:

On the job:

- ☐ Seeking a promotion or raise.
- ☐ Swaying team decisions.
- ☐ Obtaining greater autonomy.
- ☐ Motivating an employee to improve performance.
- ☐ Being asked for advice by colleagues.
- ☐ Winning others to your side at meetings.
- ☐ Leading a change process.
- ☐ Closing a sale to an important account.
- ☐ Making a business proposal.

On the home front:

- ☐ Getting your children to listen to your advice.
- ☐ Encouraging your partner to give up some bad habits.

☐ Persuading the family to be more conscious of money.

☐ Achieving the intimacy you want from others.

☐ Being a respected person in the community.

☐ Convincing a relative to visit more (or less) often.

☐ Motivating friends to join you in an activity important to you.

☐ Being seen as a trustworthy source of help.

Learn It
Three Ways to Influence People

High PQ individuals like Andrea are adept at influencing others by being patient and persistent. Their success is a function of three key skills. By **connecting with others**, influential people establish a genuine rapport with those they are trying to influence. Influential people take time to **assess needs** by finding out the viewpoints, needs, concerns, and problems others have. Finally, they use this knowledge to **make a persuasive presentation** that appeals to the needs of others so that they see the benefits for themselves.

By looking at each of these skills in more detail, you will get a clearer image of what they involve and how to do them.

1. Connecting With Others

It's hard to influence people without first making a personal connection with them. Otherwise, why should they care about what you think or believe? This requirement is as true in front of an audience of strangers as it is with those who are emotionally close to you. Even in a television infomercial, there are always some people in the role of consumers so that you, the viewer, can vicariously sense the bond between the seller and the customer.

There are various ways of connecting with others, but each works only if *you are genuine when using it.* Most of the time people can spot a phony a mile away. Here are four tools for making connections:

"I've got something for you."

Let others know about your expertise and your willingness to share it with them. Don't be boastful, but let them know that you are confident about your knowledge and skills. For example, you may have already been a successful fundraiser whose tips for success any novice fundraiser would certainly want to obtain. Let the person know your credentials.

"I've been through this, too."

If you have been through the same kinds of experiences as the people you are trying to influence, let them know. For example, you may have raised children and suffered all the anxiety that experience entails. If you were counseling younger parents, it would comfort them to know that you have traveled the same road and survived.

"I admire you."

Maybe you don't have the credibility of being someone who has walked in the other person's shoes. Instead, you can express your admiration for qualities that you respect in the people who have had different experiences than you. Praising their efforts, their intelligence, and their goodwill can help you to build positive rapport. For example, you may lead a cancer support group despite not having been a cancer patient yourself. Genuinely admiring the courage of the cancer patients in the group might establish a productive relationship between you and them.

"You interest me."

Get to know people who are different from you and express interest in their backgrounds, life experiences, and concerns. The more that you let participants know that you care about who they are, the more they will care about what you have to offer to them. For example, maybe you are a manager who recently had a person from another country join your staff. Your interest in his or her country of origin and its culture may enable you to form an effective coaching relationship with that person.

Think how these paths of connection may serve you even in hostile circumstances. When communicating with a rebellious teenager, for instance, consider the fact that you have some wisdom to give him or her, or that you've been through similar experiences, too, or that you admire things he or she deals with that were never part of your adolescence, or that you want to show interest in him or her in ways you have not done before. The only hope for establishing a connection when you are distrusted is to try one of these approaches.

2. Assessing Needs

Picture the insanity of trying to sell cat food to a dog owner, convincing a priest to subscribe to a dating service, or asking a person whose child was recently a victim of gun violence for a contribution to the National Rifle Association. Yet this kind of thing happens every day. Time and time again, people try to persuade others without finding out whether the suggestion has a chance of being welcomed.

Interpersonally intelligent people know their audience. They find out what needs other people have before spending time trying to influence them. They do so in three ways: they *observe behavior, ask skillful questions*, and *obtain reactions*.

Observe Behavior

Recently, we were given this quotation but the source is unknown: "People will sit up and take notice of you if you will sit up and take notice of what makes them sit up and take notice." As we suggested with PeopleSmart Skill 1, careful observation of other people's body language, style, personality, and values can help you discover who they are and how to be effective in relating to them. You may find it useful to review that material as you learn about influencing others.

Think of someone you want to influence. What have you observed about this person? Here are some things to consider:

What seems to be the best time to talk with this person?

Does the person prefer you to get right down to business or to schmooze first?

In what situations does this person smile and seem enthusiastic?

What nonverbal signals does this person give to let you know he or she is receptive? Not receptive?

How does this person use language? What are some pet expressions?

What does this person value? (success? loyalty? teamwork? dedication? hard work?)

What motivates this person? (praise? respect? attention? activity? peace and calm?)

What do you know about the person's tastes and preferences, interests, and beliefs?

Can this person stand back and listen? Does the person like a lot of give and take?

Is the person formal or informal?

Your observations will help you decide the best way to approach this person with your ideas, advice, and suggestions.

Ask Skillful Questions

The most direct way to find out about other people's needs is to ask them. Although that sounds simple enough, it's often very difficult. People are not always sure what they are looking for and even when they are, they may find it hard to put into words. The art of asking skillful questions can be developed by paying attention to the following guidelines:

Ask questions that promote reflection. It's better for a salesperson to ask, "What colors do you like?" than to say, "Do you like this color?"

Ask questions so that the response will be clear. It's better for a spouse to ask, "Do you agree with me?" rather than, "OK?"

Ask *what* before *why*. For example, it's better for a campaign worker to ask, "What do you like about our opponent?" than to ask, "Why are you voting for him?" Asking why often makes others uneasy and defensive.

Emphasize the words in your question that invite a response. For example, it's better for a consultant to ask, "What do *you* think about my proposal?" rather than, "What *do* you think about this proposal?"

Most important of all, frame your questions so that you will receive good information. Get some background first. Find out what needs or problems the other person is facing. Find out what the person has done already to solve them before giving your own suggestions.

Imagine that you are a pharmaceutical sales rep. You are meeting with a pediatrician who treats children with poor attention spans. Notice how you might assess the situation first before offering your own recommendations:

Sales rep: *How often do you see children who have very poor attention spans for their age?*

Pediatrician: *At least once a week.*

Sales rep: *What concerns do you have about the drugs you have prescribed for poor attention span?*

Pediatrician: *They work for a while, but I don't like the side effects I am seeing, such as irritability and nausea.*

Sales rep: *So what are you doing now?*

Pediatrician: *I'm backing off prescribing anything unless the problem is severe.*

Sales rep: *Would you be interested in a new product we have that does not have these side effects?*

Now imagine that you are a manager who is concerned about the quality of the reports you are getting from an associate:

Manager: *I've not been happy with the quality of your reports lately. They seem rushed and incomplete. This hasn't been the case in the past. Your reports have always been terrific. Could you give me some background first? What's the situation as you see it?*

Associate: *Yeah, I agree with you. I'm just not getting the same cooperation I need from my support staff to pull the reports together.*

Manager: *Can you give me more specifics?*

Associate: *Well, Sam's still out on family leave and Bianca's been pulled away by IS for a few hours a day, and I just don't have the support I can normally depend on.*

Manager: *So, what are you doing in the meantime?*

Associate: Well, I'm crunching a lot of the numbers myself,
but with all the other things on my plate, it's hard to
produce the same quality reports.
Manager: Would you like some suggestions I might have to
get you through this?

As you can see, asking skillful questions not only helps you to understand the person you are trying to influence, but also helps to open the door to the influence message you want to convey.

Obtain Reactions

Most people give advice and then wait for others to agree with them. It is much more effective to obtain someone's reactions immediately after you have finished speaking. You not only receive immediate feedback but also learn what else you need to do to be better received. Consider this exchange between a doctor and a patient:

Doctor: I can't find anything wrong with you that would
explain the headaches you are having. You probably
have had too much stress lately. Why don't you cut
down on your workload?
Patient: Well, maybe.

Now replace the exchange with this approach:

Doctor: I can't find anything wrong with you that would
explain the headaches you are having. It may be due
to stress. Perhaps you're working too hard. What do
you think?
Patient: Well, maybe. But I don't think that's the problem.
It's my marriage that's stressing me. My husband
and I have been arguing continually.

129

Think of any situation in the next day or so in which you want to give advice to someone. Here are some follow-up questions to check out how your advice will be received:

How does that sound to you?

Will that work for you?

Have I been helpful?

What's your reaction to what I'm suggesting?

Such questions also stop you from talking on and on in hopes of winning the person over. The best way to find out how to win the person over is to find out his or her reactions to what you have said thus far.

3. Making a Persuasive Presentation

Whether you are talking to one person or 100, once you know your audience, you are ready to make your pitch. So much has been written about how to create powerful presentations that many books can be devoted to that topic alone. In our opinion, however, it all boils down to two skills: *reduce resistance* and *make your message appealing*. We will look at each separately, but in reality they are hard to separate. The more you make the receiver comfortable, the more open he or she will be to what you have to say. The more appealing your message is, the more receptive the receiver will be.

Reduce Resistance

When people sense that you are trying to convince them of something they have not been convinced of before, they will dig in their heels before you ever get to your main point. This may happen even if you've already established good rapport. Fortunately, many strategies can reduce resistance or prevent it in the first place.

One approach is to take the *indirect route*. Ask questions that might lead the other party to explore your concerns without pressing them yourself. Let's examine a case in point. Geoff would prefer that he and his wife Lori had sex more often than they do. It's been a battleground between them for a long time. One day, while taking a walk, Geoff turns to Lori and the following dialogue ensues:

> *Geoff: Lori, I've been meaning to ask you: Do you feel that I'm disappointed in you sexually?*
>
> *Lori: (miffed) Look, Geoff. Your wanting to have sex several times a week is your problem, not mine!*
>
> *Geoff: You're right. It's my issue. I certainly got this discussion off on the wrong foot! (pause) Do you resent me for wanting sex with you a lot?*
>
> *Lori: Of course, not. It's flattering. But, I'm just not as into sex as you are.*
>
> *Geoff: Do you wish I would adjust to you rather than the other way around?*
>
> *Lori: That would be nice.*
>
> *Geoff: OK. I'm willing to go along with that. Do you have any other suggestions?*
>
> *Lori: Well, it's fine with me if you would just hold me or give me a massage sometimes when normally you want to have sex. And if it turns out that I become interested in going further, I'll let you know. I just want to be in charge more.*
>
> *Geoff: Fair enough. That's a good suggestion. (pause) Thanks for listening to me. I love you.*

With some people and in some circumstances, the best approach is to take the *direct route*. Before presenting your message, you might say such things as:

Let me get right to the point.

It's not fair to you to beat around the bush.

I know your time is short, so I'll tell you what I have on my mind.

Let me be up front.

Choosing the direct route is especially effective when you are communicating upward, that is, with people who have power or authority over you. It gets their attention, sounds confident, and yet respects who they are. Best of all, it may take them by surprise and give you time to speak before they build resistance to your message.

Another possibility is to request something that is so small it's hard for the other person to refuse. In sales lingo, this is called gaining a foot in the door. You might employ this approach by doing one or more of the following:

Inviting someone to read something before you talk about it.

Requesting someone to try something once.

Urging someone to deal with one specific issue rather than the whole ball of wax.

Encouraging someone to do something as an experiment or as a pilot.

Asking someone to give you five minutes to hear what you have to say.

Don't manipulate people with this approach. Adopt the attitude that they need time to come to your side. Moreover, treat them like a consumer. Give them the power to decide if they want to "shop in your store" or go elsewhere:

The supervisor was urging the toll booth collectors to be friendlier to drivers when they paid a toll. The collectors resisted. "If we talk like they do in stores and hotels these days," they argued, "the public will think we're crazy or just forced to do it. It's not what people expect." The supervisor wisely responded: "OK, I'll make a deal with you. Try to say hello or say thank you or smile to the customers for one week, and we'll get back together to see if it works for you." The next week, the toll collectors reported that they did not know what effect the experiment had on the customers, but they all reported that they liked their jobs better. [No doubt, the customers returned their friendliness in kind.]

Along with giving up efforts to control others, emphasize the positive over the negative. When you are dealing with someone who makes you feel as if you are banging your head against the wall, it's tempting to say things like: "You're being ridiculous," "You're acting crazy," or "You don't make any sense." However, negative communication just doesn't get ideas across as well as positive communication. Saying *you can*, develops positive energy in someone else; saying *you never* engenders anger. Saying, "If you do x, you will benefit" is more convincing than saying, "If you don't do x, you will be sorry."

Despite all these suggestions, of course, you will still get resistance as soon as you say something that requires a change from old habits and prior beliefs. When a person disagrees, try to stop yourself from getting into an argument. Even if the other person eventually backs down, he or she will not be convinced. The person is merely surrendering—for the moment. Instead, acknowledge the existence of the other person's views and even their validity. Says things like:

You've got a point there.

I see how strongly you feel about this.

You make sense.

That may be.

I understand what you're saying.

That's true.

Then pause for a few seconds before explaining your views. By doing this, you are far less likely to arouse resistance. The door is now open for further discussion.

Make Your Message Appealing

Remember Maureen? She was more interested in being right than finding a way to win you over. There is no question that being prepared with facts and points of evidence to back up your message is important. But don't hammer them home, one right after another. It's far better to present one point at a time and let it be digested. If you must, repeat it, but say it in a different way.

Typically, examples are more powerful than statistics or narrative. Think about this: You will probably be more influenced by the examples contained in this book than by the comments and suggestions we make. That's because a good example focuses your attention and paints a picture you can see. For instance, imagine that you are urging someone to stop smoking. All the arguments and all the statistics in the world will not be as persuasive as examples of people who successfully kicked the habit and are healthier and happier for it.

The danger of using examples, of course, is that your audience may not find that they apply to him or her. To lessen objections, say upfront that the example you are about to give may not fit. To make our point, take a look at this example and be fore-warned:

> *Doris was listening to her elderly mother's ongoing com-plaints about arthritic pain in her knees. She asked her mother why she was not taking the medication her doc-tor prescribed. Her mom countered, "I don't want to keep taking medications. I want my doctor to figure out why the pain keeps coming back." Doris, in exasperation, replied, "But, Mom, don't you get it? There is no way to cure arthritis. All they can do is offer drugs that lessen the symptoms. Lots of people take the medication your doctor prescribed and get relief. I know your sister Rose takes it and she is doing well." "Yes, but her pain is in her ankles, not her knees," Mom retorted. Now beyond frustrated, Doris snapped back: "What difference does that make?! Arthritis is arthritis!! I give up with you."*

As Doris has demonstrated, you are better off not staking your entire message on one example.

A visual metaphor is also a powerful tool of persuasion. Think, for a moment, how vivid the question, "Is your cup half empty or half full?" is to the person hearing (and visualizing) it. Consider the kind of images that make you receptive to a product. What works for you—a hyperactive bunny rabbit? A sex symbol? Or when we want to gently discourage someone from giving us new work to do, we say, "I wish I could, but I have so much on my plate already that there's no room for more." Images also inspire others and give them direction. For example, we urge volunteers to "rally the troops," we ask managers to "use a carrot rather than a stick," and we encourage senior citizens to "enjoy the autumn of their life." Images also affect us emotionally. If a busy woman says to her busy partner, "I feel sometimes like we are two ships passing in the night," the request to consider spending more time with each other may get immediate attention.

Metaphors have to fit the audience to be successful. A Baptist preacher can uplift his flock by proclaiming, "It may be Friday now, but Sunday's coming!" but the same metaphor will mean nothing to a non-Christian. A Texan might turn off an animal lover if he says, "I'm as upset as a pig in kerosene overalls at a prairie fire."

Another way to make a message more appealing is to reframe it. Reframing is a technique used by psychologists to help people consider something in a new light. For example, a therapist might say to parents who have been indecisive about bedtime rules, "Do you want to confuse your child?" The recasting of their indecisiveness as something that creates confusion may jar the parents into examining the impact of their behavior. Likewise, when a team leader says to a team member who is not pulling his or her weight, "I'm confused about why you don't want to be part of the team," the behavior is interpreted as an act of separation rather than irresponsibility. Sometimes, merely a word change reframes how things are perceived. The quality control function is now referred to in user-friendly terms as "quality services." Realizing that "role playing" makes many people anxious, corporate trainers often use the term "skill practice."

Perhaps most important of all, your message will be appealing if it is cast in terms of its benefits to the other person. Some people say that the most listened-to radio station is **WIFM**: "What's in It For Me?" The idea of WIFM is illustrated with humor in this story:

> *A matchmaker goes to see a poor man and says, "I want to arrange a marriage for your son." The poor man*

replies, "I never interfere in my son's life." The match-
maker responds, "But the girl is Lord Rothschild's
daughter."

"Well, in that case . . ."

Next, the matchmaker approaches Lord Rothschild. "I
have a husband for your daughter." "But my daughter is
too young to marry." "But, this young man is already a
vice president of the World Bank."

"Ah, in that case . . ."

Finally, the matchmaker goes to see the president of the
World Bank. "I have a young man to recommend to you
as a vice president." "But I already have more vice presi-
dents than I need." "But, this young man is Lord
Rothschild's son-in-law."

"Oh! In that case . . ."

In a serious vein, imagine that you wanted a raise from your boss and said to her, "I have been working here for over a year for the same salary and I would like to ask you if it would be possible for me to have a raise? I think I've done a good job." Now, imagine you said instead: "I have been working here for over a year for the same salary and as a result, I've been working nights to make ends meet. If you give me a raise, I'll be able to quit my night job and be even more productive than I currently am." Or imagine that you are the appointment secretary in a hospital with a slow computer system. You might say to your manager, "If we could get a faster system, I could handle scheduling appointments more quickly than now. As it is, my time gets wasted listening to patients' complaints when they are put on hold while the computer takes its time." If you put the issue in terms of how the manager might benefit, your request would probably be given serious consideration.

Our final advice is to give others the time and space to decide whether they agree with you. Influential people don't pressure others but instead, give them room to accept or reject what they suggest. In sales lingo, they understand that selling has a long cycle. The more eager you appear to want someone to agree with you right there and then, the less influential you will be. Don't come across as too eager if you want to be persuasive.

Try It
Exercises for Developing Your Influence

Armed with all these tips, it's time to "try it." We encourage you to test the waters by experimenting with one or more of these practice exercises.

Connecting With Others

1. Make it a special project to take time to develop rapport with someone you want to influence. Think about how to show interest in that person. Also, think of how you can be more interesting to him or her. Avoid giving advice during this time. Develop trust by letting the person see that you are not out to remake them in your image. Also, accentuate the positive. Seize every opportunity to compliment the person. It's hard to influence someone you have criticized a lot.

2. Evaluate what knowledge or skill you have that would be of value to someone else. Approach that person and inform him or her of your willingness to share that knowledge or skill. If your offer is welcomed, arrange a time to meet.

Assessing Needs

1. Think of two people you want to influence as your "customers." Devote a week to working on asking questions rather than giving advice. Learn more about their needs, wishes, and preferences, and store that information for later use.

2. Select someone you want to influence who gives you a hard time. Think about how you and the other person are alike and not alike. Observe the person's behavior, using the checklist on page 126. Then develop a plan of approach so that this person will likely be receptive to you.

Making A Persuasive Presentation

1. For one week, try to lessen your eagerness to influence people right away. Every time you are in a situation where you want to be persuasive, try to be patient with yourself and with others. Give yourself time to think before you speak, and give others the space and elbow room to consider what you're saying without responding right away. See if you like the results.

2. Identify a person to whom you want to be more persuasive. Develop a plan for encouraging that person to accept your idea. Prepare yourself with information about the benefits of your ideas. Think about how you might make your suggestions more appealing by using good examples, reframing, and metaphors. Try out your plan.

Live It
Overcoming Your Own Barriers
to Lasting Change

If influencing people were easy, you'd have long ago sold the Brooklyn Bridge. Here are some common pitfalls to expect along with our suggestions for coping with them:

I haven't been very influential in the past. I am afraid that my ideas will be dismissed if I start now.

> It will take time to build your influence power. Start by selecting an issue on which you feel you can be very convincing. Express yourself. Don't press others to agree with you, but persist a little longer than you usually do and see what happens. Accept rejection and try again. As soon as you have some success, you will feel encouraged to move on to other issues.

I don't know how to read other people well.

> It's possible that you are somewhat self-absorbed and haven't focused enough on the other person. This is when it is important to take time to observe a person you find difficult to understand. Go back to the suggestions in PeopleSmart Skill 1 (Understanding People).

I get overly anxious about getting someone to agree with me right away.

> It's good that you recognize the fact that pressuring someone to agree with you is a sign of insecurity. Make a conscious decision to end a discussion with someone as soon as you sense that the other person is not convinced. Ask the other person to think about your message even if he or she doesn't accept it. If your advice has merit, people will often

agree with it later on and to themselves. With some people, this is a way to save face.

I hate to be pushy.

You don't need to be. Think of your advice as something of value to the other person. It's a kind of gift. It's someone else's choice whether to accept the gift.

I often don't have enough time to prepare what I'm going to say.

Unfortunately, there are no shortcuts here. If you want to be influential, you must be well prepared. Consider that every time you have developed an effective argument for an issue, you can use it over and over again. Also recall that examples are usually more effective than statistics and may take less time to prepare.

Others often shoot down my logic.

Sharp-minded individuals can be difficult to win over because they are adept at exposing gaps in your arguments. Don't try to argue with them on the spot. Think about their comments and come back later with better logic. Also, keep in mind that people are emotional as well as rational. Reread the suggestions on appealing to emotion that were discussed on pages 123 to 125.

Some people are just plain stubborn.

It's likely that they believe that what you are advising them will lead to a problem. Spend some time listening and asking questions to assess their concerns. (Refer to the section on asking skillful questions, pages 127–129.) And consider the tactic of getting your foot in the door described on page 132.

I get better results by getting angry at someone than by being nice.

> You can get results from intimidation. However, the person may silently resist your influence. If you truly want another person to be convinced, there is no substitute for positive reinforcement. People will do more things for those who build them up than for those who tear them down.

Remind yourself that influence takes perseverance. Keep practicing and honing your skills, without dwelling on short-term setbacks. Gradually, you will find that the techniques of influencing others become more automatic and familiar. You will be well on the way to becoming a persuasive person. And that will come in handy when resolving conflicts.

Resolving Conflict

As long as you keep a person down,
some part of you has to be down there to hold him down,
so it means you cannot soar as you otherwise might.

—MARIAN ANDERSON

If we invited you to free associate to the word *conflict,* would you think of war, destruction, divorce, turmoil? Probably many people would. Even as we write this, the effects of conflict cast shadows on the world: children murdered, people hated because they are different, nations torn apart over ethnic and racial feuding. It is hardly surprising that many wish that life could be entirely free of conflict.

Of course, this is impossible. As long as there are differences among people, there will be conflicts and competing interests. This is not entirely bad: Out of conflicts have come our most enduring institutions, governments, and religions. Nations have all been forged out of the struggle to express our needs, resolve our disputes, and accept our differences. Like sun and rain or day and night, conflict is part of the rhythm of life. Our challenge is to master it and grow through it.

Fortunately, most of us do handle conflict without resorting to violence. Let's consider a fairly typical case example:

If you asked Jim to describe his own conflict style, he'd admit to some confusion. He's been called both avoidant and aggressive. Jim's basic stance is that conflict makes him uncomfortable, so his usual approach is to smooth things over and play peacemaker. A case in point is the way Jim deals with his wife's ongoing complaints about his mother. Jim often finds himself caught in the middle of their disagreements, reluctant to offend either, but satisfying neither. When his frustration gets the better of him, Jim blows up and yells at his wife to leave him out of her fights. Then she acts hurt and betrayed, Jim feels anxious and guilty, and the cycle begins again.

At work, Jim is generally deferential, especially to management, who perceive him as loyal and cooperative. He accepts last-minute projects, sometimes venting his irritation with a sarcastic remark. In fact, on the job, sarcasm is Jim's weapon of choice when he's dissatisfied. He has a rapier wit, which others find amusing but disconcerting. Colleagues aren't always quite sure when Jim is seriously displeased.

Last week, Jim had a rare burst of explicit anger at work when he learned that a young subordinate he himself had trained received the promotion he'd been hoping for. Steaming, Jim dashed off an e-mail message to his boss that just dripped with venom. He even included a remark about how his boss had been "swayed by youthful enthusiasm rather than experience." Now his boss has asked him to come to his office to discuss the situation, and Jim feels like a nervous wreck.

Do you see any of yourself in Jim? Or are you more people smart about conflict, like Stu:

People usually know where they stand with Stu, a middle manager in a large communications company. He's direct with others, and likes them to treat him the same way. He tries to deal with issues promptly, rather than push them under the rug. Stu is observant with others and tends to pick up the signals when they're upset or annoyed. When he engages someone in discussing a conflict, he makes it a point to be calm and direct, even if he needs to talk himself down before he goes to confront the person.

Stu has a knack for setting the stage for dealing with conflict by inviting people to find solutions. He'll say something like, "Let's sit down and see if we can figure out how to improve communication between our departments," even if his first impulse was to say: "What is it with your people, anyway?" Before he goes to the negotiating table, Stu prepares himself by thinking through his own wants

145

and needs and doing some detective work, whenever possible, to know where the other guy is coming from. Experience has taught him not to try to win the battle at the expense of the war, so he tries to show respect for the other party. He's skillful at brainstorming possible solutions to conflicts that will allow everyone to walk away with something they want, even though this isn't always easy.

Stu tries to apply the same conflict resolution skills at home. Recently, he found himself at odds with his wife, April, about where to go for their next vacation. April was adamant about wanting to go to Paris, while Stu really preferred the beaches of Hawaii. Stu asked April what it was that she found so appealing about Paris and learned that her real need was to take a vacation someplace with lots of new sights to see and things to do. Stu, on the other hand, wanted to go somewhere quiet and scenic, where he could just veg out.

They brainstormed options and came up with several: They could take separate vacations, alternate their preferred destinations each year, or figure out places to go that combined some of the features each wanted. They ended up deciding to visit the Outer Banks of North Carolina this year, which they determined offered a combination of beaches and historical sites. Both are looking forward to the trip.

Want It
Motivating Yourself to
Resolve Conflict Better

What would motivate you to improve your ability to resolve conflict? There are limitless opportunities to use conflict resolution skills. Check the examples that are meaningful for you:

On the Job:

☐ Negotiating deadlines.

☐ Reconciling differences about job performance.

☐ Confronting gossiping or backstabbing colleagues.

☐ Addressing workload issues with superiors and colleagues.

☐ Resolving budget arguments.

☐ Dealing with angry or dissatisfied customers.

☐ Coping with bullies.

☐ Addressing schedule problems with suppliers.

☐ Resolving labor-management disputes.

On the home front:

☐ Negotiating responsibilities and privileges with children and adolescents.

☐ Planning vacations and leisure activities that accommodate different preferences.

☐ Agreeing on saving and spending priorities.

☐ Dividing household chores.

☐ Resolving disputes about in-laws and other relatives.

☐ Working out issues with neighbors.

☐ Intervening in sibling rivalries.

☐ Dealing with jealousy.

☐ Handling problems with contractors.

You can probably think of other specific circumstances when the ability to manage conflict effectively would make your life easier and more productive. Recognizing these situations can help energize you and motivate you to improve your skills.

If you are open to improving your conflict resolution abilities, closely reviewing the three skills described in the next section will be an important step in that direction.

Learn It
Three Ways to Be an Effective Conflict Resolver

Rather than shy away from conflict, people smart individuals use three key behaviors to constructively navigate their differences with others. They **create a climate of mutual interest** by confronting disagreements without *being* disagreeable. They take a positive approach and elicit cooperation from others. High PQ people are adept at **putting the real issues on the table**. As negotiators, they focus on the important needs and concerns, instead of bogging down or getting sidetracked. They strive to **negotiate win/win solutions**, being creative and persistent about finding ways for all parties to meet at least some of their needs. They know how to handle setbacks and deal with curve balls in the negotiating process. Let's take a closer look at each of these three conflict resolution skills.

1. Creating a Climate of Mutual Interest

Conflict resolution poses the most gain and the least pain when we are able to take a cooperative rather than an adversarial approach to working out differences. For this to happen, both parties need to own the problem and recognize that they have a stake in solving it. Three behaviors are helpful in promoting a mutual approach to conflict. We need to *surface the conflict, take a positive approach*, and *foster partnership*.

Surface the Conflict

Conflicts occur when two parties perceive their interests as incompatible. Differences in needs, goals, or values, or competition for scarce resources, are potential triggers for conflict. Sometimes these issues are immediately apparent and quickly settled, as when two people run for the same taxi on a rainy day. Whether one yields the cab to the other or they share it, it's unlikely their dispute will continue for long. But often conflicts simmer over time without resolution. Either the differences are not addressed openly or occasional skirmishes erupt, but neither party pursues the problem to resolution. We all know couples who have been having the same fights for years. We could practically choreograph their arguments. But arguing repeatedly is not the same as defining a conflict and facing it directly. When we surface a conflict, we bring it out into the open, state it in neutral terms, and own it as a mutual problem.

Problems are not defined in mutual terms when one or both parties simply blame the other guy. If Joe and Harry have a long-standing disagreement, and Harry's explanation is that Joe is a stubborn S.O.B., then Joe has been defined as the problem. How likely is it that Joe will accommodate Harry by changing his personality? Not very. In order to be willing to deal with a conflict, we need to get to "we:"

> *"We are at odds about_____"*
>
> *"Our problem is_____"*
>
> *"The conflict we're having is_____"*
>
> *"The issue between us is_____"*
>
> *"Where we are bogged down is_____"*

Until the conflict is acknowledged as "ours," little will happen in the way of cooperative resolution.

Stating the conflict in descriptive, neutral terms also facilitates joint ownership. It is easier to do this if we can get a handle on the type of conflict we're facing. Jean Lebedun (1998) identifies four basic categories of conflict:

Over facts or data. A basic misunderstanding or misinformation is the easiest type of conflict to resolve.

Over process or methods. People have the same goals, but differ on how to achieve them, a situation where compromise is often possible.

Over purposes. People have different goals or agendas, which sometimes can be merged.

Over values. Differences in basic beliefs or principles create the most difficult conflicts, and sometimes people must agree to disagree.

Identifying the category of conflict involved in a specific situation makes it easier to frame the problem in a neutral, mutual, and descriptive way. Here's how such statements might sound:

Surfacing a *facts* conflict: "Our budget projections are not in sync because you're using next year's salary levels and I'm using this year's. Let's decide how to reconcile our figures."

Surfacing a *methods* conflict: "We agree that Valerie's work performance needs to improve, but we disagree about how to accomplish this. You want to offer her more support and counseling, while I want to take a harder line. Let's get together and talk about it to see what we can come up with."

Surfacing a *purposes* conflict: "We seem to have a major difference about Jeff's curfew. You think the kids should have opportunities to develop their judgment and independence, while I'm really worried about their safety. What ideas do you have about how we can resolve this?"

Surfacing a *values* conflict: "The big problem in our relationship right now is that you believe premarital sex is fine and I think it's wrong. But we want to stay together, so I want you to work with me to find a way we can live with our differences."

Surfacing the conflict at the appropriate level helps eliminate irrelevancies and distractions, posing the crux of the matter in a clear and descriptive way.

Take a Positive Approach

Conflict can produce benefits, including more creative solutions to problems, greater respect for the knowledge and skills of others, and closer and more trusting relationships. Outcomes like these are more likely when we show respect and consideration for others during our controversies with them.

A critical requirement for staying positive and respectful is emotional self-control. Managing anger, fear, and hurt feelings may be the toughest part of dealing with conflict for many people. Our nervous systems are wired for fight or flight responses when we feel endangered. Small wonder that we vent our tempers or run away from conflict. Nature didn't design us to willingly submit ourselves to harm. On the other hand, we're also endowed with the ability to reason and make choices, and these are the skills we need to call on during disagreements. We will handle conflicts much more effectively when we *act*, rather than *react*.

One of the simplest, and most overlooked, ways to manage emotions during a conflict is to take a time-out to cool down and collect your thoughts. Few people are at their best when they feel on the spot. Negotiating expert William Ury (1991) calls the time-out technique "going to the balcony." Your balcony is a place where you can get some distance from your impulses, get another view of the conflict proceedings, and prepare yourself to reenter the fray in a calm, positive, and strategic way. As Ury points out, the danger of reacting impulsively is that, when we're in that mode, we tend to lose sight of our own interests and blow our objectivity, hardly a formula for negotiating success.

Time-outs are not just for formal negotiations. Many couples could minimize resentments and hurt feelings by tabling disputes until one or both parties have had time for some quiet reflection. "Never go to bed mad" shouldn't mean screaming at each other until dawn. Parents trying to work out issues with their children sometimes paint themselves into corners by pronouncing draconian punishments during the height of their anger ("Go to your room until you're 21!"), only to end up reversing themselves after they calm down. E-mail is another arena where time-outs can be crucial. It's easy to vent from the safety of your desk, but once you hit that *Send* key, there's no turning back! Before sending a red-hot message, re-read it after you've cooled down. Don't mistake time-out for capitulation—it's a way to hit the pause button before returning to the action.

Taking a positive approach to conflict also involves being flexible. People have different styles of dealing with conflict. The more we understand about our own and others' conflict styles, the more prepared we can become to respond to a range of behaviors. Which of the following typical approaches to conflict is most characteristic of you?

Confrontive: You take the bull by the horns and have a strong need to be in control.

Persuasive: You stand up for yourself without being pushy and are willing to negotiate.

Cooperative: You listen more than you argue and are willing to be conciliatory unless the conflict involves something really important to you.

Avoiding: You withdraw from conflict and suppress feelings that might make the other person angry.

Obviously, the confrontive and avoiding styles are the extremes, posing the greatest challenge to effective conflict resolution. Confrontive people may use blaming, attacking, or bullying tactics, which are difficult to meet with a positive approach. Alan, the CFO, confronts Rita, the manager of the word processing department:

> *You've done it again! You didn't have my approval to increase Victoria's hours. When are you going to get it about how things operate around here? Are you stupid, or what?*

What Rita would like to say is:

> *Who the hell are you, the Shah of Iran? I don't report to you, you bean counter!*

But Rita knows she's going to have to work with Alan and this will only get harder if she escalates the conflict. So she tells him she's on the way to a meeting and will call him later. After she calms down, she calls Alan and resumes their discussion:

> *Rita: All right, I guess we both can see that we need to find a better way to work together, Alan. We both want the company to work efficiently. Let's see if we can get clear, once and for all, about the procedures we're going to follow to deal with staff and budget changes.*
>
> *Alan: We already have procedures! You just don't follow them.*
>
> *Rita: Alan, I don't usually have difficulty following*

procedures when they're clear to me. Let's slow
down and go through the sequence from step one to
make sure we're on the same page.

Rita keeps her cool, stays respectful and focused, and doesn't let Alan put her in a reactive mode. He may never be her favorite person, but she has the flexibility to deal with him when she must.

Where confrontive people are "in your face," avoiding types may need to be flushed out of the woods in order to engage them. Avoiding a conflict doesn't solve it. Instead, the issues may fester, ultimately causing more damage when they finally do come out in the open. Moreover, avoiders often end up venting their dissatisfaction in indirect ways, such as sniping, gossiping, or sabotaging:

Carol: Jennie, I think we need to talk about the carpool
arrangements. You were scheduled to pick up the
kids after soccer practice yesterday and you didn't
show up. Luckily, Phil was home and came to get
them after Sean called him on his cell phone. What
happened?

Jennie: Carol, I'm sorry. I guess I just forgot.

Carol: Uh huh. Sure, it happens. But, Jennie, I'm wondering
if there's more to it than that. When he dropped off
Sean, Phil mentioned that you'd been complaining to
him about feeling you're doing more than your fair
share.

Jennie: No, no, it's nothing like that, really . . .

Carol: We all have such hectic schedules. If we're going to
depend on each other, we need to be able to tell each
other when we're feeling overloaded. We can be flex-
ible and back each other up as long as we know

> *what's going on. Is there anything I can do to make*
> *it easier for you to tell me directly if you want to*
> *change the schedule?*
>
> Jennie: *(sighs) No, Carol, not really. I have been kind of on*
> *overload this week. Maybe that's why I forgot.*
>
> Carol: *So let's talk about next week. How does your schedule*
> *look?*
>
> Jennie: *Well, actually . . .*

Positive persistence, rather than confrontation, helps someone with an avoiding style to acknowledge a conflict and begin to address it. Pointing out similar past episodes, in a gentle way, may help promote more open discussion.

It's rare that any of us *always* uses just one conflict style, though we all have our preferred mode. When someone with an extreme style happens to approach you more cooperatively or persuasively, make a point of telling him or her how much you appreciated the way he or she approached you. An ounce of reinforcement is worth a pound of criticism.

Foster Partnership

In a climate of mutual interest, people negotiate differences side by side, rather than head to head. Sometimes this literally means sitting next to, rather than across from, each other to create a less polarized atmosphere for problem solving. Side by side also means taking a cooperative instead of an adversarial approach to conflict resolution.

A common piece of negotiating wisdom is to be "soft on people and hard on problems." All conflicts involve both issues and relationships. In the next section, we'll look at how to focus on issues in conflict resolution. On the relationship side, effective conflict resolution is about respect, consideration, and promoting a joint stake in the process.

People smart negotiators use their skills at tuning in and explaining things clearly to encourage acceptance and understanding. Empathy, tact, and humor can go a long way to foster partnership. And when we approach conflict resolution as partners, rather than adversaries, we can avoid wasting time bogging down in extraneous battles, saving our energy for the real issues at hand. The idea is to fix the problem, not the blame.

Unfortunately, we all bring biases and negative attitudes to conflict situations, which skew our perceptions and hamper our ability to forge partnerships. Here are some of the distortions that can interfere with collaboration:

Mirror image: Both you and the other person feel you are a victim of the other's injustice.

Double standard: You feel that what is legitimate for you to do is illegitimate for the other person to do.

Polarized thinking: Each side has an oversimplified view of the conflict in which everything they do is good and everything the other person does is bad.

Self-fulfilling prophecy: One person's defensive actions intensify the other person's hostility and decreases his or her positive feelings toward the first person.

We can minimize our use of these distortions by stepping into the other person's shoes, acknowledging their points and reminding ourselves that our goal is to find a way to work together. Conflict will always be challenging, but it doesn't always have to be painful. When we have created a climate of mutuality and respect, it frees us to deal with the issues effectively.

2. Putting the Real Issues on the Table

Few things are more frustrating than a pointless argument. Yet people have them all the time because they fail to focus on the real needs and interests at stake in the controversy. There are many ways we can get derailed in the negotiating process:

We go off on tangents and lose our way.

We bog down on details.

We dig in our heels and refuse to listen or change.

We don't understand what the other person wants.

We haven't really thought through what we want.

We can deal with issues more flexibly and productively if we can do three things: *focus on interests, set our own targets,* and *study the other party's situation.*

Focus on Interests, Not Positions

In a typical conflict, each side takes a position, a stance about what it wants. In a labor dispute, for example, the union's position might be, "We want higher wages," while management's position might be, "We can't increase wages without reducing benefits." As a rule, the positions of two parties in conflict are directly opposed, and usually extremely difficult to reconcile.

In reality, however, the parties in a conflict also hold basic interests, which may be even more important to them than the positions they've taken. Interests are our needs and motivations, the *reasons* for our positions. When we understand and address the basic interests each of us brings to the table—what we really need to get from negotiation—we greatly expand the possibilities for effective conflict resolution.

When we left Rita and Alan, they were at odds over an apparent procedural conflict. Alan's position is that, as CFO, he needs to approve any budget changes, so Rita, as unit manager, should consult him before taking any actions that will result in budget modifications. Rita's position is that she knows how much money is in her budget, so she should simply inform Alan of changes, not seek his permission before she takes any action.

What are Alan's and Rita's basic interests in this controversy? They both seem concerned about self-esteem and want to be recognized for the important work they do. Alan wants respect for the authority of his position; Rita does, too, and she's also sensitive to any slights related to her gender. They both want control. Rita has an interest in being able to implement decisions in a timely manner. Alan is feeling some job pressure because the CEO has warned him not to allow units to overspend their budgets. All of these factors are driving forces in their conflict—and they are opportunities for potential solutions.

The kinds of interests people bring to controversies may be concrete (time, money, titles, privileges) or intangible (respect, trust, appreciation, control, acceptance). Whereas positions are usually very difficult to reconcile, interests present opportunities for mutual gain. By putting interests on the table, instead of bogging down on positions, we expand the possibilities for creative solutions in which everyone comes away with something he or she wants.

In any conflict, ask yourself: "What are my real interests in this situation? What are the other person's?" It may be easier to identify interests by considering why each of you has adopted your position and why each of you opposes the other's. List as many interests as you can identify for yourself and the other party. When you are ready to brainstorm solutions, these will become key bargaining pieces.

Set Your Targets

There are times to be purely spontaneous, but negotiating a conflict isn't one of them. Even if you're good at thinking on your feet, you'll undoubtedly negotiate more effectively if you think through ahead of time what your needs, wants, and interests are. Set your targets by identifying the following:

Your maximum position: the best outcome you can hope to attain

Your goal: what you'll be satisfied with

Your bottom line: the minimum outcome you'll accept

Even more detailed preparation can include identifying your starting point, your options, the concessions you will and won't make, your strengths, and your deadlines. When you've thought through these considerations ahead of time, you can respond more flexibly in the moment and free yourself to focus on the other party.

Suppose Rita, the unit manager, were preparing to negotiate her conflict with Alan, the CFO. She has already identified her interests. Her targets might look like this:

Rita's maximum position: Alan agrees to authorize her expenditures, without advance notice, as long as they don't exceed her unit budget.

Rita's goal: Alan authorizes all routine expenditures and she sends him advance notice, with budget projections, via e-mail for any unusual expenditures.

Rita's bottom line: Alan authorizes all routine expenditures and she calls him for advance approval for any unusual ones.

Rita has decided she will not concede to seeking Alan's advance approval for routine expenditures. She is willing to further meet his control interests by sending him quarterly budget reports. And if she has to settle for her bottom line, she will push for Alan to promise her a 24-hour response time when she calls him for advance approval.

Setting targets is especially useful in a conflict situation like Rita's and Alan's, where tempers have been known to flare. It will be easier for Rita to keep her cool if she doesn't have to sort out her goals and cope with Alan's attacks at the same time.

Study Their Situation

The flip side of setting your own targets is discovering the other party's interests and goals. To use an analogy, if you were going to an important job interview and wanted to make an effective presentation, you might very well research the company ahead of time. Perhaps you'd review the company's website, read their annual report, or at least network to find someone knowledgeable about the company. At the interview, you'd ask careful questions and pay close attention to the interviewer's responses in order to understand the demands of the position and the qualifications they were seeking in a candidate. You couldn't change your own qualifications to meet their needs, but you could certainly tailor your presentation to highlight areas with a good fit.

In a conflict, it's equally important to understand as much as you can about the other person's situation: his or her needs, targets, options, and constraints. Sometimes doing a bit of detective work ahead of time will enhance your knowledge. Often, just putting yourself in the other person's shoes and thinking through his or her perspective will be helpful. It's also critical to ask open-ended questions to learn what the person wants and needs, and why. Examples of questions that can facilitate understanding during a conflict are:

What do you want?

Why do you want that?

What's concerning you?

What would you do if you were in my shoes?

What if we were to_____?

How can we work this out?

Why not do it this way?

What makes that fair?

Whereas statements often generate resistance during a conflict, questions can generate answers, allow the parties to get their points across, pose challenges, and diffuse attacks. Consider how Alan might respond to Rita if she asked him some of these questions:

Rita: Alan, why do you want me to seek your approval before I spend money that's already in my budget?

*Alan: You may **think** the money's in your budget, but you might be wrong. Do you know how many units exceeded their budget limits last fiscal year?*

Rita could then ask Alan to share more with her about this situation, so she understands the problems he's facing with budget overruns. If she showed appreciation for the situation Alan's accountable for, he might then be more receptive to Rita's reminder that her unit has never exceeded projections and to any suggestions Rita may have to help him monitor the budget in a less obtrusive way. In addition to asking questions, requesting feedback from the other party also helps you understand his or her situation and interests:

161

Rita: What if we were to try this: I could send you quarterly reports of our expenditures, so you'd have ongoing information. I could attach an addendum to let you know if we anticipated any unusual expenses coming up in the next quarter, and if you wanted more information, you could contact me.

Alan: I don't know. There's so much crossing my desk.

Rita: How can we work this out? Do you think we might try this system for three months and see how it works?

Alan: I suppose so.

By using these people smart abilities to get the important issues on the table, you can make conflict resolution less painful and more productive, avoiding wasted time and energy. Only when the real issues are out in the open is it possible to generate solutions that allow everyone to take away something valuable.

3. Negotiating Win/Win Solutions

In most conflict situations, there's the potential for both parties to meet at least some of their basic interests. If you can accept that conflict resolution can be a cooperative process, rather than a battle to the death, you can promote win/win outcomes. To do this, you need to *generate mutual gain options, develop a joint plan,* and *use contingency strategies.*

Generate Mutual Gain Options

If you want to multiply your chances of solving a conflict to the satisfaction of both parties, you need to create options, options, and more options. Once everyone's interests are on the table, it's time to generate a range of solutions that meet at least some of each person's needs. Usually the best way to do this is to brainstorm.

Most people are at least somewhat familiar with the brainstorming process. The basic rules are as follows:

- **Invent ideas**. Participants list as many alternative solutions as possible. Having each party alternate expressing his or her ideas is usually helpful. The parties should feel free to piggy back variations onto each other's suggestions and come up with creative ways to integrate interests. Listing should continue until each person sees several solutions he or she would be willing to work with.

- **Withhold judgments**. During the brainstorming process neither party may discuss, reject, or evaluate any suggestion. The decisions come later.

- **Evaluate the solutions**. Discuss the list and star the most promising ideas. Try to improve and elaborate these suggestions. Consider each solution in terms of whether it will really solve the problem and what it would cost each party.

- **Choose the best solution**. Often this step is best deferred until each party has had time to think about the alternatives. The best solution should at least meet each party's bottom line and satisfy some basic interests on both sides.

Negotiating experts recommend expanding the pie to increase possible win/win solutions. Instead of narrowing the options, add interests and resources to the picture to enhance the likelihood of mutual gain. Let's look at how the win/win process might go with Alan and Rita:

Rita and Alan get together and negotiate a way to work together more cooperatively. Since they will have to share their solution with the CEO, they have no choice but to sit down and brainstorm ways to resolve their ongoing conflict. They start the list with some of their usual proposals, but to their surprise, they find themselves getting more creative as they go along. Their list of potential solutions looks like this:

- *Rita will send Alan quarterly reports so he can monitor her routine budget expenditures.*

- *Rita will e-mail Alan to request his preapproval for any unusual expenditures or expenses in excess of $1,000.*

- *When Rita requests Alan's authorization for an expenditure, he'll respond within 24 hours.*

- *Alan will agree to let Rita make expenditures within the scope of her budget without his preapproval, but if a quarterly check shows that she has exceeded her budget limits, Rita will agree to seek Alan's prior approval for all subsequent expenses.*

- *Alan and Rita agree to meet monthly to discuss the status of her program, air concerns, and generally work on improving their communication.*

- *Alan will conduct a seminar for all the managers on Rita's level on "Pitfalls in Budget Management."*

- *Rita and Alan will resolve their disputes without involving the CEO.*

  When they review their list, Rita and Alan are surprised at how many of the options make sense to them. They agree to combine all of the proposals, except for the one about monthly meetings, since neither has time for another meeting.

  Now all they need is a plan.

Develop a Joint Plan

Planning begins with selection of the best solutions, but doesn't end there. An action plan promotes follow-through by incorporating specific information about who will do what, and when. It's also a good idea for the participants to schedule a subsequent meeting to evaluate how their solution is working out. This not only makes the plan more real, it ensures an opportunity to make any needed modifications after the participants have given their solution a trial run.

An action plan for Rita and Alan might specify that Rita will send Alan her first quarterly budget report in April, but begin requesting his preapproval for major expenditures immediately. Alan will schedule the seminar for next month and Rita will encourage her colleagues to attend. They might agree to meet after Alan has reviewed Rita's first quarterly report to evaluate how their arrangement is working out.

If we can agree on win/win solutions, and the means to implement them, we can turn conflicts into opportunities. But we all know that conflict resolution doesn't always go smoothly. There are times when we need to deal with curve balls in the negotiating process.

Use Contingency Strategies

Conflict situations become the most stressful when the other party employs tactics that push our hot buttons. Although there is a wide range of provocative behaviors people may use, William Ury (1991) groups them into three broad categories: *stone walls* (obstructive tactics), *attacks* (offensive tactics), and *tricks* (deception). When faced with one of these tactical approaches, the first line of defense is to recognize it, rather than just react to it. If we pause and take stock of the situation, we can choose a more strategic response.

Stone walls include extreme positions, ultimatums, and rigid deadlines. When confronted with a stone wall, Ury's advice is to go around it. You can do this by ignoring it (continuing to negotiate a solution to the problem at hand), testing it, or reinterpreting the extreme demand as a wish, rather than a realistic expectation.

Parents sometimes find themselves presenting stone walls to their teenagers. Liz, the mother of 16-year-old Jason, took a hard-line position about getting his chores done:

Liz: You cannot go out, under any circumstances, until you have finished all of your homework, cleaned your room, and fed and walked the dog!

The first strategy adopted by Jason, an aspiring criminal lawyer, was to reinterpret Liz' position as a wish:

Jason: You're right, Mom. I do need to be more consistent about doing my chores. And I promise I'm going to work on that. Can we talk about special circumstances that might arise, when we might both want to modify the arrangement?

Liz: Such as? (Notice that Jason has already disarmed her and inched her away from her original position.)

Jason: Well, the visiting hours at the nursing home are so strict, and I'd really like to get over to see Grandma next week. Maybe I could finish my homework after I get back.

Liz: Well, we'll see.

Having taken a few steps around his mother's stone wall, Jason's next strategy will be to test her position by finding another plausible reason to go out before his chores are completed, say, to get to the library before it closes.

Attacks can take the form of blame, insults, or threats. Many people find such tactics extremely uncomfortable. The best approach to an attack is to deflect it. This can be done by ignoring it (continuing to focus on the issues, while tuning out the offensive noise) or reframing the attack in several possible ways. You can reframe an attack as behavior directed at the problem rather than yourself, or define the attack in terms of the past, while shifting the focus to the future. You can also reframe by shifting to "we" terms:

Chris, a division manager, is notorious for her short temper and bullying style with subordinates. Fred is a newly promoted supervisor who has just started reporting to Chris since the resignation of his former boss and mentor, Rick. Chris didn't like working with Rick, an assertive guy she couldn't boss around. She's determined to remedy this situation with Fred and starts their meeting accordingly:

Chris: So, am I finally going to get some accurate project reports around here? You know, Rick used to lie all the time to cover up for your group!

The attack on Rick, whom Fred liked and respected, is hard for Fred to swallow. But, recognizing the tactic for what it is, he pauses, takes a sip of his coffee, and reframes Chris's attack by shifting the focus from past to future, and from "I/you" to "we":

Fred: Chris, I hope that you and I won't stay bogged down in past problems. What can we do to improve the communication flow?

Fred silently apologizes to Rick for not defending him. But Rick was Fred's teacher, and Fred was a pretty good student.

Tricks range from outright lies and falsifying data, to a variety of ploys (such as "good cop/bad cop," a familiar staple of crime shows). Tricks may be particularly difficult to recognize, but, once spotted, need to be exposed. Asking clarifying questions and paying careful attention to discrepant body language are helpful techniques for identifying deception. Making a reasonable request can be a way to test out the other party's sincerity. When you do expose a trick, don't do it in an aggressive way; that merely escalates the situation. However, it's fair game to use a trick to your own advantage:

Tricia, a nurse, hates the endless documentation that seems to be an increasing part of her job. Being on the passive-aggressive side, she tends to take a sneaky approach to conflicts. Rather than do all the paperwork, or negotiate some other arrangement with Candice, her supervisor, Tricia creates projects that take her away from the dreaded documentation. She cleans out supply closets, volunteers to run errands that take her to other floors, even slips out for extra breaks or extends her lunch hour.

Candice, however, is nobody's fool. When she finds Tricia sorting out the magazines in the waiting room, she calmly questions her about how she came to be doing this project. Tricia responds that she heard some visitors complaining about the out-of-date magazines and thought she'd do the customer-friendly thing. Candice responds: "I'm glad to see you have some extra time. There are some patient status reports that Linda couldn't get to last night. I was going to do them, but since you're free, I'll give them to you!"

While staying calm and strategic can often keep the conflict resolution on track, there are times when negotiations either break down completely, or simply don't go our way, despite all efforts. It's important to recognize when we need a walkout option-an alternative solution outside of the other party's control. In work conflict, the walkout option is often to take another job. In marriages, it's sometimes a separation. There are times when we need to go, and, in many instances, having walkout options gives us the confidence to stand up for our needs and negotiate more effectively.

Try It
Exercises for Developing Conflict Resolution Skills

Practice makes perfect—or, at least, better! Here are some ways to enhance your abilities and your confidence in dealing with conflict.

Creating a Climate of Mutual Interest

1. Identify a long-standing disagreement you have been having with someone. How have you been defining the problem? See if you can state the problem in mutual terms such as, *"The conflict we are having is_____."* or *"Our conflict is_____."* Do the issues look different when you frame the conflict this way? Decide what type of

conflict you are having with this person. Is it over facts, methods, purposes, or values? Are there any different approaches to the conflict you might take, based on your analysis?

2. Identify your own usual style of dealing with conflict. Are you primarily confrontive, persuasive, cooperative, or avoiding? List some examples of conflict situations where you relied on this particular style. What were the consequences? Choose an alternative style you might have used in each of these situations. What would you have done differently?

Putting the Real Issues on the Table

1. Select a current or recent conflict you have been dealing with. Write down the positions taken by you and the other party. Now brainstorm your own interests in the situation, as well as those of the other party. Have these issues been addressed at all in your efforts to resolve the conflict? How might you put them on the table?

2. For a current or recent conflict you have faced, identify your targets. Write down your maximum position, goal, and bottom line. See if you can think of what the other party's targets would be and write these down, as well. Decide whether you want to do some negotiating with the other party, based on your understanding of your respective targets.

Negotiating Win/Win Solutions

1. Choose a current conflict situation and brainstorm as many mutual gain options as you can. Do you think any of these solutions might be workable? Consider sharing your list with the other party and inviting him to add his own ideas.

2. Think about which type of negotiators you find most difficult: stone

wallers, attackers, or tricksters. Review the examples of response strategies and identify two possible ways you might respond to future tactics of this type.

Live It
Overcoming Your Own Barriers to Lasting Change

As you work on using your conflict resolution skills in the real world, what pitfalls should you anticipate? See whether any of these situations are likely to pose problems for you.

I really believe that conflict inevitably leads to bad feelings and bitterness. It's better to avoid it whenever possible.

> Just because a belief is strong doesn't make it true. Examine the evidence to support your avoidant attitude. Have you found that conflicts actually go away if you don't deal with them? You may also have had too much experience with badly managed conflicts that distorted your expectations. Approach new conflicts with a conviction that you can resolve them more cooperatively. Pick small disagreements to deal with openly at first. Pay attention to the outcomes and notice improvements.

I've got a quick temper and can't seem to control my anger in conflict situations.

> Time-outs were meant for you. Make it a priority to slow down the action to keep yourself from losing control. Try to recognize your early signs of anger, so you can take a break and calm yourself before you lash out.

I have trouble thinking on my feet during a conflict and don't do a good job of defending my position.

> Prepare, prepare, prepare. Define your interests and map out your targets before you go to the negotiating table. Anticipate the interests and possible tactics of the other party. If you're still caught off guard, call a time-out to collect your thoughts and plan your response.

My spouse always brings up a hundred past transgressions when we argue.

> Stay focused. Don't let yourself be drawn into arguing about the past. Calmly acknowledge that you've both made mistakes and redirect the discussion to how you can make it better in the future.

My boss can't seem to tolerate any difference of opinion. There's no way to win in a conflict with him short of resigning.

> Listen, acknowledge, and ask clarifying questions to show your boss you take his perspective seriously. Give him control in constructive ways, such as by asking, "How can we work this out?," or "What would you do if you were in my shoes?" Invite him to brainstorm a range of solutions instead of acquiescing to the one solution he offers. Appeal to his interests: "You often have creative ideas about solving problems. Would you be willing to take a few minutes to generate some alternative scenarios for us to think about?" Look for ways to help him save face by, for example, pointing out how new circumstances might indicate a change in his approach to a problem.

I seem to have the same conflicts with my partner over and over again. Even when we do agree on a solution, nothing ever changes.

> Analyze what the conflict is really about. Are you arguing about procedures, competing goals, conflicting values? If

you don't address the conflict at the appropriate level, you won't resolve it. Try to get the real issues on the table, so you aren't just battling about positions. Probably one or both of you has basic interests at stake that aren't being addressed. Make sure your agreements meet both of your interests, at least to some extent. Plan out all the specifics of how you'll follow through, including a face-to-face evaluation of how it's going.

Some people are just too sneaky and indirect to deal with openly. I try to be up-front, but they deny the problem, then stab me in the back.

Acknowledge to them that, like many people, they might prefer not to engage in conflict, but calmly insist that you do have some issues to deal with, and cite the evidence. Sometimes you can nip future sabotage in the bud by predicting it. Try asking the person, "What do you think will happen in the future if we don't deal with this now?" If the backstabbing happens anyway, remind the person that this was predictable.

I can't stay calm or positive when someone attacks or insults me.

Try to change your thinking about the attack so you won't take it personally. Recognize it as a symptom of the other person's distress or concern about the problem, and not as a reflection on you. If you can't ignore the attack, try to reframe it. If necessary, negotiate about how to negotiate. Calmly suggest you both focus on the issues, or propose that you take a break and resume negotiations when you can do so more productively.

It's hard to think of win/win solutions, and I don't know if I'd trust the other person to stick to an agreement.

One reason people have difficulty generating solutions is that they start evaluating potential outcomes before they've allowed themselves to brainstorm fully. Make a strict rule, for yourself and others, against judging any possible solutions before you've developed a long list of options. If you're both stuck for ideas, consider inviting neutral parties to suggest alternatives. Remember that the best solutions will address interests, rather than positions, allowing a greater range of possibilities. When you do identify the most promising solutions, allow time to think about them before making a final choice. And be sure to develop a clear implementation plan.

Keep forging ahead, even if you do backslide. With patience and persistence, you'll find that conflicts begin to seem more like opportunities and less like threats. Remember that the oyster produces a pearl by tolerating friction! And keep in mind that learning to deal with conflicts will help you in many situations. It will, for example, help you as you learn to become a team player.

People**Smart Skill 7**

Being a Team Player

Ask not what your teammates can do for you.
Ask what you can do for your teammates.

—MAGIC JOHNSON

Are you involved in some kind of teamwork at work, with the family, or with a community, civic, or religious group? If you are, you surely have found out that being a member of a team really tests you because you have less personal control over the outcome than in a one-to-one relationship. It's often frustrating since you have fewer opportunities to get your point across and persuade others when participation has to be shared among many. On the other hand, being part of a team effort, even with its frustrations, can often be exciting and productive.

Think about it: When you work with one other person, there is only one relationship; when you work with three people, there are *six* relationships:

1. A's relationship with B.

2. A's relationship with C.

3. B's relationship with C.

4. A's relationship with B and C.

5. B's relationship with A and C.

6. C's relationship with A and B.

Just imagine how many relationships exist in a group of six people. Several hundred!

As a team player, one works hard to advance the group's goals. This can be a daunting challenge for those of us who were raised in a culture that values individual rather than group effort. It involves an attitude shift in which we must transcend our egos and desire to advance our own agenda in favor of giving our ideas readily to the group.

A person we know named Angela has not made the shift from individual performance to group collaboration:

Angela is a third grade teacher with lots of creative teaching strategies. Her classroom is alive with activity while other classrooms in
her school are less exciting. But at faculty meetings Angela keeps
pretty much to herself. She holds her colleagues in low regard and
thinks meetings are something to endure rather than to enjoy. Her
principal has urged her to acquaint other teachers with some of her
approaches, but Angela believes that any advice from her would be
wasted. Angela also holds the parents of her students in low regard.
She would like parents to spend more time reading to their children and helping them with their homework, but she has given up
much hope of seeing that happen. She is content that her classroom is a place of rich learning and hopes that her efforts will make
a difference in her students' lives.

Interpersonally intelligent people, on the other hand, have a
knack for contributing to the team's effectiveness. Take Tina, for
example:

Tina is a floor nurse in a large urban hospital, with many patients
to attend to. Some have important needs; others buzz her for the
most trivial of reasons. All the nurses on Tina's floor help each
other out when assistance is needed or when one nurse is occupied
with another patient, but Tina is especially quick to aid her colleagues. She sees them as partners, not simply people in need of
assistance. Not only is this appreciated but others are also apt to
help her in kind without much hesitation. What goes around,
comes around.

Recently, the nurses on her floor were asked to volunteer for
a process improvement committee involving nursing and the hospital pharmacy. Their task was to discuss ways to speed delivery of

medications to patients. Tina volunteered. Unfortunately, the first few committee meetings were pretty much a waste of time with blaming occurring more than problem-solving. The committee was about to fall apart when Tina, who had been rather quiet, pointed out that the group was very large and perhaps, should spend some time brainstorming in groups of four containing two representatives from each function. (Tina got the idea from a church board on which she served.) Desperate for some process that would work, the committee agreed. This change in group format allowed the committee to get beyond blaming and work through many sticky issues together. Tina was an invaluable team member throughout the process. She kept the group focused and productive by frequently summarizing what others had said so that the group had a running account of its ideas.

Want It
Motivating Yourself to Be a Team Player

In what groups do you want to be more collaborative? Check any of the following that remind you of places in your life where you want to be a team player.

On the job:

☐ Participating in meetings.

☐ Partnering with colleagues.

☐ Enhancing project teams or committee work.

☐ Connecting with people in different departments.

☐ Including those who have been excluded.

☐ Assisting others in times of need.

☐ Developing a mission statement or a strategic plan.

☐ Coordinating a sales meeting.

On the home front:

☐ Sharing parenting responsibilities.

☐ Engaging in family activity.

☐ Participating in civic, religious, or community groups.

☐ Partnering with teachers and other personnel at the schools your children attend.

☐ Instituting family meetings.

☐ Collaborating with your neighbors.

☐ Coordinating child or elder care with others.

☐ Working in a political campaign.

We hope these examples prompt you to pinpoint circumstances of your own where collaboration skills could pay off for you. Think about where, when, and with whom you could be a better team player, and see whether these skills can help you make the grade.

Learn It
Three Ways to Become a Team Player

People with high PQs are successful as team players because they are adept at **joining with others** to seek ways to contribute to a group effort. They are also effective at **facilitating teamwork** by employing techniques to enhance group activity. And finally, they are skilled at **building consensus**, the process of making decisions that everyone supports.

1. Joining with Others

Each of us comes to a group with our own talents. Team players come with something else: the ability to blend their talents with the skills of others around them. Team players also balance interest in what they are advocating with interests in what others are saying. They see themselves and others as group resources rather than individual egos. They act as if they are part of the group's pool of knowledge, skills, and ideas and are successful in getting others to act that way themselves. Key steps in joining with others are: *observing what's going on in the group, making contributions where needed*, and *building a climate of dialogue*.

Observe What's Going On in the Group

Many people in group situations are oblivious to what is happening around them. They are focused on themselves and fail to pick up cues from or about others. Perhaps someone has been excluded. Perhaps someone has a good idea but hasn't expressed it well. Perhaps the group is on a tangent or caught up in debate when it should be brainstorming. Here is a list of things to watch for in a group:

- Does everyone have the same understanding of the group's goals? Does everyone support them?

- Do people seem free to express themselves?

- Do people listen to each other?

- Is there equal opportunity for participation?

- Is the group floundering and without energy?

- Are members in the group building on each other's ideas?

- Is conflict accepted and handled?

- Do group members know about each other's needs?

Based on your observations, you are in a position to be helpful to the group.

Make Contributions Where Needed

Picture a basketball team in which each player looked exclusively for an opportunity to shoot instead of passing the ball to an open player, setting screens for teammates, or getting into position for the rebound. As we have said before, people who are not attuned to the team concept focus on their own needs and ignore the needs of others. If you have made some accurate observations of the group situation, however, you have uncovered opportunities to contribute to the group effort. In basketball terms, you have good "court awareness" and can sense what you need to do to help the group be successful. Here is a list of things you might contribute:

- Assist someone else when appropriate.

- Offer to take minutes at a meeting.

- Share information.

- Ask quiet members for their opinion.

- Objectively describe the different viewpoints in the group.

- Bring together members who are in conflict with each other but are using others to air their grievances.

- Express appreciation for the efforts of others.

- Offer to facilitate discussion.

- Share credit you receive for a job well done.

- Summarize the group discussion.

- Suggest problem-solving techniques you may know.

- Relieve tension with gracious humor.

- Check decisions you are about to make to see how they might affect others.

- Include everybody in the information loop.

- Seek information and expertise of others.

- Communicate your own activity so that it is public knowledge.

- Tell others what they can do to support your efforts, and ask them to do the same.

- Seek out the talents of others.

Build a Climate of Dialogue

We use the expression, "Everyone is entitled to his or her opinion" when we want to support freedom of speech. However, there are social limits to this right in team situations. Too often, team discussion becomes a debate of my idea vs. your idea. People advocate for the causes dear to their hearts, hoping to gain support from others. By contrast, when a climate of dialogue exists, team members listen to each other, react to and build upon each other's idea, and look for and acknowledge real differences of opinion. The purpose of dialogue is to enlarge ideas, not diminish them. Here are ways you can help to build a climate of dialogue:

- Ask questions to clarify what others are saying. Invite others to seek clarification of your ideas.

- Share what's behind your ideas. Reveal your assumptions and goals. Invite others to do so in kind.

- Ask for others to give you feedback about your ideas.

- Give constructive feedback about the ideas of others.

- Make suggestions that build on the ideas of others.

- Incorporate the ideas of others into your proposals.

- Find common ground among the ideas expressed in the group.

- Encourage others to give additional ideas beyond those already expressed.

2. Facilitating Team Work

Whenever you are in a leadership position in a group, it pays to examine your leadership style. If you are a traditional leader, you may be used to directing, controlling, and monitoring. As a team-oriented leader, your role shifts to coaching, motivating, and empowering. Also, you may be accustomed to developing individual strengths among the members of the group you lead. As a team leader, you need to develop those strengths within the team.

You don't have to be the leader in a group, however, to play a facilitative role. Anyone can offer suggestions that might help the group to work more effectively.

A religious organization applied to a municipality for permission to build a group home for adolescent girls who had come from homes where they had been abused.

*The organization wanted to buy one of a series of man-
sions that lined the main street of the town. The night the
plan was introduced before the town council, a small
but outspoken group of neighbors fought the idea fever-
ishly. The neighbors complained that the organization
wouldn't have the funds to keep up the property. They
said the girls were bad and might be thieves, would
surely be a bad influence on younger children and boys
of their own age, might party all night, and subsequently
destroy the neighborhood. They refused to listen to the
religious organization's plans and even booed its repre-
sentative. It was apparent to someone in the crowd that
the meeting was going nowhere. He suggested the town
council select three people from the minority group and
have them meet with three people from the religious
organization to iron out some of the problems. After a little time to cool down, the two groups met and struck a
deal. The organization got its group home, and the neighbors received the safeguards they wanted.*

In order to facilitate teamwork, there are three important
steps to take: *promote a common vision, encourage participation,*
and *stimulate creative problem solving.*

Promote a Common Vision

When people join a group, there may be no clear goals around which
to coalesce. Or the announced goal may be interpreted differently by
various members. Also, people may come to a group with their own
individual goals that may or may not be supportive of the group goal.
Given all these possibilities, most groups don't begin with a common
vision. Many remain that way for months or years.

Effective teams are united in purpose. Whatever you can do to facilitate the creation of a common vision will be invaluable to the group. Here are some suggestions:

- If you are the team leader, suggest a few goals that will excite the group and ask for their reactions. Don't settle for business as usual, teams thrive when there is "business as *unusual*." You could raise some specific targets for the coming year, identify some special projects for the team to undertake, or announce your commitment to changing work conditions.

- If you are a group member and sense that the group is not unified around clear and exciting goals, ask for permission to set aside time for creating a common vision.

- Raise any of these questions for discussion:

  — Imagine the meetings were coming to an end. What would you like to see as our accomplishments?

  — Imagine coming to work here with your heart beating and your feet skipping. What would be going on here? What would the place look like? What would staff members be doing that is exciting and worthwhile?

  — How could you state in a brief sentence or two the end results we might obtain if we work together? Some sample statements: For a customer service unit: "We make customers glad they bought our product." For a hospital dialysis unit: "Because of us, patients feel more dignity and hope." For a manufacturing plant: "Our customers know when they operate one of our machines they are operating the finest equipment money can buy."

Encourage Participation

Teamwork falls flat if the group is reluctant to participate or certain persons dominate. A wide range of methods can be used to obtain active team participation. If you use a few of them on a consistent basis, you will avoid hearing from the same people all the time. Here are several possibilities:

Open discussion: Ask a question and open it up to the entire group without any further structuring. Use open discussion when you are certain that several people want to participate. Its voluntary quality is also appealing. Don't overuse this method. If you do, you will limit participation to people who are comfortable about raising their hands. If you have a very participative group and are worried that the discussion might be too lengthy, say beforehand: "I'd like to ask four or five people to share." If you are worried that few people will volunteer, say: "How many of you have an idea?" vs. "Who has an idea?"

Response cards: Pass out index cards and request anonymous answers to your questions. Use response cards to save time, to provide anonymity for personally threatening self-disclosures, or make it easier for shy people to contribute. The need to state yourself concisely on a card is another advantage of this method. Say, "For this discussion, I would like you to write down your thoughts before we talk together." Have the index cards passed around the group or have them returned to you to be read at a later point. Be careful to make your questions clear and encourage brief, legible responses.

Subgroup discussion: Form people into subgroups of three or more to share and record information. Use subgroup discussion when you have sufficient time to process questions and issues. This is one of the key methods for obtaining every-one's participation. You can assign people to subgroups randomly (e.g., counting off) or purposively (e.g., one member from each department represented). Pose a question for discussion or provide a task to complete. Often, it is helpful to designate group roles, such as facilitator, timekeeper, recorder, or presenter, and obtain volunteers or assign members to fill them. Make sure that people are in face-to-face contact with each other. Separate subgroups so that they do not disturb each other.

Partners: Form people into pairs and instruct them to work on tasks or discuss key questions. Use partners when you want to involve everybody but do not have enough time for small-group discussion. Pair people up either by physical proximity or by a wish to put certain people together. Often, it is not necessary to move chairs to create pair activity. You can ask pairs to do many things, such as reading and discussing a short written document together, responding to a question, or developing a solution to a problem.

Go-around: Go around the group and obtain short responses from each person. Use this method when you want to hear from each person and equalize participation. Sometimes sentence stems (e.g., "One thing we could do is____") are useful in conducting go-arounds. Invite people to pass when they wish. Avoid repetition, if you want, by asking each person for a new contribution to the process.

Calling on the next speaker: Ask people to raise their hands when they want to share their views and request that the present speaker in the group call on the next speaker (rather than have the facilitator do so). Say, "For this discussion, I would like you to call on each other rather than having me select the next speaker. When you are finished speaking, look around to see who has a hand raised and call on someone." (Do not allow people to call on individuals who have not indicated a desire to participate.) Use this method when you are sure there is a lot of interest in the discussion and you wish to promote person-to-person interaction. When you wish to resume as moderator, inform the group that you are changing back to the regular format.

Fishbowl: Ask a portion of the group to form a discussion circle and have the remaining people form a listening circle around them. Use a fishbowl to help bring focus to large group discussions. Although time consuming, this is the best method for combining the virtues of large and small group discussion. Bring new groups into the inner circle to continue the discussion. You can do this by obtaining new volunteers or assigning people to be discussants. As a variation to concentric circles, you can have people remain seated at a table and invite different tables or parts of a table to be the discussants as the others listen.

Bear in mind that you can combine some of these methods of obtaining participation. For example, you might pose a question, form partners to discuss it, and then obtain the group's reaction through open discussion or by calling on the next speaker. By inserting the partner exchange first, you will have more people ready to participate in the full group setting. Or begin with response cards, followed by a go-around or subgroups.

Stimulate Creative Problem Solving

A group's creativity is fostered by thinking outside the box—looking at issues in new ways and developing novel solutions to problems. Brainstorming is a well-known technique for coming up with new ideas about goals, projects, solutions, whatever. Most people think of brainstorming as a way of getting many ideas in a very short period of time, but brainstorming can be done at a leisurely pace as well. Here are two alternatives:

Fast brainstorming can be compared to making popcorn. Kernels form in people's minds and out pop ideas (some of which may be corny). If things go well, you get a lot of ideas and then the process gets exhausted. The process typically involves the following guidelines:

Participants are urged to *go for quantity*; the more ideas, the better.

Participants are encouraged to *think freely*. In some cases, the crazier the ideas, the better.

Participants are invited to *express* ideas when they occur.

Participants are required to *withhold comments* about the ideas until the time for brainstorming is up.

As a result of the above, the pace is usually frenzied and uninhibited.

Slow brainstorming has a different tempo and feel. Participants are expected to be thoughtful and responsive. As a result, fewer ideas might be developed, but the quality may improve. However, there are still rules that qualify it as a form of brainstorming:

Participants are asked to *wait a few seconds* before expressing their idea.

Participants are sometimes requested to *write down ideas first* before making them public.

Participants are sometimes required to *limit themselves* to one contribution until everyone contributes or passes.

Participants are urged to *ask clarifying questions*. When an idea is offered by someone, others are allowed to seek more information about the idea as long as they don't make judgments. For example, you might ask, "How much do you estimate that will cost?" (said in a friendly tone of voice), but you would not ask, "Don't you think that's expensive?"

Participants are encouraged to *add to an idea*. ("Maybe we could also_____".)

The key to either type of brainstorming session, fast or slow, is open, nonjudgmental interaction. Of course, however the ideas are produced, they must eventually be listed, discussed, and evaluated. One way to quickly sort out the participants' reaction to the brainstormed ideas is to group them into these categories:

- Keepers (implement immediately)

- Maybes (promising enough to warrant serious consideration)

- Hold-offs (put aside for now)

Often, brainstorming new ideas is difficult because the size of the problem taxes the creative imagination of the group. One way to overcome this situation is to break the problem, issue, or goal down into its constituent parts and examine each part separately. Then participants can brainstorm ideas involving each part. Doing this will help to loosen up participants and they may produce some truly novel and productive ideas.

As the meeting begins, state the problem, issue, or goal about which you want to have a brainstorming session. Next, ask the participants to think about all the elements or parts of the problem, issue, or goal *by breaking it down*. (Or, you may do this analysis for them prior to the meeting.) As an example, consider the planning of a successful fundraising race. These are some aspects of the project to be considered:

- A slogan

- The course to be run

- A length for the race

- A date for the race (Is Saturday better than Sunday? Rain date or no? Maybe a holiday weekend?)

- Prizes

- A deadline for entries

- Emergency services

- Publicity before, at, and after the race.

Take each part, and think about the alternatives. New ideas in each of the areas could be so powerful that next year's race could be a real winner or it could change into a different kind of event and not a race at all, as a result of the planners looking at the project from a different perspective.

A third strategy to encourage creative problem solving employs a technique called scenario thinking. Participants are asked to set aside present realities and dream up a wide range of new possibilities.

To use scenario thinking, select an issue, problem, or creative project facing the group. For example, a group might be discussing employee morale, slackening productivity, or customer service. Tell the group that you would like them to set aside their current concerns about things the way they are and to think about a range of future possibilities to resolve the issue, problem, or project. Display one or more of the following sentence stems and say to participants, "Let's dream a little together. How could we expand our thinking about this? "

> *I wonder_____*
>
> *What if_____*
>
> *Maybe, we_____*
>
> *I have a dream that_____*
>
> *If only we_____*
>
> *I wish_____*
>
> *Why can't we_____*

Allow participants to speak whenever a thought comes to mind. Encourage participants to accept silences between contributions. Insist that people listen but not comment on ideas until several have been made.

3. Building Consensus

It's now crunch time. Your group has been exploring ideas and debating its options. Some ideas will have to be discarded, at least for now. Difficult decisions need to be reached and priorities need to be established. Agreement and commitment are the order of the day.

Most experts agree that groups should make important decisions by building consensus as opposed to taking votes. A consensus exists when all participants are willing to support and commit themselves to a specific decision. It may not be everyone's first choice but everyone can live with the conclusions being reached. When a group builds a consensus, there is greater commitment to implement the group's decision. With voting, a disgruntled minority usually winds up upset and lags in their commitment to the implementation phase.

While many people agree in principle with the value of consensus, they voice practical objections. Having participated in groups that took ages to reach consensus, they have serious doubts that it is worth the trouble. There are ways to counteract these concerns. When building consensus, consider three steps: *narrowing down ideas, polling the group*, and *checking for commitment*.

Narrow Down Ideas

Multivoting is an efficient way to narrow the choices from a long list of decision options. Once the list is narrowed, it is often easier to obtain consensus. The members of the group prepare a list of possible solutions to a complex problem and are permitted to narrow the list themselves by individual voting. This has the effect of reducing the list to items that are acceptable to most voters. The process continues, if necessary, until only a few proposals remain. This procedure reduces the loss of many good ideas, one of the problems created by a single vote on a long list of items. On a flip chart list all possible alternatives that could solve the particular problem, along with their attendant difficulties and advantages. If two or more alternatives are very similar, combine them if the group agrees they should be combined. Tell the participants to think carefully about what options they can accept. Pass out ballots and ask the participants to vote for each alternative they find acceptable. *They may vote for as many as they want*. Inform them, however, that only alternatives receiving half of all the possible votes will remain in contention and be placed on a second ballot. Hold a discussion of the remaining choices. Then, vote again. The alternatives that receive half of all the possible votes on the second ballot remain on the list; others are dropped. Determine at this point whether more voting is needed to narrow the choices to reach a consensus.

When many solutions to a problem have been suggested, probably the most effective way to select the best ones is to have the group weigh them against specific standards. The process can be as simple or as comprehensive as necessary in order to achieve consensus. It can be used by small groups as well as large ones.

On a large flip chart, prepare a list of all the proposed solutions to the problem on which the group is focusing. Before going any further, propose a set of standards against which the group can evaluate its options, or ask the group to produce a set of standards for judging the choices available to them. Such standards might include cost, feasibility, time needed, impact on results, and so forth. Ask the participants to discuss each option according to the standards you have suggested. Be sure to go through each option, collecting judgments. The options can also be weighted on each standard, using a simple rating scale, to generate favorability scores. Don't allow the process to get bogged down in a campaign for a particular option.

Poll for Consensus

Polling for consensus is one good way to get the pulse of the group. When you survey the group, you are better able to pinpoint the degrees of difference in the participants' opposition or support of an idea or action and assess how close the sides really are. Your polling results will tell you whether further discussion is needed or if the opposing groups are ready at this point to seek a solution.

Tell the participants that they have reached a point in a meeting when no new ideas are being presented and the participants are essentially recycling the same opinions and positions. This is the time to conduct a poll to see if a decision is near. Explain to the group the different stages of consensus readiness, graded from A through D:

A Willing to accept the plan.

B Admitting the plan is a fair solution but not one that the participant can get really excited about.

C Not fully agreeing with the plan and feeling the need to explain why it is not acceptable, but not willing to try to block the idea.

D Disagreeing with the decision and feeling strongly enough about it to try to exercise all of his or her influence to block the plan.

Ask the participants to indicate where they stand on the readiness scale. You can ask them to raise their hands as you call out the grades or to write the grade on an index card to be collected and tallied. The grades will show you whether more work needs to be done. If there are a lot of A's and B's, then you and the group will determine that consensus has been reached. If the grades are mostly C and D, then more discussion time is needed.

Check for Commitment

When a group is attempting to build consensus, it is important to provide some kind of forum for the minority to speak as well as to collect any splinter ideas they might have that could be extremely important to the project. Providing a way for the minority to be heard can be a healing experience that will help the group work together in the future.

One way to do this is to provide time for the apparent minority to make a statement. You might set aside 15 minutes or half an hour at a meeting when consensus seems near. After hearing from the minority, ask the total group if there are suggestions for alleviating the concerns expressed.

If a consensus is finally reached, ask participants to think about what they can commit themselves to do to implement decisions that have been made. If the team effort has required a long series of meetings, consider sending a letter or e-mail to participants with a summary of the main decisions and accomplishments. If group members will be involved in implementing the course of action decided on at the meeting, encourage them to keep in touch with you and offer your expertise to help them solve any unexpected problems.

Try It
Exercises for Developing Your Collaborative Skills

Ready for the next step? Here are some experiments you can undertake right away to work on your collaboration skills and find out if you like the results.

Joining with Others

1. Spend one week taking notice of what's happening in a group of concern to you. Listen to what others are saying and watch the group's behavior. (You may want to follow the suggestions on pages 180–181.) What conclusions do you come to? In what areas can you be helpful?

2. Make a list of things you do independently of others at home or at work. Examine the list and identify items where it would be helpful if you involved others rather than doing things alone.

Facilitating Teamwork

1. If you are a leader of a group, examine your leadership style. Think about how you could become a more team-oriented leader. Consider possibilities such as developing a common vision in the group, connecting staff members with each other, and asking for input on policy and procedure. Does your staff respond positively?

2. If you are member of a group that you would like to see improve, suggest using interactive discussion formats and creative approaches to problem solving. Identify roles that you could play to help facilitate teamwork, such as heading a subcommittee, publishing group accomplishments, or even leading a meeting.

Building Consensus

1. Think about how your group makes decisions. Is it by voting? Do powerful members express their preferences, and everyone else simply goes along? Talk up the advantages of reaching decisions by consensus. Listen to people's concerns about the time required and other issues. Suggest ways these concerns can be alleviated.

2. Observe how minority opinion is dealt with in your group. Are people with dissenting opinions brushed aside? Identify specific steps you can take to help the group hear from the minority.

Live It
Overcoming Your Own Barriers to Lasting Change

As you attempt to become a team player, you will inevitably hit some snags along the way. It's never easy to change your behavior, and you will have other people's bad habits to contend with as well!

But hang in, and don't give up. Here are some of the difficulties people typically encounter in being team players, along with our suggestions for addressing them:

I don't think anything can be done to save the group I work with. It's too late.

Established groups develop habits that are as difficult to break as are individual habits. However, take the attitude that it's never too late but there is no better time to start than now. Don't complain that the group is not productive. Your message will either be resisted by some or accepted with an air of resignation by others. Instead, ask the group to evaluate itself. Ask questions such as:

- How well is our group meeting everyone's expectations?
- What are we taking away from this group?
- How have we worked together? What has been helpful? not helpful?
- If we were to start all over again, what, in hindsight, would we do differently?

I don't have the power to change things.

Remember that just one recommendation might turn things around. Look for these opportunities. You also can speak to others with more power and authority than yourself, and give them suggestions they can act on.

We are a team, but we hardly ever see each other. People travel a lot or have other reasons to be away from the office.

This phenomenon is becoming more prevalent than ever. Explore how to increase e-mail communication and conference calls or use meeting shareware to keep your team-members communicating.

I'd like to partner with some of my colleagues, but they seem busy doing their own things.

> Develop a small project you would like to do with someone else. Present it so that the other person can't reject your invitation to collaborate. Maybe greater collegiality will grow from there.

I wind up doing all the work.

> The group has become used to your rescuing it from disaster. Select the very next opportunity in which you think it's worth the risk to insist that others have to contribute. Stay positive by saying something like, "I would like your help here. When I do the grunt work myself, I start to feel resentful. I want to feel good about our working relationship."

Keep forging ahead, despite the difficulties. Remind yourself daily of the benefits you will gain by being a better team player. Encourage others to give you feedback about your progress.

Now, we will turn to the eighth and final People**Smart** skill—shifting gears.

Shifting Gears

If you never budge, don't expect a push.

—Malcolm S. Forbes

It's often good advice to be yourself. If you are in your fifties, you would not pass as a cool teenager in the company of adolescents. If you are a formal person, you would probably look and feel ridiculous being flamboyant. It's hard to pretend to be the kind of person you aren't, and it's often counterproductive. You lose your genuineness and dampen the many strengths you've taken a lifetime to develop. You also confuse other people who know you for who you are and are disconcerted when you behave differently.

Nevertheless, high PQ people know that there are times when it's necessary to shift gears. They don't change with the winds like most politicians but they appreciate that when things are stuck, behaving in new ways can get things moving again. The Bible provides interesting cases in point:

The Biblical Jacob represents an intriguing example of someone with many personal strengths who had difficulty shifting gears. The younger twin brother of Esau, Jacob pretended, at his mother's urging, to be Esau so that his nearly blind father, Isaac, would bestow upon him the blessing of inheritance. If he had not done so, Esau, the firstborn but of questionable character, would have succeeded Isaac. At the same time, Jacob's deceit created a nearly fatal estrangement from his brother Esau. To his credit, Jacob did well with his responsibility. He spiritually wrestled with the angel of God and survived. He became a vital link in the transmission of the Biblical covenant between God and the Israelites. Through his two wives, Leah and Rachel, and his concubines, he had twelve sons who became the heads of the Twelve Tribes of Israel. However, his own life was marked by anguish and pain, especially over the apparent death of his favorite son, Joseph, who, in fact, was sold into slavery by his jealous brothers. The tragedy occurred because

Jacob did not learn from his own childhood experience of sibling rivalry and gave his favorite son a "coat of many colors" and a special place in his heart.

The Biblical Moses, on the other hand, became the greatest leader of the Israelites by shifting gears. Raised in the household of Pharaoh, he became a prince of Egypt. But on discovering Pharaoh's harsh treatment of the Israelite slaves, Moses gave up his royal home and became a shepherd in the wilderness where God revealed Himself to Moses and gave him the mission to lead the Israelites out of Egypt. Not sure that he had the talent to persuade Pharaoh to "let my people go," he nonetheless accepted the leadership role in which God placed him. With the help of ten plagues, Pharaoh relented and let the Israelites leave for a forty-year journey to the Promised Land. During the wanderings, Moses adopted the only leadership style he had ever known and took on the responsibility to be the sole arbiter of all matters and complaints the Israelites brought to him. When the burden became too great once again, Moses shifted gears. He was receptive to the sage advice of his father-in-law Jethro and created a council of elders to administer to the people. This act allowed the Israelites to make the transition from a generation of slaves to a vibrant nation.

Shifting gears when necessary is smart. If you think about it, most conflicts between people (and even nations) persist because each side is waiting for the other to change. As a result, nothing changes. Everything stays the same. The intelligent way to create change is to change yourself first. Even if you think it is unfair to have to make the first move, it's still people smart to do it. We all know that when relationships are not going well, each party tries to satisfy itself by proclaiming moral superiority or virtue. But the situation is still frozen and new growth can't occur. A change in your behavior may be the catalyst for a change in the other person's behavior.

In every relationship, so many interactions have occurred that the people involved fall into a pattern of behavior. Eric Berne coined the phrase "games people play" to describe some of the interpersonal ruts we get into. Recognizing the game being played at any given moment is quite difficult. People become so caught up in the game on an emotional level that they become blind to what is happening right in front of their eyes.

Other psychologists evoke the image of a dance to make this point. At a subconscious level, each party knows the other's moves. Even in a destructive relationship the dance works. Often it isn't a pretty sight, and it may feel awful to the participants, but each party knows what steps to follow, and the familiarity of movements brings some security to each side and some stability to the relationship. However, when one takes a new step, the other is thrown off balance; he or she may continue to do the old dance, but if the partner persists in changing the dance, there is the possibility of real change in the relationship. The result may be positive or negative, but at least the relationship changes.

We often hear people say in dismay, "I've tried everything but nothing works." That may be what people believe, but probably they have made short-term changes and then returned quickly to their habitual patterns. Unfortunately, it is not so easy to truly shift gears. Interpersonally intelligent people know that their commitment to change must endure. In addition, they know they will not make things better if their new behavior is simply a variation on an old theme. For example, if they listen a little longer to someone but don't really show interest in what that person has to say, nothing changes. The same is true if they assert themselves on small matters within a relationship but back off on bigger ones or periodically treat someone as a partner but then return to being a soloist. Transforming a relationship requires shifting gears long enough that a new dance emerges.

Want It
Motivating Yourself to Shift Gears

The ability to shift gears pays off in a variety of situations. Do any of these situations strike a chord with you?

On the job:

☐ Your organization is going through a massive change.

☐ Your boss ignores your requests.

☐ An employee returns to his or her errant ways after a few days of better performance.

☐ A colleague seeks your help so often you can't get anything done.

☐ No one volunteers for jobs that need to be done.

☐ A fellow staff member constantly complains to you about someone else.

☐ Your boss doesn't keep you in the information loop.

☐ Your supervisor is not clear about his or her expectations.

☐ Team morale is very low.

On the home front:

☐ You and another member of your family are uncomfortable with each other.

☐ You are not as close as you would like with a member of your family.

☐ You get frequently caught up in fights and power struggles with a family member.

☐ You and your partner have frequent conflict over little things.

☐ Most conversations with your parents are repetitions of earlier conversations.

☐ You have tried every way you can think of to get your child to listen to you, but nothing seems to work.

☐ Your relationship with family members is limited to only one or two activities.

☐ You always take the initiative in your relationship with a good friend.

☐ You dread the weekends.

As you read the next section, choose a situation to keep in mind. See if our tips work for you.

Learn It
Three Ways to Shift Gears

What does it really take to get unstuck in a troubled or frustrating relationship? Interpersonally intelligent people utilize three skills to stimulate change. They begin by **accepting the challenge**: They recognize when things are not going well in a relationship and seek to improve it. Next high PQ people try to **figure out what's stuck** by uncovering the ruts in a troubled relationship. And finally, interpersonally intelligent people change the dynamics by **acting in novel ways** instead of waiting for others to make the first move. We know it sounds like a tall order. Let's focus on each of the skills in turn.

1. Accepting the Challenge

If you are open to shifting gears when a relationship is not going well, you have won half the battle. To accept the challenge you are facing, it is important to *face reality, take responsibility*, and *apply high standards*.

Face Reality

At first glance, it would seem that anyone would recognize when a relationship is not productive. The fact is, however, that few people like to think about a relationship that is not going well. It's painful to come to terms with unpleasant reality. It's easier to pretend that things are going well enough or will get better soon. One way to avoid the truth is to act bewildered or powerless. People ask themselves:

Why is this happening to me?

I just don't understand what's going on.

Another way is to procrastinate. People may say to themselves:

It's best to lie low for awhile.

I'll wait till they get their act together.

A third possibility is denial. People think:

The situation can't be as bad as I think.

This change isn't for real; it will blow over.

Those who are people smart have the courage to look at things the way they are. When relationships are not going well, they ask themselves:

- What's going on in this relationship or situation right now? How do I feel about it?

- What can I do to deal with the problems that are occurring?

Take Responsibility

When things are not going well, people are quick to place the blame outside themselves. It's a convenient coping strategy because blaming others gets the pain we feel off our chests. Unfortunately, the pain associated with unproductive relationships returns again and again and continues to gnaw away at us.

People smart individuals accept that a relationship is a two-way street. Even if the other party's behavior is particularly toxic, one always has the choice of how to react. The classic example is the partner of an alcoholic. Rarely, if ever, does one individual cause another to drink. However, the alcoholic's partner can support the drinking habit by such behaviors as keeping it a secret or assuming the responsibilities of the alcoholic when he or she is incapacitated. As long as the partner stays in a relationship with an alcoholic, he or she influences—for better or worse—what goes on. That is a fact, not a criticism.

Imagine that every interaction you ever had with another person were videotaped from the beginning of the relationship. Who's at fault in the relationship becomes an absurd question if someone were to rewind the tape and stop it several times at random intervals. At the moment of viewing, it may appear that person A is the bad guy, but it is just as likely that person B would get that title at another time; who's at fault depends on when you stop the tape. Relationships are entangled and complicated. It's smart to acknowledge this fact, accept that almost all problems are "between people" rather than "within people" and accept the challenge to work on the relationship even if the other party is slow to do so.

Apply High Standards

It's amazing what people will put up with. We all know couples who stay together for years with only anger and resentment to show for it. We also know groups and organizations that allow individuals to wreak havoc on principles of decency. If you want to improve troubled relationships, however, it's critical to set standards high. You should not be unrealistic, but you should aim high.

Those who are people smart understand the power of self-fulfilling prophecies. When we expect someone to be a certain way, that person may very well live up to our expectations. That's because we convey our perceptions by the way we interact with him or her. Distrust someone and that person may become untrustworthy. Have confidence in someone and that person may succeed.

By establishing high but attainable standards for a relationship, you help to move it forward. Here are some suggestions:

- Expect communication from someone with whom you want to have a good relationship.

- Insist that the relationship get reviewed periodically.

- Demand that all conflicts are negotiable.

- Require the elimination of abuse.

- Count the past as over. Here and now are what count.

- Believe that relationships are about love, support, and growth, not just obligation.

2. Figuring Out What's Stuck

Once you accept the challenge of improving a troubled relationship, it's time to figure out what's getting in the way. The key is to evaluate how you and the other person are "dancing" so that you can find a way to change it. Most people ask, "What should I do with this person?" It's better to ask, "How am I currently behaving in the relationship? How is the other person responding?" When you ask such questions, you are opening the door to real change. Three ways to assess the relationship are *evaluating emotional closeness, looking for style differences*, and *detecting cycles of behavior*.

Evaluate Emotional Closeness

A powerful way to assess the dynamics of personal relationships is to think about how emotionally close or distant you and the other person are. In an *enmeshed* relationship, people are deeply entangled with each other. Each person cares too much what the other thinks and feels. There is little privacy or opportunity to think and behave in ways different from each other. In *connected* relationships, people tend to make decisions together. They have a lot in common and are actively involved in each other's lives. Outside interests exist but the relationship is primary. In *separated* relationships, people keep themselves busy with their own individual activities. They come together to share at periodic intervals as opposed to a joint activity on a daily basis. There is an allowance for an individual to develop tastes and preferences that differ from the other person. In *disengaged* relationships, there is little if any involvement with each other. Important information about the welfare of each person is usually not divulged. Tensions may flare when conflicts of interest occur, but they are usually short-lived and unresolved. Everyone is free to make his or her own decisions and to feel unencumbered by bonds of loyalty.

Problems occur most often when relationships are enmeshed or disengaged. Accordingly, it is useful to think in these terms if you are involved in a troubled relationship. If you recognize that there is too much entanglement in the relationship, it may be helpful to find healthy ways to separate yourself emotionally from the other person. On the other hand, it may be helpful to find healthy ways to connect with that person if there is too much distance in the relationship. Here are some suggestions to reduce enmeshment:

- Allow the other person to deal with his or her own problems; you should do the same.

- Listen more and talk less.

- Give the other person and yourself more space, privacy, and autonomy.

- Don't do for the person what he or she can do without your assistance.

- Accept the other person's differences.

- Don't look for the other person's approval for everything you do.

- Reduce the number of concerns and complaints you normally communicate to the other person.

To reduce disengagement:

- Give support to help the other person get over a really tough hurdle.

- Communicate more frequently.

- Involve the other person in decisions you make.

- Do activities together.

- Encourage the other person to give you feedback and return the favor.

- Show interest in the other person's thoughts, feelings, and experiences.

- Do something you know will please the other person.

211

- Give the other person information he or she may need, and ask him or her to keep you in the loop as well.

Look for Style Differences

While people who are alike can easily get stuck in an unproductive relationship, problems occur more frequently when people are different. For example, people can be different from each other in terms of what they value, how they make decisions, how they manage time, how they pace themselves, how much they disclose, how they like to work, how they handle emotions, how they deal with conflict, how they think, how they talk, and how they respond to change, among other things.

Sometimes, the differences between people complement or balance each other. For example, an overly enthusiastic person can be steadied by someone who is even-keeled. But when things are stressful, differences can cause a lot of friction. So, when a relationship is not going well, think about whether the culprit may be incompatible styles.

If you sense that your preferred style is incompatible at times with the style of the other person, experts suggest that you try to flex your style. This involves making strategic accommodations when you are with that person so that your approach causes less friction. For example, if you are very sociable and you are working with someone who is results oriented, you may need to get down to business more quickly than you normally do.

There are many discussions about style differences in business and self-help books. One approach is to look at social style. Based on a model developed by David Merrill in the 1960s, Robert and Dorothy Grover Bolton (1996) describe four social styles: *analytical, amiable, driving*, and *expressive*.

Analytical people focus on facts and logic. They hesitate to act until they are convinced acting is appropriate. They are sticklers for detail and set very high standards. When dealing with analytical people, it's important to be well-prepared and to get right down to business. Don't rush them, however, and don't come on too strong. Patiently provide the factual information analyticals need to make decisions.

Amiable people exude friendliness and empathy. They are supportive to others and make excellent teammates. Others experience them as low-keyed, conscientious, and sometimes indecisive. When dealing with amiable people, it's important to make genuine personal contact, slow your pace, focus on their feelings, and express sincere appreciation. It's also helpful to define what you want them to do. They are more comfortable with structure.

Driving people are comfortable taking charge. They make quick decisions, like challenges, and focus on results. Drivers tend to be demanding of themselves and others. When dealing with drivers, it's important to be task-oriented and fast-paced. Don't get bogged down in details and theories. Speak to them in practical, action-oriented terms, and be sure to follow through on your own responsibilities.

Expressive people create excitement and involvement. They enthusiastically share their ideas and motivate others to go along with them. They can also be flamboyant, impulsive, and restless. When dealing with expressives, it's important to be casual and informal. Allow them to think out loud and be open to their fun-loving side. Also, give them recognition and considerable freedom.

Besides adapting to the style of other people, it's important to make adjustments in your own style. Analytical people need to be more flexible, spend less time gathering data, show concern for people, and be more expressive of their feelings. Amiable people should consider learning to be more assertive, less sensitive, and more willing to take risks. Driving people might be more effective if they work on being more sensitive to others, practice active listening, and exercise more caution in making decisions. Expressive people need to tame their emotions and gear down their energy level. They might also improve their organizational skills.

Yet another approach to style differences is to look at learning style. The most popular model is to view the way people learn best in terms of whether they have an *auditory, visual*, or *kinesthetic* style. To familiarize yourself with these styles, examine the chart below.

Type of Activity	Visual	Auditory	Kinesthetic
Approach to Learning	learns by watching others	learns through verbal give & take	learns by activity
Approach to Problem Solving	deliberate; plans in advance	talks self through problems	is hands on; trial-and-error
Approach to Communication	quiet, does not talk at length	enjoys listening but cannot wait to talk	gestures when speaking, impatient listener

Accommodating people whose learning style is different from yours requires shifting gears. Here is a case in point:

> *Gloria is a visual person and her husband, Ben, is kinesthetic. Gloria gets upset when Ben doesn't write down a shopping list before he treks off to the supermarket to buy the family groceries. She prepares lists for him, but Ben often forgets to take the list with him. Ben and Gloria recently took dancing lessons together. Gloria watched as the instructor performed several steps and immediately was able to follow. Ben stopped the instructor in mid-stream and insisted on doing each step by himself until he felt confident that he knew it. Gloria implored Ben to*

*just sit back and watch carefully but Ben persisted in his
routine. When they are together as a couple, Ben likes lots
of activity and prefers to go to highly stimulating environments while Gloria prefers a walk in the woods or
taking a scenic car ride. With such contrasting styles, it
is unlikely that Gloria and Ben can maintain a happy
marriage without a lot of give and take. Sometimes that
means that they each must be more accepting of the
other's preferences. At other times it means that they
must change their own style to get along.*

If you supervise or manage other people, you would profit
from learning about the situational leadership model of Ken
Blanchard (1997). He is well known for describing four such styles:
directing, coaching, supporting, and *delegating.*

A directing style provides clear supervision. The leader
defines roles, sets goals, organizes, plans, hands out assignments,
and gives specific directions. A coaching style is somewhat directive but also uses two-way communication, help, feedback, and
explanation to motivate follower involvement. The leader also
encourages a follower to take some initiative. A supporting style is
less directive and more supportive of the follower's self-direction.
The follower is asked for input and feedback and begins to share in
decision-making. A delegating style is low-profile. Little direction
or support is provided once the leader identifies the goal or problem. Followers run the show, decide the how, when, and where,
and take responsibility for carrying out assignments.

Think about your style of leadership. Blanchard suggests that
it may not match the characteristics of the people you are leading.
A directing style is best for leading people who are unable and
unwilling to take responsibility, are not competent or confident. A

coaching style is best for people who still need to be developed but show some self-confidence. A supporting style works best for people who are becoming increasingly competent but still lack the confidence to direct their own activity. A delegating style is appropriate for people who are able, confident, and willing to take on considerable responsibility. Your challenge is to change your style based on the maturity level of the people you are leading.

Detect Cycles of Behavior

It's tempting to look at human relationships in cause-and-effect terms: Person A does something that causes person B to do something. For example, you might conclude that someone is driving you crazy or someone is controlling your life. A better model of looking at human relationships is multiple-causality. It recognizes that not only does person A's behavior determine person B's behavior, but that the reverse is also true. People are caught up in a cycle of behavior in which each party is influencing the other to behave the way they do. A cycle is a transaction that occurs between people over and over again. Once started, cycles are hard to stop. People engage in cyclic behavior all the time. It gives people a familiar script with which to interact with each other. It also has payoffs—both to the individual players and the relationship as a whole. Unfortunately, the cycle has its costs as well. For example:

> *Bill, a guilt-ridden husband, frequently wants a "night out with the boys" and knows if he mentions it to his wife, Sally, she will object. Often, Bill starts an argument with Sally about some other matter. As the argument takes off, Sally becomes angry, both begin to shout, and Bill walks out. This repetitive sequence could have multiple payoffs: Bill might feel justified about leaving; Sally*

is able to vent her anger; and the couple avoids the harder struggle of working out how they will balance their needs for closeness and freedom.

The way to detect a harmful cycle is to identify times when a problem gets resolved in ways that feel emotionally draining. For example, imagine you have a child who wants things exactly his or her own way. To avoid temper tantrums, let's say, you anticipate your child's demands, and prepare yourself in advance to meet them. Having now learned how far you will go to appease him or her, your child makes even more demands. The cycle is now complete. The more the child demands, the more he or she is appeased. The more the child is appeased, the more the child demands.

3. Acting in Novel Ways

Armed with awareness of the ruts you have fallen into, you are now in a position to get out of them by changing your behavior. While there is no guarantee that a change in your behavior will elicit a change in someone else's behavior, it is certainly worth a try. If you change your dance, your partner eventually has to change. It may not be the change you want, but it will be a change. To act in novel ways involves *testing the waters, assessing the benefits*, and *making a commitment.*

Test the Waters

The first test is to challenge your own assumption that what you are doing in the relationship doesn't need changing. This is especially hard to do when you believe that your own behavior is positive. For example, someone who is anxious may have sought your assurance that everything will be all right and you readily gave that assurance. However, the other person may be better off facing his or her fears without your assurance. Such a change in your behavior, despite its risks, could empower the other person to find his or her own inner strength.

Having challenged your own assumptions, it makes sense to take some time to explore what a change in your behavior will mean to you and the other person. Will it take you out of your comfort zone? Does the risk seem worthwhile? Will the other person try to dissuade you from acting in new ways? Questions such as these will help to prepare you for the new directions you might take. There is a joke that the only one who likes change is a wet baby. Change is uncomfortable and sometimes even scary, but it also provides an opportunity for renewal.

Rarely does only one option for change exist. For example, if you have been unsuccessfully trying to deal with the poor performance of an employee by expressing your disappointment, taking a different approach might create a climate of change. Several different approaches are available to you:

- **Requesting**: Asking for rather than demanding a change in behavior. (E.g., *"I've been unhappy about your tardiness. Would you be willing to make a concerted effort to get here on time?"*)

- **Backing Off**: Stopping comments about the undesired behavior for a short time to assess whether you have unwittingly been reinforcing the negative behavior by giving it attention.

- **Monitoring**: Keeping closer than usual tabs on the employee's behavior and perhaps reminding her or him more frequently what behavior you expect.

- **Encouraging**: Suspending any criticism for a while and looking for every opportunity to praise the employee and maintain a positive focus.

Finally, it is time to select a new approach and test it out. Be careful, however, to give your new approach a chance to succeed. Keep with it for a few days or even weeks to see if it gets the results you are seeking.

Assess the Benefits

When you have taken a new approach, watch and listen for how it is working. Don't expect that things will change overnight. Look for signs that change is starting to occur:

Harry was dismayed that his suggestions were rarely taken seriously by his boss. When he evaluated the situation, he realized that, once rebuffed, he would lay low for a while, even for weeks at a time, before offering new ideas. Harry decided that he should try to give suggestions more frequently, even if they were rejected. Each time he was rebuffed, he graciously accepted the rejection with the comment, "Maybe my next idea will be better." This change in tactics still led nowhere, but Harry noticed that each time he made a suggestion, the boss made more of an effort to explain why it would not work for him. Next, he noticed that his boss would sometimes act on one of Harry's suggestions without saying so. Although Harry wanted credit where it was due, he nonetheless was grateful that he was starting to have an impact on his boss. It wasn't until months later that Harry's boss finally began thanking Harry for his ideas.

Remember that it takes time for your efforts to bear fruit; be patient.

Make a Commitment

If your experimentation shows signs of success, you should probably feel the confidence to make a more permanent commitment to the changes you have made. Don't be surprised, however, if the other person does everything in his or her power to return you to your former behavior. After all, you may have taken that person out of his or her own comfort zone. Harry's boss, for instance, was comfortable rejecting Harry's occasional suggestions. By increasing their frequency, Harry put his boss off balance; to get back on his feet, the boss may initially be even more rejecting than before. Only by staying the course will Harry find out whether his experiment brings the results he is seeking.

Try It
Exercises for Shifting Gears

By definition, if you've been feeling stuck, you're finding it difficult to change your behavior in a relationship. That's why practice is imperative. Try one or more of these experiments in change to heighten your awareness of where and how you're stuck and to start thinking out of the box about how to change.

Accepting the Challenge

1. Identify a relationship that is in a rut. Think about the part you play in keeping it stuck. Keep a diary for one week in which you reflect on interactions between yourself and the other person. Work hard at describing what the other person did and what you did in response. Avoid casting blame or venting your feelings. Remain objective, as if you were an anthropologist studying an unfamiliar culture.

2. Ask yourself if you have given up on another person with whom you

have a troubled relationship. Have you lowered your expectations so much that you maintain little hope that anything will change? Challenge yourself to establish higher expectations for the next week. Use some of the suggestions on page 209 to guide you in formulating renewed goals.

Figuring Out What's Stuck

1. Select a relationship that feels stuck. Take an honest look at the emotional closeness or distance between the other person and you. Are you enmeshed or disengaged? If so, take steps in the next week to reduce enmeshment or disengagement. Use the list on page 211 and 212 to identify helpful steps you can take.

2. Identify at least two people in your family or at your workplace. Assess how your social, learning, or leadership styles are similar or different. Choose one of these relationships and create a plan to make accommodations in your style where you think it will do the most good.

Acting in Novel Ways

1. Select one of the following approaches: requesting, backing off, monitoring, encouraging. (See pages 218–219 for details.) Keep using the approach for one week with a person with whom you are experiencing difficulties. Select the one that is most unlike your normal approach. Evaluate the results.

2. Think about a time when you tried a different approach with someone but your experiment was short-lived. Examine why you gave up so easily. Give particular attention to what the other person did to get you to be your old self. Try the experiment again, but this time, persist.

Live It
Overcoming Your Own Barriers
to Lasting Change

As we have indicated throughout this book, lasting change requires that you confront some of the reasons why you might return to your former habits. Select the statements below that describe you and consider our suggestions for overcoming these barriers.

I don't think anything can be done to save this relationship. It's too late.

> That may be true. However, that fact doesn't suggest doing more of the same. It's still important to make some change, including the possibility of even greater distance between you and the other person. But before you take that direction, check that the failing relationship isn't a victim of low expectations. Rethink whether some renewal might occur if you set higher goals. That, of course, begins with the belief that the other person isn't hopeless.

I have trouble looking at myself objectively.

> We all do. As we suggested earlier, imagine that someone were videotaping interactions between you and another person. The camera doesn't distort reality or play favorites. Play back the tape in your mind. If you find this too hard, then imagine the camera is recording you the next time you interact with that person. It may feel a little weird, but you may find it easier to be objective when you are part of the drama. Better yet, actually tape an encounter between yourself and the other person—with that person's permission, of course.

I have a hard time accepting my responsibility in a relationship where the other person's behavior is horrid.

> No one is saying that you caused that person's behavior. He or she owns the ultimate responsibility for that. But you may be doing something to keep the behavior going. Simply letting yourself be victimized by the other person encourages that person to continue his or her ways. Think of yourself as someone who refuses to dance the same way.

I'm so burdened by other problems that I can't put effort into this troubled relationship.

> We all have limits to our ability to handle several problems at once. Be sure, however, to avoid the mistake of being so overwhelmed that you don't take action anywhere. Focus on one thing at a time and try to accomplish something positive.

I have been burned by risks I've taken in past relationships.

> Think of a risk as an experiment rather than a plunge into the unknown. Carefully decide what you are going to do to shift gears in a relationship. Also, be clear in your mind how long you will stick to your experiment. Call off the experiment whenever you sense it's getting nowhere.

I have difficulty with a person whose style and temperament are exactly like my own.

> The similarities between two people can also be a source of tension. Both of you may be butting heads because you are both asserting yourself. Or your relationship may be floundering because you are both indecisive. However, it only takes one of you to act in novel ways to untangle where you are stuck. That person might as well be you.

I know that my relationship is stuck because we get into repeated games with each other, but I have a hard time understanding what's going on.

> Even if you cannot detect the problem pattern, try a different response than the first one that comes to mind. If you succeed in changing the dance, it doesn't matter whether you understand why the original one happened.

We hope you have found our suggestions useful and feel inspired to work at those relationships that just aren't as rewarding as they should be. Of all the issues raised in this book, dealing with troubled relationships requires the most courage and effort. It also offers the greatest potential for rewards.

Putting It All Together

In the Introduction to this book, we promised a four-step development plan to promote significant change in your PQ. After reading page after page of advice, checklists, and exercises, however, you may feel a bit overwhelmed. We'd like to put the whole back together again by giving you a short review of the book and some action plans to build PeopleSmart skills into your life. Here is a concise summary of the eight skills. Look over the list. If you want to clarify any items, go back to the appropriate chapter.

1. Understanding People

When they are confused by people's attitudes and behavior, high PQ people:

Listen and Observe by:

putting the other person in the spotlight

showing interest

reading body language

Clarify Meaning by:

asking open-ended questions

paraphrasing

responding to feeling

Interpret Behavior by:
> evaluating goals
> assessing personal style
> recognizing differences

2. Expressing Yourself Clearly

When they want to be understood, high PQ people:

Get the message across by:
> thinking before they talk
> orienting and summarizing with the listener
> painting with words

Talk straight by:
> standing behind what they say
> making the listener comfortable
> being consistent

Include the listener by:
> speaking the listener's language
> letting the other person speak
> confirming understanding

3. Asserting Your Needs

When they need to set limits or advocate for themselves, high PQ people:

Are decisive by:
> separating needs from wishes
> taking a stand
> communicating their position

Remain calm and confident by:

staying on track

giving reasons nondefensively

watching their body language

Are persistent by:

reminding

requesting

encouraging

4. Exchanging Feedback

When they want the perspectives of others or believe others can benefit from hearing theirs, high PQ people:

Invite others to give them feedback by:

conveying receptiveness

making people comfortable

broadening the circle

Get invited to give feedback to others by:

asking for permission

sharing rather than insisting

timing their input

checking perceptions

Are informative by:

referring to concrete behaviors

limiting the amount of feedback

offering suggestions for improvement

5. Influencing Others

When they want to have an impact on others or encourage them to change, high PQ people:

Connect with them by:
> offering their expertise
> identifying with others
> admiring others
> getting to know others

Assess needs by:
> observing behavior
> asking skillful questions
> obtaining reactions

Make a persuasive presentation by:
> reducing resistance
> making their message appealing

6. Resolving Conflict

When they find themselves at odds with others, high PQ people:

Create a climate of mutual interest by:
> surfacing the conflict
> taking a positive approach
> fostering partnership

Put the real issues on the table by:
> focusing on interests, not positions
> setting their own targets
> studying the other party's situation

Negotiate win/win solutions by:

> generating mutual gain options
>
> developing a joint plan
>
> using contingency strategies

7. Being a Team Player

When they need to work in groups, high PQ people:

Join with others by:

> observing what's going on in the group
>
> making contributions where needed
>
> building a climate of dialogue

Facilitate teamwork by:

> promoting a common vision
>
> encouraging participation
>
> stimulating creative problem solving

Build consensus by:

> narrowing down ideas
>
> polling the group
>
> checking for commitment

8. Shifting Gears

When they find themselves deadlocked in a relationship, high PQ people:

Accept the challenge by:

> facing reality
>
> taking responsibility
>
> applying high standards

Figure out what's stuck by:
> evaluating emotional closeness
> looking for style differences
> detecting cycles of behavior

Act in novel ways by:
> testing the waters
> assessing the benefits
> making a commitment

Your Personal Action Plan

Schedule specific dates to start using the skills you've decided to try out. Decide on ways to monitor and evaluate your progress by getting feedback, keeping logs, or retaking the *PeopleSmart Scale* at regular intervals. The following steps provide a framework to guide your efforts. Fill in the blanks to create your personalized change plan.

My PeopleSmart strengths are: _____

_____

_____

_____

_____

_____

_____

The areas in which I most want to improve are: _____

_____

_____

_____

_____

_____

_____

_____

The specific skills I need to work on to improve in these areas are:

_____

_____

_____

_____

_____

_____

_____

_____

_____

_____

The key situations in which to use these skills more effectively are:

_____

_____

_____

_____

_____

_____

_____

I intend to do the following practice exercises to enhance my skills:

_____

_____

_____

_____

_____

_____

_____

_____

_____

The barriers I'm most likely to encounter are:

_____

_____

_____

_____

_____

_____

The strategies I plan to use to overcome these barriers are:

_____

_____

_____

_____

_____

_____

_____

My personal action plan is to begin using my target skills in my selected situations by _____(supply date).

Eight-Week Reminder Plan

Besides creating your own action plan, we have also developed an eight-week reminder list for your convenience. Make a copy and post it where you will see it often.

Week One: Understanding People

- Give others your undivided attention whenever possible.
- Eliminate or reduce distractions and refrain from interrupting.
- Paraphrase and summarize what you hear.
- Ask open-ended questions to clarify what people are saying.
- Acknowledge people's good points and have empathy for their feelings.
- Notice other people's body language and interpret it.
- Respect and respond to people's different styles and personalities.
- Look beyond surface behavior to understand a person's needs.

Week Two: Expressing Yourself Clearly

- Speak clearly and slowly enough to be understood.
- Use expressive language.
- Speak fluently (avoids filler words).
- Get to the point.
- Make others feel that you are talking to them, not at them.
- Check to be sure you are understood.
- Be open to give and take.
- Speak in your own name (not in others).

Week Three: Asserting Your Needs

- Be straightforward and direct.
- Get proactive rather than reactive.

- Don't get into power struggles.
- Stay focused on what you are trying to achieve.
- Don't overapologize and overjustify.
- Keep calm and remains confident under pressure.
- Say "no" when you need to.
- Speak up and don't be afraid to ask for things.
- Above all, be clear and decisive.

Week Four: Exchanging Feedback

- Don't be afraid to ask others for feedback.
- Make it comfortable for others to share their reactions.
- Be open to the feedback you receive.
- Describe how you feel about some behavior.
- Be specific and give examples.
- Develop a good sense of timing and fairness.
- Show interest in the other person's welfare.
- Invite others to share their own self-appraisals.
- Offer constructive suggestions for improvement.

Week Five: Influencing Others

- Take the time to connect with people you want to influence.
- Be enthusiastic about your ideas.
- Ask lots of questions and seek the opinion of those you are trying to influence.
- Present your ideas one at a time.
- Provide strong evidence to support your position.
- Tailor your message to the listener's background and style.
- Appeal to the subject's self-interest; focus more on benefits than features.
- Give others time to mull over what you have presented.
- Don't be overeager to win people over.

Week Six: Resolving Conflict

- Believe that conflict can produce benefits for all parties involved.
- Bring your concerns out into the open and encourage others to do so.
- Show respect and consideration.
- Think through your own needs and interests before you start negotiating.
- Persevere with the negotiating process, in spite of any initial negative reactions.
- Brainstorm mutually beneficial solutions with others.
- When possible, suggest objective criteria for decision-making.
- Follow up on solutions.

Week Seven: Being a Team Player

- Observe what's happening in the group to understand what is needed.
- Time your contributions to the team when they are needed the most.
- Include everybody in the loop.
- Take on roles that are not being taken by others.
- Focus on the group goal rather than your personal self-interest.
- Share credit you receive for a job well done.
- Express appreciation for the efforts of others.
- Check decisions you are about to make to see if they might affect others.
- Seek information about the talents of others.

Week Eight: Shifting Gears When Relationships Are Stuck

- Recognize when your relationships are in a rut.
- Look for the patterns you fall into with certain people.
- Avoid blaming others.

- Take the initiative when a relationship is not going well.
- Change your behavior in order to change the behavior of someone else.
- Be resilient. If things don't work out, bounce back.
- Don't give up easily once you try to change what's happening in a relationship.

As you work on developing People**Smart** skills, be patient with yourself. As Confucius once said, "It does not matter how slowly you go, so long as you do not stop." So, if you wish, take a month or even a year to work on each skill. We promise you that the investment will be worth it.

References

Ball, P. (1996) *Straight Talk Is More Than Words*. Granville, Ohio: Knox.

Bell, C. and Shea, H. (1998) *Dance Lessons: Six Steps to Great Partnerships in Business and Life*. San Francisco: Berrett-Koehler.

Berne, E. (1996) *Games People Play (Reissue edition)*. New York: Ballantine.

Blanchard, K. (1997) *Situational Leadership II*. Escondido, CA: Blanchard Training and Development.

Bolton, R. and Bolton, D. (1996) *People Styles at Work*. New York: Amacom.

Carnegie, D. (1994) *How to Win Friends and Influence People (Reissue edition)*. Pocket Books.

Covey, S. (1990) *The 7 Habits of Highly Effective People*. New York: Fireside (Simon & Schuster).

Fensterheim, H. and Baer, J. (1975) *Don't Say Yes When You Want to Say No*. New York: Dell Publishing.

Gardner, H. (1993) *Frames of Mind: The Theory of Multiple Intelligences (Tenth anniversary edition)*. New York: Basic Books.

Gilligan, C. (1993) *In a Different Voice (Reissue edition)*. Cambridge, MA: Harvard University Press.

Goleman, D. (1995) *Emotional Intelligence*. New York: Bantam Books.

Gray, J. (1992) *Men Are from Mars, Women Are from Venus*. New York: Harper Collins.

Jakubowski, P. and Lange, A. (1978) *The Assertive Option*. Champaign, IL: Research Press.

Johnson, D. and Johnson, F. (1999) *Joining Together (Seventh edition)*. Needham Heights, MA: Allyn & Bacon.

Kolb, D. (1983) *Experiential Learning*. Englewood Cliffs, NJ: Prentice Hall.

Kouzes, J. and Posner, B. (1995) *Credibility*. San Francisco: Jossey-Bass.

Lazarus, A. and Lazarus, C. (1997) *The 60 Second Shrink: 101 Strategies for Staying Sane in a Crazy World*. San Luis Obispo, CA: Impact Publishers.

Lebedun, J. (1998) *Managing Workplace Conflict*. West Des Moines, IA: American Media Publishing.

Lepsinger, R. and Lucia, A. (1997) *The Art and Science of 360° Feedback*. San Francisco: Jossey-Bass.

Merrill, D. and Reid, R. (1981) *Personal Styles and Effective Performance*. Radnor, PA: Chilton.

Myers, I. (1993) *Introduction to Type: A Guide to Understanding Your Type on the Myers-Briggs Type Indicator*. Center for Applications of Psychological Type.

Nichols, M. (1996) *The Lost Art of Listening*. New York: Guilford Press.

Nirenberg, J. (1963) *Getting Through to People*. Englewood Cliffs, NJ: Prentice Hall.

Parker, G. (1996) *Team Players and Team Work*. San Francisco: Jossey-Bass.

Satir, V. (1988) *The New Peoplemaking*. Mountain View, CA: Science and Behavior Books.

Silberman, M. (1999) *101 Ways to Make Meetings Active*. San Francisco: Jossey-Bass.

Silberman, M. and Wheelan, S. (1981) *How to Discipline Without Feeling Guilty*. Champaign, IL: Research Press.

Tannen, D. (1991) *You Just Don't Understand*. New York: Ballantine.

Toropov, B. (1997) *The Art and Skill of Dealing With People*. Paramus, NJ: Prentice Hall.

Ury, W. (1991) *Getting Past No*. New York: Bantam Books.

Verderber, R. *Communicate!* (1999) Belmont, CA: Wadsworth.

Wall, B. (1999) *Working Relationships*. Palo Alto, CA: Davies-Black Publishing.

Watzlawick, P., Weakland, J., and Fisch, R. (1974) *Change*. New York: W.W. Norton.

Wheatley, M. and Kellner-Rogers, M. (1996) *A Simpler Way*. San Francisco: Berrett-Koehler.

Zemke, R., Raines, J, and Filipczak, B. (1999) *Generations at Work: Managing the Clash of Veterans, Boomers, Xers, and Nexters in Your Workplace*. New York: Amacom.

Index

acceptance, asserting your needs, 92
acknowledgment
  listening skills, 28–29
  of speaker's meaning, 35–37
action plan
  conflict resolution, 165
  personal, 230–233
admiration, building rapport, 124
advice
  acceptance by others, 140–141
  unsolicited, 28, 48
age cohort, recognizing differences, 44
amiable people, dealing with, 213–214
analytical people, dealing with, 212–214
Anderson, Marian, resolving conflicts, 143
anger
  body language, 30
  conflict resolution barriers, 171
  controlling when listening, 49–50
  feeling levels, 35–36
anxiety, body language, 29
apologies, keep it simple, 85
approaches, positive conflict resolution, 151–155
arguments, asserting your needs, 92
assertion, needs
  expressing, 3, 6
  improving skills, 71–94, 226–227
  self-assessment, 14, 139
assumptions
  challenging, 217–219
  getting in the way of listening, 48
attacks, resolving conflicts, 167–168, 173
attention
  keeping a listener's, 68
  personal style, 40–42
  span lengthening, 48

  on speaker, 25
audience, needs assessment, 125–130
auditory learners, dealing with, 214–215
avoidance
  conflict resolution barriers, 171
  conflict resolution strategy, 154–155

backing-off, changing behavior, 218
balance, enmeshed relationships, 210–211
Ball, Patricia Ann, *Straight Talk Is More Than Words*, 27
barriers
  asserting your needs, 92–94
  conflict resolution, 156, 171–174
  exchanging feedback, 115–117
  expressing yourself clearly, 67–70
  shifting gears, 222–224
  to influencing others, 140–142
  to teamwork, 197–199
  understanding people, 47–50
behavior
  changing your, 7
  concrete, 109–111
  conflict resolution, 148–169
  cycles, 216–217
  experiments in changing, 10
  expressing your true feelings, 81–82
  focusing feedback on, 116
  interpretation of speaker's, 37–44, 46
  observing, 126–127
  studying nonverbal, 45
  unacceptable, 87–90, 110–111, 218–219
  understanding a speaker's, 46
benefits, changing behavior, 219
Bera, Yogi, understanding people, 19

Berne, Eric, games people play, 204
Bible, shifting gears, 202–203
Blanchard, Ken, situational leadership styles, 215–216
body language
    congruent verbal messages, 61
    controlling your, 85–86
    focused listening, 27
    identifying deception, 168
    interpretation, 45
    listening and observing, 22
    reading, 29–30
    videotaping, 61
Bolton, Robert and Dorothy Grover, social styles, 212–214
Boyd, Susan, relating new information to known subjects, 62–63
brainstorming
    conflict resolution, 162–164
    fast vs. slow, 189–192

cards, response, 186
Carnegie, Dale, *How to Win Friends and Influence People,* 1200
categories
    basic conflict, 150–151
    feelings, 35–36
challenge, accepting, 206–209
change
    creating within yourself, 203–205
    focusing on positive, 223
    group habits, 198
    lasting, 10–11
    resistance to, 8–9
    risks, 218–219
    stimulating, 206–219
choices, consensus building, 193–194
circle, feedback resources, 104–106, 116
clarification
    exchanging feedback, 114–115
    key techniques, 31–37
    puzzling behavior, 40
    skill improvement, 45–46
    techniques for listening, 49

clarity
    assuring, 63–64
    checking your message, 60
closeness, emotional, 210–212
coaching leadership, situations, 215–216
codes, *MBTI* personality style, 41–42
collaboration
    avoiding distortions, 156
    partnering, 199
    rating ability, 16
    sharing feedback, 107
    teamwork, 5, 7
comfort zone
    exchanging feedback, 103–104
    testing your, 8–9
commitments, changing behavior, 220
communications
    congruent verbal and nonverbal messages, 61
    direct route, 131–134
    improving group, 198
    unclear information, 52–53
competence, basic personal goals, 38–40
compliance, asserting your needs, 94
composition, message, 55–56, 65
confidence, under adverse circumstances, 82–83
conflict, surfacing, 149–151
conflict resolution
    improving your skills, 143–174, 228–229
    rating ability, 16
    skills, 4–5, 7
connections
    basic personal goals, 38–40
    influencing others, 123–125, 138–139
    reducing hostility, 125
consensus, building group, 192–197
contributions, group efforts, 181–182
control, personal basic goals, 38–40
conversations, monopolized, 49

criticism, limiting negative feedback, 116
culture, recognizing differences, 43
cycles, behavior, 216–217

data, conflicts over, 150
decision-making
  improving your ability, 76–82
  personal style, 41
decisions, asserting your needs, 93
defenses, to feedback, 106
delegating leadership, situations, 215–216
denial, feedback, 106
details, relating the pertinent, 68
dialogue, building a climate of, 182–183
dictionary, proper word choice, 68
differences, recognizing, 42–444
directing leadership, situations, 215–216
disagreement, while understanding the speaker, 49
disclaimers, avoiding, 70
discounting, feedback, 106
discussions, facilitating group, 186–188
disdain, body language, 30
disengagement, relationships, 210–212
driving people, dealing with, 213–214

e-mail, time outs, 152
effectiveness, contributing to the team's, 177–178
emotions
  asserting your needs, 93
  conflict situations, 151–155
  exchanging feedback, 111
  retaining control of, 91
encouragement, positive reinforcement, 89–90, 218–219
enmeshed relationships, balance, 210–211
ethnicity, recognizing differences, 43

evaluation, opportunities for change, 209–212
examples
  exchanging feedback, 110–111
  using good, 134–138
exchanging feedback, improving your ability, 95–117
experience, sharing prior, 124
expertise, sharing your, 124, 139
explanations
  straightforward, 84–85
  of your position, 91
expression
  ability rating, 14
  clearness of, 3, 6, 51–70, 226
expressions
  idiomatic, 20
  soliciting feedback, 104
expressive people, dealing with, 213–214
eye contact
  focused listening, 27
  nonverbal behavior, 86

face, nonverbal behavior, 86
facilitation, teamwork, 183–192, 197
facts, conflicts over, 150
feedback
  exchanging, 4, 7, 95–117
  giving constructive, 28–29, 97
  inviting, 99–100, 113–114
  negative, 96–97, 116
  rating ability, 15
  soliciting, 84
  summary, 227
feelings
  categories, 35–36
  explaining in enough detail, 67
  response to the speaker's, 35–37
  sharing feedback, 117
  towards unacceptable behavior, 81–82
fishbowl, group discussions, 188
fitness, interpersonal, 8–10
flexibility
  conflict resolution, 152

flexibility *(continued)*
    rating ability, 17
    shifting gears, 5–7
focus
    attention span, 48
    on basic interests not positions, 157–162
    broad picture, 26
    conflict resolution, 172
    conflict resolution strategy, 154
    critical feedback, 116
    limiting feedback, 111–112
    listening ability, 25
    on main points, 67
    messages, 55–56, 65
Forbes, Malcolm S., on shifting gears, 201
fright, feeling levels, 36

gears, shifting, 201–224, 229–230
gender, recognizing differences, 43
generation gaps, recognizing differences, 44
gestures, nonverbal behavior, 86
go-arounds, group discussions, 187
goals
    advancing the group's, 176
    evaluating speaker's personal basic, 38–40
    setting teamwork, 185
    understanding people, 23–24
group
    efforts, 181–182
    minority participation, 195–196
    observation, 180–181, 196–197
    participation, 186–199
    relationships, 176–178
growth, change, 47
guidelines, establishing, 127–129

habits
    changing group, 198
    changing personal, 10–11
happiness, feeling levels, 36
hedging, avoiding, 60
honesty, expressing yourself with, 69

hostility, establishing a connection, 125

illustrations, improving persuasiveness, 134–138
images
    mirror, 156
    visual aids, 135–138
implementation, conflict resolution action plans, 165
improvement, feedback with suggestions for, 114–115
incompatibilities, relationships, 212–216
influencing others
    ability rating, 15
    attributes, 4, 7
    improving your ability, 119–142
    summary, 228
information
    framing questions, 127–130
    unclear communications, 52–53
intelligence, improving interpersonal, 10–11
intensity, feeling levels, 35–36
interactions, person-to-person, 187–188
interest
    body language, 29
    conflict resolution, 173–174
    creating a climate of mutual, 148–156
    focused listening, 27–29
    influencing others, 125
    teamwork, 180
interpersonal style
    assessing, 8
    improving, 9–10
interruptions
    focusing on speaker, 25
    improving listening, 21–22
    listening and speaking without, 47
    of speaker, 25, 45
intimidation, influencing others, 142
invitations, for feedback, 99–100, 113–114

involvement, body language, 30
IQ (intelligence quotient), vs. PQ
    (people quotient), 12
issues
    determining areas of conflict, 170
    focusing on, 157–162
    rating acceptability of, 79–80
    resolving at the appropriate level,
        172–173

Jacob (Biblical), shifting gears,
    202–203
Jakubowski, Patricia, asserting your
    needs, 71
Johnson, Magic, on teamwork, 175
judgment
    getting in the way of listening, 48
    rushing to, 28
Jung, Carl, assessing personality
    preferences, 40–42

kinesthetic learners, dealing with,
    214–215
Korean proverb, on influencing oth-
    ers, 119

labeling, exchanging feedback,
    110–111
language
    tailoring for your audience, 62
    using more colorful, 58–59
leadership
    styles, 215–216
    teamwork, 183–192
learn it
    asserting your needs, 74–75
    being a team player, 179–186
    changing habits, 10
    conflict resolution techniques,
        148–169
    exchanging feedback, 99–106
    expressing yourself clearly, 55–64
    influencing others, 123–138
    shifting gears, 206–217
    understanding people, 24–44

learning
    personal style, 41
    styles of, 214–215
Lebedun, Jean, basic conflict cate-
    gories, 150–151
limits, communicating your, 72–73
listener
    including in conversation, 61
    making the situation comfortable,
        60–61
    opportunities for response, 63
listening
    ability improvement, 20–21, 24–30
    common barriers, 47–50
    fishbowl group discussions, 188
    skill improvement, 44–45
    with your "answer running," 27
live it
    asserting your needs, 92–94
    being a team player, 197–199
    changing habits, 10–11
    conflict resolution, 171–174
    exchanging feedback, 115–117
    expressing yourself clearly, 67–70
    influencing others, 140–142
    shifting gears, 222–224
    understanding people, 47–50
logic, influencing others, 141

matrix, feeling, 36
MBTI (Myers-Briggs Type Indicator),
    personal style assessment, 40–42
meaning, acknowledgment of
    speaker's, 35–37
Merrill, David, social styles, 212
messages
    audience appeal, 134–138
    composition, 55–56, 65
    softening harsh, 69
    stating clearly, 3, 6, 14
    WIFM (What's in It For Me?),
        136–138
metaphors, as visualization aids,
    135–138
methods, conflicts over, 150
minority group, participation, 195–196

monitoring, behavior modification, 218

Moses, shifting gears, 203

mutual interest, conflict resolution skills, 169–170

Myers-Briggs Type Indicator (MBTI), personality types, 40–52

needs, asserting your, 3, 6, 71–94, 226–227

needs assessment, influencing others, 139

negative feedback
    accepting, 96–97
    limiting criticism, 116

negotiations
    conflict resolution, 155–156
    win/win solutions, 162–171

"No"
    asserting your needs, 93
    learning to say, 79–80
    saying it gracefully and tactfully, 84

nonverbal signals
    congruent verbal and, 61
    controlling your own, 85–86
    focused listening, 27
    interpretation improvement, 45
    listening and observing, 22
    reading, 29–30
    videotaping, 61

novel ways
    acting in, 217–220
    changing behavior, 221

objections, considering any, 84–85

objectivity, self-assessment, 222

observation
    group, 180–181, 196–197
    reading people, 126–127, 140–141
    relationships, 221
    skill improvement, 24–30, 44–45

opinions, differences of, 172

opposition, researching the, 160–162

options
    change, 218–219
    mutual gain, 162–164
    walkout, 169

orders, giving, 80

organization, messages, 56

orientation
    clarity of your message, 65
    personal style, 41–44
    preparing your listner, 56–57

overreaction, avoiding, 83

ownership, conflict, 149–151

paraphrasing, clarification of meaning, 32–34

participation
    group, 186–188, 199
    minority group, 195–196

partnering, inviting collaboration, 199

partners, group discussions, 187

partnership, fostering, 155–156

patience, influencing others, 120–122

patterns, problem relationship, 224

pauses
    listener response opportunities, 63
    word selection, 67

people, social styles, 212–214

people, understanding
    benefits, 6
    rating your ability, 13
    skills improvement, 19–52
    success, 2–3
    summary, 225–226

PeopleSmart Scale, 12–18

perceptions
    acceptance of feedback, 108–109
    reception of feedback, 117
    reframing questions, 136–138

perfectionism, exchanging feedback, 96–97

permission, sharing feedback, 106–107, 114

persistence
    asserting your needs, 93
    behavior modification, 87–90
    discussing conflict, 155
    influencing others, 120–122
    practicing and grading, 91
personal style, assessing individual,
    40–42
persuasion
    examples as illustrations,
      134–138
    WIFM (What's in It For Me?)
      messages, 138
pitfalls, influencing others, 140
plan
    eight-week reminder, 234–237
    personal action, 230–233
polling, reaching consensus,
    194–195
position, taking and communicating
    a, 79–82
positive reinforcement, 218–219
posture, nonverbal behavior, 86
power struggles, asserting your
    needs, 92–93
PQ (people quotient), vs. IQ (intelli-
    gence quotient), 12
PQ rating
    interpreting scores, 17–18
    PeopleSmart Scale, 12–17
preparation
    conflict resolution, 145–146
    influencing others, 141
    resolving conflicts, 172
presentations
    persuasive, 130–139
    tailoring, 66
pressure, influencing others, 138
priorities, setting personal, 77–78
privacy, exchanging feedback, 108
problem solving, stimulating group,
    188–192
problems
    anticipating your reactions to
      predictable, 75–82
    verbalization of, 26

process, conflicts over, 150
prophecy, self-fulfilling, 156
pseudo-acceptance, listening skills,
    28
purposes, conflicts over, 150

questions
    clarity of message verification, 64
    direct, 31
    eliciting solid information,
      127–130
    encouraging feedback, 97
    leading, 32
    listening and asking, 22
    open, 186
    open-ended, 31
    reaction to adivce, 130
    reframing for clarification,
      136–138
    rhetorical, 81
    sharing feedback, 106–107
    skillful, 127–129
    soliciting feedback, 102–103
    studying the opposition, 161–162

race, recognizing differences, 43
rapport
    building, 124
    influencing others, 138–139
rating, PeopleSmart Scale, 12–18
reactions, obtaining immediate,
    129–130
readiness, stages of consensus, 195
"reading" people, 140–141
reality, facing, 207
receptiveness
    barriers, 115
    to feedback, 100–103, 106–107
references, unclear, 59
reflection, body language, 30
reinforcement, positive, 89–90, 142
relationships
    actively changing, 206–217
    asserting your needs, 92
    balancing, 210–212
    changing your behavior, 220–221

relationships (continued)
   enmeshed, 210–211
   failing, 222
   shifting gears, 203–220
   within groups, 176–178
   your PQ rating, 12–17
religion, recognizing differences, 44
reminder plan, eight-week, 234–237
reminders, behavior modification, 87
repetition, reducing, 48
requests
   changing unacceptable behavior, 88–89, 218–219
   exchanging feedback, 113–114
   making and responding to, 90–91
research, background, 160–162
resilience
   rating ability, 17
   shifting gears, 5–7
resistance
   focusing on goal, 83–84
   minimizing, 130–134
resolution
   conflict, 4–5, 7
   improving skills at conflict, 16, 143–174, 228–229
resources, circle of feedback, 104–106
response cards, group participation, 186
responses
   listener opportunities for, 63
   remaining calm and confident, 82–83
   taking time to formulate proper, 69
   to speaker's feelings, 36–37
responsibility, taking personal, 208
restatement, staying on track, 83–84
risks
   change, 218–219
   changing relationships, 223

sabotage, predicting, 173

sadness, feeling levels, 36
safety zone, exchanging feedback, 99–106
Sartre, Jean Paul, understanding people, 20
scenario thinking, brainstorming, 191–192
secretiveness, body language, 30
self-assessment
   asserting your needs, 73–74
   being a team player, 178–179
   communication skills, 54–55
   conflict resolution skills, 146–148
   exchanging feedback, 98–99
   influencing others, 122–123
   objectivity, 222
   PQ rating, 12–17
   shifting gears, 205–206
   understanding people, 22–24
   your conflict style, 152–153
self-control, conflict resolution, 151–155
self-improvement, achieving, 10–11
sensitivity, conveying your stance, 82
sentences, finishing the speaker's, 47
setbacks, asserting your needs, 94
sharing, group discussions, 186
shifting gears
   improving your skill at, 201–224
   summary, 229–230
signals. See nonverbal signals
situational leadership style, 216
situations, upsetting, 77–78
skills, people smart, 2–7
social styles, personal attributes, 212–214
socioeconomic status, recognizing differences, 44
solutions, conflict resolution, 162–171
speech, taping to improve habits, 68
spotlight, putting speaker in the, 24–26

stand, taking a, 78–80
standards
    considering options, 194
    double, 156
    setting high, 208–209
statements
    talking straight, 59–60
    using straightforward, 66
stone walls, conflict resolution
    strategies, 166–167
Straight Talk Is More Than Words
    (Ball), 27
strategies, contingency conflict reso-
    lution, 165–169
stress
    body language, 30
    remaining calm and confident,
    91
styles
    conflict resolution, 144–146
    interpersonal, 8–9
    leadership, 183–192, 215–216
    learning, 214–215
    personal conflict resolution,
    152–153, 170
    social, 212–216
subgroups, group participation,
    186–187
subjects, introducing new topics,
    56–57
suggestions
    exchanging feedback, 112–113
    for improvement, 114–115
summarization, closing communica-
    tions, 58
supporting leadership, situations,
    215–216

talking straight, clear statements,
    59–60, 66
targets, setting conflict resolution,
    159–160
tasks, giving clear explanations,
    65
Teague, Jr., clearness of expression,
    51

teamwork
    being a team player, 175–199
    collaboration, 5, 7
    rating ability, 16
    summary, 229–230
techniques, conflict resolution,
    148–169
tension, changing relationships, 223
tests, clarity of orientation message,
    65
thesaurus, varying word use, 68
thinking
    polarized, 156
    scenario, 191–192
thoughts, explaining in enough
    detail, 67
3D mode, feedback, 106
time outs
    cooling down emotions, 151–152
    resolving conflict, 171–172
timing, sharing feedback, 107–108
Toastmasters, improving your
    speaking abilities, 59
tricks, conflict resolution strategies,
    168–169
try it
    asserting your needs, 90–91
    being a team player, 196–197
    changing habits, 10
    conflict resolution, 169–171
    exchanging feedback, 113–115
    expressing yourself clearly,
    64–67
    influencing others, 138–139
    shifting gears, 220–221
    understanding people, 44–46
tuning in, focused listening, 27–29

understanding
    confirming, 63–64, 66–67
    idiomatic expressions, 20
    paraphrasing to improve, 32–34
    without agreeing with speaker, 49
Ury, William
    conflict resolution obstacles,
        165–169

Ury, William (continued)
"going to the balcony" time out
technique, 151–152

validation, of opposing viewpoints,
133–134
validity, denial of speaker's, 28
values, conflicts over, 150–151
verbal messages, congruent nonverbal and, 61
verification
feedback acceptance, 108–109
feedback perceptions, 117
victimization, relationships, 223
videotaping, body language, 61
viewpoints, validation of opposing,
133–134
vision, promoting a common,
184–185
visual learners, dealing with,
214–215
visualization aids, persuasive,
135–138
vocabulary, expanding your, 59, 65,
68
voice, and nonverbal behavior, 86

walkout option, conflict resolution,
169
want it
asserting your needs, 73–74

being a team player, 178–179
changing habits, 10
conflict resolution skills,
146–148
exchanging feedback, 98–99
expressing yourself clearly,
53–55
influencing others, 122–123
shifting gears, 205–206
understanding people, 22–24
Ward, William Arthur, on feedback,
95
what, vs. asking why, 127
WIFM (What's in It For Me?), messages, 136–138
win/win solutions, negotiating,
162–171
wisdom, conflict resolution,
155–156
wishes, vs. needs, 76–78
word
painting with, 58–59
pausing to select the proper, 67
workout programs, appropriate,
17–18

Zeno (Greek philosopher), on listening, 25

About the Authors

Mel Silberman, Ph.D.

Mel Silberman, Ph.D., is professor and coordinator of the Adult and Organizational Development Program at Temple University where he received the "Great Teacher" Award. He is also president of Active Training, a provider of cutting-edge business and personal development seminars based in Princeton, NJ.

A licensed psychologist, he specializes in training and development, marital and family health, performance improvement, and team building. Dr. Silberman has written a dozen best-selling books for parents, business people, educators, and trainers, including *Active Training, Active Learning, How to Discipline Without Feeling Guilty, Confident Parenting, 101 Ways to Make Meetings Active,* and *101 Ways to Make Training Active.* He is also editor of *The Team and Organization Development Sourcebook, The Training and Performance Sourcebook,* and *The Consultant's Toolkit.* Dr. Silberman is a widely sought-after speaker and seminar leader for educational, corporate, governmental, and human service organizations.

Freda Hansburg, Ph.D.

Freda Hansburg, Ph.D., is a psychologist and facilitator of change both for individuals and for organizations. She currently maintains a clinical practice with individuals and couples and directs the Technical Assistance Center, a consultation and training program at the University of Medicine and Dentistry of New Jersey. A popular trainer and conference presenter, Dr. Hansburg has provided consultation to numerous behavioral health and human service organizations, taught in university settings, and published professional and popular articles.

About PeopleSmart Seminars

Seminars based on *PeopleSmart* are available to business, educational, and community groups throughout the United States and Canada. They include:

Working PeopleSmart

Living PeopleSmart

Understanding People

Expressing Yourself Clearly

Asserting Your Needs

Exchanging Feedback

Influencing Others

Resolving Conflict

Being a Team Player

Shifting Gears

For further information, visit:

www.activetraining.com

or contact:

Active Training

26 Linden Lane

Princeton, NJ 08540

800-924-8157

Mel Silberman and Freda Hansburg are also available for speaking engagements.

800-924-8157 or mel@activetraining.com

When
Dating
Becomes
Dangerous

A Parent's Guide to
Preventing Relationship Abuse

Patti Occhiuzzo Giggans, M.A.,
and Barrie Levy, M.S.W.

HAZELDEN®

Hazelden
Center City, Minnesota 55012
hazelden.org

Based on the book *What Parents Need to Know About Dating Violence*

Library of Congress Cataloging-in-Publication Data

Giggans, Patricia Occhiuzzo.
    When dating becomes dangerous : a parent's guide to preventing relationship abuse /
  Patricia Occhiuzzo Giggans, M.A., Barrie Levy.
       pages cm
    Based on the authors' book, What parents need to know about dating violence.
    Includes bibliographical references.
    ISBN 978-1-61649-471-1 (pbk.) — ISBN 978-1-61649-502-2 (e-book)
    1. Dating violence.   2. Dating violence—Prevention.   3. Parenting.   I. Levy, Barrie.
  II. Title.
    HQ801.83.G54 2013
    362.88—dc23
                                                                    2013031095

Editor's note
The names, details, and circumstances may have been changed to protect the privacy of those mentioned in this publication. In some cases, composites have been created.
    This publication is not intended as a substitute for the advice of health care professionals.
    Alcoholics Anonymous and AA are registered trademarks of Alcoholics Anonymous World Services, Inc.

16 15 14 13   1 2 3 4 5 6

Cover design: Theresa Jaeger Gedig
Interior design: Kinne Design
Typesetting: BookMobile Design & Digital Publisher Services

I dedicate this book to my children Ally, Chris, and Ruby:
I've learned so much from you and because of you; and also
to Ellen, my partner in life and in parenting.

—Patti

To Linda, Nisa, Johanna, Jedd, Ethan, Katie, Julia,
and Sammy—you are my inspiration and the
source of so much wisdom and love.

—Barrie

CONTENTS

Foreword xi

Preface xv

Acknowledgments xix

Chapter 1: What Is Relationship Violence? 1

    Emotional Abuse 4

    Physical Abuse 7

    Sexual Abuse 7

    Technology Abuse 8

    What Teens Say about Ways They Have Been Abused 10

Chapter 2: Dynamics of Abusive Relationships 13

Chapter 3: Recognizing the Warning Signs 21

    Signs of Abuse 21

    If Your Daughter Is Seeing a Gang Member 26

    If Your Son or Daughter Is in a Same-Sex Relationship 27

    Recognizing Trauma 27

    Helping Your Teen to Recognize Warning Signs 29

Chapter 4: Speaking the Unspeakable: Talking to Your Teens
about Sexual Violence 31

    Teen Attitudes 32

    Teens at Risk 34

    Sexual Coercion 35

    Sexting and Texting 35

    Reproductive Coercion 38

    Coerced Sex for Money 39

    Effects of Sexual Abuse 41

    What Parents Can Do 43

Chapter 5: What Keeps Them Together? 45

Why He Abuses 45

Why She Stays... 51

Chapter 6: Skills for Healthy Relationships 59

Characteristics of Healthy Relationships......................... 60

Skills for Sustaining Healthy Relationships....................... 61

Chapter 7: Parenting for Healthy Relationships 73

Developmental Vulnerabilities and Strengths.................... 74

Parents' Roles.. 78

Guidelines for Conversations with Teens 83

Chapter 8: Teaching Teens to Be Safe............................... 87

Teaching Your Teens to Protect Themselves 87

Chapter 9: Effects on the Family 97

Effects on Parents 98

Effects on Siblings 101

Chapter 10: Getting Off the Rollercoaster......................... 105

Dialing Down the Drama... 107

Gathering Information 110

Getting Help for Yourself 111

Setting Limits.. 112

Managing Your Reactions.. 114

Chapter 11: Strengthening Your Relationship with Your Teen........... 123

Accepting Teens' Choices.. 126

Open Communication 128

Effective Listening 131

Recognizing Your Feelings 135

Using Your Influence as a Parent................................. 136

Avoiding Power Struggles.. 138

Chapter 12: Taking Action to Intervene 143

Assessing the Situation... 143

Planning for Safety... 146

Involving Family and Friends 150

Chapter 13: Breaking Up 155

Guiding Your Teen through a Breakup 155

After Breaking Up 156

Post-Breakup Safety 158

Emotional Reactions after the Breakup 162

Chapter 14: If the Violence Stops 165

Committing to Change 167

Safety Alert 168

**Chapter 15: Getting Help: Counseling, Schools, and the
Legal System** 169

Resources for Parents 169

Schools as a Resource 175

Chapter 16: Using the Legal System 183

Current Laws 184

Restraining Orders 186

Legal Resources 188

Stalking as a Tactic of Abuse 192

Chapter 17: Cultural Strengths and Challenges 195

Cultural Influences 195

Building on Cultural Strengths 197

Confronting Your Culture 199

Chapter 18: For Parents of Abusive Teens 203

Recognizing Abusive Behavior 204

When Girls Abuse 206

Confronting Your Teen about Abusive Behavior 207

Contacting the Victim of Your Teen's Abuse 208

The Parent's Emotional Rollercoaster 209

Seeking Support 210

**Chapter 19: For Parents of Gay, Lesbian, Bisexual, or
Transgender Teens** 213

What Parents Can Do 218

Chapter 20: Healing 221

    Conclusion 227

Appendix A: Your Safety Plan Checklist 229

Appendix B: Characteristics of Healthy Relationships 233

Appendix C: Guidelines for Conversations with Teens
about Healthy Relationships 235

Resources 239

Notes 241

About the Authors 245

FOREWORD

When I began in my role as Detective Olivia Benson on *Law and Order: Special Victims Unit,* I was new to the idea of being an advocate. I understood *advocacy* in general terms—that certain individuals in our society are more vulnerable and that we have a responsibility to speak up for them. But that general understanding of *advocacy* barely scratched the surface of what that beautiful word now means to me.

My education came by way of the letters I began receiving as I worked on the show. They were much more than fan mail. The letters spoke of pain, fear, and isolation, of lives filled with deep uncertainty, deeper shame, and dim hopes for a future.

Many—if not most—of the individuals reaching out were very young girls, on the cusp of puberty. With each letter, my understanding of a "vulnerable population" came into sharper focus and took on deeper meaning. I was reading about incidents of a kind of violence that girls at this age should not even know exists. But indeed it does—too much of it, too often. These girls knew about violence because they experienced it. And then they reached out with open hearts and shared their wishes:

"I wish I had a detective like you when I was raped."

"I wish you were there last week when my boyfriend beat me up."

"I wish you were there to protect me."

They needed to connect. They needed protection. They needed an advocate, in the true sense of the word: someone who would "call out" for them, someone with a voice, willing to use it to stand up for what is right.

That is exactly what Patti Giggans and Barrie Levy have done in their years of powerful work in the anti-violence field. Their commitment, passion, and wealth of experience have changed the lives of children and families. And I am deeply grateful for Patti, who has been a blessing and a teacher on my parallel path of actor and advocate.

The wisdom they share in *When Dating Becomes Dangerous* is timely and vital. They squarely address society's ingrained victim-blaming attitudes, which are manifested in questions like "Why does she stay?" With expertise, clarity, and compassion, they help readers see the issues from multiple perspectives, all within the context of a deep understanding of the cumulative impact of trauma exposure, and the very real dangers that exist as survivors plan their exit from violent relationships. The book also offers insight from teen abusers working to address and change their behavior, an area of understanding that must deepen if we are to bring an end to teen dating violence. Particularly helpful is the chapter on healthy relationships and the responsibility of parents, educators, and professionals to ensure that children and teens have access to the information they need to build, evaluate, and maintain those relationships. Parents are the first and most important advocates in a child's life, and this book serves as a tool to support them in this pivotal role.

And if those reasons aren't enough to convey the value of this book, consider this: We all have an obligation to do everything we can to protect children and adolescents. As a mother of three, that is the most personal reason for my enduring admiration and appreciation for Patti's and Barrie's work. Every child deserves to live in a supportive, loving environment, free from violence. At this moment in time, far too many children don't have that most basic opportunity. We must all deepen our understanding of what it means to be an advocate, what it means to "call out" and stand up on behalf of this vulnerable population who is explicitly or tacitly asking for our protection. This book is vital in equipping us to step up and become better advocates.

In Gratitude,

Mariska Hargitay

President and Founder, Joyful Heart Foundation

Actor and Advocate

PREFACE

Despite their attempts to make us believe otherwise, our children need us to guide and protect them. Jenny didn't tell me what was happening to her, and I didn't know enough to ask. Don't let this happen to you and your child. Don't let another day go by where you simply wonder and worry, but take no action. . . . My family has suffered a devastating loss. We live with sadness every day. Perhaps it could have been prevented if we had only been educated.

> —Vicki Crompton, Davenport, Iowa, author of *Saving Beauty from the Beast.*
> Vicki's daughter, Jenny, died when her ex-boyfriend stalked her, broke into
> her home, and killed her. Jenny Crompton was fifteen years old.

～

We wrote *What Parents Need to Know About Dating Violence* (which this book updates and revises) in 1995 after Barrie Levy's two groundbreaking books *Dating Violence: Young Women in Danger* and *In Love and In Danger: A Teen's Guide to Breaking Free of Abusive Relationships* were published. We did so to meet the demand for information by parents who were discovering that dating violence was an issue for their children. Both of us have spent most of our careers in the field of violence against women and girls as activists, advocates, trainers, and teachers. We have started and run several organizations dealing with sexual and domestic violence, have written violence prevention curricula, have been interviewed many times on radio and television, and have been keynote speakers on the topic of teen relationship violence, as well as other related subjects. Both of us are parents.

Teen relationship abuse is a serious—sometimes lethal—problem that affects both males and females. Young men and young women have been victimized in intimate relationships, and both have perpetrated abuse. Teens and young adults may experience abuse in any intimate relationship, whether with a partner of the same or another gender.

Though relationship violence can happen to anyone, females are more often abused than males. Estimates are that as many as one-third of all girls experience relationship abuse at some time during their adolescence. Because the majority of violence and abuse is committed by men or boys, and because English is a gendered language, we refer to abusers as "he" and victims as "she" in this book. Our examples and stories, however, also include girls as abusers and boys as victims, as well as same-sex couples.

This book is for parents of teens (thirteen to eighteen years old) and transition-aged youth (eighteen to twenty-one years old). Research has shown that teen relationship violence starts even younger than originally thought. Some young people as young as eleven and twelve are beginning to date and becoming sexually active; therefore, we address parents of middle school–aged adolescents too.

We cover a broad definition of the kinds of relationships that parents may be concerned about, including close friends who are or have been intimate, teens who are casually or occasionally seeing one another, teens who are trapped in abusive relationships that they are trying to end, couples who expect to have a future together, and young people who have broken up with partners who continue to abuse them after the relationship has ended. As noted earlier, we include teens in same-sex and opposite-sex relationships.

When Dating Becomes Dangerous is informative for parents who want guidance for prevention. As parents, we want to influence our children so that they can have healthy relationships while they are growing up and learning about relationships, as well as when they get older and "settle down" into ongoing relationships. This book includes ideas about how to discuss healthy relationships with teens or young adults, and information on how teens can be safe while dating or hanging out with friends and intimate partners. It has a checklist of warning signs, which will help guide parents and their teens if they encounter or find themselves in a potentially violent or abusive relationship.

As parents, we also want to effectively intervene if our children encounter situations that can hurt them, or if they are hurting others. When a teen is being hurt by someone he or she is dating (or seeing) through violence or abuse, this book will help parents think through the crisis and help guide their decision-making process. It will help parents decide what to do about the abuse and how to deal with the struggles their teen is facing.

We have interviewed parents and teens who have been through the crisis of teen relationship violence. This book tells some of their stories, which are often inspiring but always informative. The book also helps parents to navigate the school system as advocates for their children and informs them of the options that are available to create safety for their teens.

During a crisis, it is natural to focus on the victim or the perpetrator, but couples, families, close friends, and schools are affected too. So we also offer guidance that will support good coping skills and effective intervention for everyone who is affected by relationship violence.

Since 1995, the issue of teen dating violence has become mainstream. Within the fields of domestic violence and public health, reaching young people sooner rather than later has become the recognized best practice in terms of both intervention and prevention. Informing and educating teen influencers like parents, teachers, and peers has become essential. Technology has exploded and the Internet, Facebook, texting, and the sharing of personal information have proliferated. Teens in particular are in constant communication. There are upsides and downsides of technology, so we give careful consideration to the potential for technology to be a friend, making support and information easily accessible, and a foe, giving abusers new tools for harassment and control. Resources have also expanded over the past few years, especially on the Internet, so we include national resources available for parents and for teens and young adults.

Our purpose is to give parents ideas about how to help their teen and young adult children to be safe and healthy in their intimate relationships. We think of putting skills in the hands of parents, supporting them in all the ways they can be effective:

- providing information about preventing relationship abuse

- supporting their children's skills for healthy relationships

- providing tools for coping with the emotional rollercoaster and the danger of their child's abusive or violent relationship— whether their child is the victim or perpetrator

- providing tools for effectively tackling the emotional, safety, and legal challenges of dealing with the abuse and violence

We hope that parents who read *When Dating Becomes Dangerous* will become educated and empowered with information and tools to prevent violence from happening and to cope with it skillfully if it does.

ACKNOWLEDGMENTS

This book reflects the generosity of many people who shared the stories of their experiences so that others might learn from them. Teens and parents participated in hours of interviews as they described relationship violence and how it affected them and their families. We are grateful they trusted us with the task of telling their stories. To respect their privacy, we will not name them individually, but we acknowledge our appreciation for their important contribution to this project.

We thank the following people for their assistance and support. The Youth Violence Prevention team members at Peace Over Violence (Lili Herrera, Trina Greene, Fabiola Monteil, Karen Lopez, and Emily Austin) were fantastic because of their wealth of knowledge about teens and violence prevention, and their enthusiasm in helping us. Lawyer Emily Austin, director of Policy and Evaluation at Peace Over Violence, made a major contribution to this project by writing two chapters on getting help from schools and the legal system. We really appreciate her quiet competence and excellent ability to articulate clearly.

Hazelden is a wonderful organization, providing valuable information on all sorts of issues. Marty Harding picked up our original book for parents and saw that an updated version would fit well with Hazelden's mission to help and encourage individuals, families, and communities to recover from addiction and violence. Thanks to Marty, we have had the pleasure of working with Peter Schletty as he moved this project along from beginning to end. He has been encouraging, responsive, and patient. April Ebb has made the production of the book painless for us, and we appreciate how she and her team have improved each draft. We are honored to be able to work with everyone at Hazelden. Thank you all.

Thank you to Linda Garnets and Ellen Ledley for their tireless support and love. Thank you, Jedd Mellin, for your very intelligent review of an early draft to make sure we are in sync with teen culture. And thank you to all of our children and grandchildren who, as teenagers, challenged us and taught us to be better parents.

We appreciate our movement and all of the people who have worked to end sexual and domestic violence. We have always sustained our hope and faith that young people will change the norms to prevent violence, so that future generations will have relationships free of violence and abuse.

What Is Relationship Violence?

Families who have a problem with relationship violence and abuse often feel that they're the only people going through it. But many teenagers experience relationship violence with a boyfriend or a girlfriend. It affects preteens, teens, and young adults. Approximately one in three adolescent girls in the United States is a victim of physical, emotional, or verbal abuse from a dating partner—a figure that far exceeds victimization rates of other violence affecting youth.[1] In a national online survey, one in five eleven- to fourteen-year-olds say their friends are victims of dating violence, and nearly half the youth surveyed who are in relationships know friends who are verbally abused.[2] Estimates are that 40 percent of female adolescents have experienced relationship abuse, and 20 percent of those experience sexual victimization in a relationship.[3]

We now know more about this problem. In part because girls have died as a result of relationship violence, it is now treated as a serious national problem recognized by the Centers for Disease Control and Prevention, school districts, mental health experts, domestic and sexual violence prevention advocates, and others. It is a problem that requires us as parents, along with anyone else involved with young people, to re-examine the ways we respond to teen and young adult relationships, and the ways we parent teens.

Dating violence happens everywhere and to all kinds of people. There is no particular culture or community in which it does not occur. Dating violence has been documented in large cities and in small farming communities, in wealthy neighborhoods and in housing projects. It occurs in every culture and ethnic group. It happens in gay and lesbian relationships as well as in heterosexual relationships. It happens to teens who have babies and to those who do not. It happens to teens who live together and to those who live with their parents. It happens to teens who are sexually active and to those who are not. It happens to teens who live in single-parent households and to those who live with both parents.

Dating violence is a serious issue. The potential for serious injury or murder is present in every violent relationship. According to the FBI, 20 percent of homicide victims are between the ages of fifteen and twenty-four. One out of every three women murdered in the United States is killed by a husband or a boyfriend.[4] Even an abusive boyfriend who does not intend to kill his girlfriend can accidentally kill her with hard shoves or threats with a weapon. Although young men can also be the victims of relationship violence and young women can be the perpetrators, the great majority of abusers are young men and the majority of victims are young women. The social tolerance for aggressive behavior toward girls seems to make it far more common for boys to be violent. Girls who victimize their boyfriends are more likely to be emotionally or verbally abusive, while boys are more likely to use threatened or actual physical violence.

We are seeing changes in teen culture—girls are more willing to be physically aggressive than in the past. Girls are less likely to inflict severe injuries; however, boys can be intimidated by abusive girls and afraid of displeasing or making their girlfriends angry. Often, young men are more violent once the romantic "pursuit" has ended and they see themselves as being in a "couple" relationship. The couple may or may not be having sex, but they feel committed to one another.

Sometimes abusers become more violent when they sense the relationship is going to end, or after their girlfriend or boyfriend breaks up with them. Thus, the chance of being seriously injured or killed increases when the victim decides to break up the relationship. This makes breaking up frightening for the victim, who may try to break up (and then get back together) several times before actually ending the relationship.

Many victims believe that their partner's violence is a sign of love. The abusive partners seem to accept violence and coercion as a means to get what they want—for example, to frighten or intimidate, or to force the other person to give them something. Violence and abuse can be seen as tolerable, or normal, in relationships.

In this book we use the word "dating," but teens don't use this term very often. A more accurate term would be "courtship," but no one uses this term anymore either. Teens might call it "seeing," "going with," "kicking it," or "hanging out." When we use the word "dating," we are talking about intimate (usually sexual) relationships in which two people see themselves as a couple with a potential future together.

A violent or abusive person repeatedly (1) tries to get their way by forcing or coercing the other person; (2) verbally attacks, demeans, or humiliates the other person in order to get and keep control over them; (3) uses or threatens to use physical force against the other person; and/or (4) forces the other person to participate in sexual acts.

Violent and abusive behavior is not the same as getting angry or having a fight. It happens again and again, and one person is afraid of and intimidated by the other. Controlling behavior is not always considered battering or abuse. For example, a teenage girl can be in a relationship with a boyfriend who is self-centered and controlling, frequently insists on having his own way, or criticizes a lot, but when he is confronted or told he can't have his way, he backs down. He may become angry, but he doesn't become explosive, violent, verbally abusive, or threatening. Also, his girlfriend is not afraid of him. There is some give and take in the relationship. This type of boy is not what we call a batterer or abuser.

Certain things he does might be considered abusive, but his behavior does not fit the repeated pattern of violence that characterizes battering relationships. Defining this distinction can be difficult. Controlling behavior, however, does have the potential for becoming abusive or violent.

In this book we use the terms "batterer" and "abuser," "battered teen" and "abused teen," and "violence" and "abuse" interchangeably. All of these terms refer to the full range of behavior that is emotionally, sexually, and physically injurious. We use "he" or "she" and "boyfriend" or "girlfriend" throughout the book, usually referring to the batterer as male and the abuse victim as female. We do this because it fits what predominantly occurs. We are also concerned, however, about the increasing numbers of young men who have been abused by other young men or by young women, and the high incidence of young women abused by female partners.

As a parent, it is probably difficult for you to read details about the kinds of abuse teens can suffer in a battering relationship. It is horrifying to imagine that these things could happen to your child at any age. We hope that as you read this book, you will feel supported while you deal with some of the most difficult problems a parent with a teenager can face.

Emotional Abuse

Emotional abuse is the most common type of abuse and lies underneath physical or sexual abuse. Emotional abuse can be very confusing for teens. It is confusing to be constantly criticized, blamed, and humiliated in front of others—by the same person who expresses intense love. Emotional abuse also causes wounds such as self-doubt, self-hatred, shame, feelings of going crazy, or feeling unable to survive without the abuser. These wounds are invisible to others, unlike the wounds caused by physical violence, which are more easily recognized. As a result of emotional abuse, your daughter may feel that she caused her own injuries, and that she is to blame for the problems in her relationship.

Emotional abuse is not always done in anger. It is often done in the guise of love, and accompanied by confusing expressions of caring. For example: "It's a good thing you have me to love you, because you are so [ugly, fat, crazy, disgusting . . .], no one else would want you." "I'm only telling you that you dress like a slut because I love you." "We have each other; we don't need anyone else. Your friends and parents are trying to keep us apart. No one else understands us and what we have together."

Jealousy and possessiveness that control and restrict the other person's behavior can also be emotionally abusive. The abuser's jealousy and suspicion may lead to accusations, explosive outbursts, name-calling, or interrogations about everything his victim does or says. A jealous boyfriend may constantly check up on his girlfriend. He may follow her or have friends follow her. He may contact her many times each day—by calling, texting, instant messaging, or posting on Facebook—and then explode if she doesn't reply. He may go through her messages, her bags, her room, and her personal belongings, checking for "proof" that she's "cheating."

He may call to find out where she is or show up when she is at work, at school, or spending time with others and demand her attention (for example, by claiming he has something urgent he wants her to do for him). The boyfriend's jealousy and explosive temper can make it too frightening for his girlfriend to do anything that might set him off. So, out of fear, she gradually stops doing things outside the relationship.

Jim and Alisha's story illustrates this dynamic.

Jim and Alisha

Sixteen-year-old Jim's girlfriend, Alisha, was terrified by his jealous fits of rage. Jim never hit her. He yelled at her, called her names, and interrogated her for hours about everything she said or did with anybody, going over and over the same answers to his questions and accusations. Later, Jim said to a counselor in a domestic violence program, "After a while, I got what I wanted: complete control over my girlfriend. Power."

Threats of suicide and threats of violence can also be emotionally abusive. A boyfriend may become seriously depressed, especially if he is afraid of losing his girlfriend. He may feel like hurting or killing himself, and he may actually attempt it. This can be terrifying for his girlfriend—imagine feeling that you could cause someone you love to kill himself! These threats to kill himself, however, may also be an attempt to emotionally control her. He doesn't want to get help or turn to others for support; he only wants his girlfriend to drop everything and take care of him. Worse, he may threaten to kill her or her family if she ever leaves him. These threats have the same effect of terrifying her and trapping her.

Isolation is another form of emotional abuse. By keeping his girlfriend isolated, the abuser maintains control over her. There are many ways that the abuser tries to coerce or manipulate her to keep her from seeing her family and friends. An abusive boyfriend may tell her that her friends and family are no good. He may have a fit of rage every time she talks to a friend, or he may accuse her of betraying him if she talks about him to anyone else. He may try to convince her that her family is the "enemy" of their relationship, and that talking to her parents about their relationship makes her "disloyal" to him. He may interrupt her when she's spending time alone with her family, or when she engages in activities or interests without him, by texting or calling or showing up unexpectedly to distract her, so that she refocuses her attention on him.

Physical Abuse

Physical abuse is rarely a onetime incident, but is part of a pattern in an abusive relationship. The violence or the threat of violence happens again and again. Physical abuse is used to control, restrict, intimidate, and frighten, and it is usually accompanied by verbal and emotional abuse. The violence generally escalates, becoming more severe over time. Even if the physical violence does not occur frequently, the abuser may use frequent threats of violence after it has happened once. This can be powerful and frightening to the victim.

Examples of physical abuse include pushing, hitting, slapping, kicking, choking, and attacking with an object or a weapon. Physical abuse can be lethal, whether the death is accidental or intentional. Some teen victims have been pinned down, pulled by the hair, or restrained hard enough to cause bruises. Often batterers deliberately inflict injuries in places on the body that others can't see. We have talked with teens who have been seriously or permanently injured, such as one young woman who lost an eye, another who lost her hearing, and others who were shot or stabbed. A young woman may be slapped so hard that handprints remain on her face. She may be choked until she passes out, leaving red marks on her neck. She may have been shoved or thrown across the room, causing a concussion when she hit a wall or a table.

Physical injuries may not be easy to see because victims go to a lot of trouble to hide them—by wearing long sleeves and turtlenecks, for example, or by wearing heavy makeup, avoiding contact with people until the worst bruises have faded, or telling lies about how they were injured.

Sexual Abuse

Sexual abuse is defined as any unwanted sexual activity. It includes mistreatment by sexual acts, demands, humiliation, or insults. It can include being violently forced to have sex, or being coerced or manipulated into having sex. A victim of sexual abuse is being "coerced" if she is afraid to say no because she fears being rejected, humiliated, or beaten. Coercive tactics committed within a relationship are as illegal as when committed by a stranger.

A young woman may be forced to perform sexual acts she does not want to do, or that are intended to humiliate or degrade her. She may have been told lies about what "normal" sex is, or what "guys need," or how girls are supposed to act in bed. She may never have felt anything but pain during sex in a relationship of months or years.

Some girls have reported that they have been forced to have sex with others, or to watch their boyfriends have sex with someone else. Some have been humiliated or insulted sexually, or made to feel disgusting or ugly. Many have been forced to have sex without protection from pregnancy or sexually transmitted diseases (STDs).

Some girls have been raped vaginally or anally or forced to have oral sex with their boyfriend. Teens have described other kinds of sexual abuse, such as being tied up; having breasts or genitalia cut, bitten, or mutilated; being stripped and stared at for long periods of time; and being forced to watch or enact scenes from pornographic films.

Sexual abuse can occur even when the couple is not having a sexual relationship. A girl may be subjected to unwanted groping, sexual jokes that make her feel harassed, or rumors that she is a "slut." Sexual harassment in a relationship is part of the overall pattern of abuse. Parents also should be aware that teens may not consider some sexual activity, such as oral sex, as "having sex."

Technology Abuse

Technology abuse is one of the most dynamic, constantly changing tactics of control. There are ever-evolving technology developments that give a controlling person new and powerful opportunities to invade the many aspects of a victim's life and cause emotional injury. Whatever technologies or social media outlets we describe here may be completely outdated or different compared to what your child may be dealing with. New devices and social media outlets are frequently changing and being created, but the basic concepts presented here will remain.

There are many forms of technology abuse. For example, controlling partners may constantly check up on victims by texting, tweeting, using smartphone cameras, using cell phone GPS to track them, and tagging photos on Facebook. Frequent cell phone communication is very common among teens and is usually harmless. In an abusive relationship, however, constant communication becomes restrictive and oppressive. The number of texts or posts is not necessarily an indicator of abuse. But the impact of the texts on the victim, and the texts' tone, context, and content can be intimidating and controlling. Texts can be threatening or manipulative. They can occur when the teen is with the family, at the dinner table—anywhere, at any time. Although the abusive tweeting, texting, or instant messaging can go on while the family is together, parents can be unaware of it.

We can't underestimate the value of the use of the cell phone as a safety tool, as a way for parents to keep in touch with their children wherever they are. However, we also must be aware that it can be used by an abusive person to track, retaliate, and blackmail. Many of us use smartphones more than computers, and we stay "connected" via messaging, e-mails, and information at all hours of the day. For teens who are being abused, however, constant messaging can lead to multiple forms of abuse. It is far too easy to hit the "share" button on a phone, allowing a private text, picture, or video to be weaponized.

Texting crosses a line when the teen feels her partner will "freak out" (become enraged and/or threatening) if she doesn't respond immediately. Victims will go against parents or school policy to reply to a text, because fear of the boyfriend outranks everything else.

An additional form of technology abuse is cell phone cameras, which can make a teen especially vulnerable to sexual coercion, tracking, retaliation, and blackmail. Teens often don't think about the possible long-term consequences of "sexting," or sending their partners sexual text messages or photos of themselves naked or in suggestive poses. Sometimes a partner will use threats or coercion to force the other person to take the photos; sometimes the victim will think that because the couple is in love, it's safe, and will send the photos willingly. These photos may then be used as a threat to control the victims; for example, "Have sex with me or I'll send the photo out and show everyone." The photos may be sent to everyone in school, or posted online, as a way of retaliating during a jealous rage or during a breakup.

Social media, such as Facebook, can also be used to control and track victims. The "check in" feature is used to notify people of your location. It can also be used by a controlling partner to stalk, follow, and check up on a partner, to know where that person is at all times. A controlling partner can ask friends to follow the victim, take photos, and post them on Facebook as a way of keeping track of the person.

What Teens Say about Ways They Have Been Abused

When asked, "What are some of the ways you have been emotionally abused?" teens have answered:

- yelled at
- had money stolen
- constantly blamed for everything that goes wrong
- accused of flirting with others
- verbally harassed
- publicly humiliated
- called names
- had possessions broken

When asked, "What are some of the ways you have been physically abused?" teens have answered:

- scratched
- arm held so tightly it bruised
- arm twisted
- head hit against a wall
- choked
- dumped out of a car
- beaten up
- cut with a knife
- hair pulled
- knocked down
- burned
- hit with an object
- slapped
- punched in the face

When asked, "What are some of the ways you have been sexually abused?" teens have answered:

- called sexual names
- boyfriend threatened to get a new woman
- boyfriend wanted sex after hitting
- forced to have sex or raped
- forced to watch pornography
- forced to do disgusting sex acts
- boyfriend always wanted sex, and got mad when I didn't want to
- slapped, pinched to get his way
- forced to have sex without protection
- pressured to text sexual photos

Dynamics of Abusive Relationships

"One small disagreement would lead to another. It would build to a crescendo, which always ended with Mike's violence. Then the storm would clear, and we would make up passionately and be blissfully happy for days or weeks until the next storm started to build."

—MARGE, 18

You may have noticed that there is a pattern in an abusive relationship. Abusers seem like two different people: loving some of the time and cruel some of the time. Their behavior and moods fluctuate in repeated cycles. In some relationships, the two people fight, exploding in anger, yelling or being physically aggressive with one another when they have a conflict. They are evenly matched, and either one may start a fight that turns aggressive. This is often called "situational violence."

We are describing a different sort of abusive relationship, however, in which one person uses intimidation, isolation, domination, manipulation, and threats of violence to control the other person. The pattern is often called coercive control. For some couples, it is a cycle that is repeated: Tension builds to an explosion that is then followed by remorse, apologies, and making up . . . until the tension builds again. For other couples, the tension rises and falls without following a cycle. In either case, the abuser instills a great deal of fear in the victim throughout the normal activities and on a daily basis. It doesn't always appear that abuse or violence is going on at any particular moment, but victims experience the abuser constantly undermining them and attacking their ability to make decisions, take care of themselves, and feel good about themselves. The coercive dynamic is continually present.

Victims of coercive control often find that what is actually done to them doesn't have as powerful an effect on them as what their partners prevent them from doing for themselves. Abusers gradually take over their victims' lives, undermining their relationships with family and friends, making it impossible to have any privacy, and depriving them of self-respect and autonomy. Partners who are coercive and controlling use many tactics to accomplish this.

Sometimes an abuser will control his victim by threatening to break up with her if she doesn't do what he wants. He could threaten her for a variety of reasons: for example, to have sex with him, use drugs or alcohol with him, or to commit a crime with him.

Victims often find themselves trying to stay safe by focusing the majority of their time and energy on their abusive partner's moods and needs. Victims are always trying to avoid conflict because they are afraid of what will happen if they challenge, resist, or don't comply with their partner's demands. But the "rules" about what will keep the abusive partner happy are continually changing and impossible to predict, so the victim pays more and more attention to any little changes in her partner. Because abusers know their intimate partner's vulnerabilities so well, they can target their attacks and efforts to undermine their victims in a very personal way. Manipulation and control are embedded in everyday life. The abusers' behavior appears "normal," and for some teens it may seem like a sign of love. For example, many teens believe that jealousy and not "allowing" them to do things with friends is romantic: "He loves me so much, he can't stand to be without me, even for an hour!" The message is powerful: "No one can have you but me."

Not only are victims afraid of getting hit or injured, but they also often question their own sanity, because what is "normal" or "sane" keeps changing. There is no aspect of the victims' lives that the abusers do not scrutinize and try to control. This can make it frightening for the victims to make even the most minor decisions. Unbearable anxiety can be triggered by such trivial choices as what to wear, what to buy, or whether to talk to a family member or friend after church.

The victim becomes increasingly isolated. Friendships are regulated, for example, when the abusive partner insists they go everywhere together, makes rules for how the victim must behave, and interrogates the victim after any contact with someone outside the relationship. Some victims manage their anxiety by shutting down their emotions, so they seem to be unaffected by or not remember what others readily see as the atrocious or frightening behavior of the abuser. In his book *Coercive Control,* Evan Stark describes what he calls "perspecticide": the abuse-related incapacity to "know what you know" as a result of isolation.[5] A victim might find herself believing that she is worthless or stupid until later, sometimes after talking to someone outside of the relationship, when she is able to get her own perspective of the truth. Often the validity of what she really knows to be true is impossible for her to see for a long time, because she has been so undermined for so long that it is too difficult to maintain her own perspectives, boundaries, and values.

The impact of coercive control accumulates over time, through constant undermining, isolation, and intimidation, with physical violence and threats of physical violence interspersed with daily routines. Evan Stark writes, "Intimidation instills fear, secrecy, dependence, compliance, loyalty, and shame, through threats, surveillance, and degradation. Intimidation relies heavily on what a woman's past experience tells her a partner is likely to do and what she imagines he might do or is capable of doing."[6]

These relationships are often very intense. The demands of the abuser keep the targeted teen in a hyper-alert mode, and the breakups, getting back together, the "fights," and making up afterward are dramatic and emotional.

Teens and parents often believe that breaking up with an abusive partner will end the violence, abuse, and attempts to control. However, the abuse often continues after the relationship has ended. Abusers develop new tactics when they don't have easy access to the targets of their control, and continue to use their familiarity with the victim's vulnerabilities to try to get her back.

These dynamics are difficult to understand, because relationship abuse is not simply about being hit, but is very complex. Parents must be aware of this complexity to be effective in dealing with it.

The following story about Dana and Jason will provide insight about how the cycle of violence and coercive control often take place.

Dana and Jason

Dana and Jason are both sixteen years old and have been going together for eight months. Their experience is typical of abusive dating relationships for teens.

When things are good, they get along really well. They're happy and enjoy hanging out together. Their friends say they're the "perfect couple."

However, Jason can be temperamental, edgy, and critical. He blows up easily. He constantly criticizes Dana. He "punishes" her for her "mistakes," anything he feels is wrong—no matter what she does. Jason is also jealous and possessive. He accuses Dana of dressing too sexy, or flirting, or having sex with other guys. He texts her constantly to find out where she is—or to make sure she doesn't go anywhere. Dana is aware that she can't do anything separately from him, like hang out with her best friend, and that he hurts her feelings by teasing her.

Sometimes Dana thinks Jason's demands seem to prove his love. She knows she is important to him. But she has become more and more afraid of doing something that will trigger his temper. To keep the peace, she tries to please him. When he wants to know where she's been, she attempts to tell him the truth. When he barrages her with questions, she tells him what she thinks he wants to hear. Sometimes she realizes it doesn't matter what she says. Jason twists whatever she says and just gets angrier and angrier. His anger keeps building and the tension increases.

In the beginning, sex with Jason felt special, and she enjoyed it. Recently, he has been rough with her. So she becomes quiet just to get it over with.

Jason has slapped Dana and punched her. Each time, he felt sorry afterward and was afraid that she would leave him, so he apologized and promised he wouldn't do it again.

Dana is usually a happy person, full of energy, but when the tension between her and Jason gets bad, she becomes withdrawn and depressed. She has become tense and nervous. She gets terrible stomachaches; her doctor thinks she is developing an ulcer.

Dana has broken up with Jason a couple of times, after really bad incidents ("fights" she calls them). Dana's mom, Peggy, notices the changes in her daughter's behavior. She sees that Dana doesn't care about school or her appearance. She used to spend hours in front of the bathroom mirror. She notices that Dana is jumpy, quick to answer the phone and reply to text messages, and ready to drop anything if Jason insists. She also sees Dana apologizing for everything and criticizing herself a lot. When Peggy asks Dana what is wrong, Dana either says "nothing" or jumps all over her ("Why do you always think something is wrong?").

Jason's mom, Celeste, can also feel the tension when Jason is around. She overhears Jason talking with Dana and being cruel to her and critical of her. When Celeste comments to Jason that he isn't being nice to Dana, Jason yells at her to mind her own business. Celeste cautions him, "Be careful, you'll lose Dana. You know what a bad temper you have."

As Jason's anger builds, he stops trying to cool off. Dana tries to get away from Jason each time she senses the tension building up; sometimes she can, and other times she can't. Jason stops containing his rage, and lashes out at Dana. He calls her names, hits her, forces her to have sex, and won't let her get away from him. He justifies his rageful behavior, usually over some insult or emotional injury that becomes hugely important in his mind, and Dana struggles to figure out what happened. When he is like this, he wants to humiliate and hurt her.

After he calls her names, verbally lashes out, or hits her, his rage subsides and he feels relieved—until the next time. Afterward, he often feels sorry and is afraid that Dana will leave him. He has given her bruises, which even he can't ignore. She can't stand him touching her. When he sees how he has hurt her, he cries and begs her to forgive him. Dana realizes that she has been fooling herself by thinking (again) that Jason will ever stop his violence. It's a relief for her too when the violence subsides, but it also makes her angry. No matter what she does, Jason hurts her. Like a number of times before, she breaks up with him following the attack.

Peggy and her husband, Don, are frightened when they see the bruises, and they now realize that Jason has really hurt their daughter. Until now, they had not known that he's been hitting her. They are afraid Dana will make excuses for him, forgive him, and get back together with him. Peggy and Don talk with Dana about getting away from Jason and getting her life together without him. Peggy is also worried about Don. He is furious with Jason, and threatens to "take matters into his own hands." Peggy and Dana are afraid Don will get hurt or make things worse. They file a police report and try to convince Don to let the police handle Jason. Everyone is relieved that Dana is no longer covering up for Jason.

Celeste knows that Jason has a real problem, but she can't believe that her son would hurt Dana so badly without provocation. When Jason says that Dana pushed him, and that it was her fault, Celeste wants to believe him. She feels powerless to do anything about Jason's violence and hopes that the police report will have some effect on him.

After his rage and attack on Dana, Jason is apologetic, romantic, and passionate. He promises he will change and never hurt her again. Dana still feels afraid and vulnerable, and she wants to get away from him. But he is so much like his old self, and he feels so bad, that she begins to remember the things she loves about him when he is not violent. She knows he loves her and needs her. They get back together, and Jason is not as tense. He is fun to be with again. Dana feels better, relieved, and her energy is restored. Jason doesn't feel so easily irritated and jealous, even though he continues to twist anything Dana says or does. They go to their special places and enjoy their time together. However, Dana is also aware that she once again can't do anything separately from him, like hang out with her best friend, and that he hurts her feelings by teasing her.

They both find excuses for his hurtful, mean behavior—his unhappy childhood, his failures in school, her failure to keep him happy. They may even think that his violence was justified or her bruises deserved. They deny the fact that the violence is Jason's problem. They both begin to believe that the violence was a "misunderstanding" and won't happen again . . . until Jason is tense and mean again when Dana doesn't immediately respond to his needs.

Peggy and Don feel helpless as Dana avoids them and spends all of her time with Jason again. They can't believe that Dana has forgotten her bruises so quickly and that she seems to think he won't be violent again. When they talk to her about Jason, she defends him, makes excuses for him, and gets angry with them for trying to interfere in the one thing in her life that makes her happy. They also know that Dana does not let them know about her problems with Jason until they get really bad. Jason and Dana seem bonded to each other again, and Peggy and Don are very tense and worried.

Celeste, Jason's mom, keeps hoping that this time Jason will realize his violence causes serious problems. She is relieved that he is his old self again, but she worries about Dana, because she keeps going back to him.

The worries of the parents in this story are justified. Generally, patterns of coercive control and the repeated cycle of violence continue, and become worse, unless the abusers take active steps to change or the victims take active steps to protect and take care of themselves. In many cases, this means deciding to leave the relationship and go through a process of recovery.

In the next chapter, we'll explore the warning signs that parents like Peggy and Celeste can look for.

3

Recognizing the Warning Signs

"Learn about it before you need it."

—DONNA, parent of a teen in an abusive relationship

Parents have varying experiences of finding out about their son's or daughter's abusive relationship. Some find out as soon as the abuse starts—they see the bruises, they witness the verbal or physical attack, or their child tells them. Others don't find out until the violence has become so severe they are notified of it by their child's school, a hospital, or the police. Still others don't find out until after the relationship has ended. But there are a number of warning signs that can help parents recognize if their child is being abused. Although this chapter refers to an abused daughter, it could just as well be an abused son, and it can happen in either a heterosexual relationship or a same-sex relationship.

Signs of Abuse

There are many signs of relationship abuse. The following questions can help you determine if your child is being abused.

Does your daughter come home with injuries?

Bruises, red marks (as from a slap), a limp, clumps of hair missing, torn clothes, burn or choke marks: These are visible signs of physical violence. Often the teen's explanation doesn't match the injury. And by the second or third time, the explanation is no longer plausible. By asking your daughter over and over what is going on, you may uncover the truth.

Peggy, Dana's mom, describes injuries she noticed:

> Dana is athletic, so she'd tell me that she had been injured when playing soccer. She didn't used to get so many injuries, and she never had so many soccer games either. Finally, I confronted her and asked, "What is going on? Is Jason hitting you?" She denied it at first, but then she couldn't explain how a soccer ball could have given her a red mark around her neck. She finally told me that Jason had choked her to keep her from leaving his house. This had been going on for months.

Do you see signs that she is afraid of her boyfriend?

Peggy relates an incident she had with Dana in the supermarket:

> She went to the market with me the other day, and she began rushing me through the checkout line. Jason had texted her, and she said she had to go home. She seemed to be afraid. I rushed with her and didn't say anything. I heard Dana talking to Jason. She was explaining, apologizing, trying to calm him down, and telling him, "Don't come over here! My mom's here." After she hung up, we had a long talk. That's when she told me that Jason keeps interrogating her about where she's been when he hasn't been able to reach her.

Ask your teen why she is so jumpy, nervous, or afraid to displease or disagree with her boyfriend. Does she flinch when he lifts his hand to do something? In an outburst of anger, does he hit a wall or break something? Have you heard stories in which your daughter was not threatened directly, but was frightened by his temper or his violence toward someone or something else? These and other expressions of fear are important warning signs.

Does her boyfriend check up on her?

Peggy talks about signs that Jason was checking up on Dana:

> Dana spent all of her time with Jason. She was either with him or they were texting. When they weren't together, Dana thought his friends were watching her and reporting to him. Sometimes he hung out with our family, and he was really sweet. But after a while it seemed that he was everywhere she went, which confused us.

You may see evidence that your daughter is being watched, followed, checked up on. You may see her boyfriend suddenly showing up everywhere you go. The most common sign is constant texting and tracking of the victim via technology. Your daughter may be afraid not to reply to the constant texts and e-mails. These texts, phone calls, and conversations are often tension-filled and contain repeated explanations and apologies from your daughter, as if she were being interrogated about everything she wears, does, and says. You might find out that your daughter's boyfriend is calling her siblings or friends to find out where she is or what she is doing, what she is wearing, whom she is interacting with, and so forth.

Does he verbally lash out at her, call her names, or talk mean to her or about her?

If he does these things, he is being emotionally abusive. Verbal attacks, talking in a mean and accusing tone of voice, using foul language, name-calling, and constantly criticizing, demeaning, and putting down the victim—these are ways abusers use words to hurt their partners. People often do not recognize this kind of behavior as abusive. Verbal attacks can be especially damaging because they undermine a person's self-esteem. Verbal attacks are also powerful because they are interspersed with positive, complimentary, or more sensitive ways of talking to the victim. Thus, victims never know what to expect, and when they let their guard down they are open and vulnerable to the impact of suddenly and unexpectedly being accused or attacked, usually without any warning or clue as to the reason. As a parent, it is important for you to know that often the extent of the abuse is worse than what you have witnessed.

Does your daughter seem to be giving up things that were important to her, such as time spent with friends and family, classes and activities at school, or other interests?

You may notice that your daughter is not doing things she used to enjoy, or is not doing as well in school as she used to. She may be spending so much time with her boyfriend, and be so consumed by the relationship, that she stops paying attention to anything else. Her close friends might be angry with her because they don't see her anymore. When she tries to see her friends, her boyfriend gets angry, accuses her of cheating on him, or convinces her that they don't need other friends or time apart. Parents often don't know how isolated their daughter has become until they happen to talk with one of her friends and hear the friend's perspective of what is happening.

You may find out that your daughter is having difficulty concentrating in school. Your daughter's comments or explanations may alert you: "Jason says that only really nerdy kids play soccer. And besides, he wants me to spend all of my time with him. Isn't that great?" Or: "Jason thinks all my friends are dumb and spoiled. I don't know. Maybe he's right."

Although parents might be unhappy about these kinds of behavioral changes, they may not suspect abuse. These changes are signs of emotional abuse, however, even if there is not physical abuse.

Does she apologize for him and his behavior?

You might notice your daughter apologizing and making excuses when her boyfriend does things to upset her. She may not acknowledge that she feels bad when he hurts her. Instead, she blames herself for his mistreatment and defends him, justifying why he has treated her badly. She is protective of him, seeing him as misunderstood or victimized by others.

Have you seen signs of coercive control?

You may have noticed that your daughter is having trouble making decisions for herself, doing things for herself, or trusting her own judgment. You might see that her attention is focused exclusively on her abusive partner, and rarely on herself or her family.

Have you seen him be verbally abusive or physically violent toward other people or things?

A clear sign that your daughter's boyfriend is or could be violent toward her is if you see his explosive temper or violence toward other people, animals (such as pets), or things. If you witness him throwing things or hitting walls, hurting pets, or punching people when he's angry, these are clear indications that he does not control his temper. This kind of explosiveness is intimidating, and it is just as frightening as violence directly aimed at your daughter.

Has her appearance or behavior changed?

As you saw in the last chapter, Dana started to change—she didn't care about school or her appearance. You may have noticed that your daughter no longer dresses well or pays attention to her appearance. Something is wrong when a daughter who usually spends time each morning fixing her hair, putting on makeup, and carefully selecting outfits to wear to school is suddenly having a hard time getting up in the morning and caring about how she looks. She may be covering bruises with long sleeves and turtlenecks, even in summer. Her boyfriend's emotional abuse and jealousy may be making her afraid of other guys' attention. His accusations about how she "comes on" to other guys, and her fear of his violence, may lead her to wear clothes that cover or hide her body. His constant criticisms or erratic violent outbursts, along with her isolation, may affect her self-esteem so badly that she is depressed and therefore not taking care of herself. Neglected appearance is also a major warning sign of sexual abuse or rape.

If your daughter is depressed, she may experience sudden weight loss or gain. Other signs of depression are sleeping too much or too little, inability to concentrate, withdrawing, apathy, showing little pleasure or enjoyment, and expressing thoughts of suicide.

Is your daughter using alcohol or drugs?

Sometimes behavioral change is caused by substance abuse. Alcohol and drug use is a common factor in abusive teen relationships. Your daughter may be drinking alcohol or using drugs—as a way to cope, as part of the relationship (i.e., they drink or use drugs together), at his insistence, or as a continuation of a problem she had before the relationship that has now become worse. Some parents have found out about dating violence through dealing with their daughter's substance abuse. Some abusive partners force their victim to drink or do drugs. Drinking and abusing drugs increases the risk for more violence.

One study found that, in junior high and high school, teens who drank alcohol before age thirteen were more likely to be both victims and perpetrators of physical violence in relationships. Another study found that teenage girls in abusive relationships are more likely to abuse drugs and alcohol, have eating disorders, engage in unsafe sexual behaviors, and attempt suicide.[7]

Although alcohol and drug abuse is often connected to relationship abuse, these substances do not cause it. Not everyone who abuses alcohol or drugs becomes violent, and some people are violent whether they drink or not.

If Your Daughter Is Seeing a Gang Member

If you think that your daughter is in a relationship with a gang member or at risk for being in a gang, it is important to be aware that relationship abuse is common within gang culture. The violence may be more visible and public than in non-gang cultures. The main reasons a child joins a gang are to belong and to feel protected. But being part of a gang and being in a relationship with a gang member carries a high risk for relationship violence. Men dominating women is pervasive in gang culture. Girls have also reported that the way their boyfriends related to them in private was more reasonable ("softer") than the way they behaved in front of other gang members, when they were rough and abusive with the girls to prove their status.

Surveillance, checking up, and threats are especially frightening for victims whose boyfriends are in gangs, because threats can come not only from the boyfriend but from the whole gang as well.

If Your Son or Daughter Is in a Same-Sex Relationship

Consider the possibility that your child may be in a same-sex relationship. Adolescence is a period of sexual exploration and experimentation. Parents are often in denial about whether their child is dating or in a committed relationship, even a heterosexual one. It is even more common for parents to be unaware that their child's "best friend" relationships might be more intimate than that. This is because many same-sex relationships are kept secret.

The dynamics of same-sex relationships are very similar to those of heterosexual relationships, and so are the warning signs. The major difference is that often parents don't know about the relationship unless the teen is open about it. It is also more difficult to identify who is the abuser and who is the abuse victim if parents assume that the abuser is always male and the victim is always female. See chapter 19 for more information about this.

Recognizing Trauma

Trauma results from stressful events that are prolonged, overwhelming, or unpredictable. These events are out of the victims' control. According to child psychologist Bruce Perry, nature equips us all to react to stress in one of two different ways: hypoarousal or hyperarousal. Indicators of hypoarousal are withdrawal, defiance, depression, and resistance. Signs of hyperarousal are hyperactivity, inattention, vigilance, and aggression. When someone experiences trauma, both reactions become heightened and more extreme. Stress causes confused and distorted thinking and suppresses short-term memory. When teens are stressed, they do not think clearly and their memory is impaired. When teens are traumatized, memory and thinking problems become worse. Trauma creates a heightened stress receptor within the brain. In this manner, traumatized teens are often anxious, nervous, and fearful, and subsequently are more aggressive or withdrawn.[8] They disconnect from their own emotions and from others who are usually close to them. Their attempts to disconnect can be seen in some of the ways they try to cope with trauma (e.g., cutting school, smoking, drinking, and staying busy).

These responses are normal reactions to abnormal circumstances or experiences, such as relationship abuse. Teens reacting to trauma are doing their best to cope with being overwhelmed or frightened, and having a nervous system that is overstimulated. These reactions cause parents to worry because their child isn't behaving the way he or she usually does.

Common symptoms of trauma include an inability to relax or sleep, or sleeping a lot more than usual; overeating or an inability to eat; agitation; impatience and irritability; fear or panic reactions; "freeze" responses such as being immobilized or unable to act or make decisions; hypervigilance; inability to concentrate or focus; and somatic reactions such as back or stomach pain or headaches. Parents can also develop symptoms of trauma as a reaction to what is happening to their teen. They may experience hypervigilance, physical stress responses, nightmares, panic/anxiety, inability to concentrate, or an obsessive focus on their child or on the abuser.

"Regulation" and "dysregulation" are terms used to describe the physical reactions to stress and the ability to tolerate stress. Regulation is the ability to experience and maintain stress within one's window of tolerance, generally described as being calm. Dysregulation is the experience of stress outside of one's window of tolerance. This state is commonly referred to as being "stressed out" or in a state of distress.[9]

Parents who are aware of their children's trauma symptoms as well as their own are better able to understand the seemingly extreme and changing behaviors associated with trauma. This makes it clear to parents that they must address their own need for help to become calm and more "regulated" before they can begin to solve their children's problems.

Helping Your Teen to Recognize Warning Signs

It is important to ask teens thought-provoking questions that help them to recognize warning signs of abuse—in their own relationships as well as in those of their friends. You can start a discussion at any time. Examples of good conversation starters are the following:

1. What are examples of abuse in a relationship?

2. If you saw someone treating a boyfriend or girlfriend badly or saying mean things to them, would you call that abuse? Why or why not?

3. Has anyone you know posted rumors or harmful gossip about a boyfriend or girlfriend online? What happened afterward? Do you think this was abusive?

4. Would it be weird to you if someone you were going with texted you all day to ask where you are and what you're doing? What behavior would be weird, or would upset you, and what would be okay? What if you were afraid not to reply

to repeated texts, and felt you had to respond immediately to every text? What would you do?

5. Have any of your friends ever talked to you about boyfriends or girlfriends being super-controlling?

Use the information about warning signs in this chapter to think of your own conversation starters. It is very important to have these conversations many times. Assure your teen that if they ever need to talk about anything happening in their relationships, you are available to listen.

Speaking the Unspeakable:
Talking to Your Teens about Sexual Violence

Sexual violence is the most difficult aspect of abusive relationships for teens to talk about. Forced or coerced sex is often part of the pattern of relationship violence, along with emotional and physical abuse, and it can happen repeatedly throughout the relationship. It is part of the whole pattern of abuse. Victims report that they are afraid to say no to sex, just as they are afraid to say no to anything else the abuser wants them to do. Sexual abuse can happen in any relationship, and it can also be perpetrated by someone of the same gender.

In the beginning of the relationship, the sex may be romantic, loving, and passionate, or the couple may have discussions about whether and when to have sex. Girls may feel open to having sex, or want to have sex. But willingness and consent to have sex may turn into abuse when a boyfriend suddenly forces unwanted sex, or is manipulative or threatening and demands sexual activities that are unacceptable or demeaning to his partner.

Many teens and young adults have told us that the abuse in their relationships started with forced sex, sometimes when they were just starting to date. In the confusion or disbelief that they had been raped—if they were even able to call it rape—the victims sometimes chose to reframe it as awkward sex with a new boyfriend, just "figuring out what each other likes," even if they hated the experience.

Some girls have told us that their experiences of sexual abuse started with seemingly innocent "play fighting," which then escalated to being pinned down and unable to escape. They wanted it to stop, but the boyfriend wouldn't stop.

Teen Attitudes

Many teens experiment with sex, and many feel social pressure to be casual about sexual encounters. They may experiment with bisexuality, having sexual interactions with both boys and girls. They often experiment within friendships, sometimes having sexual interactions with friends (sometimes called "friends with benefits" or "hooking up"). There are many different kinds of relationships that don't fit neatly into familiar categories, some of which are unknown to parents and make them uncomfortable. Many teens are willing to take risks as they experiment in their relationships, and sometimes they take behavioral risks that they are not developmentally capable of handling. Teens often appear to be sophisticated, maybe because of a great deal of media exposure to sexuality and sex, thereby giving the impression that they know a lot about it. But they are generally not as experienced or as knowledgeable as they appear. This fools parents and peers, and possibly even themselves.

Youth culture has a strong influence on individual teens, and it is always changing. Targeted marketing to teens and young adults promotes ideas and visualizations about sex and what is "cool." Song lyrics and the actions in video games and movies are often hypersexual, link sex to violence, and objectify women and girls, creating the impression that they are there to be used by men and boys. The sexualization of young girls and young boys in advertising, movies, music, and media influence the norms and attitudes of today's youth.

This hypersexualization of teens in our culture also makes teens more vulnerable to being targeted, controlled, and sexually coerced.

When we asked high school students what they knew about "date rape" or "acquaintance rape," here are some of the responses we got:

- That's not rape; rape is when a guy you don't know grabs you and threatens you with a knife or gun.

- She's his girlfriend; a guy can't rape his girlfriend.

- She wasn't a virgin, so it doesn't matter.

- She kissed him, so it's her fault.

- He took her out and spent a lot of money on her. What did she expect?

Many adults have these same ideas about rape. The truth about sexual assault by intimate partners and acquaintances is quite different. Rape is not committed only by "strangers." In fact, most rapes are committed by acquaintances or people who have been intimate with the victim. Agreeing to kiss or "mess around" does not mean that someone has agreed to have sex. Everyone has a right to say no to sexual activity and to have those wishes respected. Just because a woman or girl allows her boyfriend to buy her dinner or treat her to a movie does not mean she owes him sex in exchange.

Boyfriends may not accept it when their girlfriends do not want sex. They may choose to believe that when she says no it really means that she wants to be talked into it or that she is playing "hard to get." A teenage boy may think that if a girl previously engaged in sexual activity with him, he can automatically expect her to respond to any future demands for sex. Both parties may believe the myth that because they are in a relationship, it is her responsibility to do whatever he wants her to do sexually.

While you, as a parent, learn about date rape, it is important to maintain a dialogue with your teen to develop his or her awareness of these realities. Open discussion of sex and sexual violence helps your teen to recognize date rape, to say no to unwanted sex, and to challenge the pervasive attitudes in youth culture.

Teens at Risk

It's hard for parents to think about their teens having sex at any age, but we know that teens tend to be having sex at younger and younger ages. They could be developmentally unprepared for sex, having harmful or unwanted sex, or at risk for pregnancy or STDs. Parents should start preparing their children early for healthy sexuality. They should not assume that their teens are not being sexual. If they do assume this, their children won't get the support and solid information they need to be healthy.

Teens may also hide the fact that they are dating if their parents disapprove of it because of their values or culture. Teens may be seeing someone without their parents' knowledge. If teens are keeping their relationships a secret, they may not have information about sex, safe sex, or abuse, and could be at risk.

A teen who has been raped may not be able to define it that way. She may not be able to acknowledge it fully to herself. If she is sexually inexperienced, or if this is her first sexual experience, she may be completely confused about what has happened to her.

Many teens report that while they are eager to learn about sex, no one talks to them directly about it. When they don't know the difference between forced or coerced sex and consensual sex, it's easy to be coerced into sex or be abused. They may feel they can't say no to sex, or not really know what is happening to them. If they don't have accurate information, they may not protect themselves from becoming pregnant or from contracting an STD.

Many teens use alcohol and drugs, especially when socializing with friends and peer groups. This adds to the risk of abuse for teens because it is difficult to make good choices when one is under the influence. According to a recent study, teens found that alcohol helps them feel more comfortable in social situations, but they were more likely to have regrets later about sexual behavior or to have limited capacities for protecting themselves from sexual coercion when they had been drinking.[10]

Sexual Coercion

Sexual coercion is difficult to define because it is confused with seduction. Mary Koss and her colleagues defined it as ways of obtaining sexual intercourse or other sexual activities with someone who is resistant by using extreme verbal pressure, such as false promises, lies, insistent arguments, threats to end the relationship, and threats to ruin the girl's reputation by spreading rumors.[11] For example, a boyfriend might say, "If you don't do it with me, I'll get it from other girls," or "You might as well give it up because I'll tell everyone you did it anyway." The victim is worn down or deceived, and so she believes she has consented, but in reality she has been coerced. This tactic is especially powerful when the couple is in an ongoing relationship and it is done repeatedly. This situation can begin to feel normal to the victim, especially to an inexperienced teen, and it is considered sexual assault because consent to have sex was coerced, not freely given.

Sexting and Texting

Sexting is the act of sending, receiving, or forwarding sexually explicit messages or images via a cell phone. It may be forced or coerced, or it may be something that a girl does as a way to flirt or keep a boyfriend. Teens may enjoy the feeling of doing something daring and sexy. Sexting attracts many teenagers who are curious about sex and sexuality. They might not have a sense of the long-term consequences of sexting, not realizing that their photos can go viral in seconds, out of their control. They often don't understand that when they delete the text or e-mail, it is still out there and can continue to be circulated by others. What they think is an intimate act has no real safety or privacy protections.

A 2012 study found that nearly 28 percent of public high school students said they had sent a sexually explicit image of themselves on their cell phone or by e-mail, and 31 percent asked someone for a "sext." Of those receiving such a picture, over 25 percent indicated that they had forwarded it to others. In addition, of those who had sent a sexually explicit picture, over a third had done so despite believing that there could be serious legal and other consequences if they got caught.[12]

A 2012 study by the Internet Watch Foundation estimated that as many as 88 percent of images people post of themselves are "stolen" from their original upload location, typically social networks, and made available on other websites, including porn sites. This report also pointed out that "sexters" who lose control of their images are at high risk for depression.[13]

Many young women cite "pressure from guys" or their boyfriends as the reason they send or pose for sexually suggestive pictures or texts, and guys sometimes blame "pressure from friends." Still, for some teens, it has almost become normal behavior, a way of flirting, or "not a big deal." But it *is* "a big deal," especially in the context of an abusive relationship. Sometimes the abusive sexting is part of the pressure for other unacceptable sexual behavior during the relationship; sometimes the abuser does it in retaliation or out of anger because his partner doesn't do what he wants or is trying to end the relationship.

The consequences of sexting are illustrated in the following story about Tina as told by her mother, Mary.

Tina

When she was seventeen, Tina came to me sobbing. A friend had received a photo Tina had taken a year before when she was first going out with her boyfriend, Stan. She was trying to break up with him, and in a fury he texted the photo to their friends. When I asked what was so upsetting about the photo, I was horrified to find out that she was naked and in a sexy pose. I asked her how she could do that! They were fooling around and he kept saying he wanted a picture of her undressed to keep with him all the time. He kept pressuring her, so she gave in, never thinking anyone else would ever see it. Now she's trying to end their relationship because he is so controlling, and he's threatening to post it on Facebook if she leaves him, and to tell everyone that she's a slut. This could jeopardize any future career, or family and friends could come across it.

Even though it's impossible to control your children's use of technology, especially as they get older, there are steps parents can take to educate children so they are aware of the general risks involved. Starting at as early an age as possible, let your children know that once an image is sent, it is no longer in their control and cannot be taken back, and that sending images, messages, and personal information can have harmful consequences. Typical childhood and teen experimentation that in the past went unrecorded now can be captured forever, and sexting is a good example of this. Open conversations about personal responsibility, personal boundaries, how to resist peer pressure, and Internet safety should occur throughout your children's lives. Talk to your children about the legal consequences of sexting. Regional laws haven't kept up with technology, as most of them were intended for dealing with child pornographers, not high school students with smartphones. In some states, some technology-related offenses—for example, distributing sexual images—call for prison sentences or large fines. In theory, a teen could face felony charges for texting explicit photos or even have to register as a sex offender.

As part of discussions about healthy relationships with preteens and teens, parents should remind both boys and girls that someone who truly cares about them will not push them into doing things that are uncomfortable and can hurt them in the long run. There are online sites that can help your teen discover ways to deal with this kind of pressure. If they cannot talk to you about it, make sure that they have an adult they can talk to who will support them in standing up to the pressure.

Reproductive Coercion

In general, teen pregnancy is on the decline, but recent studies have shown that teens in abusive relationships have higher rates of pregnancy than non-abused teens. Reproductive coercion is not unusual in abusive relationships. Refusing to use condoms and not allowing a partner to use any kind of birth control are ways for a boyfriend to control and claim possession of a girl's body and sexuality. Thus the risk of unintended pregnancy is high for girls in these relationships. According to public health researcher Elizabeth Miller, birth control sabotage is the manipulation of the other person's birth control with the intention of undermining efforts to prevent unwanted pregnancy.[14] It consists of emotional and verbal pressure, as well as manipulation, to keep a girl from using birth control. For example, a boyfriend might say, "You want to use birth control so you can sleep around with other guys." Or, "If we have a baby we will always be a part of each other."

Using violence or the threat of force also plays a role in birth control sabotage. Miller describes teens' fear of "condom negotiation"—having to discuss and decide together whether to use protection.[15] For example, a boyfriend might tear the condom, or force her to have sex when she is not protected, or refuse to use birth control because "it ruins sex for me." Girls who experienced physical dating violence were almost three times more likely to fear the perceived consequences of negotiating condom use than non-abused girls.[16] Current involvement in a verbally abusive relationship was associated with not using a condom during the most recent sexual intercourse. Adolescent boys who abuse were less likely to use condoms.[17]

> "I told him to put a condom on; he didn't. . . . I went to a clinic, and they were like, 'Oh, he gave you chlamydia.' He said it was me messin' around with some other guy, and that's not true. . . . [I told him] 'You were the only guy I was with.' And he's like, 'Oh, that's you, you're messin' around. . . . I thought you loved me.'"
>
> —As told to ELIZABETH MILLER, personal communication, March 2007[18]

Coerced Sex for Money

Sexual abuse in an intimate teen relationship can sometimes result in girls being used by their boyfriends in prostitution schemes. Boyfriends may "turn out" girls after the couple has become sexually involved. Sometimes "boyfriends" are actually pimps and have the intention of recruiting girls for prostitution, either as part of an organized gang, or for their own profit. These boyfriends are motivated to control girls in order to make money. In other cases, boyfriends in a money crisis find that they can get cash by coercing their girlfriends to have sex with others. For example, Christine's older boyfriend had gambling debts and was being threatened if he didn't pay them. He convinced Christine that she could save him, and their relationship, if she prostituted herself "a few times." This was the beginning of her entrapment. She could never say no to him after that, because he completely controlled her by manipulating her and threatening to tell others that she was a prostitute. Some victims of this kind of sexual coercion find themselves caught up in sex trafficking with boyfriends who are gang members running trafficking and prostitution rings.

The pimp/boyfriend turns out the girl through a seductive process of targeting, luring, grooming, and coercing her into performing sex for money. Often, when the girl resists or decides not to prostitute herself, threats and physical violence escalate, until she finds that she can't escape either the relationship or the prostitution. This cycle of violence confuses and entraps victims.

This kind of sexual coercion can happen to any teen, depending on circumstances. Pimps know where to find vulnerable teens, often recruiting them at bus stations, train stations, shopping malls, schools, movie theaters, concerts, juvenile and family courts, and on social networking sites such as Facebook.

A "grooming" period begins when a boyfriend showers victims with love, affection, attention, and gifts, and/or provides for their basic needs, such as food and shelter. The boyfriend also might make false and empty promises about the future, like the couple will get married or be together forever. Or he might promise to buy the victim a car, an apartment, fancy jewelry, and expensive clothes, or even purchase these things. Victims typically fall in love with their boyfriends, and then discover they are pimps. Pimps are master manipulators. During the grooming period, a pimp will typically isolate the teen so that he is her only source of comfort and stability. Then the mental and physical abuse ensues. The process is similar to what we described in chapter 2 on the dynamics of abuse: There is the same cycle of violence, and there are similar results. The traumatic bonding that follows makes it incredibly difficult for victims to separate from the person who is harming them. Kevin Bales, president of the organization Free the Slaves and author of *Disposable People,* explained that this physical and mental manipulation often results in a "chain" around the victim's brain. Even if given the opportunity, she will not leave.[19] (See chapter 5 for more about traumatic bonding.)

This traumatic bonding not only keeps the victim entrapped, it also ensures that she will return to her pimp. She often returns even after she has been forcibly removed from the situation—being sent to juvenile probation camps for criminal charges of prostitution, for example.

Parents can recognize signs that their teens are involved in having sex for money by noticing if they have new clothes and jewelry that they couldn't have bought themselves, or other unusual or expensive gifts. Another important factor parents must pay attention to is substance abuse, and the amount of money needed to maintain it—that might be the motivation or the way in which victims are trapped. Other signs are a defiant attitude, keeping secrets, coming and going late at night, or disappearing for a few days at a time.

Effects of Sexual Abuse

If your daughter has been sexually assaulted by her boyfriend, you should be aware of the kinds of emotional reactions that often follow. She may experience feelings of guilt and shame. These feelings can be especially strong if she has continued contact with her boyfriend. She may blame herself for not being able to foresee or stop the assault, or for making the wrong choices. She may feel she did something to cause it. Other people could be contributing to her feelings of guilt as well. Friends or family members may try to find a "reason" for the sexual assault in the same way they try to find a "reason" for battering: by finding fault with her behavior, attitude, or dress. Blaming the victim is a coping mechanism that keeps people from feeling vulnerable. The thought process goes something like this: "If I find something wrong with her behavior, and I don't do the same thing, then it won't happen to me." Parents may feel so angry and powerless when they learn that their daughter has been sexually assaulted that they blame her and direct their anger at her.

The victim may have negative feelings about sex: She may feel used, she may dread sex, or she may experience it as painful. Because she does not realize that her boyfriend is using sexual violence to maintain power and control over her, she may not be able to explain why she feels so frightened and powerless. These are all natural feelings after being sexually abused in a relationship.

Isabel, a survivor of sexual abuse, describes how she felt.

Isabel

I didn't tell anyone about the rapes. After he hit me, he would want to make up. He'd feel sorry. Then he would want to have sex, but I wouldn't want to right then. I'd be upset and black and blue. But then he would beg me and get mad and frustrated. He'd throw me on the bed and have sex with me. It felt bad, and I'd imagine myself on the ceiling looking down, like I wasn't really there.

I thought there was something wrong with me. After all, he loved me so much, and he was sorry. He needed sex all the time, and I thought I was frigid or cold. It never felt good to me. Maybe this is just the way sex is.

I hadn't admitted it was rape even to myself until we had been broken up for about six months. I started having nightmares and reliving the rapes. My concentration was gone, and I started being nervous around people, especially guys. I'd freak when this guy I just started dating tried to put his arm around me. I was scared to be out with people because I thought they were looking at me, and I sort of felt ashamed of how I looked. I had trouble making the simplest decisions. I lost all confidence in myself. I felt like I was going crazy.

Isabel's reactions are part of a complex set of emotional, physical, and behavioral responses known as rape trauma syndrome (RTS) and post-traumatic stress disorder (PTSD). The experiences of powerlessness and loss of control that rape victims go through are similar to those of victims of other traumas, such as car accidents, earthquakes, and military combat. It is difficult to separate the effects of sexual assault from the effects of being isolated, controlled, and battered in a violent relationship, but sexual assault has distinct effects on the survivor's feelings about herself and her body.

Young women have told us they have stopped caring about their appearance in order to look less attractive to their boyfriend or to other guys. Others have gained a lot of weight as a "protection" against sexual aggression. Some young women have experienced physical problems, such as migraine headaches or stomach pain.

Other symptoms of RTS and PTSD are loss of concentration, sleeplessness, nightmares, flashbacks, memory gaps, fear reactions of being touched in ways associated with the sexual assault, or of being touched sexually at all, and fear of places or things associated with the sexual assault. Some teens have suicidal thoughts, and some actually attempt suicide.

By identifying the symptoms of these syndromes, the victim can realize that she is not going crazy. It is important for parents and teens to understand that these are normal reactions to a traumatic experience, they usually diminish with time, and there are safe opportunities to talk about the experience that can lead to recovery and healing.

What Parents Can Do

Even under "normal" conditions, teens are often uncomfortable talking to their parents about anything sexual. If you ask teens directly if they are having sex, they may not answer, or they may assume that you are referring only to intercourse, since many teens do not define oral sex as "sex."

Many teenage girls fear their parents' disapproval of behavior that may be associated with the rape—for example, dating without permission, being sexually active, continuing to see a boy their parents dislike, or drinking alcohol or taking drugs. They assume their parents won't believe they were raped. They are also afraid that their parents will blame them for the assault rather than offer the support and understanding they need. Teens also might not tell parents about sexual assault because they want to protect their parents from emotional distress, and they feel that they can handle the situation on their own. Some teens feel their independence will be compromised if their parents get involved, or feel their parents don't understand very much about their lives. In addition, many teens don't view sexual assault in a relationship as "real rape" because it wasn't committed by a stranger.

By becoming informed, you can help your daughter define rape and sexual assault, identify whether or not she has had these experiences, and deal with them. Ask your daughter in a supportive, non-judgmental, non-blaming way about what is happening in her sexual relationship. Ask her whether she has ever felt forced or coerced to have sex, or if she has felt afraid to say no to sex. You may both be shy or uncomfortable talking about this. But the effort to overcome the secrecy will allow room to gradually overcome the shame. You will help your daughter think in new ways about what has happened to her. It will be good for her to hear that her reactions are normal, and that she doesn't deserve to be treated this way.

If you feel that you cannot talk with your daughter about sexual abuse, help her find someone she can talk with. If you do talk with her, chances are you will become upset when you learn about her experiences. You must consider your own need for support to deal with your feelings, but you must remain emotionally objective when discussing it with her, and listen to what she has to say. You will need to talk about your concerns, fears, and feelings later, but your daughter will be unable to listen to your feelings or support you. You might both need to see a counselor. With both of you getting the support you need, you can help your daughter to heal from the sexual violence and be open to positive experiences in the future. Find a rape crisis center near you for counseling and advocacy for you, your daughter, and anyone else who has been affected by her sexual abuse. There is also a great deal of information available on the Rape Crisis Center website, www.rapecrisis.com, and at the Rape, Abuse & Incest National Network (RAINN) website, www.rainn.org.

5

What Keeps Them Together?

Parents naturally search for a way to understand why a teen would love and stay with a person who is violent toward him or her. It is also hard for parents to understand why someone would threaten and hurt someone they seem to care about.

Most battering relationships are not solely violent, but have tender moments as well. The things that keep any couple loving and needing one another is complicated in any relationship, and the dynamics of an abusive relationship are especially complex. Intermittent kindness and abuse trap the victim in the belief that the abuse will stop, even as it gets worse. These are the issues we will discuss in this chapter.

But understanding why someone stays with a person who is violent does not explain why the violence takes place. All it takes for a relationship to become abusive is for someone to be willing to use threats, intimidation, and violence to control another person. Once batterers act on their violent impulses, they find it easier to use violence again and again. The first part of this chapter analyzes the factors that contribute to a batterer's use of violence.

Why He Abuses

It is hard to explain why a person is cruel or violent to someone they love. There is no single explanation for it; a variety of factors contribute, and you might recognize some of them in your teen's battering relationship. Again, please remember that we refer to the batterer as "he" because relationship violence is most commonly, although not always, perpetrated by males. However, we have seen in recent years that teen girls have become more aggressive in relationships, sometimes to emotionally or physically defend themselves, and sometimes because of their own issues of power and control.

It is commonly believed that anyone who has an explosive temper, uses violence, or controls their partners is a victim of their own inability to control themselves and their emotions—they are "out of control." But the reality is that most of the time, abusive and violent behavior in relationships is deliberate and planned. Abusers have a purpose for their behavior: to get their needs met by controlling the person they care about.

There is some good news, however. Social norms seem to be changing, as more and more boys are recognizing when they have problems with aggression and abuse in their relationships, and deciding not to use their power this way.

Jealousy

Many high school and college students say that jealousy is the main cause of dating violence. Although it is based on insecurity, teens often think jealousy is a sign of love. The abuser says, "I love you so much I can't stand for you to have other friends. I want you all to myself."

A girlfriend or boyfriend feels flattered by this "proof" of love. But they may ignore the way an abuser's jealousy leads to restricting and controlling behavior. What starts out as romance and "special" love can become a prison for the person who is loved.

Love has already become a prison when an abusive boyfriend says to his girlfriend, "I want you all to myself," and then has jealous, angry outbursts when his girlfriend visits friends or does something by herself that she enjoys. Then, because she is afraid, the girlfriend tries to avoid the abuser's bad temper and violence. Gradually, she stops doing things she enjoys or seeing people who are important to her. She becomes more isolated and more dependent on the abuser as the only person in her life. The abuser then becomes even more jealous and violent, because he discovers that his jealousy gives him an excuse to control the person he loves by keeping her intimidated, frightened, and dependent on him.

In fact, jealousy is not a sign of love. People are jealous because they are insecure about themselves and afraid they won't be loved. Because they are insecure, they may use their jealousy to dominate, isolate, and control the person they love. They then feel free to justify their violence and abuse because they assume that their jealousy is a valid explanation for their behavior.

Asserting Power Over

In our society, teenagers can learn mistaken ideas about what is considered normal in a relationship from what they see in movies, video games, music videos, television shows, and advertising. They see many situations in which a strong person or group maintains power by using violence to control people who are less powerful. They see bigger or older kids bullying smaller or younger kids. They see governments using armies or bombs when they have a conflict. They see women treated badly in movies, video games, and on TV. They may see adults they know using violence to show they have power. So they assume that maintaining power with violence is normal.

The realities about the actual consequences of violent behavior are missing from media portrayals, while the violent behavior itself is glorified and justified. This desensitizes people so they overlook or don't react to the harmful effects of violence. Studies have shown that exposure to violent television shows, movies, and video games increases aggression in youth of all ages. One study reported, "There is some evidence that youth who are predisposed to be aggressive or who recently have been aroused or provoked are somewhat more susceptible to these effects than other youngsters are, but there is no evidence of any totally immune group."[20]

Peer Pressure and Gender Roles

Some young men believe it is their right to abuse women. They mistakenly believe that men should dominate and control women, and that women are passive, inferior, and obligated to please men. They may also believe that they have authority over women and are entitled to sex.

Young men experience a lot of peer pressure to be sexually active, and sometimes sexually aggressive, with girls. Many of them feel it is their role to be dominant and to control their girlfriends' activities and behavior.

Young men often receive approval from their friends for being "the boss," for keeping their girlfriend "in line" by pushing her around, or for insisting on sex even when she says no. They may be afraid they won't look "man enough" if they don't behave this way.

A girl will often feel pressured to do what her boyfriend wants her to do, even if it hurts her. She often becomes dependent on her boyfriend, learning to put him first, and not to have anything important in her life apart from a relationship with him. She might become judgmental and critical of girls who are not seeing one special guy. A girl feels peer pressure to be in a relationship even if it is not good for her.

Girls also feel pressured to have sex when they don't want to. If her boyfriend forces her to have sex in spite of her saying no, she may blame herself. The pressure and blame come from mistaken ideas about sex and relationships. For example, some teenagers believe that if a guy takes a girl out, she is "obligated" to have sex with him, even if she doesn't want to. Some teenagers believe that guys are justified in raping a girl if they are turned on by her, or if they have spent money on her. Once a girl agrees to have sex with her boyfriend, she may believe that she doesn't have the right to say no, change her mind, or refuse to do particular sex acts, or she may believe she doesn't have the right to turn down another date—as if he now "owns" her. Or she may be afraid that she will damage her reputation and be seen as a "slut" by other teens if she doesn't agree to his "ownership" of her.

Abuse During Childhood

Young men who were abused as children or who saw their mothers being abused are more likely to abuse their girlfriends, wives, or children.[21] This does not mean that everyone who has been abused becomes abusive, or that abusive behavior is excused because of past experiences. But a combination of factors that includes a childhood history of witnessing or experiencing physical abuse seems to lead some people to use violence.

A young man may have learned from his abusive parent to blame others for his problems and to use violence to maintain control. Situations in which he feels frustrated or powerless may trigger overwhelming rage. He may have learned to release his tension by losing his temper and exploding in anger, no matter who gets hurt. Because he considers himself a victim, he feels justified when he lashes out at those closest to him, and those around whom he feels most vulnerable. He may not have learned other ways to handle his problems and feelings.

If he has witnessed his mother being abused by his father, his stepfather, or her boyfriend, a young man might accept the mistreatment of women as normal. In such an environment, he does not learn to treat women with respect.

Insecurity and Anger

Teens who are abusive have trouble handling their insecurities and fears. Different psychological dynamics underlie each individual's use of violence, which is often caused by traumatic or disruptive childhood experiences. Three of the more common psychological factors are unmet dependency needs, the fear of abandonment or loss, and the compulsive need to have order and control. Although many other people have these fears and insecurities and do not become violent or controlling, abusers may be influenced by these factors to use violence rather than other means of coping. Insecurity and difficulty managing emotions, including anger, are common issues for preteens, teens, and young adults, especially males; but in healthy relationships, teens find ways to handle these issues without hurting or needing to control their partners.

Dependency needs surface when a batterer falls in love. He may find himself to be emotionally needy and dependent on his girlfriend. When these needs are stimulated, and he then perceives them as not being met, he becomes panicky and enraged. He may also feel that it is unacceptable and unmanly to be dependent, so he restricts and undermines his girlfriend until she becomes dependent on him, allowing him to hide his own dependency.

A boyfriend who is abusive often experiences an intense fear of abandonment, then becomes panicky and enraged at the perceived threat of loss. He may be especially afraid his girlfriend will leave him, so he has trouble trusting her. He constantly tests his girlfriend to prove her love, including the demand that she give up everything to be with him. At any real or imagined sign that she might be thinking of leaving the relationship, he may become violent.

Some abusers who need order and control fear that everything around them will fall apart if they are not in control. A boyfriend might demand that his girlfriend comply with his compulsive requirements for attention—for example, with frequent and poorly timed demands that she bring him things instantly, meet him at particular places, or rescue him from his daily troubles and inconveniences. Batterers become enraged, and violent, when they do not get their way.

Many abusers don't know how to communicate or talk about their feelings. An abuser often can't empathize or understand why his part-ner feels afraid and upset when he gets angry and mistreats her.

Alcohol and Drugs

Many teenagers who have experienced violence say that drinking al-cohol and using drugs make the situation worse. Alcohol and drugs allow people to lose their inhibitions and become violent. Research has not proven that substance abuse causes violence; however, sub-stance abuse and violence have often been described as exacerbating one another, like pouring gasoline on a fire.

Alcohol and other drugs alter a person's perceptions and reactions. Some drugs trigger violent behavior. Some people only get violent when they drink or use. For others, it doesn't make a difference; they are violent whether or not substances are involved.

For example, Sam is at a party with his girlfriend, Lila. Sam gets drunk, takes Lila home, and verbally and physically attacks her. Later he explains that he gets violent when he drinks. However, at the party, he was able to decide not to beat up other people. He saved his vio-lence for Lila. If he had decided not to drink, he says, he might have been able to decide not to beat up Lila too. So he uses his drinking as an excuse to be violent.

Abusing alcohol and other drugs is often a dangerous way to deal with personal problems. Problems with substance abuse and problems with violence must each be dealt with separately, but with equal atten-tion. As complicated as all the contributing factors can be, in order for a batterer to stop using violence, he must realize that only he can stop it. He is responsible for his violence and for making the commitment to change his behavior.

Why She Stays

The question that parents of abused girls most often ask is, "Why does my daughter put up with the way her boyfriend treats her?" A victim may be furious with her partner for hurting her, and the next day she may be in love again, or she may make excuses for him as if she had never been angry. She may go back and forth as she changes her mind over and over again.

Parents wonder if there is something wrong with their daughter, or with the way they brought her up. They may be continually trying to figure out why she goes back to her boyfriend after she has been hurt by him.

It is important to understand that many victims do eventually leave abusive relationships, even if they go back more than once before the final break. A girl's tie or bond to the batterer is only part of the picture in understanding why she stays. Leaving or breaking up can be frightening, dangerous, and complicated because of the likelihood that the batterer's violence will escalate when she tries to leave.

Ultimately, most teens do leave abusive relationships. It may take weeks, months, or years, and they may break up and go back several times before the relationship finally ends. In the meantime, there are a variety of reasons why a girl might keep seeing her boyfriend in spite of his violent behavior. In this section, we will discuss what girls have told us about why they stay, and how a phenomenon called "traumatic bonding" affects the way girls perceive what is happening to them.

Hope, Fear, and Love

Girls have told us that hope, fear, and love keep them tied to the young men who hurt them. Most of the girls we have talked with who have ended a battering relationship had tried to break up several times before finally doing so. Sixteen-year-old Karen said:

> I got so mad, I broke up with him. Then he cried and said he was sorry. He promised he'd never hit me again. This happened again and again. I'd believe him every time, because I didn't want to leave him; I wanted him to change.

A girl may hope that he'll change, or hope that her love will change him, or hope that something will solve whatever problems she blames for his violence (such as drinking, school pressure, or conflicts with his parents). She may hope that the two of them can recapture the romance of the beginning of their relationship, or that the good times will last "this time" and not be interrupted by violence. Tracy, mother of fifteen-year-old Danielle, had this to say:

> Danielle was always trying to save Jake. She'd feel bad because he had so many problems with his family. They didn't celebrate holidays. They didn't help him with school. She believed that if only she could do enough for him, or give him all the things she had as a kid, he'd change— he'd become more like her. But that didn't happen. He got worse, and she fell apart.

Fear also keeps girls from leaving abusive relationships. They often discover early in the relationship that the violence intensifies anytime their boyfriends suspect or imagine that they are thinking of separating. They may be afraid of telling their boyfriends that they want to end the relationship, fearful their boyfriends will explode in anger and become more violent than ever.

Sometimes a young woman may have tried to break off the relationship, but her boyfriend became so depressed he deliberately hurt himself, or threatened to kill himself. So she is afraid to try again. She may feel that she is the only one who loves and understands him, and that he needs her so much he won't be able to survive without her. She may feel more responsibility than love for him, and too afraid of what will happen to him to try to break up.

She may also be afraid that he will hurt friends or family members. Renee said, "Selma was afraid to leave him because he threatened to kill her or other guys she might go out with." She may be afraid that he will stalk her, follow her, harass her, or threaten her and her friends and family, especially if he has already done these things in the past.

These fears should be taken seriously, because often the threats become real, as illustrated in the tragic story of Cindi Santana.

Cindi Santana

Cindi Santana was seventeen years old when she was killed by her ex-boyfriend, Abraham Lopez, during lunch at South East High School in Los Angeles in 2011. They had been dating throughout high school, and he had become increasingly jealous, controlling, and threatening until she finally ended the relationship. He became enraged and threatened to hurt her mother and others in the family. They reported him to the police and obtained a restraining order. Cindi was frightened about breaking up with Abraham and what he might do. It turned out that her fears were realized.

A victim may have other additional fears that keep her from ending the relationship. She may be afraid to be alone, fearing the pain of loneliness without the intensity of the relationship. She may be afraid that she will never again find someone to love her (especially if her boyfriend has been telling her this). Jessica, age sixteen, said, "I felt lucky to have him, and believed that no one else would want to be with me; I was convinced that I was ugly and stupid."

Familial and cultural expectations about a loving relationship may also convince a teen to stay with her abusive boyfriend. She (and her family) may believe that enduring abuse is the "price you pay" to be in a couple. She may believe that the abuse is normal, that all relationships are like this. Or she may believe that her boyfriend's abuse means that he loves her, and his jealous tantrums show how much he cares. She may expect that once she has had sex with someone, it means they have a commitment to each other and should get married. If she is pregnant or has had a child with her boyfriend, she may believe that she must stay with him for the benefit of her child.

Her expectations about her future may affect the way she feels about staying in the abusive relationship. If this relationship is all that she has planned for her future, and she does not see other options, she may be unwilling to give it up. She may believe there are no other guys she would prefer to be with, or that she doesn't have anything else to look forward to, such as work, school, athletics, or other activities.

Being in love can make it difficult to end a battering relationship. Often the bond between the partners is intense. During times when there is no physical or verbal violence, the victim and the abuser may feel strong love or a strong bond for one another. Yvette, age eighteen, had this to say:

> After we broke up, I thought, "He was my security," and I was extremely lonely without that. So I went back. I knew that he would be there, that he still loved me. I didn't think I could be or do anything without Bruce. We had such an incredible bond with each other—we both felt it.

Traumatic Bonding

Research has shown that a phenomenon called "traumatic bonding" intensifies the ties between abuser and victim. Some people relate this to the "hostage syndrome" or the "Stockholm syndrome" that can happen to anyone under circumstances in which they feel threatened, are isolated, and don't see a way out. As a result of being traumatized and frightened (by having her physical or psychological survival threatened), the victim needs nurturing and protection. If she is isolated from others, the victim turns to her abuser. If the abuser is loving or kind, she becomes hopeful and denies her anger at him for terrifying her previously. Thus the victim bonds to the loving and kind side of her abuser and works to keep him happy, becoming sensitive to his moods and needs (and hoping he will not hurt her). She tries to think and feel as he thinks and feels, and unconsciously takes on his worldview. She sees her parents and others the way her abuser does—as hostile to their relationship, as her enemy, as trying to come between them and their great love for each other. Her own feelings, needs, and perspectives, especially her feelings of anger or terror, get in the way of her doing what she must do to survive, so she gradually loses her sense of self. Even when she has the opportunity to leave the abuser, she has an extremely difficult time doing so. She is afraid of losing what she considers the only positive relationship she has, and of losing her identity as his girlfriend—the only way she knows herself. She goes back and forth, pushed and pulled between her fear of and her anger toward her abuser and her survival-based desire to take care of and protect him.

Addictive Relationships

Many relationships start with romantic love, where everything seems perfect and the couple only sees the good things about each other. Traits that one partner instinctively doesn't like are excused, or seen as positive. For example, what one person initially sees as "suffocating" and "controlling" is instead seen as "devotion" and "attentiveness."

Romantic love is thrilling, exciting, and passionate. Feeling intensely romantic at first, a young couple wants to be together all of the time. As the relationship develops, this desire to be together can become either nurturing or addictive. In an addictive relationship, the partners gradually feel more desperate to be together. They find themselves neglecting activities and relationships that are good for them, just so they can be together. They feel threatened by anything one of them does apart from the other. If one person is addicted and the other is not, the addicted person becomes desperate, jealous, or threatened by the other's activities that do not include him or her.

To parents of a teen in an addictive relationship, their child seems obsessed. They can't get him or her to focus on anything except the relationship. Either this relationship becomes part of their family life, or their child stays away and they hardly see him or her. Their teen is texting or waiting for a message whenever he or she is not with the object of their affection.

An addictive relationship, though not healthy, may or may not turn into an abusive one. It usually goes on for a prolonged period of time because both partners find it difficult to extricate themselves from each other. If the teen, preteen, or young adult is the target of addictive love, he or she may have a terrible time convincing the other that they should do things separately, and suggestions of breaking up may provoke a huge, dramatic crisis. If the teen is addicted to the relationship, he or she may experience a life-threatening panic at the thought of losing his or her partner ("life-threatening" because of the threats of violence or suicide that are often involved).

A healthy, nurturing relationship, on the other hand, doesn't rely on dependency to sustain the couple. The people involved encourage one another to have friends and to enjoy activities they do separately as well as those they do together. They support each other to do well in school, work, and other activities. If they have an argument, neither is afraid of the other. If one wants time alone, the other can accept it. Although they love each other, they know they can survive the painful feelings after a breakup and go on to other relationships if this one ends.

Alcohol and Drugs

Sometimes addiction to drugs and/or alcohol plays a major role in keeping a young woman in a battering relationship. Teens whose partners are addicted to drugs or alcohol are at high risk of violence from their partners. Sometimes a girl will continue to see a boyfriend who is violent because he is her source of drugs. She may choose to return to the familiarity and security of doing drugs with her boyfriend rather than searching for drugs on the street.

Sometimes the couple will drink or use drugs together to sustain the connection between them or to support her caretaking role. For example, some girls have told us that they drink or use drugs in an effort to make their partners drink or use less; others have told us they drink or use drugs when forced or coerced by their partners; and still others have told us that the powerful bond between them and their abusers includes using drugs and/or drinking together.

Sometimes the substance abuse stops when the relationship ends because it has been tied to the relationship. But often, there is an ongoing problem with substance abuse that requires addiction treatment as part of the recovery from the abuse after the relationship ends.

Skills for Healthy Relationships

Parents want their children to have healthy, happy relationships—as teens and as adults. Parents might assume that teens know what a "good" relationship looks like and also how to develop one. But teens need to learn not only about "violence-free" relationships, but also about what it takes to engage in healthy relationships. It takes information, awareness, attention, and—above all—the intention or deliberate plan on the part of parents to be sure their children know what a healthy relationship actually is.

An unhealthy relationship may be hurtful because of the partners' inability to communicate well, handle their emotions, or tolerate closeness. Not all unhealthy relationships are abusive or violent, however. In an abusive or violent relationship, one person is afraid of the other, and afraid of doing anything that will upset the abusive partner, who might lash out at them, or punish or humiliate them.

Talking with teens about what they are looking for in their relationships helps them to be aware of the differences between unhealthy and abusive relationship behavior, as well as healthy behavior. They can then begin to understand what it takes to be a healthy relationship partner: to be treated with respect and to treat the other with respect.

Characteristics of Healthy Relationships

A healthy relationship includes more than feelings of love, passion, affection, and shared likes and dislikes. Engage your teen in a discussion by emphasizing the following characteristics of healthy relationships:

- Both partners *give and receive,* each getting their way some of the time and compromising some of the time.

- They *respect* each other, value one another's opinions, and accept each other for who they are. They don't feel pressured to do things they are not comfortable with, such as drinking, using drugs, or having unwanted physical contact.

- They *support* and *encourage* one another's goals and ambitions and want what is best for each of them. They encourage each other to have friends and activities outside the relationship.

- They *trust* one another and learn not to inflict jealous and restrictive feelings on the other if these feelings should arise.

- Neither is afraid of the other. They feel *emotionally safe;* for example, they feel comfortable being themselves without fear of being put down. When one of them is upset, they feel safe enough to talk things out in a respectful manner. They feel *physically safe;* they are not afraid of being hurt or pressured into unwanted physical or sexual contact.

- They *communicate openly and honestly* and make their partners feel safe in expressing themselves. They listen to each other and talk face-to-face (not just text) about their feelings.

- They share responsibility in decision making. They have an *equal say* in choosing activities and friends.

- They accept the differences between them. They can be themselves and have their own *individuality,* without pretending to like something they don't like or be someone they are not.

- They respect each other's *boundaries*. If one says "no" or "stop," the other listens. This applies to sex as well as other activities. When they are together, they feel connected, not controlled.

- They are each *responsible* and *accountable* for their own behavior and don't blame others to justify their bad behavior. They accept the consequences of their actions and try to repair them.

- They express *appreciation* of one another to one another.

- Although they may be sad or even brokenhearted if the relationship ends, they know they will *essentially be okay,* and they aren't fearful about the relationship ending.

These characteristics were adapted from the book *Fifty Ways to a Safer World* and are also listed in appendix B for easy reference.

Skills for Sustaining Healthy Relationships

Communicating respectfully, resolving conflicts, and managing strong emotions are all important relationship skills that everyone can learn. Parents can model and teach teens (starting at a young age) behaviors that are constructive in maintaining mutual respect through the good and bad times in a relationship.

Conflict and disagreement are normal and expected in relationships. Resolving conflicts in a manner agreeable to everyone involves special skills that anyone can learn. It is important to practice conflict resolution and problem solving in your family and teach these skills to your teen, who can apply them to other situations outside your home. "Fighting," or having disagreements, can happen in a healthy way, if both partners know how to "fight fair." When parents provide models of effective interpersonal interactions, they are teaching violence prevention skills. If you feel you aren't able to provide models of these skills, you can find other ways for your teen to learn them, such as through classes or groups offered at community centers or in their school.

Resolving Conflicts and Solving Problems

Successfully resolving conflicts involves honest communication, willingness to listen to others, assertiveness, compromise, and problem-solving skills. You can teach your children the following five-step technique for problem solving.

Five steps for problem solving:

1. Discuss and define the problem from each person's point of view (by listening and communicating clearly).

   Jane: "I want to spend Christmas Day with you, and I want you to come to my house."

   John: "But I want to spend it with my family."

   Jane: "The problem is we both want to be together on Christmas, and we both want to be with our families too."

2. Brainstorm possible solutions.

   John: "We can go to my family's house this year and to yours next year."

   Jane: "I can go to my family's and you can go to yours."

   John: "We can spend half the day with each."

   Jane: "We can spend the day by ourselves and avoid the whole thing."

3. Evaluate and choose a solution that is acceptable to both people (by negotiating).

   John: "We can't go to your family's house and not mine because my family will be too upset and I can't deal with that."

   Jane: "The same is true for my family."

   John: "So . . . we can't avoid our families, and I really want to be with you."

Jane: "Let's split the day between our two families, or go to your family's house on Christmas Eve and to mine on Christmas Day."

John: "Okay. Let's go to my family's on Christmas Eve and to yours on Christmas Day."

4. Implement the solution that has been negotiated.

5. Evaluate the outcome at a later date.

   John: "I'm glad we saw both our families the way we did, but my mother didn't like it that I wasn't there for Christmas dinner."

   Jane: "This worked out just fine for me."

   John: "Maybe next year or for Easter we'll have the holiday dinner with my family."

"Fighting Fair"

How a couple argues can determine the success of a relationship. Fighting fair means communicating respectfully during the process of resolving conflicts. When the goal is to resolve a conflict, you aim not to win but to come to a mutually satisfying solution to the problem. You don't want vengeance, punishment, or control, or to be the one who is "right" so that you make the other person "wrong." A fight is not an excuse to attack your partner about everything that has gone wrong in the relationship or a reason to threaten your partner to get your way. This means being thoughtful about what you say.

There are several things to keep in mind when trying to be fair in a conflict or fight. Parents can use the following principles in conflicts with teens, and they can point out these principles as a way to teach teens these skills.

Ten principles of fighting fair:

1. Keep it real: Focus on the topic or problem at hand (not the person)—no old grudges, and don't use the past as ammunition.

2. Be respectful: No personal attacks, cursing, name-calling, or hitting below the belt.

3. Listen carefully: Try to see your partner's point of view.

4. Express appreciation: Acknowledge when your partner is right or understands what you are saying.

5. Look for compromise, not to win: Seek solutions that satisfy everyone.

6. Avoid exaggerating: Refrain from saying "you always . . ." or "you never . . ."

7. Stick it out: Stay focused until the issue is resolved. Do not walk away unless you agree to take a break to calm down and talk about it again at an agreed-upon time.

8. Refrain from ultimatums or threats: They escalate tension.

9. Pick your battles: Not everything you disagree about is earth-shattering or worth a fight. Sometimes it's better to "let it go."

10. Keep it short: Arguments shouldn't go on for very long. Don't allow the stress of the argument to drag on indefinitely.

Communicating Respectfully

Communication in healthy relationships is most challenging when emotions are high or when feelings are hurt. You can help your teen learn the essential skills for effective communication: how to express opinions, thoughts, and feelings so that they can be heard clearly, and how to listen effectively so that others are heard. Listening well and expressing one's feelings are most important at moments when people are trying to sort out a problem, tension, or emotion. Poor communication can lead to misunderstandings and hurt feelings that create problems, tension, or intense feelings. Abusive communication can be used to punish, hurt, and control the other person.

Parents teach effective communication by modeling and practicing it within the family. A respectful and calm way of responding to one another can allow for clarification and empathy. Teach teenagers how to communicate effectively by practicing the skills yourself.

Use the following guidelines to practice clear and effective communication in healthy relationships.

Ten guidelines for effective communication:

1. Calm yourself so you don't over-react to something someone says or does. Give yourself room to think about how you want to respond.

2. Stop yourself if you have the urge to defend yourself—if your response is defensive, the other person may defend him- or herself too. Then strong feelings could escalate and communication could be blocked.

3. Ask for clarification before responding, to be sure you understand what the other person has expressed. For example, ask, "Do I understand that . . . ?" or "I am hearing that . . . ?"

4. Establish agreed-upon ground rules: for example, not allowing personal attacks, insults, or name-calling, and agreeing that the conversation will stop and be restarted later if this occurs. Another example of a ground rule is to turn off cell phones during the conversation.

5. Show that you are interested and be attentive by maintaining eye contact and avoiding distractions. Sometimes making eye contact doesn't work, especially if the other person is uncomfortable with the subject. In those cases, looking at something else or sitting side-by-side while engaging in the conversation works better. Be aware that people are discouraged from expressing themselves when someone cuts them off, denies their feelings, rolls their eyes, or lectures them.

6. Emotional issues are sometimes best discussed in person rather than by text or e-mail. Talk with your teens about the pros and cons of communicating by text. It's easier, quicker, and abbreviated. It allows for time to think before responding, thus avoiding emotional flare-ups and making emotional conversations easier and more effective. Texts offer a way to begin difficult conversations (e.g., "I need to talk to you about school when I get home"). On the other hand, texts can also be easily misunderstood and may not convey the emotional tone that the sender intends.

7. Encourage communication by asking open-ended questions that can invite conversations; avoid asking questions that only require a "yes" or "no" answer, or answering with only an immediate "yes" or "no" before you understand or thoughtfully respond to the question.

8. Be aware of your nonverbal communication. People often don't listen to words as much as they watch facial expressions or gestures, or hear the speaker's tone of voice. Teens in particular often express themselves with body language and facial expressions more than with words. Teens can learn how to pay attention to their own and others' nonverbal communication.

9. Communication problems sometimes occur when one person makes a request of the other, and it is interpreted as a "demand." Requests become demands when the other person thinks they will be blamed, punished, or made to feel guilty if they don't comply. Marshall Rosenberg, author of *Nonviolent Communication,* notes: "When people hear a demand, they see only two options: submission or rebellion. Either way, the person requesting is perceived as coercive, and the listener's capacity to listen compassionately to the request is diminished."[22]

10. Listen carefully, and express yourself with a combination of empathy and honesty (though not "brutal" honesty). Listen for other people's feelings and needs, trying to understand their feelings about what they are telling you.

Managing Emotions

Healthy relationships require a balance between having and expressing feelings, and being able to handle them so they don't control and overpower the people involved. According to Heather Forbes, "regulation" and "dysregulation" refer to our varying abilities to be in a state of stress and to tolerate stress. As mentioned earlier, regulation is the ability to experience and maintain stress within one's window of tolerance, generally defined as being calm. "Dysregulation" is "the experience of stress outside your window of tolerance," which is often called distressed or "stressed out." Stress, fear, and being overwhelmed interfere with a person's ability to be connected with others.[23]

Parents can help teens develop healthy relationship skills by encouraging them to be engaged, focused, and calm when confronted with intense feelings, fear, or stress. The most beneficial and effective way to "self-regulate" and to manage intense emotions is to practice tools for becoming calm. You can develop your own personal "tool kit" while helping teens to develop their own. Help yourself and your children to develop ways to restore a calm mind and body as part of daily life.

Practice these calming and self-regulating strategies together:

1. Breathe. Because we breathe automatically, we rarely pay attention to it. To calm yourself, guide yourself to pay attention and take deep breaths from the diaphragm or belly. Exhaling is as important as inhaling. One example of a breathing technique is to inhale, expanding the belly, to the count of four, and then bring the breath from the belly to the lungs,

expanding the chest. Then exhale while silently counting to eight. Do this at least three times.

2. Find the stress spot. Locate as precisely as possible where you feel tension, tightness, discomfort, distress, or fear in your body. Where does it show up? Mindfully breathe into that part of your body, become aware of your body's responses, and then release the tension. This brings you to the present moment, stops your thoughts from spinning and agitating, and helps you physically calm your nervous system.

3. Use imagery. Imagine a place that is peaceful, safe, warm, and secure. Imagine yourself in that place, and focus on your feelings, enjoying the benefit of those feelings.

4. Connect with yourself on an ongoing basis. What do you do that gives you a sense of being centered and feeling peaceful, safe, and secure? For many people, spending time in nature does this. For others, listening to music calms them. Daily meditation is another powerful way to connect with yourself.

5. Connect with others. Find sources of emotional support, safety, and security among your friends and relatives, or through organizations such as AA or other support groups.

6. Take time-outs to physically and mentally calm down. Take a walk or go to another room to breathe and work on soothing yourself when agitated or stressed.

Expressing Anger

Anger is a normal feeling that is neither "good" nor "bad," and it needs to be expressed in healthy ways. Repressing anger, hurting oneself, or raging at someone else is not constructive. Healthier ways of expression include verbally communicating your feelings to someone, using artistic expression, writing in a journal, exercising, or taking action to change a situation.

Here are some steps to making safe choices for expressing anger:

1. Recognize the physical signs (for example, increase in heart rate, racing thoughts, feeling hot) when you are feeling angry.

   Joseph was waiting for his girlfriend, Sara, to arrive at the coffee shop. After ten minutes, he started worrying about her, then he became angry that she hadn't shown up or texted him that she'd be late. He started imagining that she wasn't going to show up and was going to leave him hanging there. Then he started imagining that she was with her friends ("who are more important than I am!") or, worse, with another guy. He realized that he was pacing and obsessing, and getting more and more agitated.

2. Calm your body's reaction. The best way to do this is to pay attention to your breathing and take deep breaths.

   He stopped himself and took a few deep breaths.

3. Identify your judgmental and/or blaming thoughts (violence is often a result of the belief that other people cause our pain and should be punished) and reframe your thoughts ("Is there another way to understand what is happening?").

   He decided to stop assuming that Sara intended to hurt him . . .

4. Recognize what has triggered you, especially needs of yours that aren't being met.

   . . . and realized that he liked her a lot and he felt insecure, afraid that she might not feel the same way about him. He even thought that maybe he could talk to her about how he felt about her when they would have time alone together later.

He remembered that it was more likely that she was delayed at school and couldn't use her phone.

5. Stop and think so that you can make good choices. Think about how your actions and reactions may have an impact on the other person.

   Feeling calmer, he decided to listen to music on his phone while he waited for her. When Sara got there, the urge to yell at her for being late had gone away.

6. Come up with a safe way to express yourself. Find a way to channel your anger into healthy ways of expressing it or taking action to meet the needs that aren't being met.

   He told her that he had felt mad at her when he had to wait so long, but he figured that she had a good reason. He asked her what happened, and listened to her story.

   Joseph found a way to accept his feelings, make choices about how he thought and behaved, express his feelings about Sara and about her being late, and listen to her.

Appreciating the Other Person

People often overlook the opportunity to express appreciation, regardless of their age. We tend to be quicker to express what is wrong rather than what is right. Everyone needs to know that a person who is important to them appreciates them. So often people feel that the "gifts" they give and bring to a relationship are taken for granted. Marshall Rosenberg, author of *Nonviolent Communication,*[24] describes the components to expressing appreciation in relationships: "This is what you did; this is what I feel; and this is the need of mine that was met." He also emphasizes that appreciation is important to "celebrate" a good moment or action between people, not to manipulate it or to get something one wants. Beware of adding "but" at the end of an appreciative statement, because it negates the positive remark.

Receiving appreciation gracefully can be difficult for many people. Rosenberg says to accept appreciation "joyfully," and with empathy, showing that you have heard the feelings the other person has expressed.[25]

Teach your teen how to express and receive appreciation by noticing and expressing the things you appreciate about him or her, and by explaining how important it is to show and express this in all relationships, especially intimate ones.

Parenting for Healthy Relationships

As parents, what can we do to prevent relationship abuse from happening to our teen? What can we do to prepare our children for healthy relationships? How can we teach them not to be abusive toward or to be abused by someone they love? This chapter will be helpful for parents of preteens, teens, and young adults who are in an abusive relationship, or for parents of teens who are just beginning to date.

One possible challenge for parents is that they might not have spent much time thinking about what makes relationships healthy, or how to talk about relationships with teens. It is also challenging for parents to think about their own relationships in this way.

Teen relationships provide a way to experiment and practice for future long-term relationships and marriages. It is critical for parents to pay attention and help teens use this time to develop their healthy relationship skills, in dating and in general. Parents have an important role: to model, teach, and support these skills for developing good relationships as well as preventing abuse.

You have already taken the most important first step in preventing relationship abuse: By reading this book, you are acknowledging that abuse can happen in teen relationships. You are also finding out that it can happen not only to "other people," but also to families just like your own. Denial, or the "not my daughter syndrome," hinders parents from preparing their children to be on the alert for relationship violence. The best approach to preparing children for this is (1) to teach them skills that form the basis for healthy relationships, which we will cover in this chapter, and (2) to teach them to think about their own safety, which we will address in chapter 8.

Developmental Vulnerabilities and Strengths

Adolescence is a time when tremendous growth takes place—physically, socially, and mentally. Research based on imaging of teen brains has revealed that the brain takes much longer to develop and mature than we had previously thought. There are substantial brain changes during adolescence. Teens do not have all the hardware yet to think like an adult; the adolescent brain goes through major remodeling that starts around puberty and continues into the early twenties. Teens need parents and caregivers in their lives more than ever to help them with their brain development.[26]

Teens and young adults undergo a major developmental reorganization between the ages of twelve and twenty-five. Their brains don't grow so much as undergo "pruning" and become more efficient, allowing them to get better at integrating memory and experience into their decisions. David Dobbs, a writer for *National Geographic* magazine says, "When this development proceeds normally, [teens] get better at balancing impulse, desire, goals, self-interest, rules, ethics and even altruism, generating behavior that is more complex and, sometimes, at least, more sensible. But at times . . . the brain does this work clumsily. It's hard to get all those new cogs to mesh. . . . The [new] 'adaptive-adolescent' story casts the teen less as a rough draft than as an exquisitely sensitive, highly adaptable creature wired almost perfectly for the job of moving from the safety of home into the complicated world outside."[27]

Not all teens develop in the same ways and same time frames, and there are many steps forward and backward during these years.

One day a parent may be talking to their stable, mature, thoughtful seventeen-year-old, and the next day a cranky, emotional thirteen-year-old shows up.

Adolescents are frequently curious and open to new experiences and risk taking, which can be useful. They reason about risks as much as adults do, but they weigh risks and rewards differently: They value the reward more heavily than adults do. This gets them to try new things and expands their learning.

Social connections are especially rewarding to teens; these connections help them mature as they invest in the future and learn new ways of engaging others and being themselves. All of these characteristics of adolescence help teens accomplish a very difficult challenge: learning how to negotiate their surroundings so that they can move successfully from family to the outside world, where they will function as adults. This is not an easy process, and this time of life is full of potential challenges that can throw off healthy development, such as alcohol, drugs, violence, difficulties in school, and problematic relationships.

David Dobbs emphasizes the importance of parents in this process. "When parents engage and guide their teens with a light but steady hand, staying connected but allowing independence, their kids generally do much better in life."[28] Parents must adapt their ways of parenting to accommodate their changing teens.

Psychologists have divided adolescence into three stages: early (ages 11–14), middle (ages 15–18), and late (ages 19–21). The brains of young adults are still developing and maturing between the ages of 22 and 25, which could be considered a "late, late" adolescence stage.

Early Adolescence (Ages 11–14)

Preteens and young teens experience huge hormonal and physical changes, accompanied by awkward feelings about their bodies and worries about being normal. They may feel like hiding their developing bodies, or they may feel proud that they are becoming "grown up." Girls tend to mature faster than boys, and sometimes girls physically develop before they are emotionally ready to deal with their new, womanly bodies. Scientists have recently documented that puberty is starting younger than it did years ago. Because of these physical changes, preteens and young teens may suddenly demand more privacy.

Children this age have emotional highs and lows as their hormones fluctuate. Their conversations with peers often seem overly dramatic. Peer groups have increasing influence, and they may learn about sex from their peers. They become more interested in popular culture, media, video games, and the Internet. They may turn more to peers than adults for information, and peers are not the best source of information about sex and relationships.

This stage of adolescence is challenging for parents for many reasons, but especially because preteens and young teens begin to test rules and limits.

Middle Adolescence (Ages 15–18)

Fifteen- to eighteen-year-olds are self-involved, concerned about their appearance and sexual attractiveness, and preoccupied with fitting in to a peer group.

Intellectual interests gain importance for this group, and their capacity for moral reasoning grows. They become more focused on school and more anxious about their academic performance (striving to do well, having too much interference to do well, or withdrawing out of frustration at not doing well). They might have unrealistically high expectations of their abilities and worry about failure. Parents may appreciate these teenagers' improved capacity for setting goals, abstract thought, and thinking about the meaning of life.

Adolescents in this age group tend to spend more time away from home and with peers, and they demand more autonomy and independence. They negotiate new boundaries and test limits with their parents. They complain that parents interfere with their independence, and that parents don't trust their capabilities to handle things by themselves. They appear to have a low opinion of their parents and other adults, and withdraw from them.

This age group begins to have intimate, often sexual, relationships and frequently changes relationships. They more clearly define their sexual orientation.

Late Adolescence (Ages 19–21)

During this stage, identity becomes firmer. These young adults are better able to delay gratification, and they have greater concern about their futures. They aren't as self-involved, and they show more concern for others. They are thinking about their lives as "grown-ups," what kind of work they might want to do to support themselves, and their roles in life. Their emotions are more stable, they are more focused in their work, and they are better able to make good decisions. They are more independent and self-reliant. They get along better with their parents, and value them again. They are able to express ideas, and to negotiate and compromise. Sometimes the stresses of the transition to adulthood—for example, going away to college—can make this age group vulnerable to serious emotional distress, binge drinking, and drug abuse.

Young Adult (Ages 22–25)

Young adults are ready for intimacy and commitment in their relationships. They may be preoccupied with their own growth and goals—in relationships and education, careers, and jobs. Their relationships with their parents improve. When teens enter young adulthood, their thinking capacities, relationship skills, and ability to regulate emotions have improved, but they still aren't fully prepared to cope with the demands of a diverse, global, technological, rapidly changing world and the pressures to function independently as adults. If all goes well, biology and environment bring a surge of growth paralleling those of childhood and adolescence. The vulnerabilities to binge drinking, suicide, school problems, mental illness, and other risks continue from late adolescence, but gradually young adults become more stable.

Parents' Roles

Parents have an important role to play in a teen's developing ability to have good relationships both with peers and with intimate partners. Parents' roles and how they influence their children change as teens grow and develop more capabilities, autonomy, and independence. As their children go through the stages of adolescence, parents evolve from being "managers" who are actively in charge of almost everything in their children's lives, to "consultants" who provide an important connection, along with values, information, and feedback, supporting their children's increasing abilities to make decisions for themselves.

Even though peers are important in all the stages of adolescence, and cultural messages support the idea that peers are paramount and parents are irrelevant to teens, parents are more important than peers. Psychiatrist Gabor Maté, in his book *Hold On to Your Kids,*[29] makes a valuable point that parents too often give up influence to their teens' peers, which leaves teens without adult connection and influence during a time when they need it. The ways they need parents may change, but the need is still there.

Parents remain important influences in the parent-child relationship, as teens experience their parents' gradually increasing respect for their children's ability to make their own decisions. By adapting parenting styles to teens' developmental changes, parents maintain connection.

According to Michael Riera, author of *Staying Connected to Your Teenager,* teens want to change the terms of parents' influence and engagement. Teens want to run their own lives. Parents have trouble understanding this shift in power, and thus the battle lines are drawn. Parents generally want more control than teens are ready or able to relinquish. In a consultant role, parents give up the illusion of power in favor of real influence. Teens still want their parents involved in their decisions, but it is a matter of degree. "During adolescence, teenagers need to extend away from their parents all the while staying connected to their parents. Their job is to extend, [the parents'] job is to connect."[30]

The only exceptions to the consultant role are when teens' health and safety are endangered; in these cases, parents must actively intervene. Of course, determining when health and safety are in danger is a matter of perspective that most parents and teens disagree on. Riera does not suggest "laissez-faire parenting; in fact . . . consultant parenting is more demanding and time-consuming than managerial parenting. Here's the payoff, though: it is more rewarding for both adolescent and parent."[31]

This approach successfully avoids two common errors that can occur when parenting teenagers: treating them like children (over-parenting or overmanaging) or treating them like adults (underparenting or abandonment). Overparenting is avoided by understanding that this consultant role involves much less doing; underparenting is avoided by being present and actively listening in order to make the most of your "consultations."

When teens are in trouble, especially in their intimate relationships—which they protect from parents' interference more than any other aspect of their lives—overparenting or underparenting doesn't work. Parents who try to control their teens, maintaining the illusion that they have more power over them than they actually have, inadvertently lead teens to accept sneakiness and lying as viable strategies in their relationships with their parents.

Self-Reflection
To be authentic and effective when talking with teens about healthy relationships, parents must first think about what a healthy relationship means to them. Parents can do this by examining their own

values, feelings, and experiences with relationships. They can ask themselves: What have I modeled? What were my first relationships like? What problems came up? How did I resolve conflicts when I was young, and how do I resolve them now? What are my children learning from the media? Do I show them ways to think critically about what they see? Am I communicating my values and allowing them to develop their own?

Teens learn about navigating relationships and treating others more from watching what parents and other adults *do* than from anything they *say*. This does not mean parents have to be perfect. It simply means they need to be honest about their own experiences, successes, and failures—especially if they want teens to be honest about theirs.

Challenging Values and Attitudes

Parents have an active role to play in preventing violence. We all must challenge the attitudes and institutions within our own cultures and communities that create and sustain a tolerance for violence in intimate relationships, and violence in general.

If we do not take action when we witness violence in our families, communities, or the media, we are actually contributing to the problem. When ignored, violence can get worse. The idea of being an "upstander" is important for parents and teens. Parents can speak up and get involved, and they can teach teens to speak up and get involved.

Parents may be aware of the extent to which children are exposed to justifications for violence. We are all surrounded by violent images: in our neighborhoods, in movies, on television. Violence is accepted as a way to resolve conflicts and as a means to retaliate against wrongdoing. "He made me so mad, I hit him." "They started it, but I finished it." These statements are often uttered between peers and, in different contexts, between countries at war.

Parents can prevent violence by challenging these mistaken ideas and the damaging images of "justified" violence. When they recognize the presence of these attitudes, they can speak up. If they do not, violence in relationships remains invisible, tolerated, and accepted. Many girls have told us that when they were hit by their boyfriends in school or in a public place such as a mall, people walked by and said nothing. Both the boy and girl then believed there was nothing wrong with the boyfriend's behavior. Silence reinforces the impression among teens that violence in relationships is normal.

In everyday family life, there are opportunities to challenge mistaken assumptions about violence. Parents can help children critique what they see in the media and discuss alternatives to what they see. They can repeatedly assert that no one deserves to be emotionally, verbally, or physically abused, and that violence is never justified. During this process, parents usually find they have to confront some of their own values and attitudes. We must all learn to expand our awareness of the messages about violence that surround us.

Parents also have an important role in influencing policies in their children's schools and in their communities. Schools and communities must have educational programs, policies, and protocols in place to inform everyone that relationship abuse is a real problem, how to recognize it, how to prevent it, and how to intervene when it occurs on campus. Dating violence prevention policies should be incorporated alongside other school safety policies.

Teaching Teens about Healthy Relationships

The teen years are a time of exploring and learning about relationships. Teens often don't know what constitutes a healthy relationship, or have not defined what this means to them personally.

Parents can encourage children to think about their relationships, both present and future, by talking to them about healthy relationships, pointing out features of good relationships they see around them or in books and movies, and opening a dialogue in which teens can think about what they look for in a boyfriend or girlfriend. To identify the differences between relationships that are built on respect and those that are not, describe examples from your own experience. Support teens for thinking for themselves if they express an opinion different from yours.

Of course, experience is the best teacher, but parents can help teens develop their own ideas and good judgment about what is healthy for them. Parents can't prevent broken hearts from failed relationships, but they can help their teens to strive for what is healthy and positive, and to seek it in all areas of their lives, including relationships.

Violence prevention measures can be implemented in a multitude of ways and settings. Skills for healthy relationships can be encouraged and learned from many different sources, including friends, school, media, and families. As parents, we can be a tremendous resource for our teens when we are aware and informed, foster good self-esteem, encourage assertiveness, talk about sensitive and volatile issues with teens, empower them, communicate openly with them, and respect their ideas and feelings.

As noted in the pamphlet "Healthy Relationships Protect Teens," children of all ages need reliable and accurate information about healthy relationships: what a healthy relationship feels like, looks like, and sounds like. One of the most effective ways of teaching a child about healthy relationships is to model positive qualities in your own relationships. Parents must not forget that even when they think teens are not listening to or watching their parents, they often are.

Preteens and young teens start to explore the idea of a boyfriend or girlfriend by interacting at school or through cell phones, instant messaging, or social networking sites. They often have relationships with someone they consider a boyfriend or girlfriend, but do not consider themselves "dating." Parents should consider "hanging out" with friends at the mall or going to a movie in a group as an early form of dating.[32]

Guidelines for Conversations with Teens

The following section contains guidelines for having conversations with teens about healthy relationships, what teens are thinking about, and what's going on in their lives. (These guidelines are also provided in appendix C for easy reference.) Although the information parents uncover is important, the process of having these conversations is equally critical. It is important for parents to be seen by teens as available whenever something comes up that requires adult assistance. Teens need to know that it is safe to tell their parents about problems that arise in their relationships.

Create Opportunities

Parents can create opportunities for discussion by doing the following:

1. "Show up" in a relaxed manner when you know that your teen is available. For example, hang out with him or her late at night or drive someplace together. Make yourself available.

2. Ask questions about something you read or saw, and be curious about your teen's opinion. For example, "I read about teens dating at age thirteen. Have you heard about that? What do you think about that?"

Take Advantage of Opportunities ("Teachable Moments")

Parents can use moments when the subject of relationships comes up to discuss healthy relationships.

1. After seeing a movie with your teen, ask about the relationships in the movie and what your teen thought worked and didn't work. Would he or she like to be in a relationship like that? What is your teen looking for in a boyfriend or girlfriend?

2. When you see something in the media about famous actors, sports figures, or others, discuss their healthy or unhealthy relationships.

3. If there is a situation involving the relationship of someone you know, engage your teen and find out what he or she thinks about the situation.

4. Notice when your teen is quiet and hanging around, as if he or she wants to ask you something. Sit with your teen and wait, sharing space. This will encourage him or her to talk without feeling pushed.

Conversation-Starters

Use open-ended questions to start a conversation with your teen, and then listen to his or her feelings and opinions. Have a relaxed dialogue about your different points of view. Here are some examples of open-ended questions you can ask your child:

1. "What do you think about _____ [a situation in a TV show or YouTube clip about a family or relationship]?"

2. "By the way, I saw your friend at the mall with her boyfriend. They've been going out for a while. How do you think their relationship is going?"

3. "I saw a story in the news about that pop star and her boyfriend getting back together. What do your friends think about it?"

4. "What if your date drinks at a party and wants to drive you home? How would you handle that?" Think of vignettes or scenarios that your teen is likely to encounter.

5. "Did you hear about _____ [a news or neighborhood story]? What do you think about it?"

6. "What are all the ways to look at _____ [a relationship situation]?" Ask about ways teens might act with girlfriends or boyfriends, and brainstorm ideas. For example, "He wants to spend all of his time with her, and wants her to spend all of her time with him. What do you think?"

7. "Did you notice how different guys treated _____
   [a woman in a movie you watched together]? Which guy do
   you think did the right thing? Why?"

Tips

1. Talking with young teens about difficult issues isn't a single
   or onetime conversation; it's an ongoing dialogue. Keep the
   lines of communication open.

2. To have an effective conversation, carefully select the time
   and place (private). Choose a moment when you can give
   your undivided attention and listen without being overly
   emotional or judgmental.

3. Avoid critical comments even when you don't agree. To keep
   a dialogue going, make sure to show that you respect and
   welcome your child's opinion.

4. Allow your teen to ask you anything. Listen to his or her
   comments and questions. If you don't know the answer, say
   so. Don't worry about being an expert. Be honest and find
   the answer together.

5. Ask direct questions, but don't overwhelm your teen with too
   many questions. It's a conversation, not an interrogation.

6. Talk at your teen's level and use examples. Share your own
   mistakes and what you learned from them.[33]

Teaching Teens to Be Safe

As parents we may say something like, "I'll kill anyone who hurts my daughter," as if saying these words creates a circle of protection around our children. But this attitude may keep us from teaching children skills of their own that are necessary for preventing violence.

We must teach our children not only to be cautious of the danger that can come from a stranger, but also to be prepared for potential violence from someone they know. The majority of incidents of violence against women and girls are perpetrated by acquaintances and intimate partners. Our daughters and sons need to have information about abuse and how to prevent it.

For example, a teen who has learned not to get into a car with a stranger (good advice at any age) will need more complex strategies to handle being in a car with an acquaintance who becomes violent. Violence prevention strategies for dating situations that take place in a car may involve getting away to a safe place, getting help, or defending oneself physically.

Teaching Your Teens to Protect Themselves

Although there is a great deal parents can do to protect children and teens from violence, it is also important to be realistic about what parents cannot do. It is impossible to completely control teens' environments as they venture out into new situations. Parents can't eliminate danger, but they can help their children think about reducing the risks they take. The best safety strategies are not based on parental protectiveness or rules, but on teens' ability to think about choices and options for taking action to protect themselves. Teaching teens to be aware, alert, and assertive gives them the ability to think and take action. Parents can empower teens by encouraging them to take self-defense training.

Awareness

Awareness is the foundation of self-protection and personal security. It involves paying attention to what is happening in a given situation, with a mind free of misconceptions.

Parents can talk to preteens and teens about the myths and realities of dating violence. Sometimes teens—and adults as well—are lulled into a false sense of security: "It can't happen to me." Misconceptions and stereotypes reinforce and justify the use of violence and keep people from taking action to prevent or stop it. Some common misconceptions are the following:

- Girls like abuse or they wouldn't put up with it.
- Guys hit and yell to show their love.
- A guy has to show his girlfriend who is boss.

As you become more informed about what is true and what is not, you can discuss these harmful misconceptions with your teen.

There is other information in this book that you can discuss with your teen. Teens can learn the warning signs of an abusive relationship (chapter 3) and the patterns that can be recognized, such as the cycle of violence (chapter 2). You might also suggest that your teen read *In Love and In Danger: A Teen's Guide to Breaking Free of Abusive Relationships* by Barrie Levy.

In order to stay safe, it is important for teens to be aware of vulnerability and potential risks in relationships. Teens must be empowered to take care of themselves by thinking about the risks inherent in their activities and then making their own plans for their safety. It helps to begin this process with children when they are young, because as they get older teens resist acknowledging their vulnerability, both to themselves and to their parents.

There are many ways to start this process. When a teen asks for permission to go somewhere, before saying yes or no, a parent can ask him or her to evaluate the safety of the situation. Asking teens to think about the situation in advance, and to think about the concerns of parents, is helpful because teens learn to think clearly rather than waiting for their parents' reactions. It also teaches them to think of the situation's impact on their parents. Ask teens: "What precautions are you taking?" "How can I be assured you are planning for your own safety?" "How am I going to have peace of mind while you are out?"

For example, if the teen wants to go to a party, ask: "How are you getting there and back?" "If _____ [friend's name] is going to drive you back, what if he [or she] decides to drink? Then what will you do?" "What kind of backup plans do you have for ensuring your safety or for reacting to an emergency?" In this way the teen is encouraged to think about his or her own safety. Another way to teach teens to think about their safety is to brainstorm all the possible ways to handle a variety of scenarios. For example, you can ask your teen, "What if . . . ?" and describe a scenario or a situation he or she might encounter when out with friends, on a date with someone new, or when out with a boyfriend or girlfriend. Another way to prompt discussion is to bring up events that have actually happened, for example, a news report or the experience of a neighbor or a friend. Without having a predetermined right or wrong answer, you can brainstorm together all the possibilities for handling the situation. Similar discussions can take place after seeing a movie, a television show, or something your teen has seen and is curious about.

Another kind of awareness—self-awareness—involves knowing what we want and don't want, what we like and don't like, what is important to us, what our values are, and what motivates us. Developing self-awareness is as important for teens as it is for adults. Parents can help children gain self-awareness by talking with them about what they believe, what they care about, and what they value. If we are intent on imposing our values on our children, we keep them from developing their own values and learning to think for themselves. It is important to support teens' sense of autonomy in order to encourage them to think, choose, and make decisions for themselves. They can be encouraged to think about the different ways to handle love and sexual relationships, what the consequences are of each, and how they can decide what is best for them in a relationship. They need to know that they have real choices about the way they will lead their lives.

Assertiveness

Assertiveness is an important skill in preventing violence. In rape situations, for example, assertive responses have proven a successful self-defense technique in the majority of resisted assaults. Assertiveness is the ability to exercise one's own rights while respecting the rights of others. Being assertive means communicating exactly what you want and don't want, standing up for yourself, and stating your opinions, thoughts, and feelings without abusing others.

Developing assertiveness skills can be as challenging for adults as it is for teens. One mother reported to us, "I realized that I would do anything to defend my children, but I could not imagine standing up for myself. I had to take a long, hard look at the values I was taught."

This mother was also referring to the values taught in a society that defines assertiveness according to stereotyped expectations of masculine and feminine behavior. When boys learn to behave in stereotypically masculine ways, they feel that they are supposed to be aggressive and to expect to get their way despite how anyone else feels.

When girls learn to behave in stereotypically feminine ways, they feel that they are supposed to accept what others want from them, to be passive, and that it is selfish to be direct about what they want. With these kinds of expectations, neither boys nor girls learn to be assertive.

Boys and girls must learn the differences between passive (under-assertive) behavior, aggressive (over-assertive) behavior, and assertive behavior. Parents can help teens develop assertiveness skills by pointing out these differences and by demonstrating assertive behavior. They can also encourage their teens to communicate assertively with family members.

Passive, or under-assertive, people tend to make excuses for their actions and behavior and often speak in a soft, inaudible voice. They apologize for what they are about to say, and they are afraid to disagree with others. They have trouble saying no when someone wants something from them. They frequently blame themselves when something goes wrong, and they may look away from the person they are talking to. They give mixed messages about what they want or what's bothering them. They focus too little on their own wants and needs, and focus more on the wants and needs of others.

Aggressive, or over-assertive, people often don't allow others to speak, and act overbearing and intimidating. They yell or speak loudly and blame others when there is a problem. In a conflict or a disagreement, they frequently take the offensive without listening to others. They ignore other people's needs or wishes, and they sometimes resort to verbal abuse or physical violence when they don't get their way.

Assertive people communicate their feelings clearly and state their opinions directly. They look directly at the other person and give honest feedback. They give clear messages with their words as well as with their body language. They do not attempt to control or manipulate others. They accept the consequences of, and responsibility for, their assertiveness. Assertive people recognize that openly expressing feelings and opinions to others is risky, and they choose to behave either under-assertively, assertively, or aggressively according to the particular situation.

Teens can learn to decide what the most appropriate response is in a given situation. Deciding when to be assertive is as important as knowing how to be assertive. Sometimes it may be necessary to de-escalate an explosive situation by replacing an assertive response with an under-assertive one. Sometimes it may be necessary to change from an assertive stance to an aggressive one—to protect oneself and get away from a physically violent situation, for example. It takes practice to develop assertiveness skills and the flexibility to use them well.

Encourage your teen to take a self-defense course to develop assertiveness skills. A good self-defense course trains people to prepare for and to be able to think in dangerous situations. In addition to teaching safety strategies and physical self-defense techniques, these courses help people to develop their awareness, to assess a situation, and to make good choices.

You can practice the following technique: Ask your teen, "Have you ever said yes when you wanted to say no?" Describe some of your own experiences. Discuss how you felt afterward, the feeling that "I should have said [blank]." Practice with each other, describing what you might have said or done if you were given another chance in each situation. Don't worry about whether your teen comes up with the "right answer." The point is for your teen to practice effectively articulating what he or she wants or needs.

Safety in Social Situations

Strangers quickly become acquaintances in social situations, and teens may wind up "dating" someone they barely know. When they know a person, however superficially, teens might ignore their instincts or let their guard down. Guide your teen to understand that in a social situation, it is wise not to assume that he or she is safe.

Unfortunately for today's teens, due to the prevalence of dating violence and date rape, prepping for a party or date involves more than choosing an outfit or doing their hair. They need to be aware of the potential risks in each social situation and take precautions. Make sure your teen knows about the following tips for safety in social situations, whether meeting new people or going out with someone they know well (and might trust). These precautions are important even when going out with someone they have been dating for a while.

1. Before leaving on a date, know your plans and make sure a parent or friend knows the plans and when you'll be back.

2. Always have enough cash with you for an emergency (for example, a cab ride home).

3. Make sure your cell phone is fully charged before you go out.

4. If you're going out in a group and in a car, choose a driver who will stay sober so everyone will get home safely.

5. Make an agreement with friends to keep track of one another and to be sure everyone is safe before leaving a party, dance, club, or other social situation.

6. If you leave a party with someone you don't know well or that you didn't come with, be sure to tell another person you are leaving and with whom. Ask a friend to call you later to make sure you arrived home safely.

7. Plan ahead how to get home or to a safe place if you might find yourself in an uncomfortable or threatening situation.

8. Always meet someone you haven't dated before in a public place rather than in someone's home. If you are living with your parents, have a new date meet your parents before going out.

9. Be aware of your alcohol tolerance, since coerced sex and sexual assaults often occur when the victim and/or perpetrator uses alcohol. Resist the pressure to drink excessively or use drugs at a party or on a date; it is easier to take care of

yourself if you are not under the influence. Be aware of how much your date drinks too. Be aware that drugs and alcohol are sometimes used deliberately to incapacitate victims.

10. Set clear sexual limits, even in ongoing relationships. If you are being pressured to have sex or engage in certain sexual acts when you don't want to, recognize that this is abusive. Be firm in your refusal and extricate yourself as quickly as possible from the situation.

11. Always trust your instincts! They are more likely to be right than wrong, and if they are wrong, you can always apologize. If a situation makes you uncomfortable, try to be calm and think of a way to remove yourself from it.

12. Maintain your independence. Don't allow your date to make all the decisions about where you go, and don't rely only on your date for transportation. Make sure you have alternative transportation or ways to get home.[34]

Using Technology Safely

Social networking is a popular form of communication for both teens and adults. Parents often use it to keep in touch with their children for safety reasons, to communicate about changing plans, and to know where their children are and what they are doing. Teens are connected to one another, and to the larger world, via digital technology. Even though teens easily navigate the digital world, they have limited maturity and life experiences, so they are susceptible to getting into trouble with these ever-evolving ways of socializing. Preteens and teens often have boyfriends or girlfriends they haven't met or talked to in person. It is more challenging for parents to pay attention to this aspect of teens' lives because using technology to socialize is less visible to parents.

Parents' involvement in their teens' use of technology evolves as their children get older. As soon as teens start using social media, parents must talk to them about its benefits and risks, and monitor their use of social networking sites as they learn to use those sites. Discuss good judgment, what it means, and the consequences of using poor judgment. Here are some other tips for technology safety:

1. Tell preteens and teens never to give out personal information online.

2. Sexting (sending sexually explicit messages or nude photos of yourself or anyone else) is never safe and can cause serious and long-lasting harm. It may even be illegal.

3. Remind preteens and teens that once something is posted on the Internet, it can't be deleted. It is there forever.

4. Establish limits that fit the teen's age, such as requiring everyone in the family to leave cell phones in the kitchen overnight. Not being allowed to sleep next to a phone can reduce opportunities for relationship abuse.

5. Remind teens to set appropriate and safe levels of privacy on social networking sites.

6. Alert your teen to the ways that technology can be used to cause harm, such as bullying, stalking and tracking, spreading rumors, sexting, hurtful gossip, threats, and harassment.

7. Try to keep up with what teens know about technology. Ask them to teach you, and talk with other parents.

8. Ask your teen to invite you to be a "friend" on their social networking sites.[35]

9

Effects on the Family

A battering relationship can cause an emotional rollercoaster for every member of the family. Margaret's nineteen-year-old daughter Molly has been seeing William for two years. Margaret says:

> We're walking on eggshells. I'm afraid to tell my husband about her new bruises. I worry about her brothers getting in trouble because they want to beat him up. Molly tells her sister things and makes her swear not to tell me. Then when she gets hurt, her sister feels guilty and I get mad at her for not telling me sooner. When Molly and William are getting along, she invites him over and she wants us to act as if everything is okay. We've called the police, we've been to the hospital. She breaks up with him. We go through so much, and then she goes back.

If your daughter is in a battering relationship, she probably does the same thing. She feels close to her batterer when he is not being abusive, and she is secretive or angry with you. Then, after he has been violent, she feels hurt and angry, and may seek support from you. Eventually they make up, and she gets close to him again. As her relationship with him goes back and forth, so does her relationship with you.

It is emotionally wrenching for parents to see a child going through this. The usual teenage emotional rollercoaster of drama and moodiness is difficult enough, but dealing with a battering relationship as well can be a nightmare for parents.

Your reactions to your daughter and her boyfriend engage you in their emotional rollercoaster. Everyone in the family—other children or extended family who are close—responds differently, so you not only react to your daughter and her boyfriend, but to one another. The entire family is eventually on the rollercoaster.

Often parents expend considerable effort and hard work to confront the violence. It is a natural response to try to protect your child. The stress and strain of figuring out what to do, and of dealing with your daughter's unwillingness to cooperate or her resentment of your "interference," can be exhausting. Adaliz, age nineteen, describes what her parents went through:

> My parents found out I was still seeing him. My friends would tell their mothers, who would tell my mom. She would question me, but I would lie about seeing him. My father tried to tell me he's bad for me. They did everything they could to stop me from seeing him. [They] hunted for a different school for me. My dad would take me and pick me up [from school] every day. I couldn't go anywhere. I couldn't make calls. My parents answered the phone, and wouldn't let me talk to Richard if he called. All I wanted was to be with Richard. So I ran away from home to be with him. I thought my dad was a mean person. Now I realize that he didn't . . . want me to be hurt. I realize what my parents went through.

Effects on Parents

The communication between spouses/partners can be challenging when so much focus is on their child's dramatic ups and downs. Conflicts with your spouse about your child's situation may seriously affect your relationship as a couple. Think about how this is affecting both of you. Do you feel conflicted about your alliances, feeling torn between your spouse and your child? Perhaps you want, or demand of each other, a united stand in dealing with your teen, but disagree about which approach to take. You may be upset with the way your spouse deals with your teen, or your spouse may be upset with your approach. Do you keep secrets from your spouse to protect her or him? For example, you may try to keep her or him from being frightened or worried, and hide information about how serious the violence really is. Or you may hide information to keep your spouse from becoming upset. Do you try to keep your teen from being rejected by your spouse? Are you and your teen's other parent separated or divorced? Sometimes old conflicts, difficulties communicating, or some other problem from a past relationship interferes with parents being able to understand or empathize with one another, or to work well together to deal with a situation. Divorced or separated parents may be seeing the teen's relationship or the abuse very differently or may be getting different stories about what is happening. Many parents find themselves in a mediating role, trying to keep trouble from starting between family members.

Don, father of fourteen-year-old Patty, says:

> My wife and I are two opposing forces. She talks to Nick, even though he's so cruel to our daughter, Patty. I feel like we should take a stand. I have no patience with them, and my wife and I end up fighting about what to do. On the other hand, while I can't talk to Patty or Nick, my wife knows what's going on. Patty confides in her. I hope my wife and I can make it through this.

Two parents may react very differently to a child's abusive relationship, and to each incident or situation that arises. One parent (often the father) may be angry and feel betrayed when the child defies rules in order to see her abuser. The other parent (often the mother), afraid of pushing the child away from the family and toward the abuser, may be more willing to compromise on the rules. One parent may refuse to get involved, and the other may be preoccupied with the child's being in danger. One parent may be working hard to help the child after everyone else in the family has washed their hands of the situation.

Many mothers have told us of their fears about their husband's violence toward their daughter's abusive boyfriend—even if their husband had never been violent before. They had never seen him so enraged, explosive, and ready to do harm to another person. Fathers have told us they feel defied, pushed to the limit, betrayed, and unable to cope with the intensity of their anger. However, sometimes it is the father or stepfather who remains calm as the mother becomes enraged.

What Parents Have Told Us about Their Feelings

- I am vigilant, dreading a call from a hospital or police.
- When I can't deal with it anymore, I catch myself thinking it's not so bad.
- I feel I have lost my daughter. I don't know her anymore.
- I feel so angry and manipulated when, after helping her, she goes back to him.
- I feel guilty. What did we do to her that she puts up with this?
- I've done the best I can. There isn't anything else I can do.
- At times I feel hopeful that she's getting stronger.
- I feel so relieved when she's safe and acts like her old self again.
- My husband and I can't talk about this anymore.
- I'm so stressed I can't sleep, I've lost weight, and I'm smoking two packs a day.

***What Mothers Who Have Been Abused Themselves Have Told Us
about Their Feelings***

- I can't believe that my son is hurting his girlfriend the way his father hurt me.

- I feel so guilty. I must be responsible in some way for what my children learned from me that they have this in their lives like I did.

- I feel angry all over again with my ex-husband who abused me.

- I try to talk to my daughter about what she's going through because I have been through it too, but she won't listen to me. She says it's not the same, and gets mad at me, blaming me for what happened to me.

There may be more than two parents in your family—for example, if parents have divorced and remarried. There may be other adults involved besides parents—for example, if your child is also being raised by grandparents or other extended family members. Parental relationships may not be legally defined as "married"—for example, if the parents are gay men or lesbians in states that don't legally recognize same-sex marriage, or if a parent is newly involved with someone who participates in the parenting. While a more complicated constellation of family members can make it more difficult to deal with the abusive relationship, it can also offer more sources of support. A teen may find it easier to seek help from a stepparent, a grandparent, or another adult in the family. You, as a parent, may find it easier to get support from an adult who is not the other birth parent of your child. If both birth parents are overwhelmed and blaming themselves and each other, another parenting adult may provide a clearer perspective.

Effects on Siblings

As normal family routines are repeatedly disrupted by an abuse victim's situation, her sisters and brothers get less attention. Depending on how old they are, siblings may not know much about their sister's problems, but they cannot avoid being affected by the repeated crises.

Some children begin to act extraordinarily well behaved, as they try to avoid causing further trouble. Other children act in ways that will get parents' attention, as if they are trying to compete with their sister. And still others seem to go on with their own lives as if nothing is happening—coping well, but covering up their feelings.

If your daughter's siblings are older than her, they may know a great deal about what is going on, and they may get involved as her confidante, as a witness to her abuse, or as part of her social circle. If they know more than you know, they may feel guilty or conflicted about telling you what they know. They may be trying to help and feel overwhelmed because they are too young to do anything about it. They may not understand the seriousness or the complexity of their sister's problems. Some siblings might feel angry with their sister and her boyfriend, and not know how to deal with their anger. They might feel protective of her and angry with her at the same time. They might feel confused about how to respond to you and your emotional ups and downs, wanting to be supportive of you at times and finding themselves angry or upset with you at other times.

What Sisters and Brothers Have Told Us

- I'm scared by how upset my parents get with my sister.
- Sometimes I feel as if I've lost my sister. She has changed.
- What do I have to do to get attention around here?
- My dad's right. They should kick her out. I don't get why they put up with her.
- My sister used to be fun, and now all she can think about is her boyfriend.
- She's so moody: happy one minute and miserable the next.

- What's the big deal? He's an okay guy. He's nice to me.
- I can't tell my parents. She'll kill me if I tell.

Siblings who have the urge to be overprotective and restrictive with the abused teen are usually not helpful. This usually leads a victim to hide what is really going on, or to "go underground." Parents should be careful not to encourage other children, particularly older brothers, to act on their anger by being aggressive to the abuser. Siblings can be encouraged to be alert to danger and actively engage in being part of a safety net for the abused teen without putting anyone in danger or "taking matters into their own hands."

Parents should pay attention to all the children in a family when a crisis such as relationship abuse is going on. Siblings need support and opportunities to talk about how the situation affects them. They need to know that even if they feel protective and responsible, it is too much of a burden for them, and you, as parents, don't need them to take on a parental role. They need to be taken care of also.

Getting Off the Rollercoaster

Victor has been stepfather to Emilia, fifteen, and Gloria, twelve, since he married their mother, Rosa, five years ago. Emilia was just starting to date, and Victor and Rosa were worried she was in a situation that she was too young to handle. Victor describes the situation as follows.

Victor

I didn't like Thomas from the beginning. Why would a twenty-three-year-old guy be interested in a fifteen-year-old girl? He could only want one thing. Emilia was head-over-heels crazy for him. Her mother and I tried to give her rules. She had a curfew; no calls after 9:00 p.m.; she could only go out one night a week. She kept defying us. She climbed out the window to be with him.

Then we decided this was crazy, and we let him pick her up at the house. At least she wouldn't keep sneaking out.

Then one day he picked her up, and I heard yelling outside. I went out, and I saw Thomas yelling at Emilia, trying to push her into the car. She was scared and didn't want to get in the car. I headed toward them, and I saw him grab her arm real hard. I was livid, and I got in his face. 'You want to hit somebody? Hit me!' Rosa called the police. That's how we found out.

On top of everything else, this guy had been pushing Emilia around and threatening her all this time. He hadn't punched her or anything like that, but he was always scaring her and manipulating her, playing mental games. For the next couple of months, things kept escalating as we tried to keep her away from him. We even thought of sending her to Mexico to live with her grandmother for a while.

Then we realized this wasn't working. We couldn't keep her under lock and key, and it was consuming us. We didn't do anything as a family anymore. We were so busy policing Emilia, we were missing Gloria's soccer games all the time. Gloria was upset and moody, and she began acting up to get our attention. Rosa and I were always fighting about what to do about Emilia.

So we decided to get off the rollercoaster we were on. We had to slow down and get our minds off this. Rosa and I talked. We realized we had been so busy fighting Emilia, we hadn't even noticed that she had pushed away not only us, but also her friends. Her life was falling apart. We decided that every week we were going to do something as a family, and also take time for ourselves. We started to take time out to talk with Emilia and Gloria more. We were determined to have fun again. For the first time in months, we went to the movies. Sometimes Emilia would come with us, and sometimes she even enjoyed herself. No matter what, we went to Gloria's soccer games. We even arranged to go away for a weekend.

Victor is convinced that this was a turning point in his and Rosa's ability to understand and protect Emilia and their family from the chaos caused by Emilia's relationship with Thomas. He also believes that after this, Emilia began to notice the effects of her relationship on her family, and tried to slow things down with Thomas. Emilia continued seeing Thomas, although he became increasingly violent. She tried to break up with him twice, and a year later, she made the final break.

Dialing Down the Drama

We often overlook the impact of our "quieter" actions. The drama of your child's situation can make you feel you are doing nothing if you are not directly confronting the violence or physically moving your child away from the abuser. Or the drama may make you feel frozen and passive, unable to think clearly and take any kind of action when you need to. We believe that quiet, positive actions, far from "doing nothing," can have a positive impact. These are times when, alert and aware, you are able to gather, use, or share information.

Whenever you can, get off the rollercoaster for a moment. When you feel overwhelmed with pain or fear, take a deep breath and have a quiet conversation with yourself. Tell yourself, "I am doing the best I can." Tell yourself, "Quiet moments are as important as dramatic actions, and right at this moment, I am doing a great deal."

Quiet moments with your child can create space for loving gestures and expressions of appreciation. They can allow you to connect or communicate about aspects of your life together that have nothing to do with violence. They can give both of you strength.

The way you manage your reactions and make decisions about your actions will influence the rest of your family, including the teen who is being abused. At times, dramatic actions can be effective. At other times, silence is most effective. Your intense reactions can motivate you to be alert, think creatively, and act quickly. It is important to plan and to take major steps when needed to keep your daughter safe. It is important to be ready to act when necessary, or when your daughter is ready.

Your observations will help you figure out what your child needs from you, and your heightened awareness will help guide your decisions and actions. Quiet comments about your observations help your child know that you see the abuse that is going on. Such comments give your child a chance to look at the situation as you might see it. An empathic comment is nonconfrontational. For example, "Toni, I noticed that when you told John you were going to study with Linda tonight, he accused you of going out with some guy. It must be upsetting when he gets so jealous." A statement like this accomplishes three things: (1) Toni knows that you are aware of what's going on; (2) she feels that you understand; and (3) she is allowed to feel upset about John's jealousy, even if she was about to minimize and deny it. An additional statement of encouragement can strengthen Toni's ability to resist John's controlling jealousy: "I'm pleased to see that you are going to study with Linda for that exam tomorrow, even though John is angry with you. It's so hard to decide to do something that might upset him."

Similarly, an expression of concern based on your observations can go a long way. "Toni, I've noticed that in the last two days John has been mean and texting you a lot. You seem upset after you get his texts. I'm worried about how he affects you. You're so anxious." This allows Toni to know that you know what's happening and care about her, and to notice for herself that John's mean talk has an effect on her.

Reach out to your other children as well. Assume they are affected by the disruptions caused by their sister's violent relationship, even if they don't express it. Make sure they understand why you are upset, and help them cope. Talk to them about what's happening using words that they can understand at their age. Help them express their feelings about their sister and, if appropriate, her boyfriend.

Asking and Listening

Asking and listening are quiet, positive actions. Seeking information requires asking questions and listening carefully to the answers you receive. Ask your daughter about what is happening to her, how she perceives it, and how she feels about it. Try not to accuse or challenge her, or require yourself to do anything about what she is saying (except to ask questions and listen to her answers). You may learn a great deal.

By passively listening and saying nothing, you demonstrate support and acceptance of your daughter, but not of the violence. This type of "potent nonverbal message" communicates acceptance and fosters constructive growth and change. For example:

Parent: "Toni, you look upset."

Teen: "I am upset. John gets so jealous! He doesn't want me to study with Linda tonight!"

Parent: "Oh?"

Teen: "He can be so mean! He actually thought I would lie to him and go out with somebody else."

Parent: "I see."

Teen: "He doesn't trust me. I hate it when he doesn't trust me. He's making such a big thing of this. Maybe I shouldn't go to Linda's."

Parent: (Silence)

Teen: "I don't know how to make him trust me."

Parent: "That's hard."

Teen: "He has to believe me. I can't deal with this. I'm afraid I'm going to fail my exam tomorrow. I have to study with Linda tonight. She said she'd help me. John will just have to believe me. I want to pass this exam. I'm going over to Linda's."

In this situation, the parent's ability to listen without judgment—and with implicit acceptance and support—allowed Toni to express her feelings, to think about the problem (trust), and to make her own decision.

Asking Friends

When you have the opportunity, ask your daughter's friends and other people who see her with her boyfriend to tell you what is happening. If they are reluctant to tell you what they know, ask them again. Let them know that you are worried about your daughter, and that they might be able to help her if they confide in you.

They may be relieved that you asked. They may have been afraid to take the initiative to tell you because they didn't want to betray your daughter. After ending battering relationships, several girls have told us that they were relieved their friends told their parents about the violence, even though at the time it made them mad. Often the friends didn't know what to do and felt burdened with the responsibility. People at your daughter's school—teachers, nurses, counselors, or the principal—may know about the violence, but don't tell you because they assume that you also know. By openly asking about it, finding out whatever you can, and making connections with others, you make it possible for everyone in your daughter's life to work together to help her.

Gathering Information

Gathering information from all kinds of sources and becoming as informed as possible are other forms of quiet, positive action. You are already doing these things by reading this book. Gather information from the Internet, other books, and videos and television shows. Search the Internet under such key words as "teen relationship abuse," "teen dating violence," "safe breakups," "safety planning," "domestic violence," or "parents of abused teens." Contact your local domestic violence program and hotline for information to help you begin to develop strategies for your particular situation. Talk to a domestic violence advocate. They are available to your daughter, to yourself, or to the abuser. In many states, like California, domestic violence advocates receive specialized training and certification.

Often the information you obtain is not immediately useful but will prove useful at some point later on, and you will be prepared when you need to be. The story that follows illustrates the importance of gathering such information.

Joan

Joan's daughter, Trudy, recently broke up with her boyfriend because he was possessive and had beaten her up. He was harassing her by showing up at work and threatening her. The first time Joan called the police, they did not intervene because they didn't think there was enough evidence of an assault. Then Joan went to the police again, not to make a report, but to get information about what she could do. She talked to a helpful detective who told her about a prior arrest of her daughter's boyfriend for beating up another girl. She also got information about what the police need to make an arrest. The next time she called to make a report, she was better equipped to convince the police to take action.

Getting Help for Yourself

Getting help for yourself is also important. You cannot go through all of these crises alone. Your child is in danger, you are deeply affected, and you need to talk about it. You are limiting your effectiveness and undermining your strength if you keep the abuse and your feelings about it a secret.

If both you and your spouse are present and involved in the life of the child who is being abused, it is essential that you support each other. You also need support from family members and friends. You might consider getting help from a counselor, a domestic violence advocate, or a support group. You may already have thought about counseling for your child. How about counseling for yourself and/or others in your family who are being affected by the violence? See the resources section of this book for hotlines and organizations that can help.

Setting Limits

The constant ups and downs of your daughter's relationship have a negative impact on your family. To get off the rollercoaster, you must set boundaries to limit this impact.

When you find yourself rushing to rescue or punish your daughter, stop and ask yourself, "What am I doing? Do I want to police my daughter every minute to make sure she does what I want her to do? Do I have to stop everything and respond this minute? Am I being effective?"

You are not being effective if you allow the chaos of your daughter's relationship to control you. You don't have to be thrown into a crisis every time she is. Rather than over-react or become over-involved, you can choose to (1) limit your availability to being drawn into the crisis beyond the point that you can be effective, and (2) set clear expectations and consequences of your daughter's behavior. By setting limits, you also make room for maintaining other relationships in the family.

Paula and her husband, Frank, had experience with setting limits. As Paula said, "There's a limit to how much I will allow my life to be disrupted. There are times when you have to walk away and go on about your life." Paula and Frank were able to have a relationship with their daughter, Sandy, seeing her every day, living in the same house, without being totally controlled by Sandy's boyfriend, Alan, and his drug abuse and violence. Sandy knew what she could expect from her parents and saw Alan away from their house. She knew that she could live in her parents' house, but they would not allow Alan to be part of their lives or to come into their house.

There are several elements to effectively setting limits with your teen. You can let her know what is expected of her and why, and what she can expect from you. The expectations must be realistic and clear, and they must focus on specific behavior. The consequences if she does not meet your expectations must also be clear, logical, and natural. Of course, you must be able to follow through with the consequences, provided they fit logically with the expectations. For example:

Parent: "I expect you to be home by midnight or to call by 11:30 from wherever you are."

Teen: "I can't control when we get home. It's up to Bob."

Parent: "You are responsible for getting home on time or calling. Do you mean that you can't come home because Bob won't let you?"

Teen: "Why do you have to make so much trouble? Can't I just go out and have fun? I don't want Bob to get mad."

Parent: "Are you afraid to make Bob mad? Is that why this is upsetting you?"

Teen: "Yes. I wish you didn't have to get so worried."

Parent: "Let's see how we can work this out so that you can be home on time. If we do not hear from you or see you at home by midnight, we will worry. We will be awake and assume that you have been hurt. I will call Bob's house, the hospital emergency room, and then the police to try to find out if you have been hurt. You have a couple of choices. If you like, I will tell Bob that I take this seriously, and that I expect him to. Or I can pick you up at midnight. Are there any other ways to make it possible for you to be home on time?"

Teen: "If he won't bring me home, can I call you to come pick me up?"

Your tone of voice during this exchange is crucial. It reflects your attitude, and it can make the difference between sounding firm and sounding punishing. It can also make the difference between conveying the message "That is my limit" and the message "I dare you to push me past my limit."

When parents are distressed about their children's behavior, they often focus on the problem behavior, and teens tune out. Abused teens need encouragement and reminders of their strengths. To foster a positive interaction, use comments that are specific to the situation. For example, "You were so clear in that phone call to John!" or "I appreciate that you have been doing the dishes in the middle of this turmoil." Comments like these are more effective than general positive comments such as "You are so beautiful."

It takes time to effectively set limits and follow through on them, especially if you have not used this approach previously. Allow yourself time to practice and be patient.

Managing Your Reactions

Anger is a common, natural reaction, especially when your child is being treated badly. Anger can signal you to pay attention when something is upsetting or threatening. It can also be an overpowering emotion. Often parents and siblings, especially fathers and brothers, experience an intensity of anger they have never felt before. It can be frightening, both to yourself and to others who are afraid of what your anger could lead you to do. Dealing with anger can become a problem in itself. When your anger controls you, you can't think or act clearly, and you can't be helpful to your family. Anger can magnify and compound the other problems of dating violence.

The Cabrillo family experienced this problem. Family members were so afraid of how Mr. Cabrillo would react to his daughter's abuse that they didn't tell him about it for five years, when his daughter was out of high school. He said, "It was difficult for me. I didn't find out about it until two years before it ended. My wife needed my support, but I couldn't give it to her because I didn't know what was going on. When I did find out, I was furious. I challenged her boyfriend. I wanted to see if he would do the same thing to a man. I started to do the very thing that they were afraid I would do."

When one person in a family is controlled by his or her anger, the whole family can get pulled into escalating tension, fear, and violence, mirroring that of a battering relationship. The family focus then turns away from the victim and toward the potentially violent family member. Many parents have told us that this has been one of the most frightening aspects of the way their teen's battering relationship has affected the family.

This fear became a reality for Julia's family, which was torn apart when her seventeen-year-old brother, Anthony, killed her boyfriend, Ernie. Anthony had become enraged at Ernie for beating up his sister. Anthony was convicted of first-degree murder, and it was considered premeditated because he went looking for Ernie after he saw Julia's bruises and black eye. Anthony said he intended only to scare Ernie, to get him to leave Julia alone. But he lost control and stabbed Ernie to death.

Dealing with Angry Feelings

We can feel angry without going out of control, being reckless, or becoming verbally or physically violent. Strong emotions need to be taken care of and released somehow; suppressing anger can be unhealthy. It is important to find healthy ways to express and handle your anger while you feel it. You have choices about how you deal with your anger, as well as what to do to contain it rather than let it escalate. For example, if you are angry and more likely to unleash your anger in destructive ways after you have been drinking, then it is important to make the choice not to drink. Mixing anger with alcohol or drugs is dangerous.

Without outlets for your anger, it builds up. A buildup of anger activates your body's nervous system, flooding you with stress-response hormones, such as adrenaline and cortisol. Notice how your body reacts to anger, and then choose how to respond in a healthy way. The simplest technique is to take deep breaths and to pay attention to your breathing rhythms. Deep breathing helps to calm the nervous system. Another technique is to use physical outlets for the tension associated with anger: for example, physical work (such as yard work), running, batting baseballs or hitting tennis balls, or practicing martial arts. Some people find they can release their anger by going somewhere by themselves (perhaps to the bathroom) and yelling. These are all safe outlets for expressing anger.

Distractions can help too. Give yourself a break from the situation and focus on something else. Do something to take care of yourself and calm down. When you feel your anger building, you can do something to cool off, such as taking time out from an intense conversation and doing something else. Some parents find that taking a walk, writing, keeping a journal, listening to music, meditating, or praying helps to calm them. Other parents choose activities that distract them, such as hobbies, cleaning, cooking, or going to the movies. Try to find your own way to relax or calm yourself.

You can also use your support systems to help you deal with your anger. Talking and venting with a friend or a family member can help. Family talks about the situation and discussing feelings about it can be constructive. You can use an Alcoholics Anonymous (AA) approach by seeking support when you feel you might lose control. For example, you can arrange to call a friend (the equivalent of an AA sponsor) anytime you are afraid you are going to lose your temper. The friend can help you talk through what you are feeling and help you find alternative ways to handle your anger without hurting yourself or someone else.

Another way for family members to help each other deal with anger is to make a plan to ensure that everyone can vent their anger safely. Anytime a family member feels overwhelmingly angry, or anytime an incident occurs that triggers anger in all of you, you can do the following: Give each person four or five minutes to vent their feelings while everyone else listens without commenting, other than with noncommittal responses. This means not taking each person's anger personally, but simply listening. This technique can leave everyone free to problem-solve.

It may seem odd to be reading about how to manage your anger toward someone who, because of that person's inability to manage his or her anger, is hurting your family. But it is important to manage your anger so that you don't escalate an already tense situation.

De-escalating Anger

We have been discussing managing anger on an ongoing basis over a period of time, which is necessary if a battering relationship is prolonged. But how can you manage your anger in particularly explosive incidents? If you are in an argument with someone, or face-to-face with someone who is being defiant—either your teen or the batterer—what can you do to de-escalate the situation?

There are several ways to approach someone who is argumentative and explosive so that you are not provoked into losing control over your anger. Sitting down is less menacing than standing up, and it can defuse the confrontation. Do not respond to baiting or argumentative comments; let the other person vent until he or she is worn out. To do this effectively, do not disagree or argue, but respond by acknowledging the other person's feelings: for example, "I know that makes you mad" or "That's really terrible." If you disagree with what the person is saying, acknowledge that you understand how he or she feels, and save your feelings for later.

Respond in a quiet voice. Do not attempt to be heard over the other person's yelling by shouting. A softer voice invites the person who is yelling to stop and listen. You might ask the other person to sit down or to take a walk while you talk. Never get in a car with someone who is in a rage. If the person tries to leave, let him or her go. Don't corner or restrain them. Don't try to touch or enter their physical space, even to try to calm them down. You can only do this when the tension is winding down.

Let the person cool off. It is essential that you resist your own urge to blow up or to insult the person. If you feel your own anger escalating, take deep breaths, silently count to ten, come up with an image of a peaceful scene—whatever you can do to keep yourself from losing control. Sometimes walking away or leaving can cool down an explosive situation, but sometimes it can escalate it. Use your judgment. If you do walk away, tell the other person that you are taking a break to cool down and will be back to talk again later.

These techniques apply to an argument, not to a violent situation. Once physical violence starts, you must focus on your own safety and forget about trying to do anything else. If you are a parent of an abused teen, you might help her learn the previous techniques to help her de-escalate a confrontational situation. She may need to examine ways in which she contributes to escalating the situation rather than taking care of her own safety. It is natural for someone who has been abused to get angry, and because it is often dangerous to express anger directly, the anger can build. But if your teen's anger builds and then explodes, she may not be in the frame of mind to make wise choices about how to deal with that anger safely. This can trigger an escalation of the batterer's anger to the point that your teen gets hurt. For example, if the batterer is enraged or tense, and your teen gets "in his face" and escalates the argument, then she is not taking care of herself. If she doesn't allow him to cool off or leave when he needs to, she may be endangering herself.

This *doesn't* mean that she provokes violence. She has no control over whether or not he becomes violent, but she can be as careful as possible not to be in his "line of fire." In a battering relationship, it is usually not safe for the victim to express her anger directly. In a healthy relationship, there is room for arguing and disagreement without fear, control, intimidation, threats, and beatings.

Parents can discuss with their teens ways in which they can protect themselves, and how to handle their anger in situations in which they could be hurt because of the threat of violence. Although this does not stop the violence, it does help to manage incidents that have the potential for escalating into violence.

Resolving Conflicts with Your Spouse or Partner

You and your spouse or partner may not agree about how to handle day-to-day conflicts with your teen and her boyfriend. Talk to each other. Try to come to some understanding about how each of you feels. Try to accept one another's feelings and limits, validating the struggle each of you is going through. Try to give each other breaks from the tension and take turns interacting with your daughter and/or her abusive boyfriend. Take turns taking the lead in solving problems that arise. If you are divorced, you may need to focus extra attention on setting your past or current conflicts aside in order to be on the same page concerning your child's abusive situation.

If you are the spouse of someone who needs help managing his or her anger, or if you are frightened by the other person's anger, assess the situation. Does (or would) he or she act on their anger in a way that hurts someone? If not, allow their feelings to be expressed. If your spouse's anger is potentially harmful, however, set limits regarding your tolerance of his or her behavior. For example, you can say, "I understand how angry you feel, but you must stop this. You can't blow off steam this way. Everyone's afraid of what you'll do. You're making the situation worse." Of course, this won't work in the middle of the person's rage when he or she can't listen. At a quieter time, apply the techniques for managing anger described earlier in this chapter.

Instructions for Time-Outs

When you are not having a problem or conflict, make an agreement that either you or the other person can ask for a time-out when one of you feels too upset to talk about a problem in a constructive, respectful way. Commit to continue the discussion when the upset person is calmer. The "appointment" to return to the discussion is an important part of taking a time-out.

Then, when a difficult conversation or conflict comes up, either person can say, "I need a time-out" and take a break to calm down, prepared to continue the discussion later. The time-out shouldn't last more than a couple of hours, unless there is a good reason to resume the discussion after a longer time.

Steps for taking a time-out:

1. Notice the physical signs—such as muscle tension, heart rate pumping, and shallow breathing—that tell you that you are getting too agitated, angry, or frustrated to be reasonable in a conflict or conversation.

2. When you recognize that you aren't able to have the conversation until you are calmer, pause and consider taking a break.

3. Say to the other person, "I want to discuss this with you, but I'm too [angry, agitated, upset . . .], so I want to take a time-out to calm down. Let's talk about this later. I'm going [for a walk, to take a shower, to sit quietly . . .] and I'll be ready to talk about this again [in twenty minutes, in two hours, after dinner . . .]. Is that okay with you?"

4. Listen to the other person's preferences about when to talk about it again, and come to an agreement about a time that will work for both of you to continue the discussion.

5. Take a break to physically and mentally cool down.

    a. Have a positive talk with yourself. For example, you can say to yourself, "I want to solve this problem," "I'm glad I stopped before saying something I'd regret," or "I know we can work this out." Avoid negative thinking that stops you from getting calmer. Switch to positive thoughts.

b. Do something to physically calm and cool yourself down. For example, take a walk or run, listen to calming music, sit quietly in a room with soft lights, do twenty minutes of breathing and stretching, or take a hot shower.

6. At the appointed time, take the initiative to continue the discussion, now that you are better able to listen and reflect on the other person's point of view, and express your point of view respectfully.

Strengthening Your Relationship with Your Teen

What makes a strong relationship between parents and children so important when dealing with a teen's abusive relationship? Abuse often involves patterns of secrecy and isolation that further endanger the victim after the abuse has started. The more teens keep the emotional, sexual, and physical abuse secret from family and friends, the more ashamed they become. The more ashamed teens become, the more isolated and the more protective of their abusers they become.

If, in addition, an abusive boyfriend threatens his girlfriend with more severe violence or even death, then she becomes increasingly isolated and terrified. The abuser may also isolate her through jealousy, restrictiveness, excessive criticism, and humiliation. This pattern often results in the alienation of the victim from her parents and other people who had been important to her. The more the abuser succeeds in isolating his victim from her family and friends, the less protection she has from both the physical violence and the effects of the brainwashing or emotional abuse. As isolation increases, violence tends to become more frequent and more severe. As a parent, by maintaining your communication and connection with your child, you may be able to interfere with these attempts to isolate her.

Tanisha and Tyrone's story illustrates the importance of maintaining communication and connection with your child.

Tanisha

Tanisha met Tyrone when she was seventeen, in her last year of high school. Tyrone was nineteen and working as a mechanic. Barbara, Tanisha's mother, describes their relationship and the family's way of dealing with it:

> Tyrone seemed like a nice guy. He was certainly devoted to Tanisha. He was calling and coming over all the time. Then one Sunday we were going to church, and Tanisha was wearing sunglasses and a big hat that hid her face. I saw bruises on her ankles, and I asked her what happened. She said, "Don't worry, we were just in a little car accident last night." She showed me her black eye, and I said to myself, "This girl is not telling the truth." After denying it, she finally admitted that Tyrone drank too much at a party the night before. He beat her up because he thought she was looking at another guy.
>
> Later, we talked some more, and it turned out that Tyrone drinks a lot. He is also very jealous, and there had been other instances of his getting out of control. Tanisha is a girl who stands up for herself. She's outspoken.
>
> But around Tyrone, she loses her voice. I told her, "You deserve better. What are you going to do about this?" She said, "I won't put up with this. It'll never happen again."
>
> Well, over the next two years, it happened again and again. She moved in with him. She'd still come around because we're a close family. She'd cry to me and ask my advice. I'd say to her, "You need to find the strength to get out." I'd tell her to pray. She knew she could come to me. I understood what she was going through.

I prayed a lot; I was so worried about her. I was glad she also had her grandma to talk to. She's her favorite. We had family meetings. Tanisha's younger brother and sister, her uncle, her grandma, and I would talk about what to do. Tanisha was always welcome in our home, but Tyrone wasn't. Tanisha wanted us to at least be civil to Tyrone. We all disagreed about what to do. Her uncle refused to speak to either one of them. But I got everyone to realize that Tanisha is making her own choices, and we have to accept that. She's made her bed, and she's going to have to lie in it until she decides she doesn't want to anymore. My mother said, "You can't tell people what to do because they won't listen. She knows we don't like this, that we're scared for her." We, as a family, will never turn our back on her. Having family discussions helped us get through it.

After two years, Tanisha realized she was going home to her family more and more often, and finally ended her relationship with Tyrone.

Witnessing a teen or young adult go through the ups and downs of an abusive relationship often means helplessly watching as she makes foolish, even dangerous choices. It may mean watching the effects of being treated badly for a long time: serious signs of stress, lack of confidence and self-respect, clinging to scraps of kindness from her boyfriend, sacrificing herself while he seems to thrive. It may mean seeing her feeling powerful and ready to take charge one moment, and defeated or beaten down the next.

As she goes through this, other people tend to withdraw from her, depriving her of the one thing she needs more than anything else: connection to people other than her boyfriend. While the abuser is trying to keep her away from other close relationships, her connections with healthy people who support her strengths become more important.

Accepting Teens' Choices

Children sometimes make choices that are contrary to their parents' values and what their parents have taught them. In situations like this, parents have a valuable position in their teen's life, even as the person who abuses her becomes more and more important to her. Parents don't want to cut off their connection to a teen who is going through this, or stop their willingness to listen, hear her out, and acknowledge her perspectives, even if parents disagree with those perspectives. This may mean parents hold back, not saying what they think, in order to pay attention to what their child is telling them.

By doing these things, parents maintain the connection and make it possible to have some impact. Parents are a resource, and a teen in an abusive situation must see his or her parents (or another adult) as people to turn to. By acknowledging and supporting their teen's autonomy and the independence that their teen has, whether or not they think their child is ready for it, parents are acknowledging reality and dealing with what *is* rather than how they would *like* things to be. This is a challenge! But no one wants to lose the connection with his or her child to the power of an abusive relationship.

Parents can ask their teen about her point of view, her feelings, and her opinions, as well as tell her their own. This can be done in such a way that they are exchanging and sharing perspectives without one party being proven right and the other wrong.

When parents are thinking about how to deal with the violence, they should include the teen in the conversation: "How can we deal with this together?" She may be doing the best that she can at that moment; an effective approach must take that into account and build on what else she can do. Parents can aim to help their teen make her own decisions rather than make decisions for her and risk pushing her away. It is important to problem-solve, brainstorm, and make safety plans together, helping her see that she doesn't have to go through this alone.

Parents may not be able to use this approach if their teen is so isolated and trapped that she is beyond the point of allowing anyone to talk with her about her relationship. Even so, it is usually possible to find some way to show acceptance, caring, and appreciation of her strengths. It is also possible to help her find another adult to talk to if she doesn't want to talk to a parent.

It is important to find all possible ways to build on a teen's strengths: to notice and appreciate what is working well for her, and to encourage her to focus on aspects of and activities in her life besides the relationship—especially areas that have not yet begun to deteriorate, such as school, after-school activities, sports, lessons, hobbies, or other friendships. If she can do this, she can become strong enough to be free of the grip of the battering relationship.

Valerie, mother of a teenage daughter, had this to say:

> My fifteen-year-old daughter, Jessica, is a dancer, and when she was seeing Bruce, she began to give up her dancing. I reminded her how much she loves to dance and how strong it makes her feel. I encouraged her to continue dancing. She did, and after the relationship ended, she was relieved to be able to dance without any restrictions imposed by Bruce.

Parents can notice healthy and positive ways their teen is coping with the stress and resisting being controlled. It is empowering to teens when a parent acknowledges how difficult things are under these circumstances and that they appreciate how she is trying her best. Parents must recognize and appreciate the ways in which she handles tension, conflict, fear, and restricted options. For example, parents could say the following:

- "It must be hard to concentrate on schoolwork, but I am glad you are doing as well as you are."
- "I appreciate that you chose to have dinner with your grandparents in spite of the pressure from Jason to see him tonight."

- "I know that at times you feel pressure from us to do things with the family at the same time you feel pressure from Jason not to."

Parents can strengthen their relationships with their teens by spending time with them or having conversations that have nothing to do with the battering relationship. It can be a relief for teens to have the kinds of parent-child interactions they used to have before the abuse. The family might actually have some fun together—watching TV, going to a movie, or shopping. These activities let an abused teen know that the family values the time together. If parents can do this without having a fight about her boyfriend, they will be allowing room for their parent-child relationship to be free of his interference.

If a teen only hears negative comments or criticism from parents, their bond with her will weaken, and she will be less able to resist the abuse. When parents keep their resentment under control so that it doesn't inhabit every corner of their relationship with their teen, it strengthens the parent-teen relationship. In the long run, supporting her abilities and strengthening the relationship between parents and teens can go a long way toward helping a battering victim believe in herself and get away from the violence.

Open Communication

It is very important to keep the paths of communication as open as possible. In addition, what parents say and how they say it is key to maintaining strong relationships with teens.

Tanisha's boyfriend Tyrone picked a fight with her every time she went to her family's house for Sunday dinner. Tanisha's mother said, "We knew that he was trying to get her to stop seeing her family. We kept encouraging her to come. I knew that you have to keep the door open or your child will be lost."

Abuse can lead to emotionally charged interactions between parents and children that make it easy for communication to be cut off. When both a parent and a teen are afraid of their temper or of becoming overwhelmingly upset, the conversation can stop. Sometimes a situation that could be handled in a straightforward manner becomes a crisis because of a parent's over-reaction. One parent's advice to other parents is, "Don't yell. Hold your tongue. Suck it up."

Because such intense feelings and reactions are involved when dealing with violence, extra efforts to initiate and sustain communication are often required of parents. Rosa, eighteen years old, said, "I can see my mom trying not to yell at me, like she did when he gave me a black eye. I get it—I'd also be upset if that happened to my daughter. But I then just tried to keep her from finding out what was going on. Then she tried harder to talk to me. Now she talks to me, she hears me, she gives me advice, and she tells me, 'I know the way you feel.'"

Even under the best of circumstances, teens often keep their feelings or details about their intimate relationships from their parents. Once a teen knows her parents disapprove of her boyfriend, she will assume that she cannot tell them anything about him or what is going on between them. She may be afraid of her parents' emotional outbursts about her relationship, or their interference, or that her freedom will be restricted. No matter what parents do, there is no guarantee that their daughter will talk to them about her relationship in general, or about the violence in particular. But to be an effective support for a teen's safety and for her getting free from the violence, parents need to know what she is dealing with, and she needs to know that her parents can help. Communication between parents and their daughter is essential for her safety.

In day-to-day interactions with teens, there are many opportunities to invite them to talk about what is going on. Parents can ask their teen about feelings and problems she is experiencing as well as information about her safety. It isn't necessary to focus on the specifics of her relationship to get a picture of how it is affecting her. According to Thomas Gordon in *Parent Effectiveness Training*:

> One of the most effective and constructive ways of responding to children's feelings is the 'door-opener' or 'invitation to say more.' These door-openers keep your own feelings and thoughts out of the communication process. Young people feel encouraged to open up, pour out their feelings and ideas. These door-openers also convey acceptance of the child and respect for [her] as a person.[36]

What Gordon refers to as door-openers are noncommittal responses or explicit invitations to say more in response to something a child says. Examples of door-openers are "I see," "Really?" "Tell me more," and "I'd like to hear about it."

Your attitude makes a difference when inviting a teen to talk to you. Without a receptive attitude, efforts to communicate will be ineffective. For example, parents must want to hear what the teen has to say. If they don't have time, or if they really don't want to hear it, it is better to say so, or to arrange to talk at another time. Parents should avoid inviting their teen to talk, then stopping her with judgments, telling her what to do, or over-reacting to what she says. They must also be aware of when their tone of voice and facial expressions may contradict their words. For example, there is a difference between asking, "How did you get the bruise on your arm?" with concern (inviting an open response) and asking the same question with anger and blame (triggering a defensive response to your accusation).

Parents must also want to be helpful, and feel empathic about the teen's struggles. They must be able to accept her feelings, even if those feelings are completely different from their own or from what they think she should feel. This is especially difficult to do, and may take time to develop. It also requires parents to let go of their need to control her, and to acknowledge that although they might help and support her, she is the one who must actively work on decisions and solutions to the problems she is facing.

Effective Listening

There are times when it is important to advise or instruct teens, or to let them know what you, as their parent, think or how you feel. But the most important tool in communicating with teens is effective listening. And a teen who is truly listened to is more likely to listen when you express yourself as well.

Effective listening means using open responses that acknowledge a child's feelings, as well as the child's perceptions of his or her problems. Open responses allow expression of feelings, understanding, and clarification. Open responses are nonjudgmental and empathic. They are nonverbal as well as verbal. Effective listening means noticing nonverbal cues ("You look upset" or "You're shrugging and rolling your eyes. You don't agree?"). Effective listening is a first step in problem solving.

Lucinda has been going with Robert for two years. Even though her parents are distressed about Robert's violence, she says that her friends envy the way she can talk to her parents.

> **Lucinda:** "I have had it with Robert. I told him we're finished, and I don't want him to come around here anymore."
>
> **Father:** "What happened?"
>
> **Lucinda:** "He's been calling me from jail trying to control everything I do. He gets mad if I'm not home when he calls. He has his friends watching me."
>
> **Father:** "He has? I thought we didn't have to worry with him in jail! So he's still trying to control you."
>
> **Lucinda:** "Yes, and I saw a girl on the news who got shot by her boyfriend. I don't want to see Robert anymore."

Father: "Oh, my God. Shot! You think Robert could do that to you?"

Lucinda: "His friends followed me today, and he called and he said, 'I saw you, I was watching you, I know everything you do.'"

Father: "No wonder you're so afraid of him. This frightens me too."

Lucinda: "I never want to see him again."

Mother: "Do you really believe this in your heart?"

Lucinda (in tears): "I really love him. I'm afraid I'll go back to him. But I never stood up to Robert before today. I can't live like this anymore."

Mother: "I'm afraid too. How will you get through this, breaking up with Robert, getting away from his friends and his threats, but loving him and missing him?"

Lucinda: "I don't know."

Father: "It's hard to do what you did today. Maybe you're afraid of what he'll do to get back at you, but you should also be proud of yourself."

Lucinda: "Maybe I can do this. Do you think I have to move away? What should I do?"

Lucinda's parents listened without jumping in with too many of their own reactions. They clarified what was happening to her, and acknowledged her feelings. They recognized the change in her response to Robert and supported it. By the end of this conversation, Lucinda and her parents were ready to problem-solve. They all understood that the problem was twofold: how to get away from Robert, and how to deal with the fact that Lucinda still loves him and might feel like going back to him.

Parents often react to a conversation like this by thinking, "This is all fine and well in a book, but that isn't really the way people talk!" But this example is based on an actual dialogue in a real family. Such a dialogue really is possible for any family. Each person will find their own way to communicate and can use these ideas to add to their effectiveness in a way that is comfortable for them.

Some teens resist advice from parents and respond better to a problem-solving process in which parents refrain from telling them what to do. As parents, you can reflect on your past experiences: How does your child respond when you offer advice? Your child might respond better when advice is offered rather than imposed. For example, you can preface advice by saying, "My way of doing this is . . . Would that work for you?" or "I have a suggestion."

It is often helpful to acknowledge the fact that your teen's problems create problems for you too, and for other members of the family. While at times it is better to set such feelings aside and listen to a teen, there are also times when parents need to express their own feelings. A teen must know that his or her parents are affected as well. Parents can think about how to express feelings in a way that does not close down communication among family members.

Lucinda's parents reacted to what Lucinda was telling them. They expressed their feelings and asked about hers. Some experts have recommended using "I-statements" to let children know that there are consequences to their behavior without blaming, accusing, punishing, or using other approaches that make children stop listening or become defensive. An "I-statement" consists of an observation about one's own response to something that someone else is doing and, if it fits, a request for the other person to change what they are doing. For example:

- "When I see you with bruises, I'm terrified and I worry about you."

- "When I see how Robert hurts you, I get so angry I'm afraid I'll explode."

- "When you try to keep it a secret that Robert has been pushing you around, and I can see it happening, I feel so helpless
and frustrated. Would you tell me about it? What happened
last night?"

It is often challenging to find ways to give teens information
so that they are open to hearing it. Sometimes teens respond when
parents share their own experiences. If a parent has had a similar
experience—for example, with a relationship breaking up, or having
been abused—telling a teen about it might convey understanding and
empathy. It is a way of saying, "I know what you're going through."
It also conveys the message that it takes strength to get through these
experiences, and that the parent appreciates the teen's strengths.

Parents may have a long-term perspective of a teen's experiences
that they can share with her. This can be especially true if they have
been in an abusive relationship. A parent can tell their teen, "I've been
there, and it was hard. But I've dealt with it. I've gotten out of it."
What makes the difference is how this is presented. Parents can ask
themselves, "What, specifically, is similar between my experience and
my daughter's?" Usually the details are not similar, and teens are interested in hearing about what is most relevant to them. If you aim
to tell your teen to "do as I did," you are bound to fail. Your teen will
be quick to say that the situations are not the same. What's more, it is
important for teens not to be the same as their parents.

Parents can also encourage their children to communicate with
others besides them. While most parents might like teens to come directly to them to talk about any issue, this is not realistic. Teens need
others to talk to as well, and they are safer talking with other adults
who are helpful and supportive rather than not talking to anyone at
all. It also broadens a teen's safety net if others know what is going
on in an abusive relationship and are available to help.

Parents can be supportive of their teen by acknowledging that she may want to talk to another adult besides them, especially about dating, and they can help her to identify someone. Teens might be able to seek out an older sister or brother, a grandmother, a friend's mother, a school counselor, or a neighbor who is approachable and can be trusted. They may even find out that after sharing things with someone else, they find that they are less reluctant to actually talk to their parents. The message to a teen is still the same: Open communication is important.

Recognizing Your Feelings

Parents often feel responsible for what happens to their children. Of course, parents want to protect their children from harm and help them to be happy. It is important that parents recognize these feelings and how such feelings can lead them to act in a controlling manner. Fear, helplessness, and anger—at the loss of control over a teen's and the family's well-being—these are feelings that lead most parents to want to control the people or events that are causing them. Parents can "talk" to themselves, saying things like this:

> Acknowledge your fear. Allow yourself to feel that you are terrified that your teen is in serious danger. Accept that you feel frustrated that she "allows herself" to be treated badly. Prepare yourself for the deep sense of powerlessness that comes when you acknowledge that you have no control over your child's choices.

It is difficult for any parent to see their teen in danger and have only very limited ways to protect her. Parents actually have no control over the ways in which her choices affect her future or put her in danger. By acknowledging all of this, by being prepared to tolerate these very strong feelings, and by becoming aware of the impulse to control the teen, parents can avoid power struggles. The Serenity Prayer can be helpful:

God, grant me the serenity to accept the things I cannot change, courage to change the things I can, and wisdom to know the difference.

Using Your Influence as a Parent

Even though parents feel helpless about having an impact on the situation, they are still an important influence and resource for teens. When engaging with teens about their behavior, parents influence them to make changes themselves. Even when it doesn't look like teens are listening, they usually struggle within themselves, and do have their parents' points of view in mind as they make choices.

Parents must remember that they have had—and do still have—an important place in their children's lives, and this will continue to be true. Their relationships with their children are more important and longer lasting than the abusive relationship. Most teens want to maintain their relationships with their parents, even if they want it on their own terms. They seek out their parents, especially if they can trust that their parents will listen to them and will not do battle with them or challenge their autonomy. Often parents have such an important place in the lives of their children that even if a rift occurs, children eventually want to restore the relationship.

Of course, some parents are able to control their children by making their children afraid of them. Fear that a parent might over-react or react violently can make children careful not to report or do anything that will set the parent off, or make them lie or keep a situation secret. This fear does not help children learn to make positive choices or to change their behavior, except to avoid conflict or violence. In fact, it makes it more likely that they won't be able to think clearly and will become frozen or paralyzed by conflict, control, or abuse in their relationships. A more effective approach is one that actually encourages children to learn how to think about options, risks, and consequences for themselves, and make good choices. Janeece said:

I was afraid to tell my parents the truth about what was going on with John. When they found out, I was amazed that they could listen to me without freaking out.

Teens need information in order to understand what is happening to them and to make decisions, and parents can help them get this information. Parents can learn facts about dating violence/abuse and share what they learn or help teens find it for themselves. Sometimes teens will be more likely to accept this information from other sources, even if what they find out is similar to what a parent has been telling them.

A great deal of information is easily accessible to teens, especially on the Internet. Sometimes teens will authoritatively share something they read online that their parents already told them about. Parents can be appreciative when this happens—this is evidence of their influence.

Another way to have influence with teens is to be a safe harbor for them. When teens are distressed, they are most likely to seek comfort from their abusive partners. When that doesn't work, however, they will often seek nurturing from their parents. Parents may just sit with their teen, listen if the teen needs to talk, show quiet affection, or do something together to take a break from the distress.

Many teens are defiant and refuse to cooperate or to work out solutions to their problems. Sometimes it takes time and repeated efforts on a parent's part to try new approaches that avoid power struggles before a teen changes old ways of reacting. Sometimes the influence of the batterer makes a victim hostile toward her parents, no matter what approach parents use. It is important to keep trying, because at some point the batterer's influence may weaken.

Sometimes other factors are affecting your teen's behavior, such as alcohol or drugs, or perhaps she was defiant, sullen, or hostile even before the battering relationship began. Liz had been using crack and alcohol, but her mother, Peggy, didn't know about it. "I thought her wild behavior came from an attitude problem," said Peggy. Attending a support group for parents of teens, such as Al-Anon, can be useful in situations such as this to help you change ways in which you respond to your child so that you become more steady and effective.

Avoiding Power Struggles

While parents are horrified to see their teen's abuser control and threaten her, punish her, restrict her movements, and criticize her, it may come as a surprise when they realize they are using these same tactics. Parents can find themselves in a battle for control over the teen—a battle between them and the abuser. Parents who use ultimatums ("It's either him or me!" or "If you continue to see Tim, you'll have to move out!") create or worsen a power struggle.

Jennifer said, "My mom told me if I continued to be with him, she didn't want me in the house anymore. So I ran away to my cousin's house."

Imposing one's power and trying to control teens generally backfires. The outcome is usually that the teen is not motivated to carry out the imposed solution; the teen is resentful of the parent; the parent has difficulty enforcing the solution; and/or the teen has no opportunity to experience the consequences of his or her choices. Power struggles consume energy and escalate tension—they don't solve the problems.

Using parental power and control does not work in abusive situations in particular. The abused teen feels caught between her parent and her batterer, feeling that she has to choose between them, or that she is controlled by both. Power struggles with parents make it even more difficult for a teen to make decisions and to act on what is best for her. These struggles undermine her strength and ability to think for herself. Power struggles with a parent may align a teen more firmly with the abuser. The bond between victim and abuser can become stronger as the parent becomes the enemy they have in common. The abused teen may experience all of these difficulties even if parents do not engage in power struggles about the abusive relationship. The teen's own struggles in the relationship with her boyfriend become that much harder for her if she is caught in a battle for control with her parents.

There are many ways in which parents get hooked into power struggles over abusive relationships. When parents give ultimatums, they are often doing what the controlling boyfriend does. Abusers also tell their partners that they can't do things they want to do, "or else." They may say, "It's them or me—your parents want to keep you from being happy, and don't understand what we have together."

Ask yourself the following questions:

- Are you trying to control your daughter—for example, by threatening her or threatening to do something to hurt her boyfriend?

- Are you threatening punishment? For example: "If you insist on seeing him after I told you not to, then I will _____."

- Are you endlessly arguing, bickering, and criticizing her boyfriend? For example: "See, you're failing English again. You know I've told you you'd fail in school if you didn't get rid of James. You don't care about school anymore; all you care about is James. Well, I hope he'll buy you things you need for the rest of your life because I won't."

- Do you barrage her with accusations or questions about where she has been? For example: "You think I don't know that you sneak around with that boy. Just where were you until six o'clock? You say you were at the library. Dressed like that? Where are your books? I know what you're up to. Sharon next door saw you two the other day."

- Do you make rules that cannot be enforced ("You are not allowed to see him ever again") and then find yourself policing

her activities ("You aren't going anywhere without me taking
you and picking you up")?

- Do you point out what a loser her boyfriend is every time he
calls or every time his name comes up in conversation?

A controlling boyfriend does these same things, constantly criticizing what his girlfriend says and does, what she wears, and how
she looks. He may criticize her relationship with her family members, especially her parents, perhaps telling her she is stupid to believe
that her parents have her best interests in mind. He may be constantly
suspicious and accuse her of lying. She may be afraid to say anything to her boyfriend because she is afraid to start arguments. She
may feel the same about talking with her parents, especially about her
relationship.

How can parents avoid power struggles with battered teens? They
can do this by accepting the reality that they actually cannot control
their teens, but they can influence them. They can recognize their
own feelings, manage their own reactions, and act as a supportive
resource.

Effective Techniques to Prevent Power Struggles

When a conflict is about to escalate into a power struggle, parents can
disengage. This means they set aside their own feelings so they can
listen and respond to their teen. They do not have to take their teen's
actions, reactions, or behavior personally. She is not doing anything
"to them." When parents disengage, they don't get hooked and say
things they don't mean. They can sort out their feelings after resolving the conflict with their teen, when their feelings won't interfere.

So many things surrounding the abusive relationship can consume
parents' attention: their daughter, her attitude, the emotional rollercoaster everyone is on, the threat of violence, the fear for their daughter's safety and well-being. It is important for parents to acknowledge
how overwhelming this can be. Most parents find they have to set lim-

its to how much they let their time, attention, and emotions be taken over by the abusive relationship. Setting limits and boundaries can help to avoid power struggles. Parents can also make sure they get enough rest so that they can be discerning about which battles and worries to focus on.

Another way parents can avoid power struggles and defuse escalating tension is by listening calmly and reflectively to their teen, and clarifying what the teen feels, thinks, or wants. They can ask questions to clear up misunderstandings or miscommunication. These questions can clarify everyone's perspectives of the conflict. For example:

Teen: "Bob and I are going out tonight. See you later."

Parent: "Where are you and Bob going?"

Teen: "You always have to know everything I do. I can't go anywhere! You're trying to control me. You treat me like a child! Bob's right. He says you just can't face it—your little girl is grown up."

Parent: "You feel that I am treating you like a child when I ask where you are going?"

Teen: "You don't trust me."

Parent: "I think you are very capable and sensible. It doesn't matter how old you are, I think it is safer for someone to know where you are going. That's why I often tell you where I'm going."

Teen: "Well, I don't like all your questions and rules. And I know you don't trust Bob. But everything's okay now."

Parent: "You're right. I don't trust Bob. I know you like him a lot, and that you are happy to be getting along well now. I'm glad to see you happy. But ever since he hit you, I've been afraid. I think you still have to be careful when you go out with him. Do you understand how I feel?"

Teen: "I'm not so afraid of him anymore. He's changed."

Parent: "Can we work out a way I can feel more reassured by you and you can feel more trusted by me? I will feel more reassured if I know where you are and what time to expect you home."

Teen: "Do you trust me?"

Parent: "Yes, I trust you when I know that you are thinking about your own safety."

What we are saying may seem contradictory. While we are saying that it is most effective to respect our children's choices, we are also saying that your child may be in a dangerous situation and that you must respond. We recommend an attitude that reflects your actual lack of control as well as your acceptance of your child's situation at the moment. This approach enables effective interventions, not power- or control-motivated interventions.

Taking Action to Intervene

As a parent, you instinctively want to protect your child, and to help him or her get away from violence and abuse. The most important aspect of taking action is to be thoughtful about what will work. You want to be effective at making your child safe, not just feel that you are doing something to ward off your own feelings of helplessness. You have two important tasks: to create a safety net for your child as well as a support network for you. Gathering information is an on-going effort. Your situation will continue to change as you try ways of intervening and then learn from the results. There are many ways to go about these tasks, and you will find that you have to be flexible and adaptable.

Assessing the Situation

You need to consider several factors when making decisions about what to do.

Do you have enough information?

Do you know enough about what is going on in the relationship? Do you know enough about general tactics abusers use, the particular ways your child is being controlled, and the patterns in the violence your child is experiencing? How reliable is your information? Has it been confirmed by your daughter or other sources? Be sure you aren't making decisions based on a story you tell yourself out of fear or anger.

What have you already tried?

What has already been effective? What hasn't? Have circumstances changed, so that an approach that was not helpful before might work now?

What resources are there?

Have you contacted national or local hotlines, such as the National Teen Dating Abuse Helpline or your local domestic violence shelter program? Do you have an advocate to help you think things through? Do you have a place your daughter can hide if necessary? Think of who could be helpful: your daughter's friends, the local juvenile police officers, school administrators and counselors, or other supportive adults. There is a great deal of information available on the Internet to help with safety planning and strategizing. Also see the resources listed at the end of this book.

Attitude of the Victim

If the victim is ambivalent and has periods of time when she is hurt and angry with her batterer, or periodically breaks up with him, she will respond differently to intervention or planning than will the victim who is more consistently allied with and protective of her batterer. Does your daughter participate in discussions about getting away from the violence, even some of the time? Does she acknowledge your expressions of concern, or does she resist? How likely is it that your daughter will respond to your efforts?

Risk and Danger

The harsh reality is that sometimes relationship violence leads to serious injury or death. Even if it's difficult to believe that a person you know, especially a teen, would or could kill someone, abusive relationships are often volatile and unpredictable, and "accidents" or impulses can cause serious harm.

Assess the risk of your teen's situation and of any actions you or anyone else in your family might take. Engage others in your support network in helping you evaluate additional risks. Will your actions lead to more violence? What are safety needs that must be considered?

If you're discovering that serious violence has been hidden from you, you need to assess the degree to which your daughter's safety and perhaps your family's safety are being threatened. This will make a big difference in the urgency of your interventions. If you determine that the threat of violence is serious, it is crucial to be connected to an advocate or an advocacy organization, and to assess the degree of risk.

If the abuser does one or more of the following, it can be a sign of the potential for serious injury or death:

- threatens to kill
- abuses substances
- owns a gun
- becomes increasingly violent
- forces sex
- attempts to choke his partner
- threatens or attempts suicide

Victims sometimes have a sense that their partner is capable of seriously injuring or killing them, and this can keep them trapped in the relationship. This sense or intuition is hard for everyone to understand and is why lethality assessment is so important.

Do you have support from others?

Are there friends, family members, school staff, coworkers (yours or your daughter's), a counselor, or others who are aware of your situation? Do they listen and understand? Are there ways in which they can be helpful—to help you cope, to help ensure your daughter's safety?

What else is going on that will help or hinder your efforts?

Factors such as your health, your availability, the needs of another child or family member, or any number of other circumstances can affect your decisions.

Planning for Safety

The focus of this section is on the victim's safety, whether she stays in or leaves an abusive relationship. Parents can feel empowered by helping their teen with safety issues. While a battered teen cannot control the violence or the abuser, she is responsible for doing what she can to ensure that she is as safe as possible.

If your daughter is being abused, you can help her use her strengths to plan for her safety. She knows the abuser and his patterns better than anyone—although she may not realize that until you tell her. She knows what kinds of situations are the most volatile for him—and the most dangerous for her. For example, does he become violent when he drinks at parties? What are the safest ways to leave such situations, based on his particular patterns? You can help her remember and take credit for the times she has been strong in dealing with or avoiding the violence.

Knowing patterns is helpful when planning for safety, but you must also be prepared for the unexpected. You need to be vigilant and aware, and ready to adapt to the ever-changing situation.

If she is not going to break up with him, or is considering it but isn't ready yet, you can try to brainstorm strategies with your daughter so that she is prepared with possible actions she can take when he is enraged or harassing her, or when the tension is building. If she is ready to break up, you can help her make a safety plan to prepare for his explosive reaction to the breakup and the harassment that often follows as he tries to get her to come back to him.

An important step when planning for safety is preparing yourself to take action by making a commitment to deal with the reality of the situation, and a spectrum of possible problems you may encounter. If you are prepared by being able to think clearly without being frozen or agitated by fear, you are better able to handle an emergency situation, and to think about ways to keep an emergency from happening.

There are many different ways to plan for safety. The plans that will work for you depend on the particular characteristics of your situation. Brainstorm safety plans with everyone in your family, and include others who might be key participants in helping keep your daughter safe. Some things to consider include the following:

- ways to get home safely if violence starts while she is out with her boyfriend
- safe places she can go if she can't get home
- people she can call in emergencies
- people you can tell to be on alert for signs of danger
- ways to handle specific emergencies (for example, "Go to the hospital emergency room and call me to meet you there")
- backup safety strategies for times the victim is vulnerable to violence (for example, having friends accompany her to and from school)
- how to deal with harassment by telephone, texting, Facebook, or e-mail (for example, by blocking phone numbers or Facebook, or changing accounts)
- steps she can take to be prepared for emergencies, such as spare keys and cash stored where she could get to them (for example, in a magnetic box hidden under her car)

Parents can work together with their teen to create a successful safety plan, as illustrated in Jessica's story.

Jessica

Jessica was in her junior year in college, attending a university three hours from home. She lived off-campus with her boyfriend,

Ken. At first they had fun together, but tension began soon after she moved into his apartment. He worked off and on, and had trouble sticking with one job. He had a bad temper and had fits of rage when he couldn't get his way. Jessica hated fighting, so she gave in to him. He punched her on a few occasions. He was manipulative, especially about their finances. He spent her money, buying things on impulse, and even used her credit card without her knowing it. She became more and more stressed, and started having trouble with her schoolwork. One day she called her parents, sobbing, and asked them, "What should I do?" Over the next few days, Jessica and her parents came up with a plan.

The first stage in Jessica's safety plan took place via phone calls and e-mails with her parents. Her parents advised her to put her important papers, money, and keys—anything she might need in an emergency—in a safe place. She stored some other belongings at a friend's place in case she needed to get out of the apartment to safety without much time to prepare.

The second stage of her safety plan started when Jessica decided to leave school and go home to think. The day she left, she told Ken she was going home for a visit with her parents. She left quickly, to avoid a prolonged (and possibly violent) argument with Ken. She took her emergency items with her, along with a few other valuables she feared Ken would destroy if he had an outburst of rage while she was away.

The third stage took place while she was at home with her parents. During this time, her parents listened to Jessica's accounts of what had been going on. Although they were upset and frightened, they listened calmly and realized they needed more information. They called a domestic violence hotline, and all three of them were able to get questions answered and the support they needed. Jessica started to see a counselor. On her second day at home, Ken started relentlessly calling, e-mailing, and texting Jessica, at her parents' home number as well as on Jessica's cell phone. She told him to stop contacting her, that she needed to think, and that she'd contact him when she was ready to talk. She blocked his number from her cell phone and unfriended him on Facebook, and the family started screening all their calls.

During this time, Jessica's parents saw how Ken treated her, especially when he was desperate and angry. They became anxious and frightened for Jessica, and stressed about what to do. The family agreed to take breaks from the stress, and set boundaries about times they wouldn't talk to or about Ken or think about him. They spent time on positive activities, such as exercise, outings, and dinners with family and friends. They all became better able to think clearly about what to do next.

Eventually the fourth stage became clear to Jessica. She decided to end the relationship and to begin the process of making the major changes that were involved. She decided to drop out of school for the rest of the semester and to move home. With her counselor, she prepared to tell Ken that she was leaving him, and to say good-bye to her friends and her life at school. She and her parents met with the counselor to plan a safe way for Jessica to go to the apartment to get her things and to be prepared for Ken's unpredictability. They talked with advocates and a law enforcement officer about the help available to prevent any violence—for example, going with her to move her things out of the apartment. They made a plan for how to deal with Ken's persistent efforts to pressure her to come back.

Looking back later on this difficult time, Jessica and her parents remember it as incredibly stressful, but they were all relieved that they were able to plan together so that Jessica did not get hurt.

Involving Family and Friends

Teen dating violence is everybody's business. However, you and your teen may not want other people to know about it. Maybe you are embarrassed or afraid people will think badly of you. You might feel people won't understand why the battering relationship has been going on for such a long time. You might be private about your family's ups and downs in general. Or perhaps you are afraid that family and friends might become involved in the violence. But it is a good idea to include trusted family and friends.

By involving family and friends, you expand your resources for dealing with an extremely difficult and often dangerous problem. You are creating a safety net and a support system. You are getting the problem out in the open. You are taking it seriously and getting strategic support.

Your family and friends are important resources for your battered teen. This group includes brothers and sisters, grandparents, aunts and uncles, and cousins, as well as friends of your family. They can each be helpful in many ways. Perhaps they can provide a place to stay for the victim to get away from her abuser. They can be on alert for signs of danger and for opportunities to help. They can be supportive and can listen (sometimes more objectively than parents) as your teen makes decisions (about breaking up, for example).

These support people can offer direct opinions without getting the hostile reactions a parent might get. In some instances, friends and/or family might all get together to discuss the situation openly and provide support and understanding to your daughter, to you, and to one another. People acquainted with the abuser might talk to him so he knows that his girlfriend is not isolated and that he is being watched.

Your friends and family members also have friends, contacts with other resources, and other ways to expand your network of information, support, and safety. Your daughter can feel surrounded by love and support—and by realistic perspectives about her relationship.

In chapter 11 you read about how Barbara brought her family together for discussions about Tanisha so that they could talk about the violence in her relationship, how it affected all of them, what was going on currently, and how they could handle it. Barbara's family didn't all agree on what to do, but they did agree that they thought and planned better as a group than they did individually. Barbara believes that her family stayed sane through the rollercoaster of Tanisha's two-year relationship because of these discussions.

Your Daughter's Friends

If you have some contact with your daughter's friends, they can be a resource as well. You can ask them about what they are noticing in her relationship. You can express your concern, tell them you are worried, and tell them why. They may be concerned too, and they might be relieved to talk to you. Teens tend to want to solve their problems on their own; they tend not to ask parents for help. But sometimes when they are afraid or don't know what to do, they are relieved when a parent asks for their help. Good friends of teens who have been seriously injured or killed by their boyfriends have suffered tremendously afterward when they realized they didn't tell anyone what they knew.

Your daughter's friends can be "upstanders": allies who support her by safely speaking up or getting help instead of ignoring what is going on in front of them. You may be able to give your daughter's friends information about ways to help her. They can contact you or talk to someone at school if she is in danger. They can stay close to her and get others to join them when their presence may keep the batterer from hurting her. They can encourage the batterer's friends to talk to him about the seriousness of his problem. Telling your daughter's friends that you appreciate that they are "hanging in" and keeping her from being isolated lets them know they are doing the right thing.

The Abuser's Family

There are two families involved in a teen's violent relationship: the abuser's family and the victim's family. (If you are the parent of a teen who is abusive, see also chapter 18.) If your teen is being abused, you may consider contacting the abuser's family. This might help you find out more about your daughter's situation. You may find that the abuser's family knows nothing about the kinds of problems their child is having. They may have suspected it, or they may have seen some of the violence themselves, but they may not realize the real scope of the problem. Or it may be completely hidden from them. Hearing from you might have an impact on them and lead them to take this seriously. You may find that working with the other family can successfully address the situation and get the abuser the help he or she needs.

Theresa and Joe's story illustrates how two families can work together to help a victim in an abusive relationship.

Theresa and Joe

Theresa and Joe had discovered that their daughter's boyfriend, Charles, was abusing her. They had talked with Charles's mother about his violence. She didn't think she could stop him from doing any of the destructive things he did, especially because of his serious drug problem. But several times she called Theresa and Joe to alert them that Charles was enraged and looking for their daughter, or that he had her there and they should come get her before she got hurt. With these warnings, the family was better able to protect her.

Often, the abuser's family is protective and defends their teen. They may not listen, and they may even blame the victim. Other families are overwhelmed by their teen's violence and feel powerless to do anything about it. They may listen, shrug, and say they can't do anything. They may be afraid their teen will be arrested. Other families may not see their teen very much, or perhaps he lives with a sibling or a friend, and his family doesn't see themselves as being involved in what he does.

There is no way to predict how the abuser's family will react. You may know enough about him to know that his family life is chaotic and filled with problems. You may be right not to expect them to be helpful. But talking with them is a strategy that is often overlooked, and is worth trying if there is even a remote chance that it can help either or both children.

Neighbors

Your neighbors and (if she is not living with you) your daughter's neighbors can be a part of her safety net. You can tell neighbors what is happening in the relationship, and alert them so they can respond when necessary. For example, they could help her directly or call you if they hear her crying for help. You can also learn about aspects of the abuse from neighbors who have seen incidents outside your house or in your apartment building. For example, neighbors could tell parents about an ex-boyfriend stalking their daughter outside. Neighbors may be reluctant to "get involved" until you directly ask them. Once you have talked to them, they may be more likely to come to her aid, or call you or the police if they see your daughter being harassed or beaten. Jill's story illustrates how neighbors can be helpful.

Jill

Pamela talked to a neighbor in the apartment building where her seventeen-year-old daughter, Jill, was living with her boyfriend. This elderly woman was afraid of getting involved in the violence she suspected was taking place next door. But a short time after talking with Pamela, the neighbor called her when she found Jill in the front yard, unconscious and bleeding. Taking this action saved Jill's life. That also turned out to be the incident that was the turning point for Jill, and she began to break away from the relationship as she recovered from her injuries.

13

Breaking Up

Although leaving an abusive relationship is safer in the long run, the period of time immediately following a breakup can be extremely dangerous. Often the abuser becomes more violent, or threatens to hurt himself or his ex-girlfriend. When planning a breakup, it is essential to prepare for harassment or a potential escalation of violence.

Guiding Your Teen through a Breakup

Breaking up a relationship is difficult to do, even if the relationship is not abusive or violent. But ending an abusive relationship is not like ending a healthy one, because the abuser may not accept the breakup and then react with threats and violence. The abuser will often continue his controlling behavior and try to keep in contact with her. Loveisrespect.org, a teen dating violence prevention organization, suggests the following tips for you and your daughter:

- If it doesn't feel safe, don't break up in person. It may seem cruel to break up over the phone or by e-mail, but it may be the safest way.

- If the breakup occurs in person, it should be done in a public place. You or your daughter's friends should wait nearby.

- Your daughter shouldn't try to explain her reasons for ending the relationship more than once. There is nothing to say that will make the abuser happy.

- Let friends and other family members know that the relationship is ending, especially if you think the abuser will come to your house or confront your daughter when she's alone.

- Advise your daughter that if the abuser does come to your house when she's alone, she should not open the door, and she should call someone.

- Trust your instincts, and encourage everyone else involved to do the same. If anyone feels afraid, there is probably a good reason.

- Ask for help. You or your daughter should call an advocate who is trained and ready to answer your questions.[37]

After Breaking Up

Your daughter's ex-boyfriend may be extremely upset and feel desperately lost after she breaks up with him. He may not believe or accept that the relationship is really over. Your daughter may feel torn apart and worried about him. Or, if he is explosively angry with her for leaving, she may be afraid of what he might do to her or her family. She may also find that his anger and desperation lead him to behave in ways that are disruptive, threatening, and harassing.

There are several common kinds of harassment after a breakup:

- constant texting and calling at all hours of the day and night

- having friends repeatedly pressure her during her school day or at her job "not to do this to him"

- cornering her sisters, brothers, or friends for long periods of time to talk about the breakup and get information about her comings and goings

- asking her close friends out on dates, or pursuing sexual relations with one of her close friends

- talking, starting rumors, or writing graffiti about her on school property that contains sexually humiliating lies

- having his friends sexually harass her (name-calling, crudely talking to her, physically harassing her)

- repeatedly waking her up in the middle of the night from outside her bedroom window "to talk"

- calling or coming to her house and threatening to hurt or kill her or her family members

- forcing her or convincing her to get into his car or to go somewhere where he barrages her with questions and accusations, or pleads and pressures her to change her mind, not letting her get away

The ex-boyfriend may begin stalking your daughter. Stalking is a way the abuser intimidates and instills fear by persistently contacting the victim, or making her aware of his presence and surveillance of her. It can constantly disrupt whatever peaceful moments you and your daughter may attain. Stalking contains a threat of danger to your daughter and to your family. It can go on for days, weeks, months, or years. Stalking is against the law, and it is recognized as a tactic of abuse. It is known to intensify during and after a breakup. (See chapters 15 and 16 for information on your legal options, including what to do when stalking is taking place.)

There are a number of common kinds of stalking behavior an abuser can exhibit:

- making persistent, repeated phone calls or texts to the victim at all hours

- leaving threatening messages on your phone, in your mailbox, in your daughter's school locker, and other places

- sitting in a parked car or standing outside your home for hours
- watching your daughter and letting her know in a menacing way that she is being watched
- following her or having friends follow her
- showing up wherever she goes—for example, at parties or outings with her family and friends

Post-Breakup Safety

Breaking up may involve your daughter making a clear separation from her abuser, certain that she no longer wants to be with him. Or breaking up may be a process of her telling him she wants to break up, and then trying to help him deal with it. This process might go on for days or weeks—even months—until she makes a final break and has no more contact with him, or until he accepts that the relationship is over. Another common experience is that when she suggests that they break up, he breaks up with her or goes out with someone else. She then becomes extremely upset and confused about what she wants. She may be devastated that he doesn't want to be with her and become obsessive about being with him.

In general, the major safety concern after the end of a battering relationship is how to avoid contact with an abuser who is volatile, especially if the abuser and the victim live in the same community and go to the same school. Safety planning usually focuses on her staying away from him, and keeping him away from her.

Teens who have been abused are often hooked back into the relationship because of fear or worry about the abuser: "He needs me." "He can't live without me." "It's safer to be with him where I can keep him from hurting my family." The victim needs to get away from his pressure to go back to him and get away from his harassment or stalking. She needs to get away so she can think clearly. When an ex-girlfriend is around the abuser, she often thinks the way he thinks rather than making her own safety a priority. If he is desperately upset, she focuses on taking care of him and has a terrible time taking care of herself.

Ending a battering relationship is unlike ending other relationships. It is rarely possible to maintain contact or a friendship after the breakup. It may be possible to work out ways to safely maintain contact if necessary—for example, when a child is involved. Often, though not always, extreme measures are taken to avoid contact.

There are many specific techniques for avoiding contact. Here are a few:

- No one should reply to his texts, calls, e-mails, or social network postings.
- Screen calls to the house and to her cell phone.
- Get a restraining order (also called an "order of protection" or a "keep-away order").
- Save harassing or threatening text messages or voicemails to use to get a restraining order or make a police report; keep a record of dates and times the messages were sent or calls were made.
- Change your phone number.
- Turn off phones at night when everyone is at home, or whenever you need a break.
- If he has a key to your house, or knows where you keep one, change the lock and remove the key.
- Arrange for your daughter not to be by herself when she is vulnerable; for example, if he is likely to confront her on her way somewhere, family members and friends can accompany her for a while.
- Alert people at work and school that she doesn't want to see or talk to him.

- Make sure that an adult knows where she is going if it's not part of her usual routine, and when she is expected to return; if you are especially concerned, ask her to call when she arrives at her destination and when she leaves for home.

- Remind everyone in the family of emergency procedures, with a discussion about the kinds of circumstances in which to follow emergency procedures.

- Have her stay with a friend or a family member where he can't find her.

Cooperation and coordination between your family and community resources can enhance your daughter's safety, as illustrated in Lisa's story.

Lisa

Lisa, a fourteen-year-old girl, was trying to break up with fifteen-year-old Eric. Several incidents took place at school. Eric pushed Lisa against the wall and choked her in the girl's bathroom, trapping her when she screamed and tried to get away from him. He verbally harassed her, yelled at her, and threatened her, and called her "bitch" and "whore" across the schoolyard. He didn't believe that she wanted to break up with him and persisted in following her, writing her love letters and harassing and pleading with her. His friends cornered her and accused her of ruining Eric's life.

To try to protect Lisa, a juvenile police officer worked with school administrators. The juvenile police officer and school principal and vice principal let Eric know that they would take disciplinary action according to school protocols if he did not stay away from her. It was clear to Eric that he would be arrested if he hurt Lisa in any way. Teachers and other school personnel were informed that Eric was not to be alone with Lisa. Lisa and her parents arranged for friends to walk to and from school with her. The domestic violence program in the school educated classmates in general so they were alert and aware, even though they were not told about Lisa's situation in particular. Lisa and her family received counseling through the domestic violence program. Counseling was also offered to Eric.

Everyone working out this safety plan agreed that it should not be up to Lisa alone to convey to Eric the seriousness of his problem or her wish to stay away from him. She was too frightened of him and worried about his devastated reaction to the breakup. She was better able to take care of herself with the coordinated efforts of her parents, her friends, her school, and the police.

There are cases in which the only way to end the violence after the relationship ends is for the family to take extreme measures to get the battered teen completely away from the batterer. These kinds of measures are especially necessary when the batterer's threats or behavior indicate that it is possible he will try to kill his ex-girlfriend or someone in her family.

She may have to hide from him, changing her school and residence. She may try to stay in one of the shelters for battered women that have been established for this purpose; some of these shelters accept teens. She may have to leave town for a while, sometimes for a long time, staying with relatives or family friends. She may have to keep her new residence a secret from school, friends, and others so that it will not be inadvertently revealed to the batterer.

In some cases, the whole family must move to another city without leaving a forwarding address. Occasionally, the family must also change their name and take detailed precautions so that the batterer does not find out where they are living.

The process of breaking up is very complicated in these situations. The planning involved may take considerable time and effort so that the batterer does not suspect that his girlfriend is thinking of leaving. The family must sometimes make detailed plans for her to disappear suddenly, so that when he finds out that she has left and he becomes enraged, he cannot find her.

For teen mothers whose abuser is the father of their child, this can be an especially complicated process because of legal issues regarding the custody and visitation of the child. It will take extra planning to leave town with the child.

Emotional Reactions after the Breakup

You can help your daughter anticipate her feelings about being apart from her boyfriend when she breaks up with him. What will she need? Will she want to be physically far away from him so that she can't see him (even by accident) and can avoid feeling pressured by him or letting her own feelings pull her back to him? Will she want to be with other people most of the time? Will she want to be at home and doing her usual routine? Will she need help from others to keep her from having any contact with him?

Most people leaving a battering relationship are vulnerable to going back, especially between two weeks and two months after breaking up. This is a critical period. It is not a matter of how much time it takes to get over the relationship, but of getting through the moments when your daughter feels the pull back to him. Your daughter needs continuous support. You cannot assume that her need for your support is over just because the relationship is over. Quite the contrary: She will still be emotionally vulnerable, and possibly in physical danger, for a long time after the breakup.

After things quiet down, and she has become involved in a new routine that doesn't focus on her relationship, she may feel the pull to go back. She will start missing the things that were good in the relationship and minimizing the bad times. She will feel bad about how much the boyfriend may be suffering or despairing or missing her.

She will experience the fear and intense pain of being alone, which is especially acute after the intense demands of an abusive relationship. She will be afraid of what the boyfriend will do, and the tension can be unbearable. She might seek the relief of staying close to him, watching over him, accommodating him—feeling like she is managing the situation by being in contact with him rather than coping with the fear of the unknown when she is apart from him.

Once her boyfriend is not around, your daughter may experience intense feelings she could not feel when she was with him. She may be depressed, even thinking of suicide. She may be angry with herself and afraid to trust herself in the future. Her self-esteem has been seriously undermined, and she may be having a hard time believing that she can get over this, or do better on her own, or do the things she wants to do. She may be terrified, realizing what she has been through. She may feel ashamed and guilty when she understands what her family has been through. She may be angry, realizing how badly she has been treated or how unsupportive some people have been.

Your daughter needs support to overcome the isolation she experienced during the relationship. She has to re-establish friendships and fill the gaps in her social and emotional life that were caused by the intense relationship. She needs to be embraced by her family.

What about you, the parents? She's getting over a relationship, and you are recovering from a prolonged and intense crisis. Your emotional reactions after the breakup may surprise you. Of course you will feel relieved, but you may also realize the degree to which you were traumatized. You may dwell on your past decisions and/or mistakes. You may find it difficult to trust your daughter, her judgment, or her friends. Returning to "normal" may take a while. This is a time of healing and restoration for all of you.

Your daughter needs help from you and from people at her school to regain lost ground—academically, socially, and in her other activities. She needs counseling to help her recover her self-esteem and to deal with the intense push and pull to and from the battering relationship. She needs counseling to recover from the traumatic effects of the relationship and to evaluate what she has been through, how it has affected her, and how to believe in herself once more. She can get through this and thrive again.

If the Violence Stops

So far we have focused on breakups where the abuser has gotten worse, not better. In some cases, however, the person who uses violent behavior realizes he has a problem and gets help to stop the abuse. This can happen to anyone who has used violent or abusive behavior—male or female. There are several common motivations for an abuser to make a change like this. He may be afraid he'll lose the relationship. He may realize he has an alcohol or drug problem, get sober or clean, and find out he can control his violent behavior. He may get arrested, severely injure his girlfriend, lose access to his child, or for some other reason be forced to face the very real consequences of his violent and/or abusive behavior. If he has been arrested, he may be ordered by a judge into a counseling program and learn he can change the way he treats his girlfriend. Something might change for him, on his own or in the relationship, and a long period might go by during which he finds he can calm himself and prevent his violent outbursts. The change can be permanent if the abuser is willing to transform the way he functions in relationships.

The longer and more frequently batterers have used violence in the past, the harder it is for them to stop. For this reason, younger people, especially young adults, have a better chance of stopping their violent behavior than do older people who have more entrenched patterns. Stopping one's own violence means being constantly aware of one's potential to use violence—in a current relationship or in any other relationship in the future. People who use violence to control their partners must take responsibility for how they handle situations, circumstances, or conditions that might trigger their violent reactions. They must also learn how to be a partner in creating a healthy relationship and to give up their need for control of the other person.

Because of the possibility that the abuser could resort to violence again, you, your daughter, and her boyfriend will need to keep the same safety plans in place. This is not to minimize his progress toward not using violence. Rather, this is to provide a realistic support system that reduces the risk he will disappoint everyone and hurt his girlfriend by using violence again. Your daughter may go through changes in her behavior and responses as well, making her better able to take care of herself and raising her expectations about how she wants to be treated. She will need support to sustain these changes. The couple will feel watched by you and others. Explain to them that it is normal for you as parents to be paying attention and to have expectations that the relationship will be free from abuse. Everyone will also need to pay attention to triggers and work to prevent relapses.

People can stop being violent. To do so, they must continue to be aware of their feelings, their triggers, and the circumstances around them so that they can deal with these feelings and situations in alternative, nonviolent ways. They can establish prevention strategies for themselves, such as having people to call or a place to go to cool off if they feel enraged.

A batterer may find counseling helpful to support these changes. Even if specialized help is not available, most cities have counseling programs. Group counseling, batterers' intervention programs, and anger management classes can be especially effective. Alcoholics Anonymous, substance abuse groups, and other self-help support groups assist with accountability and conscientiousness in maintaining changes. The next chapter provides more information about counseling resources.

Committing to Change

The teen or young adult who has recognized the seriousness of his problem with violence must acknowledge his responsibility for his behavior and make a commitment to change. You can look for evidence that the teen is committed to change and willing to be accountable for his behavior by seeing if he

- acknowledges that he chooses or resorts to violent and/or controlling, abusive behavior

- understands that using violence masks other, deeper problems

- refrains from justifying violence and agrees that it is never justified

- makes every effort possible to solve problems and conflicts without hurting himself or anyone else, either emotionally, verbally, or physically

- makes a commitment to know himself, his triggers, and his reactions

- commits to using counseling, support groups (such as AA), and a variety of strategies to keep himself calm and grounded

- commits to learning how to create a healthy relationship

- develops techniques—such as deep breathing, time-outs, taking a walk, or listening to music—that can be used at any tense moment

- challenges beliefs about what is expected of women and men in intimate relationships, especially his view that he is entitled to control a woman

- makes a commitment to transforming the abusive relationship into a healthy one—based on respect, mutuality, and good communication, not power and control

Safety Alert

Before assuming that the violence has stopped, consider the possibility that it might have become hidden. If the violence has truly stopped and the couple continues to see each other, you may feel relieved that things have changed for the better. You may find that when your daughter's boyfriend has his violence under control, he can be a pleasure to have around. But what if you don't feel relieved and continue to feel uneasy? Do you notice that although the physical violence has stopped, the other controlling patterns in the relationship continue? While you are relieved that your daughter is not being beaten, are you concerned that she is still being emotionally abused or sexually assaulted? Your daughter and her boyfriend may be experiencing an extended reconciliation and feeling hopeful, but the potential patterns of intimidation, isolation, and control may continue. Although the physical abuse might have stopped, the emotional and sexual abuse might be continuing. If this is the case, your daughter is still in an abusive relationship. As we discussed earlier in this book, emotional abuse is also a serious problem, and it can have a devastating effect on its victims.

15

Getting Help:
Counseling, Schools, and the Legal System

There are many resources and many legal issues for teens in abusive relationships and their families to consider, so we asked our friend and colleague, Emily Austin, J.D., to write the next two chapters specifically about these concerns and resources that are available. She is an attorney and the director of policy at Peace Over Violence in Los Angeles.

Resources for Parents

There are services for youth and awareness-raising around adolescent dating abuse in nearly every community. There is expertise and help available, and there are many ways of getting help from different agencies and systems, such as law enforcement, schools, and community organizations.

Using the Internet

The Internet can be a way to gain information and become connected with other parents, teens, and advocates who can help you and your child. It is necessary, however, to follow a few guidelines to connect to credible resources. Remember that the Internet is in a constant state of flux, with changes happening every minute. Be sure to use your common sense when getting information from the Internet, as there is very little oversight over what is published online. We suggest the following:

- Read the website's "About" section—it will let you know what kind of organization is maintaining the site's information. This part of the site will let you know if there is a local, state, or national focus for the information.

- Check the "Facts" sections for connections to studies and other types of research, as this shows that the site values solid facts.

- Look for sponsoring agencies, government connections, and logos for such places as the Centers for Disease Control and Prevention, various school affiliations, the Office on Violence Against Women, and public health agencies—this shows a connection to vetted services that are accountable for reporting to and oversight by the state or federal government.

Several online resources are geared specifically to adolescent dating abuse and have received federal and private funding to do research and outreach (e.g., www.loveisnotabuse.com, www.loveisrespect .org). These sites provide information geared to young adults, parents, and educators. "Get Help" buttons connect online visitors with chat and/or hotline numbers. Also, organizations such as the U.S. Centers for Disease Control and Prevention, Futures Without Violence, and RAINN (Rape, Abuse & Incest National Network, which runs the National Sexual Assault Hotline) have many useful online resources. See the resources section in the back of the book for more information.

To connect to more local information, every state has a coalition against domestic violence and/or sexual assault that works with the National Coalition Against Domestic Violence and the National Sexual Violence Resource Center, organizations that spearhead many national campaigns and policy efforts. Although originally founded to respond to adult domestic violence, many state coalitions have local facts and resources for prevention and response to adolescent dating abuse. Conducting a general online search for local domestic violence and sexual assault services is another way to locate regional information and find out about what services are available in your community.

Parent-focused resources are available on many of the national and local websites. Also, parent advocacy groups, such as Moms and Dads for Education (MADE) to Stop Teen Dating Abuse, can be good online resources.

Hotlines

There are many local and national programs that provide twenty-four-hour telephone response, and some of them also provide access via the Internet during work hours. Hotline counselors are trained in assessing the crisis, safety planning, and making referrals. They are a good resource for a great deal of information for adults and teens.

Counseling and Advocacy

Counseling can make a difference as a way for you and/or your teen to sort out feelings, think about how to deal with the situation, and gain emotional support. You can contact national or state-specific hotlines to be connected to the services in your community. Many free or low-cost resources are available through local domestic violence and sexual assault agencies. With parent/caregiver consent, nearly all of these services can be used by teens. In some states, such as California, mental health exceptions allow minors to access services without parent notification or consent. You can be connected to local parent and family counseling on dating abuse through your local domestic violence program.

Support groups are valuable for dealing with dating violence. It helps to hear other teens' or other parents' experiences. It is comforting and supportive to find that you are not alone, and that other people have had similar problems. Although not widespread, more and more teen-focused support groups are being held through local domestic violence programs, mental and public health agencies, and some youth-serving organizations. Many domestic violence organizations offer parenting support groups and parenting skills classes that can provide additional support and resources. Groups are run in different ways—some are weekly "drop-in" groups, and others require more commitment over a set period of time.

Counseling is also available through mental health centers, family service agencies, general counseling programs, and youth programs. Some organizations, such as YWCAs, community centers, recreation centers, athletic programs, and gang intervention/prevention services, have special programs and workshops that help young people deal with relationships, sexuality, and issues of violence. Programs for teen mothers have been an excellent source of support for teens dealing with violent relationships. Gay and lesbian centers in many cities have specialized programs for domestic violence victims and abusers.

Teen health clinics often can be a helpful resource for services. Health clinics are often attached to high schools and college campuses, or are available through Planned Parenthood and community health clinics. Teens often prefer to go to health clinics because they don't have to wait to be seen and their visits are confidential. These clinics are familiar to teens because they go to them for a variety of needs. Many specialize in working with runaway youth; lesbian, gay, and bisexual youth; or other high-risk teens, some of whom have experienced dating abuse. Calling these clinics is a great way to connect to local services for teens and support for parents who are stressed. Health clinics can also be used to treat injuries caused by battering.

Additional help can be found in religious communities. Religious institutions and leaders are often open to teaching healthy relationship skills and providing appropriate support for responding to dating abuse. If both partners of the couple are part of the same church or youth group, leaders and everyone in that environment can be involved in your child's safety and in helping both parties get the help they need. Church members and leaders, like any people who work with young people, can be alert and talk openly with young people to find out what is going on and to intervene.

Sometimes, when the violence of the situation is serious, a teen has to get to a safe place. For example, the person who abuses is threatening harm and is known to be capable of inflicting harm, and there is no other safe place for the victim to stay. Families usually prefer to send a teen in this kind of situation to stay with a relative or friends outside the area. However, if this isn't possible, a shelter can offer a safe, hidden refuge along with counseling and advocacy services for planning for future safety. Find out if the shelter nearest to you accepts teens into their program. As with the mental health services, many times it will be easier to find your child services with your consent and with you as an advocate for your child. Some shelters may be able to accommodate a parent with the teen, but not the teen by herself. You may have to go to a shelter outside of your area to find the right services.

Counseling for the person who batters should be comprehensive and must involve more than just a support group, anger management classes, or conflict resolution classes. These are helpful in conjunction with individual or group batterer treatment programs. But treatment programs should provide a more in-depth psychoeducational approach to the problem, with accountability for the violent behavior built into the program. Groundbreaking work with adult abusers is occurring throughout the nation, with many programs focusing on underlying issues that contribute to abusive behavior and mental health concerns, such as obsessive and controlling behavior, thoughts of suicide, and depression. Work with teen abusers is not as widespread, but promising programs in partnership with the juvenile justice system are increasing. Your local juvenile justice/court/probation systems are a good resource for what is happening to rehabilitate and counsel teen offenders in your community.

Couples counseling and/or joint counseling for the victim and the batterer together are not advised until the batterer's verbal, emotional, and physical abuse has stopped. Otherwise the counseling sessions can be intimidating or even dangerous experiences for the abused teen. However, couples counseling can be helpful for parents of the abuser or parents of the victim to help cope with their child's situation.

When you look for a counselor or therapist who is not on the staff of a specialized domestic violence program, there are several criteria you can use to select someone to help with dating violence. Look for a counselor who has experience in dealing with domestic violence. One way to do this is to ask for referrals from your local domestic violence program or hotline.

In the initial interview to assess the problem, your child must feel safe in describing her actual experiences. The counselor should not ask your child to discuss the relationship or the violence in the presence of the batterer. The counselor should also be interested in building a trusting, confidential relationship with the teen. This might include limiting the information that the counselor shares with the parent during sessions with the teen. Every community has professional rules to protect the confidentiality of the clients, and a good counselor will know these rules and work with them to develop a trusting relationship with the teen, while keeping parents involved.

Questions to ask a potential counselor include the following:

- Do you have expertise in teen domestic violence? What kind of training do you have in this work?

- Have you ever worked with someone who has been abused or raped in a relationship?

- What techniques do you use in working with battered teens or teen batterers that differ from those you use when working with adults?

- Do you recommend counseling as a couple when there is abuse in the relationship?

- How would you support my participation in the counseling as a parent?

- How would you deal with the ongoing threat of violence toward me and/or my child?

- How much information about the sessions with my child will you be able to share with me?

- What is your confidentiality policy?

- When would you need to report a situation to law enforcement or child protective services?

- Are you available in emergencies? How can you be reached?

Advocacy is another service that domestic violence programs, legal advocacy centers, and other community service organizations can provide. Advocacy includes support in seeking a restraining order, as discussed below, or help in talking with school officials, landlords, child protective services, church officials, and/or law enforcement. Many domestic violence and sexual assault programs provide advocacy services to teens and their parents, or they know of local resources that can better assist you and your teen in getting the help you need.

Schools as a Resource

If your child is in middle school/junior high, high school, or college, the school system is a resource and source of support in providing help for students and planning for improved safety. School personnel can be a source of information on what is happening with the abuse at school. They can participate as part of the safety net for your child.

Schools often have the resources and authority to influence the batterer to stop his violence, and they are legally entrusted with providing safe learning environments.

Your child might not like you contacting her school or your "interference" (as she might see it). She might protect her boyfriend from intervention by the school or deny that she is being abused when school personnel try to discuss the problem with her. When dealing with dating abuse, parents often, as we have discussed earlier, have to take action to protect their child at the risk of making their child angry or withdrawn from them. With reminders that you are acting out of love and her best interests, and a commitment to keeping the lines of communication open, you can maintain your relationship with your child while taking steps to protect her.

Policies and protocols of middle schools, high schools, and colleges in response to dating abuse vary widely, as do school and individual personnel responses to the issue of dating abuse. Although the situation is improving, parents and teens can still face a dismissive disbelief in the seriousness of dating abuse when working with school officials. School personnel may see this as a family/personal issue, not a safety concern for the campus. They might also not know the appropriate response or see the connection between dating abuse and their campus discipline policy. They might feel that dating abuse does not happen at their school. Much of the advocacy work in preventing dating abuse has focused on improving schools' abilities to respond to and prevent dating abuse. This includes the development of several model policies, such as the Start Strong school policy, as well as a series of state laws encouraging and/or requiring schools to provide prevention education and response protocols for dating abuse.

Getting Help from School Administrators

As a parent approaching schools for help, it is important to remember that parents can have a huge impact on schools. Parents are the de facto consumer/customer/client at schools because they represent their children's voices. Nearly all schools, especially middle and high schools, struggle with parent engagement, and all strive to improve communication with parents and caregivers. Also, many states have requirements that schools respond to sexual harassment, bullying, and violence issues on campus, and these requirements are often enforced through parents as the watchdogs of school operations.

It is important to establish contact with someone at your child's school by calling or visiting. It might be helpful for you to find out information about your child and the batterer, if he attends the same school. For example, you can ask about your child's attendance record, any changes in her behavior or academic status, any observed incidences of abuse, or any violence toward her from other students. Trusted teachers, counselors, security officers, and staff are a good resource for how your child is doing and are integral parts of a comprehensive safety net. But it is important to reach out to administrators at the school, such as the principal, dean, vice principal, and lead teacher, as well, because they will have the ability to make certain changes, and they also often hold the most responsibility to take action when they learn of a safety threat.

The school can help both the victim and the abuser. For example, schools can create stay-away contracts between parties so that they agree to avoid contact with each other, or if the abuser is not a student on campus, they can keep him away from the campus. Schools should be able to make commonsense, reasonable accommodations to requests to improve the safety of students. These can include schedule changes (so the victim's patterns on campus are less predictable), new school drop-off/pickup locations, or alerting security officers who can check in with the victim during the day and/or accompany the student. Schools can also direct the abuser to mental health resources, as well as hold the abuser accountable for his actions through discipline policies.

Getting help from schools varies widely based on the individual administrators and the campus-level knowledge of dating abuse. Even with decades of awareness-raising and education, there are still some school administrators who do not believe that dating abuse impacts their students and the safety on campus. It is important to remember some key words and strategies to make sure your school is responding appropriately to dating abuse. These are described below. Knowing about the policies and procedures at your school can assist you in getting the help and support you need to keep your child safe.

School Policies

Very few schools have policies and protocols to specifically respond to dating abuse. However, it is useful to ask school administrators if they have such a policy, and if the school personnel have any training on dating abuse prevention and response. Just asking these questions can pressure and encourage schools to look at the variety of model policies, curricula, and resources available for school response to dating abuse. If no specific policy exists, the school still must have discipline policies and codes of conduct to address violent behavior on campus. Federal and state laws require schools to have safety plans, not only for natural disasters, but also for violence on campus. Depending on the nature of the abuse, dating abuse can pose a threat to the safety of the victim and the entire school, and it can trigger a required school response.

School responses to violent incidents on campus depend on school policy and administrations' choices. Some schools may contact the police or campus security. They might report the incident to parents. Or they may work through a restorative justice model, which is a process that focuses on healing from the harm caused by the violence by conducting meetings with the victim, offender, and community members. The offenders take responsibility for the harm caused by their violence. As restorative justice models become more common in school settings, administrators and school personnel must be mindful of the intimidating and coercive control used in dating abuse. Having both victim and offender in the same meeting can be intimidating for the victim, especially in cases of dating abuse where the victim might not want to end the relationship with the abuser or might continue to be afraid of him after the relationship has ended.

All schools that receive federal money (this includes private and charter schools) have requirements to respond to sexual harassment and sex discrimination through the federal law Title IX of the Education Amendments of 1972. Each school has to designate a Title IX coordinator to respond to complaints of sex discrimination. Dating abuse may qualify as sexual harassment/sex discrimination, depending on the type of abuse. It can be very powerful to ask the administration if you can talk to the Title IX coordinator, and in many cases this could be the person who is a resource for response and prevention of abuse at school. Schools are required to let parents and students know about their response and reporting procedures for sexual harassment/sex discrimination, and to respond in a timely manner to reports.

Also, due to recent heartbreaking suicides of bullied students and the connection between school violence and bullying, schools have prioritized bullying prevention and response. Every state has its own anti-bullying school laws and/or policies. The government site www .stopbullying.gov is a good resource to find out what your state is doing to prevent bullying. Although dating abuse is distinct from bullying (due to the intimate nature of the relationship between the victim and abuser), your school's anti-bullying policies can help you locate the resources at your school that respond to systematic and repeated abusive behavior.

Many parents run into challenges when both the victim and abuser attend the same school because schools have duties to both the student who is being abused and the abuser. This is because a school has a requirement to only discipline (suspend, expel, or require a school change) when a discipline process has been completed, and this process may include a hearing before the school board where evidence is presented. We have seen many cases where the victim has to make all the changes and concessions, even changing schools, because the threat of abuse/incident of abuse was not substantiated through the school discipline process. It is important to give schools information about the seriousness of the abuse and specific information about threats. It can also be helpful to have an advocate from a local domestic violence program provide information to the school, not only to connect the school directly to knowledgeable local resources, but also so that the school better understands the issue of dating abuse.

School-Based Services

Schools are becoming a more recognized place of health and healing. Within middle schools, high schools, or colleges, there are likely to be a variety of mental health services—anything from one-on-one counseling and case management to support groups related to substance abuse (Alcoholics Anonymous/Alateen), teen pregnancy, dropout, and stress. A school counselor or nurse would know the resources available at the school.

We are also seeing an increase in school-based health/wellness centers. These centers are located either at the school or close by, and they provide different ranges of health care (from vaccinations and physical checkups to family planning). Wellness centers can be a school-based source for counseling and are often run in partnership with community health, mental health, and public health organizations, which improves the school's connection to all kinds of community services.

In colleges, there are several options for services. Many colleges have hospital-affiliated student health care services that extend to counseling and support groups, as well as physical health. Student health centers can be a resource for the campus-based services at the college. Most colleges have Counseling and Psychological Services

(CAPS), counseling programs that are easily accessible to students on campus and often have specialized services for victims of sexual and dating violence. Many schools have women's resource centers and/or women's health centers that specialize in women's health. Also, colleges often have women's studies departments that are connected to libraries, workshops, discussion groups, or drop-in centers for young women to connect to each other and resources. Colleges are a site of advocacy and awareness-raising, with all campuses required to respond to sexual assault and harassment through federal law under Title IX. College rape prevention and sexual harassment prevention programs will be connected to the campus and local services. For students living on campus or in a dormitory, there is usually an advisor whose job is to talk with students about problems they face. Some schools have peer-counseling programs, designated student advisors, or academic advisors who can help students find campus services.

Violence Prevention Programs

More and more schools have violence prevention programs and education on dating abuse. Prevention education and awareness-building in schools have been the centerpiece of advocacy to prevent dating abuse, domestic violence, and sexual assault. Local and national domestic violence programs have developed curricula for schools. The U.S. Centers for Disease Control and Prevention and various academic researchers have developed curricula as well. For an overview of some available curricula, the Indiana Department of Education launched a database online. Through a recent state law, the department reviewed several dating abuse curricula from throughout the nation in order to develop a resource for schools with rankings and reviews.

Local domestic violence programs and rape crisis centers work with many schools to provide education and resources to students and school personnel. They often try to engage parents through school activities and groups. Other organizations, such as Planned Parenthood, the YWCA, and substance abuse programs, may be conducting workshops at your school related to sexuality, healthy relationship skills, and dating and sexual violence. Other schools offer leadership and activist clubs and extracurricular activities aimed at improving the school climate and helping students. These prevention programs can serve to build your child's support networks, as well as boost her self-confidence and self-esteem.

16

Using the Legal System

The legal system can be a tool to stop abuse. A police report starts a series of legal interventions that have the potential to improve the victim's safety. Legal action not only can empower the victim of dating abuse and help connect her to the support she needs, but it can hold the abuser accountable for his actions. However, the legal system does have its limitations and is not the sole answer or resource for many victims of dating violence.

The legal system includes both criminal and civil cases. Civil cases are between two individuals—such as a divorce proceeding, or a lawsuit between two people. Criminal cases determine if an individual has broken a law and are brought to court by the government. These cases involve law enforcement offices, prosecution and defense attorneys, court processes, and probation and parole systems. Different kinds of courts handle the different kinds of claims from the two systems of law: Criminal courts hear criminal matters, and juvenile courts hear criminal matters in which a minor is accused. Civil courts hear matters including divorces, adoptions, and most domestic violence restraining-order cases. These are often referred to as "family law cases." Additionally, a separate third court system, dependency court, hears cases to determine whether the state needs to take a child into protection. In those cases, all the parties are represented by attorneys, including the child, parents, and the government agency that is concerned with the child's safety (e.g., Child Protective Services). Our overview of the legal system here will focus on the criminal and civil court processes, and not dependency court.

Current Laws

Both civil and criminal laws and processes can be helpful in responding to dating abuse. Each legal system varies state by state and city by city. We will provide a national overview of the current legal system response to dating violence, but check your local courthouse website for more information about the legal system in your area.

In most cases, a minor (defined as someone under the age of eighteen) does not have legal status. Although minors can file police reports and appear as witnesses, their legal voice is limited. For example, minors cannot bring their own lawsuits against someone else, are not put through the criminal justice process the same way as adults, and cannot legally commit to contracts or agreements. However, the court can appoint a guardian for the purpose of litigation, a *guardian ad litem,* to represent the minor in civil proceedings. The guardian ad litem can be any adult (a parent, caregiver, counselor) who fills out a form requesting to be appointed guardian and who files the order or case on behalf of the minor.

Young people face many barriers in accessing the legal system in cases of dating abuse, such as limited transportation, money, and access to teen-specific legal advocates. Another barrier is their relationship status. Individuals in dating relationships (not married or divorced) can obtain restraining orders in only forty-one states and the District of Columbia. That means that there are still states that will not issue domestic violence restraining orders when the victim is or was in a dating relationship with the abuser. For young people, who are not often living together let alone married, this is a substantial barrier.

If a teenage victim of dating violence reports the abuse to the police, there is a series of laws that the abuser may be charged under, even if the domestic violence laws in that area do not cover dating relationships.

Most states have the following crimes:

Criminal harassment: Subjecting another to physical contact, following the person around, or phoning him or her continually if it is done with the intent to harass, alarm, or annoy the person, if it has that effect, or if the behavior occurs with no legitimate purpose.

Reckless endangerment: Placing a person in serious risk of bodily injury or death.

Assault: Intentionally (on purpose) or negligently (without due precaution, carelessly) causing or attempting to cause bodily injury.

Aggravated assault: Intentionally or negligently causing or attempting to cause grave injury, as with a weapon.

You should be aware that the police can arrest someone suspected of felony criminal behavior if they have "probable cause" to believe that person has committed the crime. Felony criminal behavior is a more serious and dangerous threat to human life and/or property and is designated by federal and state laws. At the misdemeanor level (a lower-level offense, with lower amounts of danger to society), an officer must actually see the behavior in order to make an arrest. Generally, arrest is up to the police officer's judgment—whether the officer can prove probable cause for the arrest. As the result of advocacy to increase awareness of domestic violence among police officers, several local law enforcement agencies, such as the Los Angeles Police Department, have adopted mandatory arrest policies (forcing the arrest without requiring the officer to have probable cause) for domestic violence cases when officers see evidence of physical injury.

Restraining Orders

Domestic violence restraining orders or protective orders are orders of protection issued by a judge in a criminal or civil case to keep the victim safe from the abuser by ordering the abusive or violent person to keep away from the victim, or be arrested. As of 2010, minors have access to domestic violence restraining orders in forty-five states.[38] One way for parents to help their children access the legal system is by being supportive of teens in the restraining order process—only nine states allow for young people (twelve years old or older) to ask the court for a restraining order without parental notification or permission. Further, because of the legal status of teen abusers, only fifteen states allow restraining orders to be filed against teen offenders. So if the abuser is a minor as well, it might be harder to get the restraining order depending on where you live.

Domestic violence restraining orders can be temporary or permanent. Most restraining order processes begin by filing with the court, then providing notice to the person to be restrained, and then a judge decides whether to grant the restraining order request. A temporary restraining order, obtained in an emergency situation by going to a court without notice to the abuser, usually lasts one to two weeks. There must be a hearing before the order is extended for a longer period of time. Permanent orders vary in duration, from six months to years. Restraining orders in some states can contain provisions for child custody (children of the couple), division of property, requirements on how close the offender can get to the victim, and orders to stop telephoning/texting the victim.

The person whose behavior is being restrained must be notified of the order before the order becomes effective. In most states, police, marshals, or deputies will provide the notification service (called serving the defendant) for a small fee. In some states, the victim is allowed to serve the papers herself, but should be accompanied by a law enforcement officer for safety reasons. If the abuser attends the same school, school administrators and/or campus security should be notified of the restraining order. This is another opportunity to plan for the safety of your child while going to/from school and while on campus. Notification of the restraining order can also improve the response and safety planning at places of worship or other common spaces where both the abuser and victim have access.

Although civil restraining orders are most commonly utilized in cases of dating violence and domestic violence, in some states law enforcement officers can contact a judge (at any time) to issue an emergency protective order. These are issued when a law enforcement officer believes that there is a serious and immediate threat to the victim's safety. After a violent incident, if police are called, be sure to see what types of protection the officers can help you and your child obtain.

A violation of a restraining order is a crime. Teens who violate the order may be brought into juvenile court, where the penalties vary based on the situation of abuse and threat of harm. Some penalties include going to counseling/support groups, paying a fine, or juvenile detention. Abusers who are eighteen years old or older must deal with the adult justice system, and the consequences may be more severe.

Much like the domestic violence and dating violence restraining order, teens may have the option to obtain more general restraining orders under the state's civil harassment laws. Although domestic violence restraining orders often have more provisions and protections, more general civil harassment orders are available in every area and can be a good option if your state does not allow minors or people in dating relationships to file for domestic violence protection orders.

Also, some areas have domestic violence courts, and there are even a few teen dating violence courts. These courts hear only cases related to domestic violence and often have procedures for following cases, holding abusers accountable through check-ins, and keeping all cases/hearing/actions in the same courtroom. Ask a clerk at your local courthouse if there is a local domestic violence and/or teen dating violence court.

Some victims may not want to get a restraining order because of fear that the abuser will become angry. This may be true, but it may also serve as a deterrent for the abuser—now knowing that he could be arrested for the abusive behavior and that there is a record of his abuse. The legal system does have its limitations—a restraining order is a piece of paper that will not stop violence on its own. But it can be used to improve the police response to your child and can provide your school information and proof of danger. Police can make an arrest for a violation of a restraining order, even if they cannot make an arrest for threatened violence or if they have not seen evidence of the violence that has occurred. Restraining orders are a tool for safety, but they are only effective if the offender has any respect for or fear of legal consequences of the criminal justice system. They provide a legal paper trail and signal the seriousness of your teen's commitment to safety and your own. However, be aware that restraining orders should not be relied on as the only safety measure you use. They are only part of an overall safety plan.

Legal Resources

Legal resources for teen victims are limited. Some nonprofit legal assistance organizations (for example, the Legal Aid Foundation) offer pro bono services and may provide some legal advocacy and representation in court. A few domestic violence programs have legal clinics and advocacy projects that provide varied services, such as help filling out restraining order paperwork, going to the courthouse with the victim, and even providing the victim with a lawyer in the proceedings.

Also, many courthouses have in-house (located at the court) domestic violence legal help and clinics—where victims can get help and limited legal advice on their case, as well as information about the legal process in their area. Ask a local court clerk if there is domestic violence legal help available.

Reporting and Prosecuting

Reporting domestic violence and sexual assault can be difficult. When you know and love the person you are reporting about, the decision to report abuse is full of complexity and doubt. As a parent, it is important to talk to your child about the reporting process and how working with the police can improve safety and help your child move on. It can also help all of you feel you are doing something to prevent continued and future violence. Many states have developed a series of laws to protect victims of domestic violence and improve the prosecution of domestic violence, dating violence, and sexual assault cases.

A report of abuse to the police can serve as a strong deterrent for the abuser, and it can also improve and help track the case for law enforcement or school intervention. It conveys a powerful message to the teen being abused: She does not have to deal with the violence all by herself. It also puts the abuser on notice that the police have started to look into this matter, and further abusive behavior will build the case for intervention, consequences, and punishment.

Reporting domestic violence and sexual assault is an option for every person, no matter the age. Although some processes are limited when the victim and/or abuser is a minor, the law enforcement systems are in place to protect. Law enforcement agencies and prosecutors can utilize a variety of criminal penalties to improve public safety, as discussed previously.

It is important to remember that minors cannot legally consent to sex with anyone over the age of eighteen because of their limited legal status (a minor is not considered an adult in the eyes of the law)—having sex with a minor is a crime across all jurisdictions. In many states the law is unclear on whether a minor can legally consent to sexual activity with another minor. Statutory rape laws are used to prosecute consensual sex between minors and adults, and the same laws might also be applied to consensual sex between minors. Sexual assault programs and rape crisis centers are good resources for understanding the implications of statutory rape laws and the law enforcement response in your area. Different law enforcement and prosecution offices place varying levels of importance on statutory rape cases, making for very different application of the law from area to area.

Sexual assault, which is sexual activity without consent (lack of consent can include coercion, having sex while under the influence of drugs/alcohol, and forced sexual activity of any type), is illegal in all jurisdictions and can strengthen a case of dating violence as yet another form of abuse inflicted on the victim. Sexual assault may be seen as a more serious crime in some areas, depending on the state laws and law enforcement/prosecution attitudes.

Many law enforcement and prosecution teams have dedicated offices for sexual assault, domestic violence, and child abuse/endangerment cases, and have received more specialized training to work with victims and their families. Domestic violence cases are difficult to prosecute because there is often a need for the victim to participate in the process, and many victims are reluctant to provide evidence of the abuse. Furthermore, sexual assault cases are very difficult to prosecute, as we have seen in the high-profile rape cases of celebrities. The case can often turn into a "he said/she said" battle, with nasty character discrediting. In some states there are legal protections for victims of sexual assault, including having a DNA rape kit collected (which is a DNA-tested sample on file with law enforcement), the right to participate or not in the prosecution of the abuser, and being connected to confidential services. And some states continue to strengthen the protections for domestic violence victims as well. Further, many protections exist for victims of sexual assault, such as not being named in court documents and witness protection programs. Sexual assault offenders are required to register in sex offender databases in all states, which then shows up on background checks, restricts where offenders can live, and requires updating of address changes.

Although the prosecution of these crimes is an arduous process for anyone, many teens feel strengthened by pursuing this option, seeing it as a part of their healing. Others have found it traumatic (and re-victimizing) to undergo the repeated questioning about their experience. It is important to consider all sides of this complex choice and to ask your local rape crisis center or domestic violence program for support as you go through the process.

Role of the Police

Police are in our community to help improve safety. Their role is to enforce the laws. After years of advocacy by domestic violence and sexual assault experts, law enforcement officers have a better understanding of the dynamics and sensitive nature of these crimes. Most officers now receive training in their police academies about how to respond to domestic violence and sexual violence calls. And many communities coordinate responses with police officers, sending out domestic violence or sexual violence counselors/advocates to the calls with officers. If you feel you are not getting an appropriate, respectful response to your request for help, you have a right to make a complaint to the supervising commander at the police or sheriff's department.

What to Expect of Prosecutors

Prosecutors are the state or federal lawyers who build and convey a case of law-breaking to either a judge or jury. They want to see justice done in order to build a safer community. In the case of domestic and sexual violence, prosecutors are becoming more and more aware of the complexity of these cases and the need for supportive services for victims. Many prosecutors are assigned to specific fields of expertise, such as gang violence, homicide, domestic violence, sexual assault, and stalking. They often work with advocates from outside agencies to get witnesses (often the victims in domestic and sexual violence cases) the services they need.

Conversations with prosecutors, who represent the state, are not confidential or legally protected as privileged conversations. Conversations with your own attorney or advocate are privileged, and cannot be revealed without the consent of the client/victim or an order from a judge. Examples of people who can protect privileged conversations include your personal lawyer, your spouse, priests/rabbis, psychotherapists, and in many states, domestic violence counselors and sexual assault counselors. When talking to police, witness protection services, advocates, and counselors, it is important to understand the rights to confidentiality that you have and the limitations about what can and cannot be kept confidential. Be sure to ask about the confidentiality of conversations for both you as an adult and your child as a minor.

Stalking as a Tactic of Abuse

Stalking is illegal in all states. It is largely defined as criminal activity consisting of the repeated following and harassing of another person. When legitimate behavior, such as continually following your child, calling or texting constantly, and sending letters, is coupled with the intent of instilling fear or injury, this violates anti-stalking laws. More sinister stalking behavior includes ongoing threats to harm your child or your family, destroying property, harming a pet, or showing up at work or school to harass or intimidate. Stalking consists of a pattern or series of acts over a period of time, however short. The conduct is directed at a specific person and alarms, annoys, torments, or terrorizes the person with no legitimate purpose. ("Because I love you" is not a legitimate purpose to stalk someone.)

A call or visit to your local police station can help you find out what constitutes stalking in your community. Be sure to write down the stalking behavior and when it occurred; this can help you and your child remember the incidents and can make a powerful case for intervention by law enforcement. Again, restraining orders can be deterrents in cases of stalking, as well as provide clear guidelines to both the victim and offender about when the order is being violated.

For additional resources about dating violence, see the resources section.

Cultural Strengths and Challenges

The values and beliefs of a culture or a religion affect a family's feelings and responses to abusive relationships. Therefore, parents must consider their values and beliefs when making assessments and decisions about their teen's situation. Sometimes these cultural influences are barriers to a family's effectiveness—for example, when families create "stories" about what is happening that interfere with the family's ability or willingness to understand and seek help. Other times, cultural traditions provide supportive strengths and resources to the family.

Cultural Influences

Cultural values and beliefs about relationships, dating, marriage, sex, and seeking help influence every family's way of dealing with an abusive relationship. For example, the values of your culture may require marriage to the person your daughter has sex with or, if she is pregnant, to the father of her child. This presents a conflict for you if you are also worried about a marriage filled with violence.

Cultural views about dating and sexuality affect how parents react to dating violence. A family may prohibit dating or prescribe certain rules about it. This may lead a teen to keep her dating activities hidden from parents and other family members. Parents may feel angry that their teen has violated their values or broken their rules, and then become angrier when they discover she has also been hurt by the person she is dating.

Some parents' cultural traditions include views of marriage and relationships between men and women whereby the man is the head of the household, in charge and responsible for disciplining and keeping control over his wife or girlfriend. These parents may also believe that women are to blame for the problems that arise in intimate relationships and are solely responsible for fixing them (rather than this being a shared responsibility of both men and women). These attitudes affect what teens expect as normal in their relationships, and they affect how parents react to their teen's abusive relationship.

Some parents are reluctant to see the abuser or the victim get involved with the criminal justice system or other sources of help because their family is part of a group or community that has been discriminated against. This can create conflict between dual allegiances: to the teen, who may need the help, as well as to the abuser, who may be treated badly because of racism or other prejudices.

Sometimes communities or families have experienced tremendous trauma, change, or distress, perhaps due to a history of violence, poverty, or, in the case of some immigrants, war in their country of origin. In comparison to these experiences, their daughters' problems with a boyfriend may not seem as serious. Your values and beliefs about what constitutes a serious problem will affect how you react. For example, many communities, such as those from Iraq, Somalia, Cambodia, or Mexico, have experienced genocidal massacres or torture, or very difficult journeys as immigrants or refugees. Having survived enormous tragedies affects how you respond to crises that arise in your family life. You may expect your daughter to tolerate or resign herself to the situation she is in.

It is often difficult in an oppressed community to expose violence or any other problem that contradicts the image of the culture as being free of such problems. For example, Jewish cultural attitudes might consider family violence as a *shanda* (shame). Asian Americans are sometimes seen as a "model minority," which may lead some of these families to keep family violence invisible. African American families are often reluctant to report family violence because of a sense of shame and their vulnerability to discrimination based on racism.

Building on Cultural Strengths

Culture and traditions provide strength to families and individuals. The culture in which we have grown up affects our beliefs, values, behavior, and how we deal with problems. There are differences in terms of what will be effective for each of us and each of our families in dealing with interpersonal violence. Our culture, ethnic group, religion, and economic background all contribute to forming a complicated set of influences, constraints, and resources.

People often rely on cultural traditions for sanctuary and support. They offer ways of seeing problems so that people feel comforted and able to understand what is happening to them. They offer communities shared values with which to maintain a sense of belonging and connection. They offer ancestral and collective histories that form and inform identities. People benefit from rituals and traditions that help them move from one phase of life to another. Prayers, for example, can be important for healing. People find resources in cultural communities that help to solve problems. They seek support from religious and spiritual leaders, teachers, and guides.

There has been a social revolution affecting institutions that used to rely upon the "normalcy" of certain aspects of family life—for example, methods of disciplining children, rights of husbands and fathers to control their families, and courtship practices. This revolution has affected legal definitions in the United States of what constitutes abuse. Abuse is now defined by the experiences of the people who have been abused, which has challenged the perception and acceptance of abuse as an invisible and normal part of life. Previously unquestioned authority is being challenged. Girls and women have new rights, including the right to be free from abuse and violence. They don't have to accept abuse in their relationships. Relationships themselves are being redefined; for example, many states now grant same-sex couples the same rights and privileges heterosexual couples have.

The changing roles and status of women and girls in the United States have presented challenges and provoked conflict within some cultures, communities, and families. In some families that have recently immigrated to the United States, parents often form a bridge from the old to the new, wanting better lives for their children. They do not want them to experience the limitations that they themselves experienced in their own countries or cultures of origin. Forming this bridge can be complicated and difficult because parents and children go through different experiences as they adapt to a new country. But parents must make choices, and even if those choices conflict with cultural or religious values, they are important for the protection and safety of our children. Changing beliefs means taking risks.

The following are examples of beliefs related to relationship violence that exist in some cultures, including the dominant culture in this country:

- A woman must marry the man who raped her.
- A woman must stay in a marriage in which she is beaten.
- A husband has a right to beat his wife.
- Hitting or beating children to control their behavior is an effective form of discipline.
- Courtship must lead to marriage, or girls must marry the husband that parents select or prefer.
- Young people must wait until marriage to have sexually intimate relationships.
- Committed relationships are only between a man and a woman.

Confronting Your Culture

People who are conflicted about their culture's beliefs and values must make choices. Using culture as an excuse for violence is avoiding responsibility. If you say, "He or she behaves violently because of their culture," or "In our religion, she must marry him since she is with him, even if he hits her," you make the culture responsible for the violence, rather than holding individuals responsible for their choices. It is important to challenge such beliefs and to hold people who are violent accountable and responsible, whether or not the culture or social environment tolerates it. People who challenge such beliefs are less likely to "blame the victim." When parents actively intervene on their teen's behalf, the teen knows that she has the right to be treated with respect, that she doesn't deserve to be abused, and that abuse is never acceptable—in any culture.

A family's culture influences decisions about whether to act and what kind of action to take, including where to go for help. Decisions about seeking help from schools, the legal system, friends, or family depend on what fits with each family's values and beliefs, as well as the resources available within their culture and their community.

Supports that are available within your culture can be helpful and empowering, as they can provide understanding, trust, and familiarity. Seeking help within your community may be necessary because of expectations or experiences of criticism, judgmental responses, or discrimination outside the community. Language can be a barrier to seeking help outside the community. Language and communication style may be misunderstood, especially if English is not the parents' primary language and their ability to communicate is affected by stress. Cultural values may emphasize helping people within one's own community, and a family's community may offer resources for personal support. For example, in many communities, church and civil rights organizations provide a wide variety of services. Culturally sensitive services are available in many cities—for example, multilingual Asian service centers, Armenian school-based centers, Jewish family services, and Spanish-speaking programs for Latinas who have been battered.

Seeking help within the community, however, can pose problems as well. In a closed, small, or tight-knit community, privacy is limited. Cultural values can lead some families to feel shameful if a relationship problem is revealed, especially a problem such as sexual violence. Some families prefer to seek help outside their communities for privacy and confidentiality reasons.

Parents who have recently arrived in the United States face the enormous task of learning how this country's laws, institutions, and policies work, and what to expect. Getting help or planning for a teen's safety means learning new methods of dealing with those that are different from what is familiar to parents and others in the family.

Repeated experiences with discrimination affect parents' and teens' willingness to rely on institutions. For example, an African American teen who expects her boyfriend to be arrested and jailed may be reluctant to call the police because she's experienced discrimination or harassment by police, or has seen it happen to others in her community. A teen who has a young child may expect to be discriminated against if she reports abuse, because of the scrutiny teen mothers are subjected to when seen as "inadequate" parents, and possibly risk having her child taken away. Undocumented residents in the United States are frequently afraid of deportation if they seek help, even though there are legal protections for undocumented victims of crime.

Discrimination based on stereotyped expectations and misperceptions of behavior can lead to parents or teens being misunderstood. For example, if your culture and customs make it unacceptable for you to tell strangers about personal problems, your difficulty talking to a supportive person might be misunderstood as unwillingness to cooperate. Lack of communication can lead to you being judged, blamed, or criticized for your behavior when seeking help. It is important to remember that even though people who are supposed to help can sometimes be insensitive, they often have useful resources to offer.

As parents, we often find ourselves confronting the ways in which we grew up differently from our children. Our children constantly remind us that "it's different now—it's not the way it was back then." Some of us look to cultural traditions for perspectives on what is happening with our children, and others do not. But it is important for all of us to find new ways to support our children as they deal with the realities of their lives.

For Parents of Abusive Teens

You may be reading this book because you are concerned that your son or daughter (whether gay or straight) behaves abusively toward a girlfriend or boyfriend. You may suspect it, but have difficulty finding out what is really going on. You may know that your son is treating his girlfriend badly, but are not sure if what he is doing is abusive. You may know he is being abusive, but don't know what to do about it. We will continue to refer to the abuser as "he" and the abused as "she" to reflect the reality that most often young men are the batterers and most often young women are the victims.

Nancy

Nancy, mother of Matt, shared the following story:

> At first I couldn't believe it. There was a frightening similarity to what my first husband, Matt's father, did to me. Matt was definitely having a hard time. He would flare up over nothing and go slamming around the house. I heard him blow up at his girlfriend, talking mean to her. It seemed that he was calling and texting her all the time to check up on her. I didn't know why they fought so much. I tried to talk to him about it, but he put me off and told me to stay out of his business. This was very upsetting. I was worried about what kind of relationship he was having with this girl.

Then, one day she was over and they had a big fight in Matt's room. I heard things being thrown, and she went running out of the house. I saw that her nose was bleeding. I was furious! I was ashamed that my son could do that. I screamed at him that he was just like his father, and how dare he act that way. Matt stormed out of the house and didn't come back that night. I couldn't sleep. I didn't know what to do.

Matt could be so sweet. I had seen plenty of signs of his temper before, but I never believed he would be like his father. To tell you the truth, I was a little afraid of his temper.

My husband and I talked most of the night. He thinks I'm too easy on Matt. We decided to find someplace that Matt could get counseling, and to insist on his getting help. We sat Matt down and told him that he has a big problem. We said we'd help him, but he had to help himself. At first, he refused to listen. He kept saying that his girlfriend pushed him too far. "What did she expect?" he complained. I got so upset with him. I told him that if he wouldn't go for help, I'd call the police myself. I told him he couldn't hurt his girlfriend the way his father hurt me. I think he finally believed me.

Matt's been going to see a counselor, reluctantly. His girlfriend broke up with him, and he's depressed and moody. He thinks if he goes to a counselor she will get back with him. I told him he had better not count on it. I really don't know what's going to happen with my son. I'm still worried. He'll be eighteen soon, and it will be impossible to make him do anything.

Recognizing Abusive Behavior

It is sometimes difficult to recognize who the abuser is and who the victim is in teen relationships. Either partner can be aggressive some of the time and the victim of aggression at other times. Usually, one of the two goes to extreme lengths to maintain control over the other.

Parents have to pay attention to many different kinds of information and signs of abusive behavior.

Parents learn about their teen's abusive behavior in a variety of ways. For example, Nancy heard and saw Matt with his girlfriend. She saw that he was contacting her constantly, checking up on her. Parents may see or hear their teen or young adult telling a girlfriend what she can and can't do. They may see signs that he interrogates her about where she has been, whom she was with, and so forth, or overhear him becoming enraged and verbally abusive—for example, calling her names, yelling, saying cruel things, or criticizing her.

Sometimes parents have learned about their teen's abusive behavior because he has told them about it. He may tell them about the time he spends with his girlfriend, or his interactions with her, and parents can see that he is jealous and restrictive, or that he talks in a humiliating or degrading way about her appearance or personality. When they have conversations with him, he may seem obsessive about his girlfriend and unable to focus on anything else. He may tell them about fights he has with his girlfriend. He may be troubled about his violence during their fights, and tell his parents that he has a problem and he needs help. He may be blaming his girlfriend for their fights, and it is apparent that he is not seeing his responsibility for their problems.

Some parents find out about their teen's violence when they have seen him verbally or physically attacking his girlfriend, or when another family member, a friend, or a neighbor has seen him being abusive and told the parents about it.

Parents may suspect abuse after seeing their teen being violent in other situations—for example, with them, with a brother or sister, or with friends. They may suspect that their teen is violent with a girlfriend because he generally has trouble managing his temper. They may also suspect that he is aggressive toward his girlfriend because he abuses drugs or alcohol, and he becomes violent and mean when he is under the influence.

Parents may find out about a teen's abuse from his school, the police, or some other authority. Or they may find out from his girlfriend or her family, who tells the parents because they want them to intervene to stop his violence or because they want them to keep him away from her.

To summarize, parents usually notice their teen exhibiting some of the signs of bullying and controlling behavior, including always blaming others for problems, paranoid accusations, low tolerance for stress, impatience, explosive temper, rage, emotional cruelty, verbal name-calling and put-downs, cruelty to animals, temper tantrums, and demanding immediate attention and compliance. For more information on signs of abuse in a relationship, review chapter 3.

When Girls Abuse

When a daughter is abusing her boyfriend or girlfriend, finding out about it might be more complicated for parents. There is a common expectation that girls don't behave this way. Even though relationship abuse is more commonly committed by men and boys, this expectation leads us to overlook abuse by girls.

Abusive behavior by girls is very similar to boys' abusive behavior. Abusive girls may require their boyfriends to do whatever they want, be very demanding and controlling, and punish them for not complying with their demands. They can be jealous and possessive. Girls, however, are more likely to use emotional manipulation to get their way than they are to use physical aggression, although that also happens. Parents might suspect that their daughter is being abusive when the boyfriend is around all the time, even coming to every family event, because their daughter insists that the boyfriend go everywhere with her.

Henry described his daughter's abusive behavior in the following story.

Michelle

Michelle is a cheerleader. I noticed that the way she talked to Sam was mean and demanding. She insisted that he go with her to all of her practices and the games and then stay with her afterward. If he wanted to see his friends, she blew up at him, or accused him of not loving her enough. Michelle couldn't think about anything except Sam and what he was doing when he wasn't with her. She insisted that he come to every family dinner or gathering. I asked her, "Why does Sam have to be here all the time?" She blew up at me and said, "I want him to be with me, and he's my boyfriend, so he does what I want!" She acts like she's a queen. She doesn't get up to get herself a glass of water, but sends him to get it for her. Once she told me that she made Sam give her all of his passwords, you know, for his phone and Facebook, so he wouldn't have any secrets from her. I thought this was too much. Her mom, Sara, and I tried to talk to Michelle about privacy and allowing each other to have lives of their own. They're too young to be like this.

This kind of abusive and controlling behavior won't lead you to call the police to get your teen's attention. Also, because abused young men are more likely to keep the abuse hidden than young women, it may be harder to find out that a daughter is being abusive. However, controlling, emotional abuse by young women is a serious problem, and the same effort is required to get it to stop as when a young man behaves this way.

Confronting Your Teen about Abusive Behavior

When parents discover that their teen is abusive or violent toward his girlfriend, their first reaction may be disbelief. He may deny it or minimize it, saying his girlfriend is lying, or that they had a fight but it wasn't that bad. He may blame her, saying that she provokes him, or that she hit him instead, and that he is being victimized by her. Even if he acknowledges his violence, it may be hard to believe it if you feel that this can't be true of your child.

Parents can't ignore a problem like violence. They must take it seriously. If they ignore it during their child's teen years, it will probably get worse later and cause more and more harm. As difficult as this might be, parents must overcome the impulse to deny the violence and commit to dealing with it.

If parents have reason to suspect that a teen is violent or abusive, but they don't know for certain, they can try to find out. They can ask him about it and tell him the reasons that they believe it could be true. They can ask his girlfriend. They can ask his friends or someone at school. If their son denies it, they should ask again, being clear about what they have seen or heard. Many teens don't use words like "battering" or "abuse." They are more likely to respond to questions about specific kinds of behavior, such as hitting, yelling, name-calling, or interrogating.

When parents talk to their teen, his girlfriend, or his friends, they can tell them that this is serious, and they want to know what is going on so that they can do something about it. They can let their teen know that he needs help, and that they will work with him to find out how to get the help he needs. While offering to be supportive of him as a person, and of his efforts to overcome his problems, they must make it clear to him that they do not support or tolerate his violence. Parents may have to make the difficult decision to report their teen's violence to the police or to allow him to be arrested if his girlfriend reports him. If he won't listen, or if parents are overwhelmed by his persistent violence or abuse, it can be helpful to reread about setting limits in chapter 10 and avoiding power struggles in chapter 11.

Contacting the Victim of Your Teen's Abuse

If parents are having trouble dealing with their teen's violence, manipulations, or substance abuse, then they have something in common with his girlfriend. When they make it clear to him that they will not tolerate his violence, they can also let him know that they will support anyone affected by his violence—in other words, his girlfriend. Parents and their teen's girlfriend (and possibly her family) can support each other in dealing with the violence and help each other set limits on what they will tolerate.

Marilyn

A few months after her daughter Kyra started seeing Stewart, Marilyn got a call from Stewart's mother, Amy. "You and your husband had better get over here. Stewart is a mess, on crack, yelling and waving around a metal pipe. He's got my neighbor's truck and Kyra in it, threatening her, and Lord knows where he's going to take her." Together they were able to contact the police, find Kyra, and get her to safety.

Amy couldn't stop Stewart by herself, but when she involved Kyra's parents, they were all better able to handle the situation together. Kyra's parents wouldn't have known that Kyra was in trouble if Amy hadn't called. Stewart got a clear message from his mother: *I will not be silent or hide this problem, and I will do whatever I can to confront your violence.*

The Parent's Emotional Rollercoaster

As the parent of a child who uses violence or abusive behavior, you may experience the same emotional rollercoaster as the parents of a victim. You and your family may be going through ups and downs that parallel the tension and explosiveness of your son, especially if he lives with you. The relationship between spouses is often affected when parents disagree about what to do. Often one parent is protective, while the other is confrontational. If your family life is chaotic, your son's violence may be only one problem among many that you have to deal with. Dealing with violence can be overwhelming and confusing.

As Nancy's story showed at the beginning of this chapter, feelings of fear, shame, and guilt are common to many parents. After discovering that their child is violent, parents have told us that they felt ashamed because they believed they caused their son's problems. They felt ashamed of having a child with such serious problems. They were afraid that their son could seriously injure or kill his girlfriend or someone else. They felt ineffective and overpowered by their child, especially if he challenged their parental authority. They felt terrible about the consequences of and the harm caused by their son's behavior.

Parents may feel guilty because they believe that the violence is their fault. Self-reflection about how parents' past behavior influenced or affected their child and his use of violence can be helpful. But parents shouldn't get bogged down with guilty feelings—it isn't productive. They must do something about the violence. If they become immobilized, immersed in guilt, they will not be helpful to themselves or anyone else.

Parents can be held responsible for the consequences of their child's behavior, for example, any physical or financial damage caused by their child.

Their behavior or parenting may have contributed to the difficulties their teen is now experiencing. However, many children who grew up around violence or had other difficulties earlier in their lives have made the choice not to be abusive. Children can overcome the problems they had growing up around violence and abuse, and everyone can learn to make better choices about their behavior.

Seeking Support

Parents of abusers must reach out and get help and support from others. It is very important to break through the silence. There is an understandable reluctance to talk about the problem with others if parents fear being judged. But there is no chance for change if parents don't talk about the problem. It is better to take the risk and find friends, family members, and people in the community who will actively discourage their teen's violence and negative attitudes toward his girlfriend, and who will help him to confront his problem and provide support as he tries to change.

The major factor in whether or not a batterer is able to overcome his abusive behavior is motivation. A teen who is horrified by his own violent behavior will likely make the commitment to go through the difficult process of change. Unfortunately, many abusive teens minimize and deny the seriousness of their problem. If an abusive teen's girlfriend breaks up with him, he will often seek help primarily because he wants to get her back. This could result in his getting the help he needs to change, but he must make the long-term commitment to behave differently. If he only focuses on reuniting with his ex-girlfriend, the problem of violence is not addressed. If he gets sober or clean, his violent behavior may change. But teens are often violent when they are not drinking or using drugs. The underlying causes of their violence must be addressed along with their substance abuse. Counseling can help do this.

Parents must not only help find the counseling, but, to the best of their ability, insist that their teen actually gets help. They can also influence their teen's motivation to change.

To find out about counseling resources, parents can call local domestic violence program hotlines, a teen abuse prevention program, or the district attorney's office for referrals to batterers' support groups and treatment programs.

They should also find out how the juvenile justice system in their area (or the adult justice system, if the teen is over eighteen) proceeds in teen domestic violence cases. They will then have the information they need to let their teen know about the consequences of his violent behavior.

Another strategy for getting help is informing people who should know—for example, a school counselor or principal. The aim is to have the teen's abusive behavior out in the open and taken seriously, and to extend the safety net for his girlfriend.

Resources for young men who batter are currently limited but expanding in the United States. There are psychoeducational and other therapy groups available through domestic violence programs; recovery programs such as Alcoholics Anonymous, Alateen, and Cocaine Anonymous, which deal with substance abuse issues; school groups for students having problems in general; youth service agencies; and gang prevention services.

For Parents of Gay, Lesbian, Bisexual, or Transgender Teens

Parents are often surprised to find that teens can be in gay and lesbian relationships, and that battering can take place in those relationships. Many of these teens do not tell their parents about either their relationships or the battering. When teens are not being open about who they are dating, they are more likely to keep problems with violence a secret. They are also more likely to keep their relationships secret from their peers. The fear of homophobic reactions from parents, peers, and others results in isolation. So a teen may have no one to confide in about a problem with violence in his or her relationship. Jeffrey's story portrays one teen's efforts to overcome this.

Jeffrey

My name is Jeffrey, and I just turned twenty-one. I was eighteen years old when I started dating Bob, who was twenty-eight. I lived with my mother, and I knew I couldn't tell her about my relationship with Bob. There were no other adults in my life. We lived in a small town far away from the rest of the family. Mostly, I talked to my straight friends in high school. I was the only out person, and my friends were cool about it.

Bob was abusive. It was psychological at first, then it became physical. He dominated me. I was mentally brainwashed. There were certain things I couldn't do, because if I did I was in big trouble. If he was supposed to pick me up at seven, I had to be ready at 7:00, not 6:55 or 7:05, or he'd explode. If he didn't like what I was wearing, he'd tell me all day how awful I looked. I tried very hard not to make him angry. After a while, I fought back verbally, and I harped on him. When he would hit me, I'd fight back, get a few punches in. I wouldn't just stand there and let a man hit me. But he was bigger and older than me, and it would escalate. It didn't do any good to defend myself physically. Several times, I called the police. They didn't do anything. I thought they were making fun of me.

My mom was into her own stuff. She was dating and got married. She was busy. She didn't want to believe I was gay. She saw me with a black eye and thought something must have happened in school. So she asked me, "How was school?" I said, "You don't want to know." And she didn't. She never tried to find out. She knows now, but she doesn't want to talk about it.

My friends were the ones who helped me get away from Bob. They understood me and validated me. They didn't put words in my mouth. No "you should" or "you have to." They helped me think about my options. They asked me, "Do you like being a slave? Do you like being punched and battered?" I got the message. They told me it was my decision. I am very grateful to them. With my friends' support, I got strong enough to pull away and eventually break up with Bob. Bob kept pursuing me. So I got a restraining order, and he finally stayed away.

Jeffrey's story illustrates that abuse in same-sex relationships has a lot in common with abuse in heterosexual relationships. However, it also illustrates the painful reality for teens who cannot share important aspects of their lives (for example, whom they love) with their parents, and therefore cannot approach their parents when they need support to deal with dating violence.

This leads to a teen feeling isolated. Gay and lesbian teen relationships are often "invisible." Parents, friends, and other people don't notice the warning signs of abuse or violence because they don't notice the relationship. If a teen is bisexual, and dating both boys and girls, a parent may know nothing about the same-sex relationship. Some people do not consider the possibility that two girls or two boys may be intensely involved or in love. In recent years, there has been greater acknowledgment and acceptance of same-sex relationships, which may be easing some of this isolation and invisibility.

Parents often have difficulty recognizing and accepting that their child might be lesbian, gay, or bisexual. It is understandable that some teens keep these relationships secret from their parents. They are afraid of being rejected, abused, or humiliated. Even though some teens who identify as gay, lesbian, bisexual, or transgender experience acceptance and support from their families, other teens have been thrown out or have run away because of their parents' severe reactions.

Marion's story illustrates how difficult this situation can be for parents.

Marion

Marion noticed that her seventeen-year-old daughter, Suzanne, was beginning to change. Suzanne was spending more and more time with her best friend, Melissa. They were inseparable. Marion said:

> I noticed that they were fighting a lot. Suzanne would come home late, after her curfew, usually in tears. Then she wouldn't get up in the morning until just as I was leaving for work. I suspected that she wasn't going to school, so I called and found out she was absent ten days that month and had been forging my signature on notes.

I confronted her about school. I was already worried about this friendship because she was constantly upset, and now this. I told her I thought Melissa was a bad influence on her. Suzanne promised to straighten things out with Melissa and not to miss any more school.

About a month later, we were shopping for clothes and I noticed bruises on her arm and scratches on her back. I was alarmed and asked her, "Who did this to you?" Suzanne then told me that Melissa was more than a friend: They had been "involved" for six months. Suzanne said she was in love with her, but Melissa often got drunk and jealous and pushed her around.

This whole thing was very hard for me. I didn't know what to think. She was so unhappy. I didn't know if it was just Melissa, or if this was what her life was going to be like.

The night that Suzanne came home with bruises on her face, I wasn't confused anymore. I told her, "This is getting worse. You need help." She told me, sobbing, that she had been trying to break up with Melissa. Then I realized that Suzanne was trapped. She couldn't get away from her. I'd heard about this with married couples, but at her age! And with a girl! This I couldn't believe. So I started getting information. She needed my help. No one could tell me about girls who batter other girls, but I found out what we needed to do. Suzanne was torn, afraid to hurt Melissa, but she was so relieved to have some support to get out of the relationship.

Now I see Suzanne with another girlfriend, a really lovely girl. I don't know if she's going to want this—what is the word?—"lifestyle" for the rest of her life. Maybe she can be happy, but I'm sure glad she had the strength to get away from Melissa.

Many teens feel positive about their sexual orientation, and many are flexible about their sexuality. They may be open to any romantic relationship, regardless of gender. As the norms in society and in teen culture are changing, lesbian, gay, bisexual, and transgender (LGBT) people and their relationships are becoming more accepted.

The patterns in violent same-sex relationships are similar to those in violent straight relationships. They consist of emotionally, physically, and sexually violent behavior. The cycle of violence is the same. The motivation behind the use of violence by gay or lesbian batterers, as with straight batterers, is to maintain power and control over the other person. Abusers may use the myth of mutual abuse: "You yelled at me, so you're as abusive as I am."

The isolation that is so often part of any battering situation is complicated and worsened by the isolation imposed by the secrecy of a same-sex relationship. The battering same-sex relationship also becomes insular as the couple keeps their secrets, and as they rely more and more on each other to defend themselves against anyone finding out about them. In addition, to control the boyfriend or girlfriend, the abuser may threaten to "out" his or her victim—to tell others, including parents, about their relationship or that the victim is gay, lesbian, or bisexual.

Sometimes teens feel that they are being punished because they are gay, lesbian, bisexual, or transgender, and they feel that they deserve the abuse. Sometimes the abuser tells them this as well. This makes victims vulnerable and traps them in the abusive relationship.

With recent gains in the areas of same-sex marriage and equality laws, teens have more opportunities to see examples of happy, well-adjusted lesbians and gay men in relationships. However, some teens in same-sex relationships may have few norms or role models, or grow up around very negative attitudes about homosexuality, which can be confusing for them. They may assume that the abuse is part of gay and lesbian relationships because they don't have other options until they have more exposure to healthy same-sex relationships.

Teens going through the process of coming out may have mixed feelings about themselves and how they fit in socially. They may struggle with denial about being gay, lesbian, bisexual, or transgender; feel socially isolated; despise themselves; hide their true feelings from others; and fear rejection and violence. It becomes even harder for teens to develop positive feelings about their sexual identities while being hit, manipulated, and emotionally battered in a relationship.

Parents have their own issues to confront about their teen's same-sex relationships. Like Marion, you may only find out that your teen is gay, lesbian, or bisexual when you find out about the abuse. Then your reactions to learning both "secrets" at the same time become intertwined. Some parents react with negativity about same-sex relationships, assuming that they are immoral or dysfunctional. They may not take their teen's relationship seriously, seeing it as a "phase" that he or she will outgrow.

Parents might focus on their teen's homosexuality rather than the abuse, trying to change their teen's sexual orientation rather than help him or her deal with the violence. For example, when sixteen-year-old Elizabeth was stressed or bruised, her family wondered out loud why she put up with her friend's bullying. But they never asked about the relationship or confronted her about the violence until her father found a love letter Elizabeth's girlfriend had written to her. Then they became furious, punished her, and forbade her from seeing her girlfriend.

What Parents Can Do

In addition to the other suggestions in this book, parents will find it helpful to obtain as much information specific to gay teens as they can find. Find out about organizations and agencies in their community that offer resources for gay teens and their parents. Parents, Families, and Friends of Lesbians and Gays (PFLAG) conducts support groups for parents in communities all over the United States. LGBT adults they know can also offer support and information, or can provide positive examples of healthy relationships or the coming-out process.

It is important to reach out and ask questions, even if a teen projects an attitude that it is none of their parents' business. LGBT teens have told us that one of the hardest aspects of being in an abusive relationship has been the isolation. As Jeffrey said, having nonjudgmental people close to him who encouraged him to make healthy decisions made a difference in his getting away from his batterer. In order to help, parents may have to put judgments about their teen's sexuality aside. Overcoming any negative feelings they may have about homosexuality could take time, but it is not necessary to wait for that to happen before helping their teen become safe from violence. Whether straight, gay, lesbian, bisexual, or transgender, their teen needs their support to deal with a violent relationship. It is not helpful or effective to let negative attitudes about their teen's sexuality interfere with the support he or she needs.

Healing

There is so much for parents to be prepared for and to handle in the lives of teenagers. Who expected to have to deal with violence or abuse in teen relationships? Domestic violence is a reality affecting many families, and most of us are unprepared to deal with it. Whether you have experienced it directly or are learning about it to help a teen prevent it, once you know about this kind of fear and challenge, you have been changed.

Everyone who has been through domestic violence has been profoundly affected by it. They continue on, one way or another, but relationships, priorities, the ability to cope, and ways of seeing other people are often changed. How can a family not be affected, for example, when a child of the batterer is now part of the family, or when family members have lived with threats of being killed, or when parents' tension wreaks havoc on their marriage? Families can be brought closer together or torn apart. Dating violence is a serious business that can affect an entire family, testing the strengths and exacerbating the weaknesses of each individual family member, as well as the family as a whole.

For a while after the battering relationship has ended, parents may feel afraid that their daughter will see or get involved with the batterer again. Many girls try to break up several times before finally ending the relationship. The point is that breaking up is possible. The more time that goes by, and the more actively the whole family rebuilds strength, the calmer they become about this.

Similarly, parents may fear that their teen will be in a violent relationship again in the future. The reality is that most teens become acutely aware of the warning signs of abuse after having been through it, and stay away from anyone who might be like their batterer. Others, especially if they have not gone through a process to understand the battering experience, may be attracted to someone else who becomes abusive. Parents won't know for a while if this will happen, but they can support their teen in dealing with the emotional effects of the battering, and thereby reduce the risk of another similar experience.

Many parents feel they are no longer able to believe or trust their teens after realizing how many lies have been told to cover up the abuse and/or the relationship itself. They may also find that they are overprotective or hypervigilant long after their teen is out of danger, as it takes time to heal.

Healing involves rebuilding trust between parents and teens. It may also involve rebuilding trust between the parents themselves, who may have become disconnected from each other because of differences in their reactions to their daughter's situation.

One of the results of dating violence is that parents and their teen have missed out on some of the usual experiences of adolescence, and now need to fill in the developmental gaps. Some teens feel they have to make up for the missed social life and academic accomplishments of high school. Parents of a nineteen-year-old may find themselves dealing with issues that a fifteen-year-old might have.

Some parents find that their parental confidence has been shaken, as well as their confidence in their teen's capabilities, choices, and resiliency. Certainly, their sense of safety and security has been threatened. They will find it returns slowly.

Doing one's best as a parent means finding the balance between actively participating in a teen's life and accepting that they can't control their teen, the outcome of their teen's choices, or even what their teen learns from his or her experiences. Active participation means doing everything they can to teach, guide, influence, be a resource, and support healthy choices and healing.

Families can and do heal from the emotional rollercoasters of violent relationships. Healing is a process for the whole family and takes time and attention. Healing involves managing and living with the new realities that the aftermath of a crisis brings. Healing is a time of rebuilding trust, confidence, and a sense of security. The healing process involves catching up on aspects of family life that have been neglected or interrupted.

Healing goes beyond surviving crises. It allows the family to thrive, to feel a sense of strength at having overcome the effects of the crisis. Parents who have supported a teen through a violent relationship need to use the strengths, patience, and resources they have drawn upon to continue their support for their teen and for themselves during the healing process.

Through the stories in this book, you have been introduced to families who have been profoundly affected by teen dating violence. You have benefited from what they have learned from their experiences. Real-life stories about dating violence don't have neat conclusions. The healing process takes time. Sometimes months or years will pass after the violence has ended before you will fully realize its effect and the subsequent growth, building, and rebuilding that has taken place. In the epilogues that follow, we revisit Margaret, Victor, and Barbara. Their stories continue.

Margaret

Margaret's nineteen-year-old daughter, Molly, and her boyfriend, William, broke up after a particularly violent episode, and then she discovered she was pregnant. She decided to have the baby and to give William another chance, feeling differently about him now that he was the father of her child. However, their relationship continued to deteriorate as his drinking and violence got worse.

The turning point for Molly was after she left William again and was staying with her parents, and he came by to see the baby. Molly didn't feel she could deprive him of this right. He took the baby to the park, but disappeared until the early hours of the morning. When he brought the baby back, he was drunk. The baby was hungry and dirty. Margaret's whole family had been up half the night, frightened. Margaret feels Molly became closer to the family that day and that night because they all shared the experience of terror that something had happened to the baby. Margaret feels she will be dealing with the results of this relationship forever because William is the father of her grandchild. She helped Molly get custody of the baby and place restrictions on William's visitation rights. Molly is still dealing with her emotional attachment to William, and he occasionally comes around to visit. Because of this, Margaret continues to have some degree of fear. She is pleased, however, that Molly has been attending a support group for battered women. She has returned to school, is doing well, and is making plans for her future as a nurse.

Occasionally Margaret still has to be a buffer between Frank, her husband, and Molly as he continues to struggle with his anger toward William. Frank has become totally attached to the baby. Molly's brothers also feel protective of the baby. Under pressure from Margaret, they have come to terms with the fact that William is in their lives, and they are resigned to keeping their anger under control. Otherwise they don't get too involved with Molly, having become fed up with her situation. Molly's younger sister is still a confidante and often gets caught up in the drama of her sister's life. But as she is getting older, she has a busy social life and is gradually becoming less involved with Molly's.

Although it is sometimes a strain, Margaret feels she has been effective in her central role in the family. She wishes Molly had never met William. But she has come to accept that Molly makes her own choices, and that the family has to live with those choices. Margaret also expects Molly to accept that people in her family all have to live their lives too.

Victor

Fifteen-year-old Emilia tried to slow things down with Thomas, who was much older (twenty-three). Thomas became increasingly emotionally controlling, isolating her more and more. Victor and Rosa pressured her to break up with him, but she became more secretive about the relationship. She still allowed her family to convince her to spend time with them. Her stepfather Victor's persistent demonstration of his concern for her was a new experience after years of not having a father around.

One day she didn't come home. Terrified, Victor and Rosa went over to Thomas's house to find her. Thomas's parents insisted that Emilia had to go home with Victor and Rosa. After that, Emilia resisted Thomas's controlling behavior more and began to assert herself with him. He became more violent, and Victor and Rosa called the police on several occasions. After going to court, Emilia began to realize the seriousness of her situation and gradually decided that this was not what she wanted. A year later, after two attempts, she finally broke up with him.

Emilia's relationship with Thomas put a lot of strain on Victor and Rosa's relatively new relationship. Rosa became depressed. Victor would become impatient to take action, and Rosa would become immobilized. The effects of Emilia's relationship on the family at times seemed relentless.

Naturally, Victor and Rosa were facing other problems besides Emilia's boyfriend. But dealing with Emilia's abusive relationship wore them out. At one point they talked about divorce, but they continued to work at maintaining as normal a family life as possible. They were able to get through it and were relieved when Emilia finally got away from Thomas. A solid relationship developed between Victor and his stepchildren, especially Emilia, because of everything they had gone through together.

Barbara

Barbara maintained strong ties with her seventeen-year-old daughter Tanisha throughout Tanisha's abusive relationship with Tyrone. In spite of the abuse, Tanisha thought she and Tyrone would get married. She was annoyed when Tyrone stalled by making excuses. She eventually found out from a friend that he had been seeing someone else for almost a year. He had been lying to her. Tanisha was still "hooked," believing he would get rid of the other girl and marry her because she was "the one who really understands him." Then she saw them together. She was hurt and angry, and she realized he had been lying to her. She broke up with him for the last time, no longer believing him when he tried to persuade her that he would be faithful to her.

Tanisha leaned on her family for support, knowing she would need it, as she was determined to stay away from Tyrone. Her family talked and planned together, as they had throughout the battering relationship. Her uncle, who hadn't spoken to her for a year, started talking to her again. Barbara prayed a lot and was glad she had a strong connection with her church and her family. Tanisha was successful at her job, which helped her self-confidence to grow outside the battering relationship. With Barbara's encouragement, Tanisha saw a counselor.

Barbara always knew she couldn't make Tanisha do what she wasn't ready to do, and she kept her faith that her daughter would eventually come to her senses. When it was over, she was distressed that Tyrone's violence wasn't the reason her daughter left him, and distressed that she might have married him. She realized that although she had a lot of faith in Tanisha, she had experienced constant worry and fear that something terrible would happen to her before she got completely away from Tyrone.

Conclusion

As you finish reading this book, you have attained a great deal of information that can help you prevent or intervene to stop dating violence. You are now more prepared, knowing what to look for, what to expect, and what to do. Learning as much as you can, seeking support, and knowing you are not alone makes a difference. Remember, in spite of heartbreak and pain, teens recover and families are resilient. Your resilience enables you to draw upon your reserves to find the strength and capability to handle one of the most difficult problems a parent can face.

Your Safety Plan Checklist

Once you, your teen, and your family have discussed the need for a safety plan, use this worksheet to document your plan and share with those who need it.

Increasing safety in the relationship:

☐ I will have important phone numbers with me at all times.

IMPORTANT PHONE NUMBERS	Police _____
	Hotline _____
	Friends _____
	_____
	Family _____
	_____
	_____
	_____

☐ I can tell _____
and _____ about
the violence and ask them to call the police if they hear or see
anything that leads them to suspect I might be in danger.

☐ I can alert _____
and _____ at school,
work, etc., that I might need to ask them to help me be safe.

Duplicating this material for personal or group use is permissible.

☐ If I have to get away from the person who is violent toward me, I can go to (list four places you can go to be safe):

1. _____

2. _____

3. _____

4. _____

☐ I can leave money, car keys, and _____

_____

with _____

so I can get to them in an emergency.

Increasing safety when the relationship is over:

☐ I can tell _____
and _____
at school/work/other about my situation and ask them to screen my e-mails, texts, calls, visitors, etc.

☐ I can alert neighbors _____
and _____
to let me know if they see anyone stalking me or prowling.

☐ I can obtain a protection order and keep it with or near me at all times as well as leave a copy with _____

_____ .

☐ I will talk to _____
and _____ and
_____ about my
need for support when I feel frightened or don't think I can

successfully keep my ex away from me or keep myself away from my ex.

☐ I can go to stay with _____ or

_____

if I have to be safe.

☐ If I feel down, I can call _____

or _____ for

support, or attend workshops and support groups to strengthen my relationships with other people.

Adapted from Barrie Levy, *In Love and In Danger* (Emeryville, CA: Seal Press, 2006), 121–122.

Characteristics of Healthy Relationships

A healthy relationship includes more than feelings of love, passion, affection, and shared likes and dislikes. Engage your teen in a discussion by emphasizing the following characteristics of healthy relationships:

- Both partners *give and receive,* each getting their way some of the time and compromising some of the time.

- They *respect* each other, value one another's opinions, and accept each other for who they are. They don't feel pressured to do things they are not comfortable with, such as drinking, using drugs, or having unwanted physical contact.

- They *support* and *encourage* one another's goals and ambitions and want what is best for each of them. They encourage each other to have friends and activities outside the relationship.

- They *trust* one another, and learn not to inflict jealous and restrictive feelings on the other if these feelings should arise.

- Neither is afraid of the other. They feel *emotionally safe;* for example, they feel comfortable being themselves without fear of being put down. When one of them is upset, they feel safe enough to talk things out in a respectful manner. They feel *physically safe;* they are not afraid of being hurt or pressured into unwanted physical or sexual contact.

- They *communicate openly and honestly* and make their partners feel safe in expressing themselves. They *listen* to each other and talk face-to-face (not just text) about their feelings.

- They share responsibility in decision making. They have an *equal say* in choosing activities and friends.

- They accept the differences between them. They can be themselves and have their own *individuality,* without pretending to like something they don't like or be someone they are not.

- They respect each other's *boundaries.* If one says "no" or "stop," the other listens. This applies to sex as well as other activities. When they are together, they feel connected, not controlled.

- They are each *responsible* and *accountable* for their own behavior and don't blame others to justify their bad behavior. They accept the consequences of their actions and try to repair them.

- They express *appreciation* of one another to one another.

- Although they may be sad or even broken-hearted if the relationship ends, they know they will *essentially be okay,* and they aren't fearful about the relationship ending.

Adapted from Patricia Occhiuzzo Giggans and Barrie Levy, *Fifty Ways to a Safer World* (Seattle, WA: Seal Press, 1997).

Guidelines for Conversations with Teens about Healthy Relationships

Children of all ages need reliable and accurate information about healthy relationships: what a healthy relationship feels like, looks like, and sounds like. One of the most effective ways of teaching a child about healthy relationships is to model positive qualities in your own relationships. Parents must not forget that even when they think teens are not listening to or watching their parents, they often are.

Preteens and young teens start to explore the idea of a boyfriend or girlfriend, interacting at school or through cell phones, instant messaging, or social networking sites. They often have relationships with someone they consider a boyfriend or girlfriend but do not consider themselves "dating." Parents should consider "hanging out" with friends at the mall or going to a movie as an early form of dating.

Parents can point out features of good relationships when they are around them or see them in books or movies, and open a dialogue about what their teen looks for in a boyfriend or girlfriend. To identify the differences between relationships that are built on respect and those that are not, parents can describe examples from their own experience. Support teens for thinking for themselves if they express an opinion different from adults'.

Create Opportunities

Parents can create opportunities for discussion by doing the following:

1. "Show up" in a relaxed manner when you know that your teen is available. For example, hang out with him or her late at night or drive someplace together. Make yourself available.

2. Ask questions about something you read or saw, and be curious about your teen's opinion. For example, "I read about teens dating at age thirteen. Have you heard about that? What do you think about that?"

Take Advantage of Opportunities ("Teachable Moments")

Parents can use the moments when the subject of relationships comes up to discuss healthy relationships.

1. After seeing a movie with your teen, ask about the relationships in the movie and what your teen thought worked and didn't work. Would he or she like to be in a relationship like that? What is your teen looking for in a boyfriend or girlfriend?

2. When you see something in the media about famous actors, sports figures, or others, discuss their healthy or unhealthy relationships.

3. If there is a situation involving the relationship of someone you know, engage your teen and find out what he or she thinks about the situation.

4. Notice when your teen is quiet and hanging around, as if he or she wants to ask you something. Sit with your teen and wait, sharing space. This will encourage him or her to talk without feeling pushed.

Conversation-Starters

Use open-ended questions to start a conversation with your teen, and then listen to his or her feelings and opinions. Have a relaxed dialogue about your different points of view. Here are some examples of open-ended questions you can ask your child:

1. "What do you think about _____ [a situation in a TV show or YouTube clip about a family or relationship]?"

2. "By the way, I saw your friend at the mall with her boyfriend. They've been going out for a while. How do you think their relationship is going?"

3. "I saw a story in the news about that pop star and her boyfriend getting back together. What do your friends think about it?"

4. "What if your date drinks at a party and wants to drive you home? How would you handle that?" Think of other vignettes or scenarios that your teen is likely to encounter.

5. "Did you hear about _____ [a news or neighborhood story]? What do you think about it?"

6. "What are all the ways to look at _____ [a relationship situation]?" Ask about ways teens might act with girlfriends or boyfriends, and brainstorm ideas. For example, "He wants to spend all of his time with her, and wants her to spend all of her time with him. What do you think?"

7. "Did you notice how different guys treated _____ [a woman in the movie you watched together]? Which guy do you think did the right thing? Why?"

Tips

1. Talking with young teens about difficult issues isn't a single or onetime conversation; it's an ongoing dialogue. Keep the lines of communication open.

2. To have an effective conversation, carefully select the time and place (private). Choose a moment when you can give your undivided attention and listen without being overly emotional or judgmental.

3. Avoid critical comments even when you don't agree. To keep a dialogue going, make sure to show that you respect and welcome your child's opinion.

4. Allow your teen to ask you anything. Listen to his or her comments and questions. If you don't know the answer, say so. Don't worry about being an expert. Be honest and find the answer together.

5. Ask direct questions, but don't overwhelm your teen with too many questions. It's a conversation, not an interrogation.

6. Talk at your teen's level and use examples. Share your own mistakes and what you learned from them.

Adapted from Start Strong Idaho, "Healthy Relationships Protect Teens: A Parent's Handbook," http://idvsa.org/wp-content/uploads/2013/01/Middle-School-Parent-Handbook.pdf.

RESOURCES

Centers for Disease Control and Prevention, www.cdc.gov

ConnectSafely.org, "Tips to Prevent Teen Sexting," www.connectsafely.org

Futures Without Violence, www.futureswithoutviolence.org

Idaho Coalition Against Sexual and Domestic Violence, www.engagingvoices.org (Click on "Focus" at the top of the page, then choose "Healthy Relationships" from the drop-down menu; scroll down to "Parent/Caregiver Materials.")

Indiana Department of Education, "Identified Model Teen Dating Violence Curricular Materials," www.doe.in.gov/student-services/identified-model-teen-dating-violence-curricular-materials

The Legal Aid Society, www.legal-aid.org

Levy, Barrie, *In Love and In Danger: A Teen's Guide to Breaking Free of Abusive Relationships* (Emeryville, CA: Seal Press, 2006)

Love Is Not Abuse (Break the Cycle), www.loveisnotabuse.com

Loveisrespect, www.loveisrespect.org (information and live chats for help)

National Teen Dating Abuse Helpline, 1-866-331-9474

National Domestic Violence Hotline, www.thehotline.org, 1-800-799-SAFE (7233)

National Sexual Violence Resource Center, www.nsvrc.org

Peace Over Violence, www.peaceoverviolence.org

Rape, Abuse & Incest National Network (RAINN), www.rainn.org, National Sexual Assault Hotline: 1-800-656-HOPE (4673)

Rape Crisis Center, www.rapecrisis.com

Start Strong, www.startstrongteens.org/resources/policy (school policy)

NOTES

1. Antoinette Davis, "Interpersonal and Physical Dating Violence among Teens," *FOCUS: Views from the National Council on Crime and Delinquency* (September 2008): 1.
2. "Tween and Teen Dating Violence and Abuse Study," Teen Research Unlimited for Fifth & Pacific Companies, Inc. (formerly Liz Claiborne Inc.) and the National Teen Dating Abuse Helpline, July 2008, https://www.breakthecycle.org/sites/default/files/pdf/survey-lina-tweens-2008.pdf.
3. Elizabeth Miller, Michele R. Decker, Anita Raj, Elizabeth Reed, Danelle Marable, and Jay G. Silverman, "Intimate Partner Violence and Health Care-Seeking Patterns Among Female Users of Urban Adolescent Clinics," *Maternal and Child Health Journal* 14 (2010): 910–17 (published online September 17, 2009, doi: 10.1007/s10995-009-0520-z).
4. Michele C. Black, Kathleen C. Basile, Matthew J. Breiding, Sharon G. Smith, Mikel L. Walters, Melissa T. Merrick, Jieru Chen, and Mark R. Stevens, *The National Intimate Partner and Sexual Violence Survey (NISVS): 2010 Summary Report* (Atlanta, GA: National Center for Injury Prevention and Control, Centers for Disease Control and Prevention, 2011), www.cdc.gov/violenceprevention/NISVS.
5. Evan Stark, *Coercive Control* (New York: Oxford University Press, 2007).
6. Ibid., 249.
7. National Institute on Drug Abuse, "Teen Dating Violence—Help Prevent It," *Sara Bellum Blog*, February 14, 2012, http://teens.drugabuse.gov/blog/post/teen-dating-violence-help-prevent-it; Jay G. Silverman, Anita Raj, Lorelei A. Mucci, and Jeanne E. Hathaway, "Dating Violence Against Adolescent Girls and Associated Substance Use, Unhealthy Weight Control, Sexual Risk Behavior, Pregnancy, and Suicidality," *Journal of the American Medical Association* 286, no. 5 (August 1, 2001): 572–579.
8. Bruce Perry, quoted in Heather Forbes and B. Bryan Post, *Beyond Consequences, Logic, and Control* (Boulder, CO: Beyond Consequences Institute, 2006).
9. Ibid.
10. J. Livingston, L. Bay-Cheng, A. Hequembourg, M. Testa, and J. Downs, "Mixed Drinks and Mixed Messages: Adolescent Girls' Perspectives on Alcohol and Sexuality," *Psychology of Women Quarterly* 37, no. 1 (2013): 38–50.
11. Mary P. Koss, K. E. Leonard, D. A. Beezley, and C. J. Oros, "Nonstranger Sexual Aggression: A Discriminant Analysis of Psychological Characteristics of Undetected Offenders," *Sex Roles* 12 (1985): 981–92, quoted in David Lee, "CDC on Use of 'Sexual Coercion' in NISVS," CALCASA PreventConnect, February 15, 2012, http://www.preventconnect.org/2012/02/cdc-on-use-of-sexual-coercion-in-nisvs/.

12. J. R. Temple, J. A. Paul, P. van den Berg, V. D. Le, A. McElhany, and B. W. Temple, "Teen Sexting and Its Association with Sexual Behaviors," *Archives of Pediatrics and Adolescent Medicine* 166, no. 9 (2012): 828–833.

13. Internet Watch Foundation, "Young People Are Warned They May Lose Control Over Their Images and Videos Once They Are Uploaded Online," October 22, 2012, http://www.iwf.org.uk/about-iwf/news/post/334-young-people-are-warned-they-may-lose-control-over-their-images-and-videos-once-they-are-uploaded-online.

14. Elizabeth Miller and Rebecca Levenson, *Hanging Out or Hooking Up: Clinical Guidelines on Responding to Adolescent Relationship Abuse* (San Francisco: Futures Without Violence, 2012), 7.

15. Ibid., 14.

16. G. M. Wingood, R. DiClemente, D. H. McCree, K. Harrington, and S. L. Davies, "Dating Violence and the Sexual Health of Black Adolescent Females," *Pediatrics* 107, no 5. (2001): 1–4, quoted in Elizabeth Miller and Rebecca Levenson, *Hanging Out or Hooking Up: Clinical Guidelines on Responding to Adolescent Relationship Abuse* (San Francisco: Futures Without Violence, 2012), 15.

17. A. Raj, E. Reed, E. Miller, M. R. Decker, E. F. Rotham, and J. G. Silverman, "Context of Condom Use and Non-Condom Use among Young Adolescent Male Perpetrators of Dating Violence," *AIDS Care* 19, no. 8 (2007): 970–73, quoted in Elizabeth Miller and Rebecca Levenson, *Hanging Out or Hooking Up: Clinical Guidelines on Responding to Adolescent Relationship Abuse* (San Francisco: Futures Without Violence, 2012), 14.

18. Elizabeth Miller and Rebecca Levenson, *Hanging Out or Hooking Up: Clinical Guidelines on Responding to Adolescent Relationship Abuse* (San Francisco: Futures Without Violence, 2012), 15.

19. Kevin Bales, *Disposable People: New Slavery in the Global Economy* (Berkeley: University of California, 1999).

20. Craig A. Anderson, Leonard Berkowitz, Edward Donnerstein, L. Rowell Huesmann, James D. Johnson, Daniel Linz, Neil M. Malamuth, and Ellen Wartella, "The Influence of Media Violence on Youth," *Journal of Psychological Science in the Public Interest* 4, no. 3 (December 2003): 81–110.

21. D. Gil-González, C. Vives-Cases, M. T. Ruiz, M. Carrasco-Portiño, and C. Alvarez-Dardet, "Childhood Experiences of Violence in Perpetrators as a Risk Factor of Intimate Partner Violence: A Systematic Review," *Journal of Public Health* 30, no. 1 (2008): 14–22.

22. Marshall B. Rosenberg, *Nonviolent Communication: A Language of Life* (Encinitas, CA: PuddleDancer Press, 2003), 79.

23. Heather Forbes and B. Bryan Post, *Beyond Consequences, Logic, and Control* (Boulder, CO: Beyond Consequences Institute, 2006), 17.

24. Marshall B. Rosenberg, *Nonviolent Communication: A Language of Life* (Encinitas, CA: PuddleDancer Press, 2003), 186–188.

25. Ibid.

26. Linda Burgess Chamberlain, *The Amazing Brain: What Every Parent and Caregiver Needs to Know* (Philadelphia: Health Federation of Philadelphia, 2008).

27. David Dobbs, "Beautiful Brains," *National Geographic* (October 2011), 3.

28. Ibid.

29. Gordon Neufeld and Gabor Maté, *Hold On to Your Kids: Why Parents Need to Matter More Than Peers* (New York: Ballantine Books, 2005, 2006).

30. Michael Riera, *Staying Connected to Your Teenager* (Oakland, CA: Perseus, 2003).

31. Michael Riera, *Uncommon Sense for Parents of Teenagers* (Berkeley, CA: Celestial Arts Press, 1995), 7.

32. Adapted from Start Strong Idaho, "Healthy Relationships Protect Teens: A Parent's Handbook," http://idvsa.org/wp-content/uploads/2013/01/Middle-School-Parent-Handbook.pdf.

33. "Guidelines for Conversations with Teens" adapted from Start Strong Idaho, "Healthy Relationships Protect Teens: A Parent's Handbook," http://idvsa.org/wp-content/uploads/2013/01/Middle-School-Parent-Handbook.pdf.

34. Adapted from Patricia Occhiuzzo Giggans and Barrie Levy, *Fifty Ways to a Safer World* (Seattle, WA: Seal Press, 1997); Barrie Levy, *In Love and In Danger: A Teen's Guide to Breaking Free of Abusive Relationships* (Emeryville, CA: Seal Press, 2006).

35. Adapted from Start Strong Idaho, "Healthy Relationships Protect Teens: A Parent's Handbook," http://idvsa.org/wp-content/uploads/2013/01/Middle-School-Parent-Handbook.pdf.

36. Thomas Gordon, *Parent Effectiveness Training* (New York: Three Rivers Press, 2000).

37. Adapted from Loveisrespect.org, "Should We Break Up?", http://www.loveisrespect.org/get-help/should-we-break-up.

38. *2010 State Law Report Cards: A National Survey of Teen Dating Violence Laws* (Los Angeles: Break the Cycle, 2012), 7, http://www.loveisrespect.org/sites/default/files/2010-State-Law-Report-Cards-Full-Report.pdf.

ABOUT THE AUTHORS

Patti Giggans is the executive director at Peace Over Violence, a sexual assault, domestic violence, child abuse, and youth violence prevention center headquartered in Los Angeles. She has worked in the movement to end violence for as long as she can remember. An activist, advocate, and author, Giggans is the recipient of The California Peace Prize and is a Durfee Foundation Stanton Fellow.

Barrie Levy is a licensed clinical social worker in private practice and a faculty member in the Department of Social Welfare, School of Public Affairs, University of California, Los Angeles. She is the editor of *Dating Violence: Young Women in Danger* and author of *In Love and In Danger: A Teen's Guide for Breaking Free of Abusive Relationships* and *Women and Violence*. During forty years of activism to stop domestic and sexual violence, she has founded and directed four organizations and won many awards in recognition of her groundbreaking work.

RECOMMENDED RELATIONSHIP VIOLENCE CURRICULUM FOR SCHOOLS:

Safe Dates, second edition
An Adolescent Dating Abuse Prevention Curriculum
Vangie Foshee, Ph.D., and Stacey Langwick, Ph.D.
This evidence-based program helps teens recognize the difference between caring, supportive relationships and controlling, manipulative, or abusive relationships. *Safe Dates* helps young people develop the skills needed to create and foster positive relationships.
Order No. 9863

To find resources and information for safer schools and communities, visit **violencepreventionworks.org.**